SHAKESPEARE ON SCREEN

The Tempest *and Late Romances*

The second volume in the re-launched series Shakespeare on Screen is devoted to *The Tempest* and Shakespeare's late romances, offering up-to-date coverage of recent screen versions as well as new critical reviews of older, canonical films. An international cast of authors explores not only productions from the USA and the UK, but also translations, adaptations and appropriations from Poland, Italy and France. Spanning a wide chronological range, from the first cinematic interpretation of *Cymbeline* in 1913 to The Royal Ballet's live broadcast of *The Winter's Tale* in 2014, the volume provides an extensive treatment of the plays' resonance for contemporary audiences. Supported by a film-bibliography, numerous illustrations and free online resources available for download on the Cambridge University Press website, the book will be an invaluable resource for students, scholars and teachers of film studies and Shakespeare studies.

SARAH HATCHUEL is Professor of English Literature and Film and Head of the Groupe de Recherche Identités et Cultures (GRIC) at the University of Le Havre, as well as President of the Société Française Shakespeare. She has written extensively on adaptations of Shakespeare's plays, including *Shakespeare and the Cleopatra/Caesar Intertext: Sequel, Conflation, Remake* (2011), *Shakespeare, from Stage to Screen* (Cambridge, 2004), *A Companion to the Shakespearean Films of Kenneth Branagh* (2000), and has also written on television series, including *Lost: Fiction vitale* (2013) and *Rêves et séries américaines: la fabrique d'autres mondes* (2015). She is Co-editor-in-chief of the online journal *TV/Series*.

NATHALIE VIENNE-GUERRIN is Professor in Shakespeare studies at Université Paul-Valéry Montpellier 3 and Director of the Institut de Recherche sur la Renaissance, l'âge Classique et les Lumières. She is Co-editor-in-chief of the international journal *Cahiers Élisabéthains* and Co-director (with Patricia Dorval) of the *Shakespeare on Screen in Francophonia Database* (shakscreen.org). She has published *The Unruly Tongue in Early Modern England, Three Treatises* (2012) and is the author of *Shakespeare's Insults: A Pragmatic Dictionary* (2016). She is Co-editor of the online journal *Arrêt sur Scène/Scene Focus*.

Shakespeare on Screen is unique in Shakespeare studies. Each volume is devoted to a single Shakespeare play, or a group of closely related plays, and discusses how it has been adapted to the medium of film and television. The series ranges far beyond the Anglo-American sphere, paying serious attention to European perspectives and combining discussion of mainstream Shakespeare cinema with broad definitions of adaptation and appropriation. As a result, each volume redefines the limits of the field and of the play. The series provides the finest writing on screened Shakespeare by scholars of international significance.

Originally published by Presses Universaires de Rouen et du Havre (PURH), Shakespeare on Screen is now extended by Cambridge University Press to provide fresh emphasis on new media, multimedia and the evolution of technologies. A special feature of each volume is a select film bibliography, which will be augmented by a substantial free online resource.

SHAKESPEARE ON SCREEN

The Tempest *and Late Romances*

EDITED BY

SARAH HATCHUEL

NATHALIE VIENNE-GUERRIN

CAMBRIDGE
UNIVERSITY PRESS

CAMBRIDGE
UNIVERSITY PRESS

University Printing House, Cambridge CB2 8BS, United Kingdom

One Liberty Plaza, 20th Floor, New York, NY 10006, USA

477 Williamstown Road, Port Melbourne, VIC 3207, Australia

4843/24, 2nd Floor, Ansari Road, Daryaganj, Delhi - 110002, India

79 Anson Road, #06-04/06, Singapore 079906

Cambridge University Press is part of the University of Cambridge.

It furthers the University's mission by disseminating knowledge in the pursuit of education, learning and research at the highest international levels of excellence.

www.cambridge.org
Information on this title: www.cambridge.org/9781107113503
DOI: 10.1017/9781316286449

First published 2017

Printed in the United Kingdom by TJ International Ltd. Padstow Cornwall.

A catalogue record for this publication is available from the British Library

Library of Congress Cataloging-in-Publication data
Names: Hatchuel, Sarah, editor. | Vienne-Guerrin, Nathalie, editor.
Title: The Tempest and late romances / edited by Sarah Hatchuel and Nathalie Vienne-Guerrin.
Description: Cambridge, United Kingdom ; New York, NY : Cambridge University Press, 2017. | Series: Shakespeare on Screen | Includes bibliographical references.
Identifiers: LCCN 2016044387 | ISBN 9781107113503
Subjects: LCSH: Shakespeare, William, 1564–1616. Tempest. | Shakespeare, William, 1564–1616 – Tragicomedies. | Shakespeare, William, 1564–1616 – Film adaptations.
Classification: LCC PR2833 .T4646 2017 | DDC 822.3/3 – dc23
LC record available at https://lccn.loc.gov/2016044387

ISBN 978-1-107-11350-3 Hardback

*In loving memory of our dear friend and colleague,
Mariangela Tempera, a free spirit and a pioneer in Shakespeare
on Screen studies on a worldwide scale.
This book is dedicated to her.*

Contents

Illustrations

Contributors

DELILAH BERMUDEZ BRATAAS received her PhD in English at Tufts University in Massachusetts and is Associate Professor of English at the Norwegian University of Science and Technology in Trondheim (Norway) in the Faculty of Education. Her dissertation 'Shakespeare and Cavendish: Engendering the Early Modern English Utopia' explores the development of utopianism and utopic themes through the early modern in several works of William Shakespeare and Margaret Cavendish. Her varied research interests consider aspects of gender in utopia from its earliest expressions in early modern literature to its contemporary incarnations in science fiction and fantasy. She is currently working on several articles on Cavendish and Shakespeare. Her latest article, 'Shakespeare's Presence and Cavendish's absence in *League of Extraordinary Gentlemen*', appeared in the journal *Shakespeare* in May 2015.

VICTORIA BLADEN teaches in literary studies and adaptation at The University of Queensland (Australia) and received a Faculty award for teaching excellence in 2015. She has published four Shakespearean text guides in the Insight Publications (Melbourne) series: *Measure for Measure* (2015), *Henry IV Part 1* (2012), *Julius Caesar* (2011) and *Romeo and Juliet* (2010). She co-edited *Supernatural and Secular Power in Early Modern England* (2015) and *Shakespeare on Screen:* Macbeth (2013). She has published articles in several volumes of the *Shakespeare on Screen* series, including *Shakespeare on Screen:* Othello (2015) and is on the editorial board for the *Shakespeare on Screen in Francophonia* project in France. Other publications include articles on tree and garden imagery in early modern poetry, on Jane Austen and on the pastoral genre.

JUDITH BUCHANAN is Professor of Film and Literature and Director of the Humanities Research Centre at the University of York. Publications include *Shakespeare on Silent Film: An Excellent Dumb Discourse* (2009), *Shakespeare on Film* (2005), and *The Writer on Film: Screening Literary*

Authorship (2013). She has written widely on Shakespearean performance histories (stage and screen) and on silent cinema. She speaks regularly to public as well as to academic communities and is Director of Silents Now (silents-now.co.uk). Her voice-over commentaries can be found on Thanhouser DVDs and on the British Film Institute DVDs *Silent Shakespeare* and *Play On! Shakespeare on Silent Film*. She is currently co-writing a volume on Shakespeare and live broadcast theatre with John Wyver while researching a next book project called *Shakespeare Beyond Words*.

JOSÉ RAMÓN DÍAZ FERNÁNDEZ is a senior lecturer in English Literature at the University of Málaga (Spain). He has published articles in *Early Modern Literary Studies*, *The Shakespeare Newsletter* and *Shakespeare Bulletin* and has contributed essays to the collections *The Reel Shakespeare: Alternative Cinema and Theory* (2002), *Almost Shakespeare: Reinventing His Works for Cinema and Television* (2004), *Latin American Shakespeares* (2005) as well as all the volumes in the *Shakespeare on Screen* series edited by Sarah Hatchuel and Nathalie Vienne-Guerrin. In 2001 and 2006, he co-chaired the 'Shakespeare on Film' seminars at the World Shakespeare Congresses in Valencia and Brisbane. His volume of revenge tragedies by Thomas Kyd, John Webster and John Ford was awarded the Translation Prize by the Spanish Association for Anglo-American Studies in 2007. He has also been the principal investigator of a research project on Shakespeare in contemporary culture from 2008 to 2012.

JACEK FABISZAK teaches Shakespeare and adaptation theory as well as cultural history and theory at the Faculty of English, Adam Mickiewicz University, Poznań. His research interests include English Renaissance theatre and drama and their televisual and filmic transpositions. He has published and given papers at conferences on both Polish and English-speaking versions of Shakespeare's plays; one of his major publications in this area is *Polish Televised Shakespeares* (2005). He has also approached Shakespeare from a linguistic and sociological perspective – his *Shakespeare's Drama of Social Roles* (2001) is an attempt to interpret Shakespeare's last plays in light of the theory of social roles and speech act theory. Furthermore, he has popularized Shakespeare's works in Poland, co-authoring *Szekspir. Leksykon* [Shakespeare. A lexicon, 2003] and co-editing *Czytanie Szekspira* [Reading Shakespeare]. He has also written on Christopher Marlowe, both his plays and their screen versions (especially *Edward II*).

KINGA FÖLDVÁRY is senior lecturer at the Institute of English and American Studies at Pázmány Péter Catholic University, Hungary. Her main research interests, besides a close reading of William Harrison's *Description of Britain*, include Shakespearean tragedy, problems of genre in film adaptations of Shakespeare's plays, twentieth- and twenty–first-century British literature, and theories of visual and popular culture. Her work in screen studies focuses on the significance of the adapting cinematic/televisual genres or the oeuvres of auteur-directors in the interpretation of film adaptations of Shakespeare's plays, as opposed to traditional fidelity-based taxonomies. She has co-edited four volumes of essays, and published several articles in edited collections and journals, including *Reinventing the Renaissance: Shakespeare and his Contemporaries in Adaptation and Performance* (2013), Global Shakespeares, a special issue of *Shakespeare: Journal of the British Shakespeare Association* (2013), and *Shakespeare on Screen: Othello* (2015).

RUSSELL JACKSON is Emeritus Professor of Drama at the University of Birmingham, where his research and teaching have focused on theatre history, film and Shakespearean performance. His publications include *Romeo and Juliet* in the 'Shakespeare at Stratford' series (Arden Shakespeare, 2003), *The Cambridge Companion to Shakespeare on Film* (2007), *Shakespeare Films in the Making: Vision, Production and Reception* (2007), *Theatres on Film: How the Cinema Imagines the Stage* (2013) and *Shakespeare and the English-Speaking Cinema* (2014). In the past thirty years, he has also been text consultant, working closely in rehearsal with actors and directors, on many theatre and film productions. These have included Kenneth Branagh's Shakespeare productions on stage, radio and film. In the 2015–16 season, he was text consultant for the Kenneth Branagh Theatre Company's production of *The Winter's Tale* and *Romeo and Juliet* at the Garrick Theatre in London.

GAËLLE GINESTET teaches English at Université Paul-Valéry Montpellier 3 (France) and is a member of the Institute for Research on the Renaissance, the Neo-classical Age and the Enlightenment (IRCL). She holds a PhD on mythology in Elizabethan love sonnet sequences from Université Paul-Valéry. She is currently engaged in two collective research projects: *Shakespeare on Screen in Francophonia* and *A Dictionary of Shakespeare's Classical Mythology* (and its *Textual Companion – Early Modern Mythological Texts*). She regularly contributes play reviews to *Cahiers Élisabéthains* and is the author of articles on Thomas Watson, mythology in Renaissance poetry and Shakespeare in French cinema.

SARAH HATCHUEL is Professor of English Literature and Film at the University of Le Havre (France), President of the Société Française Shakespeare and head of the 'Groupe de recherche Identités et Cultures'. She has written extensively on adaptations of Shakespeare's plays (*Shakespeare and the Cleopatra/Caesar Intertext: Sequel, Conflation, Remake*, 2011; *Shakespeare, from Stage to Screen*, 2004; *A Companion to the Shakespearean Films of Kenneth Branagh*, 2000) and on TV series (*Lost: Fiction vitale*, 2013; *Rêves et séries américaines: la fabrique d'autres mondes*, 2015). She is general editor of the *Shakespeare on Screen* series (with Nathalie Vienne-Guerrin) and of the online journal *TV/Series*.

DOUGLAS M. LANIER is Professor of English and Director of the London Program at the University of New Hampshire. He has published widely on Shakespeare and Shakespearean adaptations, including his book *Shakespeare and Modern Popular Culture* (2002); he has also published on Jonson, Marston, Milton and the Jacobean masque. For his teaching and research, he won the Gary Lindberg award at the University of New Hampshire. A former Trustee of the Shakespeare Association of America, he is the Fulbright Global Shakespeare Centre Distinguished Chair for 2016–17. He is currently working on two projects, a history of *Othello* on screen and a book on *The Merchant of Venice* for the Arden Language & Writing series.

RANDY LAIST is Associate Professor of English at Goodwin College in East Hartford, Connecticut. He is the author of *Cinema of Simulation: Hyperreal Hollywood in the Long 1990s* and *Technology and Postmodern Subjectivity in Don DeLillo's Novels*. He is also the editor of *Plants and Literature: Essays in Critical Plant Studies* and *Looking for* Lost: *Critical Essays on the Enigmatic Series*.

MADDALENA PENNACCHIA is Associate Professor of English Literature at Roma Tre University. She has authored three books: *Shakespeare intermediale* (2012), *Tracce del moderno nel teatro di Shakespeare* (2008) and *Il mito di Corinne* (2001). She is the editor of *Literary Intermediality* (2007) and co-editor of *Questioning Bodies in Shakespeare's Rome* (2010), *Adaptation, Intermediality and the British Celebrity Biopic* (2014) and *Turismo creativo e identità culturale* (2015). She is also the author of a bio-fiction for children, *Shakespeare e il sogno di un'estate* (2009). She is general co-editor of the book series *Turismi e culture* and a member of the editorial board of *Biblioteca di Studi inglesi*; she is also a member of the editorial and advisory board of the *Journal of Adaptation in Film and Performance*.

LINDSAY ANN REID is a Lecturer in English at the National University of Ireland, Galway. Though broadly interested in issues of adaptation, her scholarship to date has primarily focused on the reception of Ovid's works in early modern England. She is the author of a relevant monograph entitled *Ovidian Bibliofictions and the Tudor Book: Metamorphosing Classical Heroines in Late Medieval and Renaissance England* (2014). She has published articles in *Translation and Literature, Early Modern Literary Studies, Etudes Epistémè* and *Spenser Studies* and contributed essays to collections including *Singing Death: Reflections on Music and Mortality* (2017) and *Ground-Work: English Renaissance Literature and Soil Science* (2017).

EDEL SEMPLE is Lecturer in Shakespeare Studies at University College Cork, Ireland. She is co-editor of *Staged Transgression in Shakespeare's England* (2013) and *Staged Normality in Shakespeare's England* (forthcoming) with Rory Loughnane, and of a special issue of *Early Modern Literary Studies* on 'European Women in Early Modern Drama' (forthcoming) with Ema Vyroubalová. Edel has published on Shakespearean drama, prostitution in Wilson's *Three Ladies of London*, the critical history of Kyd's *The Spanish Tragedy*, early modern travel literature, and Shakespeare in contemporary performance and on film. She is also a coordinator of the 'Shakespeare in Ireland' scholarly blog, promoting and reporting on early modern events and research across the island. In 2016, Edel was granted an Irish Research Council New Foundations award for the project 'Celebrating Shakespeare 400: Performing *Pericles, Prince of Tyre*'.

PETER J. SMITH is Reader in Renaissance Literature at Nottingham Trent University. His books include *Social Shakespeare: Aspects of Renaissance Dramaturgy and Contemporary Society* and *Between Two Stools: Scatology and Its Representations in English Literature, Chaucer to Swift*. His articles and reviews have appeared in *Cahiers Élisabethains, Critical Survey, Renaissance Quarterly, Review of English Studies, Shakespeare, Shakespeare Bulletin, Shakespeare Survey, Speech and Drama, Times Higher Education* and *Year's Work in English Studies*. He is one of the four co-editors-in-chief of *Cahiers Élisabethains* and a trustee of the British Shakespeare Association.

NATHALIE VIENNE-GUERRIN is Professor in Shakespeare studies at the University Paul-Valéry Montpellier 3, Vice President of the Société Française Shakespeare and director of the 'Institut de Recherche sur la Renaissance, l'âge Classique et les Lumières' (IRCL, UMR 5186 CNRS). She is co-editor-in-chief of the international journal *Cahiers Élisabéthains* and co-director (with Patricia Dorval) of the *Shakespeare on Screen in Francophonia Database* (www.shakscreen.org). She has published *The Unruly Tongue in Early Modern England, Three Treatises* (2012) and is the author of *Shakespeare's Insults: A Pragmatic Dictionary* (2016). She is co-editor, with Sarah Hatchuel, of the *Shakespeare on Screen* series.

ROBERT S. WHITE is a Chief Investigator for the Australian Research Council Centre of Excellence for the History of Emotions 1100–1800, and Winthrop Professor of English at the University of Western Australia. He researches mainly Shakespeare and has covered almost the whole canon in books and articles. He also publishes on the Romantics, especially Keats and Hazlitt, most recently in *John Keats: A Literary Life* (2012). He has published on different aspects of Shakespeare and movies (including Indian), most recently in *Avant-Garde Hamlet: Text, Stage, Screen* (2015) and *Shakespeare's Cinema of Love: A Study in Genre and Influence* (2016).

JOHN WYVER is a producer with the independent media company Illuminations which makes broadcast programmes and other media with many cultural organisations. He is Senior Research Fellow in the School of Media, Arts and Design at the University of Westminster where he was Principal Investigator for the AHRC-funded research project *Screen Plays: Theatre Plays on British Television* (2011–15). He produces the Royal Shakespeare Company's live cinema productions. In 2016 he produced *Shakespeare Live! From the RSC* celebrating the 400th anniversary of Shakespeare's death. He is the author of *Vision On: Film, Television and the Arts* (2007) and is working on a critical history of film and television adaptations of RSC stage productions.

Series Editors' Preface

Shakespeare on Screen is a series of books created in 2003 by Sarah Hatchuel and Nathalie Vienne-Guerrin. Until 2013 the books were published by the Presses des Universités de Rouen et du Havre (PURH). Each volume is a collection of essays aiming to explore the screen versions of one play (or a series of plays – such as the history cycles or the Roman plays) by William Shakespeare.

Volumes published by PURH, available from 'le comptoir des presses d'universités' (www.lcdpu.fr), are:

Shakespeare on Screen: A Midsummer Night's Dream (2004)
Shakespeare on Screen: Richard III (2005)
Shakespeare on Screen: The Henriad (2008)
Television Shakespeare: Essays in Honour of Michèle Willems (2008)
Shakespeare on Screen: The Roman Plays (2009)
Shakespeare on Screen: Hamlet (2011)
Shakespeare on Screen: Macbeth (2013)

Cambridge University Press has published one volume so far:

Shakespeare on Screen: Othello (2015)

The series thoroughly interrogates, through a diversity of viewpoints, what Shakespearean films do with and to Shakespeare's play-texts. If one film cannot render all the ambiguities of the play-text, the confrontation of multiple versions may convey a multiplicity of interpretations and produce a kaleidoscopic form of meaning.

Films based on Shakespeare fall into categories whose boundaries are always being transgressed. This collection encourages scholarly examination of what 'Shakespearean film' encompasses. It not only provides readers with diverging explorations of the films, but also deploys a wide array of methodologies used to study Shakespeare on screen – including all types of screen (cinema, TV and the computer – with digital productions and Internet 'broadcasts') and all kinds of filmic works, from 'canonical' adaptations using Shakespeare's text, to derivatives, spin-offs and quotes.

This series acknowledges Shakespeare as a repository of symbolic power and cultural authority in 'mainstream', English-speaking adaptations, while also showing how the plays' words and themes have travelled to other non-English cultures, and can be transacted freely, no longer connected to any kind of fixed cultural standard or stable meaning. The series shows how Shakespeare's western, northern, English-speaking 'centre' has been challenged or at least revisited through geographical and trans-media dissemination.

The books emphasize new media, multimedia and the constant evolution of technologies in the production, reception and dissemination of 'Shakespeare on film', especially at a time when so many Shakespearean filmic resources can be accessed online, whether it be on open platforms such as YouTube or cinema/television archives.

Each volume offers a select film-bibliography which is expanded in a free online version within the Cambridge website, where the reader can also access links to new media forms of Shakespeare.

Quotations from Shakespeare's works are taken from the Cambridge University Press editions of the plays.

SARAH HATCHUEL
NATHALIE VIENNE-GUERRIN

Acknowledgements

We first and foremost wish to thank Cambridge University Press for publishing this second volume in the Cambridge Shakespeare on Screen series. We are particularly grateful to Sarah Stanton for her invaluable support and patient advice.

This book stems from a seminar that we co-chaired at the Shakespeare 450 international congress organized by the Société Française Shakespeare in April 2014 in Paris. This volume is also the result of a long-term collaborative work with colleagues and friends who have come to constitute a dynamic international community of specialists examining the forms that screen Shakespeare can take.

We wish to express our deepest gratitude to the University Paul-Valéry Montpellier 3 and to the University of Le Havre, to our research centres, the GRIC (Groupe de Recherche Identités et Cultures, EA 4314, Le Havre) and to the IRCL (Institut de Recherche sur la Renaissance, l'Âge Classique et les Lumières, UMR 5186, CNRS Montpellier), to the Centre National de la Recherche Scientifique (CNRS) and to the Société Française Shakespeare, who helped us financially, logistically and morally in this venture, from the initial congress seminar to the final publication.

Our thanks also go to the international advisory board of the Shakespeare on Screen series: Pascale Aebischer (University of Exeter), Mark Thornton Burnett (Queen's University of Belfast), Samuel Crowl (University of Ohio), Russell Jackson (University of Birmingham), Douglas Lanier (University of New Hampshire), Courtney Lehmann (University of the Pacific), Poonam Trivedi (University of Delhi) and Michèle Willems (University of Rouen).

We warmly thank the contributors to this volume for their unfailing patience, reactivity and support, which have made our work on this book a truly collective venture.

We finally wish to thank wholeheartedly our respective families and friends for letting us spend so much (demanding but fun) time together to prepare this volume.

SARAH HATCHUEL
NATHALIE VIENNE-GUERRIN

CHAPTER I

Introduction
'What Have We Here?': Acknowledging Shakespeare's Romances on Screen

Sarah Hatchuel and Nathalie Vienne-Guerrin

Shakespeare's romances are magical. Four plays belonging to Shakespeare's late-phase work[1] – *Pericles* (1607–8), *Cymbeline* (1609–11), *The Winter's Tale* (1609–10) and *The Tempest* (1610–11) – should conclude tragically but miraculously end happily. Originally labelled as 'tragicomedies' (a term coined by playwright John Fletcher in his foreword to *The Faithful Shepherdess* in 1608), these hybrid plays were re-categorized as 'romances' in 1875 by Irish poet and critic Edward Dowden. Like the medieval tales relating legendary or extraordinary adventures, Shakespeare's romances defy narrative logic and verisimilitude; they emphasize sensational extravagance, geographical wanderings, wonderful coincidences and reunions in tense scenes of recognition. Loved ones are fantastically found again even when they were thought to be dead and lost forever. The plays do not only tell magical stories, they also reveal how ideological discourses shape the world and celebrate the magic of artistic creation, blurring the limits between illusion and the 'real' and marking the power and prominence of fiction, even over those who author and enact it.

José Ramón Díaz Fernández's select film-bibliography at the end of the volume, as well as the more comprehensive version provided in the volume's online resources,[2] show that *The Tempest* is obviously a prominant 'island' in the archipelago of Shakespeare's romances on screen, but also that the screen has long searched to accommodate the magic of *all* the romances and the incredible situations it engenders. During the pre-sound era, the romances were considered particularly well adapted to rendition in motion pictures: they contributed to celebrate the new techniques of cinema, especially the trend of *trucages* set by Georges Méliès, a stage magician turned filmmaker.[3] The pioneering 12-minute *Tempest* directed by Percy Stow in 1908 displayed some elaborate effects through editing and superimpositions and ignored the unity of time by adding flashbacks. Fades created magical effects during the shipwreck and Ariel's tricks, generating what Peter

Holland has identified as a polarity between the 'realism of the magic' and the 'magic of emotional realism', a tension which characterizes subsequent *Tempest* films as well.[4] The silent film versions produced by the Thanhouser company even strengthened 'hope in the future of kenematography'.[5] For instance, the one-reel *Tempest* (1911), now lost, was praised for its exquisite storm effects.[6]

As Judith Buchanan argues in this volume, alternative endings, which are referenced, remembered, averted or suppressed in the plays, haunt the romances as traces of what could have been, inviting productions to unearth the stories 'from within and behind the surface narrative'. The silent *Winter's Tale* of 1910 makes use of a court jester who seems parachuted right from *King Lear* to serve as an ironic commentator of the action: as Leontes and Hermione reunite, the fool replaces the missing words by blatant gestures metafictionally marking how unbelievable the events are.[7] In this volume, Lindsay Ann Reid wonders what, in the Thanhouser *Cymbeline* (1913), made Shakespeare's play seem so well suited for screen adaptation; she argues that the pre-sound version reshaped the play into a romantic comedy, eliminating *Cymbeline*'s notorious villains, emphasizing the love narrative and doing away with many of the fanciful and self-consciously excessive elements. The films were successful possibly because they were no longer romances. And, indeed, the romances' early popularity did not endure.

'Strange Stuff' (*The Tempest*, 4.1.232)

Albeit the diversity of spectacle, the display of magic and the array of emotions that characterize the romances, *Cymbeline*, *Pericles* and *The Winter's Tale* are some of Shakespeare's least-filmed plays. Even *The Tempest*, a play which might have been thought an appealing text for cinematic adaptation, has not been as repeatedly adapted for the screen as, for instance, *Macbeth*, *Hamlet* or *Richard III*. As Buchanan suggests, 'the small clutch of film adaptations that have emerged are all quirky or idiosyncratic in some way', thus reflecting their 'fantastical source'.[8] This addition to the Shakespeare on Screen series endeavours to explore these idiosyncratic adaptations from the silent versions to the television productions, from cinematic 'straightforward' adaptations to more 'spectral' appropriations. The history of adapting the romances on-screen is one of transfiguration that, each time, resets and illuminates the plays in various lights.

The romance plays have often thrived less on the big screen than on the small one. One of the very few instances, *Pericles*, was adapted to the screen for the BBC in 1983. Under the direction of David Jones, who saw in the figure of Gower some kind of 'television presenter',[9] the exterior scenes ended up looking 'more like sterile storybook illustrations than authentically gritty environments'[10] but used the TV conventions of the time, between artifice and realism, to create a unique rendering of the play, although a relatively neglected one. According to Jones, the play 'seems to have been written by many different hands but what it *is*, marvellously, is cinematographic and episodic' because it is 'cut to "meanwhile, in this place" and "meanwhile there"'.[11] Edel Semple revisits, in this volume, the BBC *Pericles* by looking at a female gaze which contributes to balance the power between gender roles. While the play frequently presents women as desirable objects of visual pleasure, the BBC production focuses on women's own looking.

Broadcasts of scenes from *Cymbeline* in 1937 and 1956 were also among the earliest British television productions of Shakespeare, as John Wyver documents in his chapter. Neither broadcast was recorded but, for both of these 'lost' productions, the BBC Written Archives Centre preserves detailed camera scripts, revealing the development of the language of television studio drama. Shot lengths, camera movements and framings – which are more complex in 1956 – are explored by Wyver and compared with the extant studio production of Elijah Moshinsky's BBC 1982 *Cymbeline*, a version which Robert S. White then analyses at length, examining both the history of the production and the stakes of its casting choices. Moshinsky appropriates a Rembrandt imagery and sets the play in Jacobean interiors, while creating stylised, snowy landscapes for the exterior scenes in Wales.

Jane Howell's BBC *Winter's Tale* (1981) was even more experimental with its deliberate rejection of naturalistic design and its emphasis, instead, on 'minimalist, expressionistic sets and symbolic costumes (a bearskin hat and cloak for Leontes in prefiguration of the famous bear in the third act)'.[12] Having directed the play twice for the stage before, Jane Howell felt less free. She described the setting she used in the BBC version as 'too harsh, unaccountably harsh'.[13] In this volume, Jacek Fabiszak compares Howell's work with Zofia Mrozowska's filming of the play for the Polish Television Theatre. Although the two TV versions do not refer to or acknowledge each other, the similarities are surprising: they both strive to render the non-realistic nature of the play through meta-televisual devices, while imagining how 'television realism' might work. From the stage to the televison screen, the framing of shots may affect profoundly our perception of scenes. Christopher Wheeldon's 2014 ballet version of *The Winter's Tale*, directed for the screen by Ross MacGibbon, is explored by Judith

Buchanan. Leontes and Hermione reunite in a tormented and redemptive *pas de deux* scene in which a statue of their deceased son, Mamillius, has been added on stage. The alternation between shots that show Mamillius's statue and shots that hide it engenders an emotional oscillation between the joy of miraculous reunion and the sadness of knowing that the child is lost forever.

The Winter's Tale has also been adapted by Stanislav Sokolov as a puppet show (1994) in the television series *Animated Tales from Shakespeare*. The animated production not only highlights the fantastic already present in the play-text, but creates more of it. Flame-like figures dance around Leontes as he banishes his baby daughter, as if he were manipulated by the devil and no longer responsible for his actions; the interpolated ghost of Hermione appears in Antigonus's boat, making her death even more certain for the viewers. The technique of stop-motion photography that is used to animate the puppets contributes to explore metafilmically 'the magical boundary between stillness and movement' in a play where Hermione's statue is revived.[14] As Laurie Osborne argues, 'By explicitly invoking the magic of puppetry where still sculpted figures come to life and move, the animators thus create the fantastic within an interplay between filmed movement and sculpture'.[15] In this volume, Maddalena Pennacchia prolongs this idea, suggesting that Paulina reviving the statue is a Prospero-like character who puts on 'magic' shows and pulls the strings of drama. *The Tempest* for the *Animated Tales* (1992), produced with puppets as well, aptly reflects on Prospero as a puppeteer and on the presence of Italian puppet theatre in England since the 1570s.

If *The Tempest* has been adapted as 'traditional' low-budget productions on television – such as George Schaefer's Hallmark *Tempest* (1960) or John Gorrie's BBC version (1980) – on the big screen, directors have instead revelled in the possibilities of playing with the illusionistic dimension of cinema itself. They have challenged our notion of realism, displaying the materiality of filming through the unreality of the special effects, as well as reproducing Prospero's powers. As Derek Jarman stated, 'Film is the wedding of light and matter – an alchemical conjunction'.[16] His low-budget, art-house 1979 *Tempest* was a reaction against, according to Samuel Crowl, the 'stale, safe atmosphere' of the BBC Shakespeare productions launched two years before.[17] Jarman took a play belonging to establishment culture and reshaped it in anti-establishment terms, bringing to it a transgressive, camp and punk sensibility. The film is presented as the complex, agitated, psychodramatic dream of an unhappy and aggressive Prospero. As Lisa Hopkins has remarked, the film's last word is 'sleep' instead of 'free', suggesting that the whole cinematic drama is 'rounded with a sleep' indeed.[18] The island becomes an eighteenth-century mansion (a critical comment on the tradition of heritage films?) in which Caliban's and Ariel's relations to Prospero become homoerotically charged. By casting a white actor as Caliban, Jarman underplays the racial/colonial issues of exploitation to concentrate on the sexual/gender ones. A flashback thus shows an adult Caliban sucking his mother Sycorax's breast. The witch Sycorax is portrayed as a huge and grotesque woman enchained, presenting maternity and heterosexuality as both repulsive and alienating.

Prospero's island becomes a series of fantastically lit rooms in which viewers lose all sense of direction, and watch the transformation of each chiaroscuro, secluded room into a pictorial and almost motionless composition. The magic of cinema is thus replaced by the elaboration of visual tableaux.[19] With this disorientation and fracturing of represented space,[20] the 'splitting' of the ship in the play's first scene, as Rothwell suggests, 'acts as metaphor for Prospero's own desperate struggle against the alienation of self from self and society, as well as self-referentially Jarman's own split from conventional movie making'.[21] The storm is created with apparently authentic, blue-filtered, black-and-white stock footage, thus standing apart from the rest of the fiction film. Prospero's unreal tempest is therefore, in Peter Holland's words, 'defiantly *real* in a film whose techniques exuberantly enjoy their often carefully campy separation from the real'.[22] Jarman explicitly presents Prospero as a magus using magic mirrors and surrounded by walls covered with cabbalistic symbols, recalling Elizabeth I's official astrologer John Dee. Magic becomes a way to evoke closeted gay sexuality and a means to subject eternally childish daughters to their fathers. The masque is turned into a spectacular, campy Hollywood musical: sailors dance in what can be read as a queering of the British navy, destabilizing both colonial and heterosexist discourses,[23] and Elisabeth Welch gives a soulful performance of 'Stormy Weather', a song which suggests Prospero's unceased power so that it 'keeps rainin' all the time'.[24] Recalling Feste's song in *Twelfth Night*, the chorus suggests both happiness and possible chaos. Harmonious reconciliation can thus also be seen as a subversion of the play's sexual politics: the normalizing marriage of Miranda and Ferdinand is first desentimentalized through burlesque, then celebrated through a queer show.[25] When Ariel leaves the mansion, he visually enacts 'the act of coming out of the closet', presenting Jarman's *Tempest*, according to Coernelis Martin Renes, as 'a pamphlet against the repression of homoerotic desire'.[26] The film, as Kate Chedgzoy suggests, 'emerges from the conjunction of magic and power, in that it is crucially concerned with the use of cinematic magic to stimulate the spectator's engagement with its exploration of power'.[27] In this volume, Peter J. Smith explores the way Jarman's *Tempest*, through the portrayal of Prospero and the performance of the masque, acknowledges the strangeness and roughness of the play, undermining the comfortable assumptions about the romances as being plays of forgiveness, resignation and restoration. Russell Jackson prolongs the reflection by addressing the masque/play relationship in three cinematic adaptations of *The Tempest*, noting that none delivers the masque as it appears in the script, as if the scene posed a real challenge on screen and demonstrated how the limits of cinema came into touch with the limits of theatre.

Like Jarman's *Tempest*, Peter Greenaway's 1991 *Prospero's Books* seems to place the entire dream-like action into the mind of Prospero, 'denarrativizing' and defamiliarizing the play through the staging of sumptuous *tableaux vivants*.[28] The magus writes and ventriloquizes all the parts until the late stage of the drama, engendering a world he controls entirely (though he does it consciously rather than unconsciously). However, in many respects, the film stands in opposition to Jarman's. Greenaway's Prospero is not just a manipulator of people and events, as Elsie Walker claims; he is their *originator*.[29] While Jarman endeavours to debunk Prospero, Greenaway elevates him as the ultimate patriarch and auteur – a Renaissance doge and scribe, whose artistic composition is inspired by literary study and who merges the competing authorities of Shakespeare as playwright, Greenaway as filmmaker, and consecrated actor John Gielgud as guarantor of Shakespearean authenticity. Writing himself into his own fiction, a God-like Prospero conjures a dense, baroque and vertiginous world of images and sounds, filled with framing effects of *mise-en-abyme*, superimposed screens, handwritten words and interpictorial references that emphasize the hypermediatic and illusory dimensions. For Neil Forsyth, *Prospero's Books* is a 'tribute to the connection of magician and playmaker'.[30] As a painter and art historian turned film director, Greenaway revels in all the possibilities offered by digital wizardry, notably the Paintbox software, to create twenty-four animated books of impossible knowledge from Prospero's island-turned-library. The twenty-four books (an allusion to cinema's twenty-four frames per second)[31] give the film its structure, but they also anticipate the shift from paper to '"magically" enhanced electronic books' while suggesting that the Renaissance 'codex volume is as much a part of our future as our past'.[32] Concepts and ideas are given shapes and movements, while 'the material presence of film' is made 'palpable', 'producing a stratification of layerings that is deliberately beyond our capacity of watch'.[33] *Prospero's Books* presents itself as both a 'faithful' version of the text and a *drowning* of the text's authority and monumentality within a very personal vision.[34] The film, therefore, exploits cinema's 'technology of magic' and 'magic of technology' while simultaneously, as Michael Anderegg argues, 'fetishis[ing] the written word (specifically, the words of Shakespeare)'.[35] To create the action and construct the characters, Prospero first offers us the material vision of textuality, from ink to quill and paper, deconstructing the very act of dramatic (and filmic) authoring and showing how written words can become cinematic material. As Prospero shoots his quill like a dart and lets the ink seep out like blood, the act of writing is presented as a violent way to performatively shape the world in one's own terms.

Authorship and Authority

If politics is a theatrical art, fiction is here shown to have political impact and effect. Through the 'Anatomy of birth' scene, we are invited to imagine that Prospero's wife died in childbirth. Contrary to what takes place eventually in *Pericles* or *The Winter's Tale*, no reunion can happen between husband and wife. The presence of the naked woman removing her skin to reveal her entrails may suggest that Prospero's rapture in 'secret studies' concerned pregnancy. As the implied vivisector of his wife's body for his research, the magus appears, in Chantal Zabus's words, as a 'master-anatomist' whose 'domination remains secure over her in life and death'.[36] For James Andreas, Greenaway even 'kills off Prospero's dead wife again' in this flashback of medical anatomy, enhancing the vision of the island as a perfected male fantasy.[37] By composing words, this Prospero creates 'sentences' that are, in fact, 'executed on Ariel and Caliban, Miranda and Ferdinand'.[38] Power is accessed through the actual magic of writing. If Gordon McMullan argues that Greenaway cuts lines to 'support the image of Prospero as benign and serene' instead of an 'insecure, colonizing tyrant',[39] Paul Willoquet-Maricondi suggests that *Prospero's Books* points to the 'inherent colonizing impulse of modernity', showing how language as a technique of abstraction may create 'totalistic and imperialistic illusions' to acquire 'power and authority over people, things, and places'.[40] As scribe and interpreter, Greenaway's Prospero is a true *dictator*. He controls the characters' speeches until they are eventually released from his spell. He appropriates (if not usurps) the maternal, life-giving body through literacy and digital technologies that offer illusions of life,[41] from the first animated Book, that of Water (matching the inaugural storm), to Shakespeare's *Complete*

Works. The First Folio includes blank pages waiting for *The Tempest* as if Greenaway imagined that the play was to be based on the film we have just seen, raising the question of sources and origins.[42] In this volume, Randy Laist explores the film's hyperreality where 'the art and the artist both inhabit a shifting landscape of ontological indeterminacy': real-world books are written within the confines of fiction; Prospero is the author not only of the other characters but of the text that includes himself, like the hand that draws itself in the M. C. Escher drawing. If Prospero throws his books into the water, Caliban rescues the Folio and the manuscript of *The Tempest*, echoing the work of the First Folio editors who rescued plays that Shakespeare had maybe decided to 'drown'. If the film suggests that some artefacts of Western civilization are redeemable, it also hints at the fact that Prospero's magic has not been fully abandoned and may have seeped into the 'real' world in the form of Shakespeare's influence on Western culture. In the film's last shot, Ariel undertakes to jump out of the screen, a move echoing Prospero's desire to be released from the play by the audience and leaving the film literally *open* to interpretation and rewriting.[43]

Julie Taymor's 2010 *The Tempest* takes great liberty with the script. If stage productions had already shown cross-dressed Prosperos played by women, Taymor changes Prospero's gender from male to female. Prospera, played by Helen Mirren, is given a new backstory in the 1.2 exposition, with a few lines of faux Shakespearean verse written by Glen Berger. With these lines, Prospera explains to Miranda that, at the death of her husband, the Duke of Milan, her scientific experimentation led her to be accused of witchcraft. With this crucial act of regendering, Prospero's aspirational and competitive anxiety concerning maternal body becomes, as Judith Buchanan suggests, less disruptive and may explain why, contrary to other film productions, Taymor's does not put Sycorax on screen: Mirren's Prospera embodies at once the magus and the sorceress, turning the story into a commentary on the way powerful women are branded as witches.[44]

Prospera's move from masculine Europe to a wild island filled with possibilities creates a feminist version of the exile from Milan, according to Samuel Crowl.[45] For Virginia Mason Vaughan too, Taymor's film offers a feminist critique of patriarchal power.[46] However, in interviews, Taymor denied a feminist motivation for the gender swap and spoke of a performance-based choice 'that in no way alter[s] the essence of Shakespeare's play',[47] an opinion shared by many reviewers of the film. As Courtney Lehmann analyses, Taymor's *Tempest* houses the sacrilegious and messy 'not-Shakespeare' within its narrative structure precisely because it is 'Shakespeare'.[48] Moreover, Lehmann qualifies the film's feminist stance. In fact, Prospera's interpolated backstory in Milan reinforces contemporary stereotypes concerning female professionals and their dedication to the workplace versus family. The events on the island then present her as an emotionally unstable victim and a revengeful, raging harpy. As Prospera relinquishes her power at the end of the film, she has to be corseted painfully again and prepare herself to return to the constraints and conventions of a world ruled by men, sacrificing her freedom for her daughter's happiness. This corseting of Prospera's power is reflected in the film's ending, which gives the last word to Ariel. Dispossessed of the epilogue, which is sung as a kind of elegy by singer Beth Gibbons in the credit sequence, Prospera never says that her dukedom has been restituted (Epilogue, 6), thus rendering her sacrifice somehow pointless.

In this volume, Delilah Bermudez Brataas revisits Taymor's film in relation to the notion of utopia and rekindles the debate concerning the protagonist's regendering, showing how Prospera's transformation makes her shift 'between patriarchal master-mage, androgynous mother-mage and masculine-Duchess within her utopic realm'. For Brataas, the regendering achieves 'less a reconciliation of the demonized other and more a reclamation of the excluded m/other', since Taymor's film reclaims not only Caliban's mother, but also Miranda's, allowing them both, through Prospera, to take part in the island's utopia. In this perspective, the fact that Prospera does not deliver the epilogue takes another meaning. She never declares her 'charms overthrown' nor does she ask to be released from the utopic space she has contributed to build.

As in *Prospero's Books*, the representation of Prospera's magic makes use of computer graphics. As the actor playing Ariel could not be present on set, his character was added in post-production, making him literally a digital drone obeying Prospera's tyrannical orders.[49] Contrary to the C3I Ariel, Caliban appears, in the film, as Nature personified and subdued. For Lehmann, through the portrayal of a skin-deformed Caliban bearing firewood on his back, Taymor's *Tempest*, shot on the volcanic island of Lanai, invokes the colonial history of Hawaii and its sugarcane plantations in which leprosy reached an epidemic scale. In being obliged to leave the island, Prospera also calls to mind the overthrow of the last Hawaiian female ruler, deposed by US businessmen. For Michael D. Friedman, on the contrary, Taymor's film more classically presents Caliban as an African (notably through the choice of actor Djimon Hounsou, recalling his previous part in Steven Spielberg's 1997 film *Amistad* on the African slave trade). The film would thus ahistorically transplant the story of African slavery to a place that never kept any African slaves, erasing the lesser-known, more racially diverse history of slavery in Hawaii.[50]

Both Greenaway's and Taymor's films dramatize how the performance of magic involves language and knowledge to exercise control over humans, spirits and nature. In this volume, Victoria Bladen revisits the magic and the supernatural in both films in relation to their aesthetic, metafictional, gendered and postcolonial implications, but also shows how each production significantly harnesses early modern ideas and iconography, eventually alerting to the central paradox of *The Tempest* – control is ultimately about the relinquishing of power. This is somehow what the process of adaptation reveals: the romance plays are more alive culturally when they are rewritten, recycled and reappropriated in other film genres.

Cymbeline has thus been revived on the big screen under the title *Anarchy*. Michael Almereyda's 2014 film rewrites the story as a gritty war between dirty cops and an outlaw biker gang. In this volume, Douglas Lanier explores Almereyda's *Cymbeline/Anarchy* as a return, a generation later, to issues which animated his *Hamlet* (2000): the fate of the hipster, the effects of social media on youth culture and the very possibilities for cultural dissidence from the American mainstream. Imogen's journey from high-school sweetheart to butch biker chick echoes Shakespeare's move from mainstream teen culture to a dissident alternative in independent cinema. According to Lanier, 'by saying goodbye to all that teen Shakespeare while himself producing a form of just such a film, Almereyda seeks to propel Shakespeare on film into a new, as yet uncharted, phase'.

A Cabinet of Filmic Curiosities

Cultivating openness and hybridity, Shakespeare's romances precisely seem to be a privileged ground for experimentation, freedom of adaptation, or for what Douglas Lanier calls in this volume acts of 'adaptational independence'. The romances are essentially what Yves Peyré calls 'protean plays',[51] 'prismatic comedies' that 'present themselves as tales to better display their own theatricality'.[52] Blending comic and gruesome ingredients, they have been defined as 'grotesque' by Barbara Mowat.[53] This strange monstrosity is a source of fascination and repulsion as well as of never-ending interrogation. This protean nature explains why they can be digested by so many film genres, as is shown by Kinga Földváry who studies how *The Tempest* has found its way into a western, *Yellow Sky* (dir. William A. Wellmann, 1948); a science fiction film, *Forbidden Planet* (dir. Fred M. Wilcox, 1956); two films that she classifies as *auteur* films, *Age of Consent* (dir. Michael Powell, 1969), and *Tempest* (dir. Paul Mazursky, 1982); as well as a television production, *The Tempest* (dir. Jack Bender, 1998). This conspicuous adaptability to various film genres also probably derives from the fairy-tale nature of the play, which rests on characteristic sketchable features such as an island, the discovery of a new world, an old man and his daughter, a monster and an elf. These elements are such sources of 'wonder' that they can be recognizable in many films that do not even mention Shakespeare, as is the case with *Yellow Sky* or *Forbidden Planet*. The film *Island of Lost Souls* (1932, dir. Erle C. Kenton), scripted from H. G. Wells's novel, *The Island of Doctor Moreau*, has also been considered a free adaptation of *The Tempest* through its exploration of the limits of bestiality and humanity – although it contains no direct reference to Shakespeare. The Shakespearean nature of such films has thus been questioned by Judith Buchanan, for example, who considers that they only become Shakespearean through 'retrovisions'[54] rather than being intrinsically so. 'Is it or isn't it an adaptation of *The Tempest*?': this question that Lisa Hopkins asks about *Forbidden Planet*[55] can certainly apply to other films. Földváry's contribution shows that 'an examination based on the films' cinematic qualities, particularly their associations with film genres may prove more fruitful than ill-advised considerations of legitimacy or the use of fidelity-based taxonomies' and that 'the particular version of the isolated location that the filmmakers chose to represent Prospero's island serves as the key to interpreting the films'.

This exceptional openness of the plays probably also explains why they have been used in non-mainstream, 'intellectual' cinema, notably in France. Jacques Rivette's *Nouvelle Vague* film, *Paris nous appartient* (*Paris Belongs to Us*, released in 1961) is what Kenneth Rothwell has called a 'mirror movie'[56] which extensively uses *Pericles* and especially the motifs of secrecy and perenigrating that are at the heart of the play. Within a film which constitutes a 'labyrinth' and is 'ultimately about itself, about its own process of making meaning',[57] the presence of *Pericles*, a play that similarly is 'impossible to grasp',[58] seems most appropriate. The play and the film comment on one another, in what Richard Burt calls a 'cultural interplay'.[59] For Rivette, Shakespeare is 'a myth', 'a continent that we know to be gigantic, extraordinary' but that 'remains *terra incognita*'.[60] The romances may be seen as a *terra incognita* within this *terra incognita* and thus particularly worth being explored. *Paris nous appartient*, whose 'central narrative is the struggle of a young director, Gérard Lenz (Giani Esposito), to put on *Pericles*',[61] offers commentaries that seem to summarize two basic opposite reactions to the play. The character of Jean-Marc (played by Jean-Claude Brialy) expresses his skepticism when he tells Anne Goupil (Betty

Schneider), who will later rehearse the part of Miranda, that 'there are a few good scenes, but it doesn't work. If it were not signed by Shakespeare...'.[62] This skepticism which suggests that the play is not part of the canon, explains why Jean-Marc quickly drops out of the *Pericles* stage project that is the leading thread of the whole film. On the other hand, Gérard, the director of *Pericles* within the film, formulates a longer analysis of the play: 'Everybody says I am mad,..., that it is an unplayable, incoherent play, but I don't give a damn. What I precisely like about it is that it seems to be made of shreds and patches and that everything hangs together, on a global scale. Even if Pericles travels the world, even if all the heroes go around the globe, they are no less trapped.'[63] This praise of a work of art in which 'nothing is *quite* certain' is debunked when Gérard Lenz is 'ousted by an artistic director (Boileau) who insists on spectacular effects'[64] and comically wants the pirates in *Pericles* to be played by dwarves to give the impression that the boat in the setting is bigger than it is. This comic realistic device for a play that precisely escapes verisimilitude will finally prevail and lead Gérard Lenz to drop the project in his turn. The film thus provides a literary analysis of the ambivalence of the play[65] but also illustrates the tension between the choices of leaving the play open in a radical way on the one hand and reducing it to a mainstream realistic performance on the other. Reducing the strangeness of the romances or resolutely taking it on board: here is the choice that film directors have to negotiate.

In this volume Gaëlle Ginestet analyses the rarely studied example of *Le Bal du Comte d'Orgel*, a 1970 film integrating some characters and motifs of *The Tempest* which were not present in the original novel from which it derives. It is not fortuitous that the film should end on a dream sequence that brings to mind both the beginning and the end of the play – the moment when Prospero orders Miranda to sleep (1.2.184–6) and Prospero's famous lines 'We are such stuff/As dreams are made on' (4.1.156–7). When Anne, the sexually ambivalent main character, orders his wife, Mahé, to sleep, saying 'And now, Mahé, sleep, I insist',[66] the film suggests that resolution can only be found in dreams. With Anne's last words, the film is 'rounded with a sleep' (4.1.158), indeed. *Le Bal du Comte d'Orgel* is only one example of the way French cinema has appropriated the romances, seeming to feel free to tackle plays that are less canonical and thus perhaps less intimidating than others, at least for a French audience.

Éric Rohmer's 1992 *Conte d'hiver* is another example of the intellectualizing treatment of the romances. Telling a story of loss and recovery, the film uses the final statue scene of *The Winter's Tale* to create a moment of *anagnorisis*. The main character, Félicie (Charlotte Véry), has lost track of Charles (Frédéric van den Driessche), a holiday love and her daughter's father and hopes to find him again. Watching a stage performance of *The Winter's Tale* and notably of the statue scene allows her to 'awake [her] faith' (*The Winter's Tale*, 5.3.95) in their final reunion, which will eventually take place at the end of the film. Cartelli and Rowe rightly note that 'at a meta-dramatic level, Félicie's subsequent reunion with Charles (and his with their daughter) surrogates the reunion of Hermione and Leontes'. For Cartelli and Rowe, 'To see Shakespeare adaptations as surrogating their predecessors in this way is to reconceive of classic works not as containers for stable meanings but as mechanisms by which a culture transacts meaning. It is in this transactional sense that we speak of the constants surrogated by Shakespeare performances as "differential"'.[67] Rohmer's insertion of the extraordinary *Winter's Tale* in the representation of an ordinary daily life illustrates the magic, heuristic effect Shakespeare's art can have on a character who claims she will never be of the 'bookish type' and who only 'wishes to be herself'.[68] Félicie knows nothing about the play that her friend Loïc (Hervé Furic) introduces to her as 'incredible' (*rocambolesque*), including many 'extraordinary events', with 'people thought to be dead or in exile who come back and are resuscitated'.[69] Thus watching the statue scene is for her a revelation, a moment of lucidity which allows her to 'see' better (*j'ai vu*). The end of the play in the film becomes a religious experience that allows the heroine to understand herself.[70] The film thus suggests that watching this tale amounts to going on an intellectual journey and leads to faith. If Shakespeare is quoted at length in *Conte d'hiver*, in its title and the crucial theatre sequence, it is not the case in *Trois Couleurs: Rouge* (*Three Colours: Red*, Dir. Krzysztof Kieslowski, 1993) which has nevertheless been recognized as an adaptation of *The Tempest*. The only clue that we have of the link between *Red* and *The Tempest* is given in the opening sequence which offers a glimpse of the heroine Valentine Dussaut (Irène Jacob) reading Aldous Huxley's 1932 *Brave New World*. The film is built on the confrontation of a Miranda-like Valentine and an old retired judge, Joseph Kern (Jean-Louis Trintignant). The latter spies on his neighbours, symbolically controlling their lives by listening to all their phone conversations, as Prospero controls his island. Miguel Ángel González Campos notes that the film is the last of the trilogy and, like *The Tempest*, constitutes its author's swan song.[71] The film does not start but ends with a storm that leads to what the spectators can see as the meeting of Miranda and

Ferdinand. Shakespeare's spectacular *Tempest* is transformed into an intimate story that delineates a moral, psychological and intellectual journey that mostly takes place in an old judge's study.

Rebooting Shakespeare's Romance Episodes

By combining the enigmatic and the spectacular, by cultivating what Alison Thorne has termed 'elusiveness',[72] the romances accommodate themselves to European intimist cinema as well as to American grand-scale spectacular popular TV shows. According to Northrop Frye, romance is characterised by its 'energetic pacing of incident' and its 'processional form'. Frye notably describes *Pericles* as 'a most radical experience in processional narrative: the action is deliberately linear, proceding from place to place and from episode to episode'. He refers to the Gower story 'with its constant "and then" beat'.[73] In her edition of *Pericles*, Suzanne Gossett notes that 'romance, as exemplified in Spenser's *The Fairie Queen*, seems always ready to accommodate one more adventure'.[74] If we consider this episodic nature of the romances, it is not surprising that they should have entered into a dialogue with contemporary TV series. Sarah Hatchuel and Randy Laist's online contribution to this volume[75] suggests that *Lost* (ABC, 2004–2010) can be considered as 'a Shakespearean romance for the twenty-first century', recycling and reconfiguring Shakespeare's play in the same way as Shakespeare adapted classical mythological material.[76] 'How does one read *Lost* in the light of Shakespeare? How, in turn, can we read Shakespeare in light of *Lost*?', Hatchuel and Laist ask. For them, '*Lost* is a version of *The Tempest* in which one does not discover the existence of the demiurgic magician until the final act'. They demonstrate how 'the perceived linkages between the series and *The Tempest* have had an impact on the world of theatre'. *Lost* seems, in fact, to become a source of inspiration on stage, renewing, and returning to, the plays through processes of 'borrowing back'. Hatchuel and Laist also explore the largely neglected links between *Lost* and the other romances, notably showing that 'like Shakespeare's romances, the world of *Lost* is marked by visions, religious epiphanies, spiritual intimations and the decoding of signs.' Being inspired by the romances, *Lost* thwarts expectations while *Paris nous appartient* avoids closure. Both works are unsettling for audiences and reflect times of anxiety and incertitude. According to Hatchuel and Laist, *Lost*, like the romances, reflects 'an awareness of the limitations of conventional narrative'.

The romances are difficult to comprehend and embrace. One can only really apprehend bits and pieces of them, pieces which may seem to take on a universal ring, as was the case when, during the opening ceremony of the London Olympic Games in 2012, Kenneth Branagh delivered Caliban's speech, 'The isle is full of noises' (3.2.128–35), rebooting it into a global message of hope and courage.[77] That is what Christy Desmet's contribution to the volume's online resources[78] suggests by describing the presence of the romances in social media as an 'art of synecdoche'. For Desmet, individual scenes, characters, and speeches become the focus of reproduction and imitation. She shows that YouTube videos manage to tackle some of the romances' episodes such as the storm in *The Tempest* or the statue scene in *The Winter's Tale*. Among the romances, *The Tempest* is the most present in social media, due to the several feature films that ensure its dissemination on YouTube. If all of Shakespeare's plays can be found on YouTube, dispersed and dismembered into a variety of sequences, the 'synecdochic' phenomenon, she suggests, is even more prominent with the romances. This enhanced trend is probably due to the romances' inherent episodic nature.

The social media thus reflect what can also be observed in films that tap and reboot the riches of Shakespeare's romances by taking samples of their material. *Theatre of Blood* (dir. Douglas Hickox, 1973) cleverly integrates *Cymbeline* by combining in the same murder sequence the two memorable episodes of Iachimo's chest scene and Cloten's decapitation; Rohmer's *Conte d'hiver* focuses on *The Winter's Tale*'s statue scene; in *Paris nous appartient*, actors rehearse act IV, scene 1 of *Pericles*, one of Marina's sequences; Al Pacino's *Looking for Richard* (1996) uses one of Prospero's famous speeches ('Our revels now are ended . . .', 4.1.148–ff) both as a beginning and an ending; in *Island of Lost Souls* Lota, the Panther woman (Kathleen Burke), drowns Edward Parker (Richard Arlen)'s books, saying 'Book take you away'. On the other hand, Greenaway's *Prospero's Books* seems to drown *The Tempest* in ever more books, echoing the impressive amount of critical literature the film has generated. This dissemination of the romances into shreds and patches and into a huge library of books shows how difficult it is to 'acknowledge' these plays, that is, to *know* and understand them.

The romances cultivate secrecy. No wonder they should remain a mystery. Their presence on screen, whether it be ghostly or more conspicuous, yet shows that we have appropriated them: *The Tempest* has been seen as 'Shakespeare's "Western"'[79] or as the first work of science fiction; the romances seem to be as much cut out for Nouvelle Vague films as for TV series, for horror films as for romantic movies. This protean adaptability reveals that the romances do belong to us, that we 'acknowledge' them ours, but also that, like Paris in Rivette's film, these 'things of darkness' can never fully 'belong to us'. Like Cleopatra, the romances make hungry where most they satisfy.

Notes

1 For a discussion on the constructed excavation of a classic 'late period' from the Shakespeare canon and the need to take into account not only the playwright's life but also his writing collaborations, the acting company's repertory and the literary, social and economic environment, see G. McMullan, 'What is a "late play"?', in C. M. S. Alexander (ed.), *The Cambridge Companion to Shakespeare's Last Plays* (Cambridge: Cambridge University Press, 2009), 5–28.

2 See Cambridge University Press Online Resources, available at: www.cambridge.org

3 See N. Forsyth, 'Shakespeare and Méliès: Magic, Dream and the Supernatural', *Études Anglaises* 55 (2002), 167–80.

4 P. Holland, 'Magical Realism: Raising Storms and Other Quaint Devices', in S. Bigliazzi and L. Calvi (eds.), *Revisiting 'The Tempest': The Capacity to Signify* (Basingstoke and New York: Palgrave Macmillan, 2014), 185–201.

5 See J. Buchanan, *Shakespeare on Film* (Harlow: Pearson Longman, 2005), 44.

6 See Buchanan, *Shakespeare on Film*, 43.

7 See Buchanan, *Shakespeare on Film*, 40–41.

8 Buchanan, *Shakespeare on Film*, 150.

9 M. Willems and J.-P. Maquerlot, 'Entretien avec David Jones, réalisateur de *The Merry Wives of Windsor* et de *Pericles*', in M. Willems (ed.), *Shakespeare à la télévision* (Rouen: Publications de l'Université de Rouen, 1987), 32.

10 P. Nelsen, 'Shot from the Canon: The BBC Video of *Pericles*', in D. Skeele (ed.) '*Pericles*': *Critical Essays* (New York and London: Garland-Taylor and Francis, 2000), 322.

11 Willems and Maquerlot, 'Entretien avec David Jones', 32.

12 K. S. Rothwell, *A History of Shakespeare on Screen: A Century of Film and Television*, 2nd edition (Cambridge: Cambridge University Press, 2004), 110.

13 M. Willems, 'Entretien avec Jane Howell, réalisatrice de la première tétralogie, de *The Winter's Tale* et de *Titus Andronicus*', in Willems (ed.), *Shakespeare à la télévision*, 84.

14 L. Osborne, 'Mixing Media and Animating Shakespeare Tales', in R. Burt and L. E. Boose (eds.), *Shakespeare, the Movie, II: Popularizing the Plays on Film, TV, Video, and DVD* (London and New York: Routledge, 2003), 144.

15 Osborne, 'Mixing Media and Animating Shakespeare Tales', 146.

16 D. Jarman, *Dancing Ledge* (London: Quartet Books, 1984), 188.

17 S. Crowl, 'Stormy Weather: A New *Tempest* on Film'. *Shakespeare on Film Newsletter* 5.1 (December 1980), 1.

18 L. Hopkins, *Shakespeare's 'The Tempest': The Relationship between Text and Film* (London: Methuen Drama, 2008), 89.

19 See R. Jackson, 'Shakespeare's Comedies on Film', in A. Davies and S. Wells (eds.), *Shakespeare and the Moving Image: The Plays on Film and Television* (Cambridge: Cambridge University Press, 1994), 107.

20 See C. MacCabe, *The Eloquence of the Vulgar: Language, Cinema and the Politics of Culture* (London: British Film Institute, 1999), 107–15.

21 Rothwell, *A History of Shakespeare on Screen*, 196.

22 Holland, 'Magical Realism', 195.

23 S. Ryle, 'Re-nascences: *The Tempest* and New Media', in his *Shakespeare, Cinema and Desire: Adaptation and Other Futures of Shakespeare's Language* (New York and Basingstoke: Palgrave Macmillan, 2014), 174–211.

24 H. H. Davis, '"Rounded with a sleep": Prospero's Dream in Derek Jarman's *The Tempest*', *Literature/Film Quarterly* 41 (2013), 92–101.

25 See S. Buhler, *Shakespeare in the Cinema: Ocular Proof* (Albany: State University of New York Press, 2002), 147; D. Harris and J. MacDonald, 'Stormy Weather: Derek Jarman's *The Tempest*', *Literature/Film Quarterly* 25 (1997), 90–8.

26 C. M. Renes, 'Whose New World? Derek Jarman's Subversive Vision of *The Tempest* (1979)'. *BELLS: Barcelona English Language and Literature Studies* 17 (2008), www.publicacions.ub.edu/revistes/bells17/documentos/582.pdf

27 K. Chedgzoy, *Shakespeare's Queer Children: Sexual Politics and Contemporary Culture* (Manchester and New York: Manchester University Press, 1995), 198.

28 D. Lanier, 'Drowning the Book: *Prospero's Books* and the Textual Shakespeare', in J. C. Bulman (ed.), *Shakespeare, Theory, and Performance* (London and New York: Routledge, 1996), 195.

29 See E. M. Walker, 'The Aesthetic Construction of Musical Forms in *Prospero's Books*', in C. Stalpaert (ed.), *Peter Greenaway's 'Prospero's Books': Critical Essays* (Ghent: Academia Press, 2000), 161–79.

30 Forsyth, 'Shakespeare and Méliès', 167.

31 See E. Tribble, 'Listening to *Prospero's Books*', *Shakespeare Survey* 61 (2008), 161.

32 P. S. Donaldson, 'Digital Archives and Sibylline Fragments: *The Tempest* and the End of Books'. *Postmodern Culture* 8.2 (January 1998), http://muse.jhu.edu/journals/pmc/v008/8.2donaldson.html

33 Holland, 'Magical Realism', 199.

34 See M. Anderegg, *Cinematic Shakespeare* (Lanham: Rowman and Littlefield, 2004), 192; Lanier, 'Drowning the Book', 196.

35 M. Anderegg, 'Greenaway's Baroque Mise en scene at the Imaginative Centre of Shakespeare's *The Tempest*: A Hypertextual Recapitulation of the Rivalry between Ben Jonson and Inigo Jones?' in C. Stalpaert (ed.), *Peter Greenaway's 'Prospero's Books': Critical Essays* (Ghent: Academia Press, 2000), 102; 104.

36 C. Zabus, *Tempests after Shakespeare* (New York and Basingstoke: Palgrave, 2002), 259.

37 J. Andreas, '"Where's the Master?": The Technologies of the Stage, Book, and Screen in *The Tempest* and *Prospero's Books*', in D. Hedrick and B. Reynolds (eds.), *Shakespeare without Class: Misappropriations of Cultural Capital* (New York and Basingstoke: Palgrave, 2000), 197.

38 Andreas, '"Where's the Master?"', 198.
39 G. McMullan, *Shakespeare and the Idea of Late Writing: Authorship in the Proximity of Death* (Cambridge: Cambridge University Press, 2007), 335.
40 P. Willoquet-Maricondi, '*Prospero's Books*, Postmodernism, and the Reenchantment of the World', in P. Willoquet-Maricondi and M. Alemany-Galway (eds.), *Peter Greenaway's Postmodern/Poststructuralist Cinema* (Lanham: Scarecrow Press, 2008), 178; 183.
41 See P. S. Donaldson, 'Shakespeare in the Age of Post-Mechanical Reproduction: Sexual and Electronic Magic in *Prospero's Books*', in R. Burt and L. E. Boose (eds.), *Shakespeare, the Movie, II: Popularizing the Plays on Film, TV, Video, and DVD* (London and New York: Routledge, 2003), 105.
42 See R. Dragan, 'Brave New Worlds: The Book, the Cinema, and Web 2.0 in Peter Greenaway's *Prospero's Books* and *The Tulse Luper Suitcases*', *Literature/Film Quarterly* 39 (2011), 99–115; Lanier, 'Drowning the Book', 197.
43 See A.-M. Costantini-Cornède, 'De *La Tempête* à *Prospero's Books*: Vertige des sens et fragmentation du sens', in P. Dorval (ed.), *Shakespeare et le cinéma: Actes du Congrès de 1998* (Paris: Société Française Shakespeare, 1998), 72.
44 J. Buchanan, 'Not Sycorax', in G. McMullan, L. Cowen Orlin and V. M. Vaughan (eds.), *Women Making Shakespeare: Text, Reception, Performance* (London and New York: Bloomsbury, 2014), 335–45.
45 S. Crowl, rev. of *The Tempest*, *Shakespeare Bulletin* 29 (2011), 177–81.
46 V. M. Vaughan, '"Miranda, where's your mother?": Female Prosperos and What They Tell Us', in G. McMullan, L. Cowen Orlin and V. M. Vaughan (eds.), *Women Making Shakespeare: Text, Reception, Performance* (London and New York: Bloomsbury, 2014), 347–56.
47 J. Taymor, 'Rough Magic', in S. Carson (ed.), *Living with Shakespeare: Essays by Writers, Actors, and Directors* (New York: Vintage Books, 2013), 472.
48 C. Lehmann, '"Turn off the dark": A Tale of Two Shakespeares in Julie Taymor's *Tempest*', *Shakespeare Bulletin* 32 (2014), 45–64.
49 *Ibid.*
50 M. D. Friedman, 'Where Was He Born? Speak! Tell Me!: Julie Taymor's *Tempest*, Hawaiian Slavery, and the Birther Controversy', *Shakespeare Bulletin* 31 (2013), 431–52.
51 See Y. Peyré's 'Introduction' (to the romances), in J.-M. Déprats and G. Venet (eds.), *Shakespeare. Comédies*, vol. III, Bibliothèque de la Pléiade (Paris: Gallimard, 2016), x.
52 Peyré, 'Introduction', xii; xx: '[elles] se présentent comme des contes pour mieux affirmer leur nature théâtrale'.
53 B. A. Mowat, *The Dramaturgy of Shakespeare's Romances* (Athens: The University of Georgia Press, 1976), 26, quoted by Peyré, 'Introduction', xxviii.
54 J. Buchanan, '*Forbidden Planet* and the Retrospective Attribution of Intentions', in D. Cartmell, I. Q. Hunter and I. Whelehan (eds.), *Retrovisions: Reinventing the Past in Film and Fiction* (London and Sterling: Pluto Press, 2001), 148–62.
55 On this central question, Hopkins, *Shakespeare's 'The Tempest'*, 59.

56 Rothwell, *A History of Shakespeare on Screen*, 209.

57 D. Morrey and A. Smith, *Jacques Rivette* (Manchester: Manchester University Press, 2009), 24–5.

58 *Ibid.*, 25.

59 R. Burt, 'Mobilizing Foreign Shakespeare in Media', in A. Huang and C. S. Ross (eds.), *Shakespeare in Hollywood, Asia, and Cyberspace* (West Lafayette: Purdue University Press, 2009), 231–9, 232.

60 1996 interview with Aliette Armel. See A. Armel, 'Jacques Rivette autour du cinéma', *La Nouvelle Revue Française* 520, Special Issue (May 1996), 64, quoted by M. M. Wiles, *Jacques Rivette* (Urbana: University of Illinois Press, 2013), 16.

61 R. Jackson, 'Three *Auteurs* and the Theatre: Carné, Renoir and Rivette', in his *Theatres on Film: How the Cinema Imagines the Stage* (Manchester: Manchester University Press, 2013), 221–68, 251–2.

62 'Oh, y a quelques bonnes scènes, mais ça tient pas. Si c'était pas signé Shakespeare . . . '.

63 'Tout le monde dit que je suis fou, même Terry, que c'est une pièce injouable, incohérente, mais je m'en fiche. Justement ce qui me plaît, c'est qu'elle semble faite de pièces et de morceaux et que tout se lit sur un même plan, sur le plan terrestre. Péricles, il a beau parcourir des royaumes, tous les héros partir aux quatre coins du globe, ils n'en sont pas moins enfermés'.

64 Jackson, 'Three *Auteurs* and the Theatre', 252–3.

65 The main character, Anne Goupil, is a student in literature who opens the film by reading the first six lines of Ariel's 'Full fathom five' song (1.2.396–401), in English, with a strong French accent, as if to plunge the spectators in the maze, amazement and the estranging effects of the romances.

66 'Et maintenant Mahé, dormez, je le veux'.

67 T. Cartelli and K. Rowe, 'Adaptation as a Cultural Process', in their *New Wave Shakespeare on Screen* (Cambridge and Malden: Polity, 2007), 25–44, 40.

68 'Je ne serai jamais une intello, j'ai envie d'être moi.'

69 'Beaucoup de choses extraordinaires. Des gens qu'on croyait morts, qui vont en exil, qui reviennent, qui ressuscitent.'

70 On this aspect, see B. Py, '*The Winter's Tale* de Shakespeare et *Conte d'hiver* de Rohmer (1992): Vers une commune destinée des sentiments humains', in P. Dorval and N. Vienne-Guerrin (eds.): *Shakespeare on Screen in Francophonia* (2013), www.shakscreen.org/analysis/analysis_conte_hiver_rohmer/.

71 M. Á. González Campos, 'An isle full of noises, sounds and sweer airs: Shakespeare's *The Tempest* and Krzysztof Kieslowski's *Red, Sederi* VII (1996), 265: http://sederi.org/docs/yearbooks/07/7_32_gonzalez.pdf.

72 A. Thorne (ed.), *Shakespeare's Romances*, New Casebook (Houndmills, Basingstoke: Palgrave Macmillan, 2003), 1.

73 N. Frye, *A Natural Perspective: The Development of Shakespearean Comedy and Romance* (New York: Columbia University Press, 1965), 26–28. Partially quoted by S. Gossett (ed.), *Pericles*, The Arden Shakespeare (London: Thomson Learning, 2004), 108.

74 Gossett (ed.), *Pericles*, 108.

75 See Cambridge University Press Online Resources, available at www .cambridge.org

76 See Peyré, 'D'anciennes histoires, mais au goût du jour' ('Mouldy tales that are up to date'), Peyré, 'Introduction', xvi–xxii.

77 The video of Branagh's speech (in the guise of Victorian industrialist Isambard Kingdom Brunel) is available at http://bardfilm.blogspot.fr/2012/07/the-tempest-in-opening-ceremony.html. On this speech in the context of Shakespeare and the Olympic Games, see P. Prescott and E. Sullivan, *Shakespeare on the Global Stage: Performance and Festivity in the Olympic Year* (London: Bloomsbury, 2015), esp. 1–38.

78 See Cambridge University Press Online Resources, available at www .cambridge.org

79 S. Simmon, *The Invention of the Western Film: A Cultural History of the Genre's First Half-Century* (Cambridge: Cambridge University Press, 2003), 268.

WORKS CITED

Anderegg, M., *Cinematic Shakespeare* (Lanham: Rowman and Littlefield, 2004).

'Greenaway's Baroque Mise en scene at the Imaginative Centre of Shakespeare's *The Tempest*: A Hypertextual Recapitulation of the Rivalry between Ben Jonson and Inigo Jones?' in C. Stalpaert (ed.), *Peter Greenaway's 'Prospero's Books': Critical Essays* (Ghent: Academia Press, 2000), 101–19.

Andreas, '"Where's the Master?": The Technologies of the Stage, Book, and Screen in *The Tempest* and *Prospero's Books*', in D. Hedrick and B. Reynolds (eds.), *Shakespeare without Class: Misappropriations of Cultural Capital* (New York and Basingstoke: Palgrave, 2000), 189–208.

Armel, A., 'Jacques Rivette autour du cinéma', *La Nouvelle Revue Française* 520, Special Issue (May 1996), 60–9.

Buchanan, J., 'Not Sycorax', in G. McMullan, L. Cowen Orlin and V. M. Vaughan (eds.), *Women Making Shakespeare: Text, Reception, Performance* (London and New York: Bloomsbury, 2014), 335–45.

Shakespeare on Film (Harlow: Pearson Longman, 2005).

'Forbidden Planet and the Retrospective Attribution of Intentions', in D. Cartmell, I. Q. Hunter and I. Whelehan (eds.), *Retrovisions: Reinventing the Past in Film and Fiction* (London and Sterling: Pluto Press, 2001), 148–62.

Buhler, S., *Shakespeare in the Cinema: Ocular Proof* (Albany: State University of New York Press, 2002).

Burt, R., 'Mobilizing Foreign Shakespeare in Media', in A. Huang and C. S. Ross (eds.), *Shakespeare in Hollywood, Asia, and Cyberspace* (West Lafayette: Purdue University Press, 2009), 231–9.

Cartelli, T. and K. Rowe, 'Adaptation as a Cultural Process', in their *New Wave Shakespeare on Screen* (Cambridge and Malden: Polity, 2007), 25–44.

Chedgzoy, K., *Shakespeare's Queer Children: Sexual Politics and Contemporary Culture* (Manchester and New York: Manchester University Press, 1995).

Costantini-Cornède, A.-M., 'De *La Tempête à Prospero's Books*: Vertige des sens et fragmentation du sens', in P. Dorval (ed.), *Shakespeare et le cinéma: Actes du Congrès de 1998* (Paris: Société Française Shakespeare, 1998), 57–76: http://shakespeare.revues.org/948.

Crowl, S., review of *The Tempest*, *Shakespeare Bulletin* 29 (2011), 177–81.

'Stormy Weather: A New *Tempest* on Film'. *Shakespeare on Film Newsletter* 5.1 (December 1980), 1, 5–7.

Davis, H. H., '"Rounded with a sleep": Prospero's Dream in Derek Jarman's *The Tempest*', *Literature/Film Quarterly* 41 (2013), 92–101.

Donaldson, P. S., 'Digital Archives and Sibylline Fragments: *The Tempest* and the End of Books'. *Postmodern Culture* 8.2 (January 1998), http://muse.jhu.edu/journals/pmc/v008/8.2donaldson.html

'Shakespeare in the Age of Post-Mechanical Reproduction: Sexual and Electronic Magic in *Prospero's Books*', in R. Burt and L. E. Boose (eds.), *Shakespeare, the Movie, II: Popularizing the Plays on Film, TV, Video, and DVD* (London and New York: Routledge, 2003), 105–19.

Dragan, R., 'Brave New Worlds: The Book, the Cinema, and Web 2.0 in Peter Greenaway's *Prospero's Books* and *The Tulse Luper Suitcases*', *Literature/Film Quarterly* 39 (2011), 99–115.

Forsyth, N., 'Shakespeare and Méliès: Magic, Dream and the Supernatural', *Études Anglaises* 55 (2002), 167–80.

Friedman, M. D., 'Where Was He Born? Speak! Tell Me!: Julie Taymor's *Tempest*, Hawaiian Slavery, and the Birther Controversy', *Shakespeare Bulletin* 31 (2013), 431–52.

Frye, N., *A Natural Perspective. The Development of Shakespearean Comedy and Romance* (New York: Columbia University Press, 1965).

González Campos, M. Á., 'An isle full of noises, sounds and sweer airs: Shakespeare's *The Tempest* and Krzysztof Kieslowski's *Red*', *Sederi* VII (1996), 265–268: http://sederi.org/docs/yearbooks/07/7_32_gonzalez.pdf.

Gossett, S. (ed.), *Pericles, The Arden Shakespeare* (London: Thomson Learning, 2004).

Harris, D. and J. MacDonald, 'Stormy Weather: Derek Jarman's *The Tempest*', *Literature/Film Quarterly* 25 (1997), 90–8.

Holland, P, 'Magical Realism: Raising Storms and Other Quaint Devices', in S. Bigliazzi and L. Calvi (eds.), *Revisiting 'The Tempest': The Capacity to Signify* (Basingstoke and New York: Palgrave Macmillan, 2014), 185–201.

Hopkins, L., *Shakespeare's* The Tempest*: The Relationship between Text and Film* (London: Methuen Drama, 2008).

Jackson, R., 'Shakespeare's Comedies on Film', in A. Davies and S. Wells (eds.), *Shakespeare and the Moving Image: The Plays on Film and Television* (Cambridge: Cambridge University Press, 1994), 99–120.

'Three Auteurs and the Theatre: Carné, Renoir and Rivette', in his *Theatres on Film: How the Cinema Imagines the Stage* (Manchester and New York: Manchester University Press, 2013), 221–68.

Jarman, D., *Dancing Ledge* (London: Quartet Books, 1984).

Lanier, D., 'Drowning the Book: *Prospero's Books* and the Textual Shakespeare', in J. C. Bulman (ed.), *Shakespeare, Theory, and Performance* (London and New York: Routledge, 1996), 187–209.

Lehmann, C., '"Turn off the dark": A Tale of Two Shakespeares in Julie Taymor's *Tempest*', *Shakespeare Bulletin* 32 (2014), 45–64.

MacCabe, C., *The Eloquence of the Vulgar: Language, Cinema and the Politics of Culture* (London: British Film Institute, 1999).

McMullan, G., *Shakespeare and the Idea of Late Writing: Authorship in the Proximity of Death* (Cambridge University Press, 2007).

'What Is a "Late Play"?', in C. M. S. Alexander (ed.), *The Cambridge Companion to Shakespeare's Last Plays* (Cambridge: Cambridge University Press, 2009), 5–28.

Morrey, D. and A. Smith, *Jacques Rivette* (Manchester: Manchester University Press, 2009).

Nelsen, P., 'Shot from the Canon: The BBC Video of *Pericles*', in D. Skeele (ed.) *'Pericles': Critical Essays* (New York and London: Garland-Taylor and Francis, 2000), 297–324.

Osborne, L., 'Mixing Media and Animating Shakespeare Tales', in R. Burt and L. E. Boose (eds.), *Shakespeare, the Movie, II: Popularizing the Plays on Film, TV, Video, and DVD* (London and New York: Routledge, 2003), 140–53.

Peyré, Y., 'Introduction', in J.-M. Déprats and G. Venet (eds.), *Shakespeare. Comédies*, vol. III, Bibliothèque de la Pléiade (Paris: Gallimard, 2016), x–xxxiv.

Prescott, P. and E. Sullivan, *Shakespeare on the Global Stage. Performance and Festivity in the Olympic Year* (London: Bloomsbury, 2015).

Renes, C. M., 'Whose New World? Derek Jarman's Subversive Vision of *The Tempest* (1979)'. *BELLS: Barcelona English Language and Literature Studies* 17 (2008), www.publicacions.ub.edu/revistes/bells17/documentos/582.pdf.

Rothwell, K. S., *A History of Shakespeare on Screen: A Century of Film and Television*, 2nd edition (Cambridge: Cambridge University Press, 2004).

Ryle, S., *Shakespeare, Cinema and Desire: Adaptation and Other Futures of Shakespeare's Language* (New York and Basingstoke: Palgrave Macmillan, 2014).

Simmon, S., *The Invention of the Western Film. A Cultural History of the Genre's First Half-Century* (Cambridge: Cambridge University Press, 2003), 268.

Taymor, J., 'Rough Magic', in S. Carson (ed.), *Living with Shakespeare: Essays by Writers, Actors, and Directors* (New York: Vintage Books, 2013), 466–82.

Thorne, A. (ed.), *Shakespeare's Romances*, New Casebook (Houndmills, Basingstoke: Palgrave Macmillan, 2003).

Tribble, E., 'Listening to *Prospero's Books*', *Shakespeare Survey* 61 (2008), 161–9.

Vaughan, V. M., '"Miranda, Where's Your Mother?": Female Prosperos and What They Tell Us', in G. McMullan, L. Cowen Orlin and V. M. Vaughan (eds.), *Women Making Shakespeare: Text, Reception, Performance* (London and New York: Bloomsbury, 2014), 347–56.

Walker, E. M., 'The Aesthetic Construction of Musical Forms in *Prospero's Books*', in C. Stalpaert (ed.), *Peter Greenaway's 'Prospero's Books': Critical Essays* (Ghent: Academia Press, 2000), 161–79.

Wiles, M. M., *Jacques Rivette* (Urbana: University of Illinois Press, 2013).

Willems, M., 'Entretien avec Jane Howell, réalisatrice de la première tétralogie, de *The Winter's Tale* et de *Titus Andronicus*', in M. Willems (ed.), *Shakespeare à la télévision* (Rouen: Publications de l'Université de Rouen, 1987), 79–91.

Willems M. and J.-P. Maquerlot, 'Entretien avec David Jones, réalisateur de *The Merry Wives of Windsor* et de *Pericles*', in M. Willems (ed.), *Shakespeare à la télévision* (Rouen: Publications de l'Université de Rouen, 1987), 31–9.

Willoquet-Maricondi, P., '*Prospero's Books*, Postmodernism, and the Reenchantment of the World', in P. Willoquet-Maricondi and M. Alemany-Galway (eds.), *Peter Greenaway's Postmodern/Poststructuralist Cinema* (Lanham: Scarecrow Press, 2008), 177–201.

Zabus, C., *Tempests after Shakespeare* (New York and Basingstoke: Palgrave, 2002).

CHAPTER 2

Thanhouser's 'Fierce Abridgement' of Cymbeline

Lindsay Ann Reid

Shakespeare's *Cymbeline* 'is singularly well-adapted', or so a 1913 piece in *The Moving Picture World* once claimed, 'to rendition in motion pictures'.[1] It would seem that posterity has not concurred. One of Shakespeare's least-filmed plays, *Cymbeline* has inspired few screen adaptations over the course of the last century: the Thanhouser Film Corporation's inaugural 1913 version – the very film that motivated the reviewer's overly optimistic forecast of the play's cinematic prospects – has been followed only by Elijah Moshinsky's BBC Television Shakespeare *Cymbeline* of 1982 and Michael Almeyreda's 2015 biker gang adaptation. Indeed, this Shakespearean play has been remarked far more often over the last hundred years for its alleged generic incomprehensibility and structural incongruities than its inherent filmability. It is with this disjunct in mind – that is, the obvious discrepancy between the anonymous 1913 reviewer's projections in *The Moving Picture World* and *Cymbeline*'s subsequent lack of cinematic exposure – that I pose three interrelated questions. Firstly, what was it about the Thanhouser film of 1913 that made Shakespeare's *Cymbeline* seem so felicitously well-suited for screen adaptation? To what degree did this relatively short, silent film reproduce the qualities and characteristics that scholars and theatrical audiences alike have typically used to describe and define *Cymbeline* as a play? And, finally, how much can a so-called Shakespearean romance like *Cymbeline* be cut and reshaped, as it unquestionably was in the Thanhouser film adaptation, before it ceases to present as a Shakespearean 'romance' and begins to look more like *something else*?

   In what follows, I thus consider the thorny questions of what kind of play Shakespeare's *Cymbeline* is and what features have particularly come to define it in the contemporary imagination before shifting focus to revisit the earliest cinematic interpretation of this Shakespearean text.[2] Examining the particular cuts, emphases, expository glosses and narrative streamlining of the 1913 film, I ultimately argue that it reworks the material of Shakespeare's generically ambiguous play into a fairly straightforward romantic

comedy – albeit one that occurs in a vaguely historicized and bucolic setting. Essentially eliminating *Cymbeline's* most notorious villains and priz-
ing an Imogen-Leonatus love narrative that bears a striking resemblance
to the Hero-and-Claudio plot in *Much Ado About Nothing*, this adaptation
does away with many of the more fanciful elements for which its Shakespearean source is most often remembered. The resultant *Cymbeline* may
seem 'singularly well-adapted to rendition in motion pictures', yet it is a
Cymbeline curiously devoid of those fairy-tale elements and 'mark[s] of
wonder' (5.4.365) that are so closely associated with Shakespeare's metatheatrical and self-consciously excessive original.[3]

In addressing the central questions posed in this chapter, it is useful to
start with a consideration of *Cymbeline's* defining characteristics. Loosely
inspired by chronicle history and often associated with fairy tales, pastiche,
melodrama, fantasy and/or parody, this Shakespearean piece is undoubtedly a 'glorious mishmash'.[4] It is brimming with ghosts and gods, coincidence and confusion, recognitions and revelations, prophecies and por-
tents. Implausibly peopled by lost heirs, Roman legions and noxious villains, it relies on such unlikely curiosities as a tell-tale mole, a drug-induced
slumber, a revelatory ring and a misconceived 'manacle of love' to further
its plot (1.1.122).

Like *Pericles*, *The Winter's Tale* and *The Tempest*, Shakespeare's *Cymbeline* is fraught with taxonomical difficulties. Known variously in academic
parlance as a 'tragicomedy', a 'romance', a 'late play', or – as the relevant
Cambridge Companion of 2009 would have it – one of the 'last plays',
this text both invites generic criticism and remains notoriously difficult
to categorize. Numerous editors and commentators have quipped that it is
'tragical-comical-historical-pastoral' and it has been widely observed that
Shakespeare's so-called 'Tragedy of Cymbeline' could just as easily have
been classed by Heminges and Condell as a comedy or a history when they
compiled the First Folio of 1623.[5] As Stephen Orgel once put it, 'the play
more or less fits all three' of the categories available to Shakespeare's first
editors, yet 'comfortably fits none'.[6]

Cymbeline's generic unintelligibility is only further confounded by the
play's unrelentingly meta-Shakespearean character: Imogen's relationship
with Cymbeline reprises Cordelia's with her similarly myopic father Lear,
another of Shakespeare's semi-legendary British monarchs; Imogen, defying her father and insisting that she marry a suitor of her own choice, shares
in Hermia's rebellious romantic determination in *A Midsummer Night's
Dream*; the odious Iachimo, who steals Imogen's bracelet, plays a role strikingly similar to that of *Othello's* Iago, thief of Desdemona's handkerchief;

the death-like trance of the play's heroine, brought on by a potion, is a device excerpted wholesale from *Romeo and Juliet*; the wager plot echoes both the opening of *The Rape of Lucrece* and the last act of *The Taming of the Shrew*; and like Viola, Julia, Portia and Rosalind before her, Imogen pluckily disguises herself as a boy mid-play. The list could go on, but suffice it to say that *Cymbeline*'s exaggerated host of thematic – and even appellative – connections with other texts in the Shakespeare canon once led Northrop Frye to quip that it might well have been subtitled 'Much Ado About Everything'.[7]

Less often criticized than it once was for its perceived aesthetic short-comings, historical anachronisms and structural incongruities, *Cymbeline* nonetheless strains (perhaps even farcically so) under the weight of an improbable, labyrinthine plot. It is, to borrow Shakespeare's own phrasing, 'a thing perplexed/Beyond self-explication' (3.4.7–8). No wonder, then, that when the imprisoned Posthumus is visited by familial apparitions in Act 5, these 'poor ghosts' (5.3.154) – who claim to have been taking in the play's action 'from stiller seats' (5.3.145) – end up metatheatrically quibbling with Jupiter over their inability to make sense of the scenes they have just watched. Posthumus's deceased relations assume that the 'king of gods' must be neglecting his directorial role (5.3.149). Given the ghosts' pleas for the restoration of order in this scene, it would appear that even the theoretically omniscient Jove is no longer following along by the play's final act: 'Thy crystal window ope; look out; no longer exercise/Upon a valiant race thy harsh and potent injuries' (5.3.151–2), these spectres implore, hoping to draw the great deity's attention to the theatrical chaos unfolding on stage.

Given the play's generic ambiguities, its over-the-top meta-Shakespeareanisms and its teasing references to its own incoherence, it is unsurprising to note that *Cymbeline*'s academic interpreters have often remarked on its conspicuously wry and riddling feel. Frank Kermode long ago suggested that it is hard to shake the feeling that Shakespeare is 'somehow playing with the play' throughout *Cymbeline*, for instance.[8] And more recently, Alison Thorne has advanced the related argument that *Cymbeline* 'reflects ironically on the question of its own illegibility' by 'staging…the problems and the pitfalls involved in interpretative practices'.[9]

The 1913 *Cymbeline* was not the Thanhouser group's first foray into Shakespearean film adaptation. Following the release of the Thanhouser Company's first commercial film in March of 1910, the New Rochelle-based studio – which would go on to create more than a thousand films before its closure in 1917 – announced its intention to create 'a strong series of Shakespearean releases...of which *The Winter's Tale* is first'.[10] Though a formalized Shakespeare series never seems to have emerged as such, over the next few years a number of Shakespearean pieces were released by the company as part of its loosely conceived series of 'Thanhouser Classics': a line of 'status-conscious literary adaptations,' to borrow Judith Buchanan's phrasing, that began, as promised, with *The Winter's Tale* in May of 1910.[11] Originally founded by Edwin Thanhouser, a man described by one contemporary critic as 'a quiet, cultured, far-seeing impresario' who had, unlike most of his counterparts, already 'made a striking success in the theatrical world' prior to beginning his career as a filmmaker, the Thanhouser Company aimed to distinguish itself from the competition by producing *quality* films.[12] To wit, an advertisement for *The Winter's Tale* bragged it had been 'Done in the Thanhouser way and produced at just three times the cost of an ordinary release'.[13] In an interview with *The Moving Picture News* published early in the company's history, Thanhouser expressed his desire to create only 'artistic productions, particularly in the field of legitimate drama and comedy'. Thanhouser, who declared himself 'strongly opposed to producing any picture that contains brutal and uncalled-for crimes, or anything with a suggestive nature,' seems to have been attracted to Shakespearean subjects for their perceived morality as well as their cultural capital and 'artistic' nature: 'There are tragedies that make great picture stories and that are in every way interesting and proper and instructive, as, for instance, many of the plays of Shakespeare'.[14]

The Thanhouser Company's earliest Shakespearean experiment, *The Winter's Tale*, appears to have been an overwhelming critical success. It was called 'an excellent piece of work', a film 'most intelligently and clearly constructed' that would indubitably appeal to 'students of Shakespeare'.[15] One reviewer suggested that 'there was nothing for us to do but give our full approval and applause', while another mused 'there is no reason why tales from Shakespeare illumined and apostrophized as has been done in *The Winter's Tale* should not be given a better reception by the public than some of the cheap, gaudy modern productions now commanding so much attention in the moving picture field', encouragingly adding 'I hope to see others of this type in the market in the near future'.[16] Such pictures did, indeed, appear. In the wake of its earliest Shakespearean triumph, the Thanhouser Company (later renamed the Thanhouser Film Corporation, following a 1912 buyout) went on to produce versions of *Romeo and Juliet* in September of 1911, *The Tempest* in November of 1911 and *The Merchant of Venice* in July of 1912 before turning its attention to *Cymbeline*. The directorial debut of Frederick Sullivan, *Cymbeline* was produced by Lucius Henderson, a former stage-actor, who, like the company's by-then-abdicated founder, was popularly perceived to have come 'from the ranks of the [theatrically] legitimate'.[17] The two-reel production, released on 28 March 1913, featured James Cruze as Leonatus alongside Florence La Badie in the role of Imogen.

Widely recognized as one of 'the finest features produced by Thanhouser', *Cymbeline* garnered both critical and popular acclaim.[18] One review in *The Moving Picture World* praised, amongst other things, the film's 'scenic effects,' 'balanced' cast, 'sumptuous' costuming and 'clean-cut staging'. A second, slightly less exuberant review from the same issue pointed to minor 'blemishes' such as the anachronistic 'obtrusion of a decidedly modern house,' yet noted the 'praiseworthy ambition on the part of the producer' who had 'laudab[ly] endeavor[ed] to be correct in historic details' and 'deserves very great credit for seeking to aim high'.[19] Meanwhile, a review in *The New York Dramatic Mirror* hailed the film as 'a beautiful piece of work [that] might do credit to any company,' echoing an appreciation for the 'the care and skill' evident in the staging and costuming.[20] Gulfport, Mississippi's *Daily Herald* reported that the Thanhouser *Cymbeline* was 'one of the most artistics [sic] films ever shown in the South', and a note in the Pennsylvanian *Wilkes-Barre Times Leader* declared that everyone who had viewed it 'praised this work as being the best of its kind that they have seen'.[21]

But what was the nature of this film that the reviewers praised? One of its most striking features is certainly its great variety of outdoor shots. This overt visual engagement with the natural world arguably replicates and cunningly transforms the pastoral dimensions of Shakespeare's original play-text. A brief comparison with how the pastoral was represented in the earlier Thanhouser *Winter's Tale* of 1910 demonstrates something of the subtlety of the later film's engagement with similar generic materials. In *The Winter's Tale*, the play's bucolic elements are represented quite literally with shots of sheep. Although there is nary a lamb to be seen in the 1913 *Cymbeline*, outdoor scenes are plentiful, with locations ranging from an enclosed garden to the seashore (see Figure 2.1) to rocky caverns to open hills and wide expanses of greenery.[22]

Moreover, as an advertisement from *The Billboard* published on 29 March makes clear, audiences were encouraged to take particular note of the scenic backdrop: along with two other Thanhouser features, *Her Gallant Knights* and *For Her Boy's Sake*, *Cymbeline*'s release was touted as part of the company's second promotional 'All-California Week'. 'Every one likes

Figure 2.1.   Pisanio contemplates killing the cross-dressed Imogen on the seashore in the
Thanhouser *Cymbeline* (1913).

the beautiful California pictures,' the advertisement proclaimed, with the
further announcement: 'Here's another week in which we release ONLY
California productions.'[23] The Thanhouser *Cymbeline* thus subtly translates some of the idyllic, pastoral aspects of Shakespeare's play through its
status as one of the company's limited number of 'California pictures'.

   A second notable feature of the 1913 *Cymbeline* is its heavy reliance on
text. Buchanan's description of the film as 'wordy' is apt, as visual scenes
of writing and reading are combined with a broader narrative strategy of
elucidating the action through the copious use of title cards.[24] Resultantly,
I would argue that this film is also tangibly imbued with a general sense of
rootedness in textual culture. Characters are frequently shown in the act of
creating, exchanging and reacting to written documents. At the moment
that the ill-fated wager is struck, for example, Leonatus (as Posthumus is
referred to throughout the film) – who has been sitting by a fountain in
Rome, imbibing with his comrades – calls over a scribe to record the terms
of the wager. Later, when Iachimo arrives at Cymbeline's court and 'The
crafty Roman presents himself to Imogen as her husband's best friend,' as
the title card informs us, we see him presenting a scroll to the King. Presumably a letter of introduction, it is read both by Cymbeline himself and

the Queen, who peers over his shoulder with interest.[25] When the treacherous Leonatus sends word for Imogen to meet him at Milford Haven, we are again treated to and asked to participate in a scene of on-screen reading as we see both Imogen's reception of the letter and its contents, clearly modelled on the similar epistle of 3.2.40–47. After she has donned her male page's garb (earlier here than in Shakespeare's play), another letter is revealed to Imogen by Pisanio as they stand at the seashore, *en route* – or so she believes – to meet her husband. Again inspired by a message found in the play-text (this time at 3.4.21–29), the textual content of this note is visually presented to the audience. In yet another scene, we find a very nervous looking Leonatus approached by a messenger as he is standing alone on a hilltop; as he opens a scroll to learn of Imogen's supposed death, we are once again made privy to the written content of a personal missive, this one signed by Pisanio.

Though the Thanhouser film's overt aura of inscriptedness arguably mirrors what Thorne has described as 'the conspicuous presence of letters in the play (which exceeds any requirements of the plot)' or *Cymbeline's* 'superfluous proliferation of letters, papers, books and tablets,'[26] it is hard to miss the authenticating implications of Shakespearean authority also conveyed by a number of particularly 'wordy' title cards that integrate pseudo-quotations into the film. The first of these, which reads 'Do his bidding: strike. My heart is empty of all things but grief' (words attributed to Imogen as she grieves her betrayal by her husband), represents a recognisable rearrangement and abbreviation of the heroine's more long-winded directive to Pisanio at 3.4.65–71. A second quotation is worked into the film when the siblings are first reunited. After the woodsmen return to find their domestic space surprisingly occupied, Imogen-in-disguise is graciously plied with food while her brothers exclaim via title card: 'But that it eats our victuals I should think here were a fairy' – a rendition of Belarius's lines from 3.6.40–1. A fast succession of further Shakespearean quotations appears in the final minutes of the second reel as the film draws to a close. Just after a title card announces 'A few brave men save the day for Britain', the victorious King Cymbeline humbly thanks them for their bravery in battle with words adopted from 5.4.1–2: 'Stand by my side, you whom the gods have made/Preservers of my throne.' This is quickly followed up with yet another Shakespearean quotation, the wounded Iachimo's title card confession 'I belied a lady. The princess of this country,' which substitutes words from 5.2.2–3 in place of the much lengthier confessions found at 5.4.153–68 and 179–208 of the play-text. Mere moments later, just before the final reunification of the lovers, a truncation of 5.1.25–7 reveals Leonatus's sentiment: 'I'll die for thee, oh Imogen, even for whom my life is.' And, finally, Leonatus's lines from 5.4.263–4, rendered as 'Hang there like fruit, my soul, till the tree die,' grace a final Shakespearean title card before the film draws to a close with the reunited lovers' passionate kiss.

In spite of the carefully cultivated sense of verbal alignment between the 1913 *Cymbeline* and its Shakespearean source that is created through the use of such title card quotations, we find a number of events represented that have no counterparts in Shakespeare's play-text. In a perceptible attempt to explain key elements of the backstory, for example, the film opens by dramatizing rumours about Cymbeline's kidnapped sons. Visual images of the missing princes eating, drinking and arming themselves demonstrate how, as the relevant title card puts it, 'The king's sons are reared as woodsmen by the former courtier who stole them'. Other information about Imogen and Posthumus, similarly relayed as court gossip in the play, is also dramatized in the film. In the first reel, we see the nascent relationship between the young lovers blooming in an idyllic garden scene; we witness Cymbeline's futile efforts to arrange his child's marriage to his own preferred suitor (here unidentified either by name or familial relationship) and, having been textually informed via title card that 'Imogen refuses to marry one that she does not love,' we are also made privy to a wedding ceremony in which Imogen's identity as a chaste bride is visually emphasized.

Conventional wisdom has it that *Cymbeline* is a play in need of cutting. And no wonder, for, amongst a flourish of other metatheatrical touches, this Shakespearean text seems presciently to highlight its own predisposition for abbreviation. What we might describe as the play's self-conscious sense of *cuttability* permeates its final act in particular: various characters attempt to 'speak truth' (5.4.274) and accurately paraphrase the play's convoluted action for the benefit of King Cymbeline (who has, in effect, been ruling *in absentia* for most of the previous four acts). 'Let *me* end the story' interrupts Guiderius at one point, discerning that Pisanio's rendition is limited by his lack of knowledge about Cloten's final fate (5.4.286; emphasis my own). Meanwhile, Cornelius cannot seem to fit everything he knows into his own miniaturized version of events either: 'O gods!', he exclaims in frustration as he realizes that he 'left out one thing which the Queen confessed' (5.4.243–4). Apprehending the propensity of those around him to cut the play's action in retelling it, the British monarch pointedly refers to his secondhand knowledge of events as a 'fierce abridgment' (5.4.382). Sensing the limitations of his individual courtiers' explanations as they try to 'Winnow the truth from falsehood,' he muses: 'When shall I hear it all through?' (5.4.134; 382). As Cymbeline recognizes, it would require 'long inter'gatories' – presumably to be conducted offstage after the play has concluded – to sort through the text's mess of 'circumstantial branches' (5.4.392; 383). By the play's end, we are left wondering if, indeed, the retrospective clarity that the king seeks is even possible.

Katherine Duncan-Jones was echoing something of the play's own concluding sentiments when, in a 1983 review of Moshinsky's BBC Television *Cymbeline*, she cautiously noted that 'any modern director...must make some positive decisions about how to deal with this clogged, often obscure and highly complicated romance'.[27] As Duncan-Jones's comment suggests, *Cymbeline* has a long history of 'fierce abridgement' in performance. The play's stage history has been notably characterized by emendation – often changes inspired by a desire to bring a greater sense of coherence, plausibility and/or narrative clarity to the Shakespearean text.[28] And, clocking in at just over twenty minutes in length, the 1913 Thanhouser *Cymbeline* is no exception to the rule; of necessity, the two-reel film participates in a wider, pre-existing tradition of abridging the play.

Shakespearean scholars have often described *Cymbeline*'s unusual structure as a triad of non-hierarchical plot strands: 1) the wager plot; 2) the dynastic plot; and 3) the political plot. While retaining elements from all three of these strands, as is obvious from my previous *précis* of the film's opening scenes, the 1913 *Cymbeline* noticeably privileges the wager plot. In fact, with the exception of the first scene dedicated to Cymbeline's missing sons, the remainder of the first reel is given over to exclusively tracing developments in the lovers' affair: the exchange of jewellery; Leonatus's banishment; the ill-advised bet; Iachimo's testing of Imogen; Leonatus's reaction to his wife's perceived infidelity; the heroine's receipt of Leonatus's letter; and Imogen's disguised departure to meet her husband. This emphasis on youthful romance and its attendant complications, as focalized through the perspective of Imogen, is carried over into the film's second reel, as well. The characters of Imogen's brothers, when we again encounter them, remain both unnamed and underdeveloped and, furthermore, when the audience is presented, nearly fifteen minutes into the film, with a title card announcing that 'Cymbeline, King of Britain, is informed of the Roman invasion,' this is the first time that we have heard about any political tensions in the British kingdom.

The primacy given in this film to representing the 'pangs of barred affections' (1.1.82) and narrating Imogen's (mis)adventures in love is perhaps unsurprising. It aligns with what Ruth Nevo has termed the prevailing 'Imogenolatry' of Victorian critics such as Swinburne, who famously hailed Imogen as 'the immortal godhead of womanhood' – sounding for all the world like Posthumus bragging that his 'unparagoned mistress' is 'more fair, virtuous, wise, chaste, constant, qualified, and less attemptable' than any other woman (1.4.65; 47–8).[29] This Swinburnian-style idolization of Imogen's spotless character maintained particular currency in the early years of the twentieth century. Writing just a few short years after the appearance of the 1913 *Cymbeline*, Arthur Quiller-Couch declared this plucky, yet ultimately submissive heroine not only to be the 'sum and aggregate of fair womanhood as at last Shakespeare achieved it,' but also 'the most adorable woman ever created by God or man'.[30]

What else, then, of Shakespeare's play-text has been cut to allow for this focus on the 'adorable' Imogen and her romantic escapades in the Thanhouser film? The internal power struggles of Cymbeline's blended family, which come to bear on our understanding of the dynastic plot strand in the play, have all but disappeared in this 1913 adaptation. This Queen, though a meddlesome tattletale, is no deadly poisoner. In fact, unlike the 'crafty devil' (2.1.46) of the play – in which she is explicitly described as 'a widow/That late [Cymbeline] married' who 'most desired the match' between Imogen and her own son Cloten (1.1.5–6; 12) – she is never explicitly identified as the mother of the rejected suitor, nor shown to have a particular interest in matters of the succession. Rather, her motives are simplified with the help of a title card reading 'Imogen's stepmother is jealous of her favor with the King'. The Queen's animosity towards her stepdaughter is thereby reduced to an anxious tug-of-war for her new husband's affections. In a related vein, the play's Cloten, 'a thing/Too bad for bad report' (1.1.16–17) is questionably included in the film at all. We may be inclined, based on prior knowledge of the play, to identify his character with Cymbeline's favoured suitor at the outset of the film, but there is no explicit equivocation made, no sign of attempted revenge for his slight, no gruesome beheading of his character and no confusion as to the identity of his corpse. Similarly, while Iachimo's character unquestionably plays an unsavoury role in the wager plot, and, though Imogen's bracelet is certainly filched by him, there is no mole for him to report back to Leonatus – or, if there were, this Iachimo never dared look beneath her breast to find it (see Figure 2.2). No doubt, it was the mole's absence that inspired one contemporary reviewer to laud the scene's delicacy as having been 'artistically presented'.[31]

The near-elimination of two of the play's three most sinister villains and the arguably increased palatability of the third, all of which unquestionably lightens the tone of this 1913 film, is coupled with an amplified sense of historical realism. This is achieved through the exclusion of many of the play's

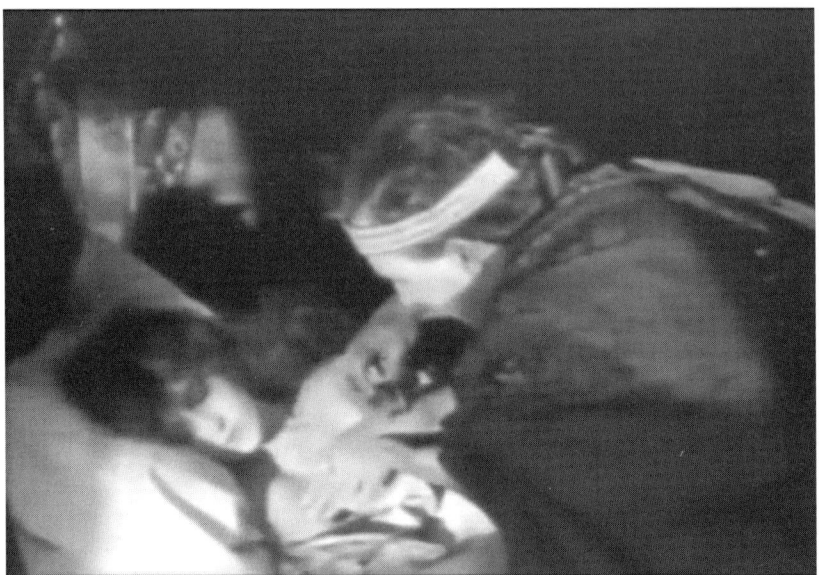

Figure 2.2.   Iachimo steals Imogen's bracelet as she sleeps in the Thanhouser *Cymbeline*
(1913).

more fanciful (and meta-Shakespearean) features. Gone from this adaptation are the play's most fantastical elements: along with Imogen's mole, the
sleeping potion/poison, the soothsayer and the *deus ex machina* entrance of
Jupiter are absent. This general excision of the fantastic from the 1913 *Cymbeline* may, indeed, have been borne of an attempt to distinguish the film
from the Thanhouser Film Corporation's 1911 *Tempest*. This earlier Shakespearean film, which reviewers generally seem to have agreed was 'not up to
Thanhouser standard,' had highlighted the fairy-tale dimensions of Shakespeare's *Tempest*, as the following review from *The Morning Telegraph* makes
clear:

> Few American producing companies have ever succeeded in the best pre-
> sentations of fantastic or fairylike subjects, and Shakespeare's *The Tempest* is
> little else than a fantasy, and of the most difficult sort to produce, either in
> dramatic or other form. So it was a bold attempt of the Thanhouser Com-
> pany to make a pictureplay [sic] of this so-seldom seen offering, and there is
> small wonder that it falls short of the mark of excellence this company has
> attained in other works.[32]

By way of conclusion, I want to again turn to the final question that I posed at the outset of this chapter: how much can a so-called Shakespearean romance like *Cymbeline* be pared down and reshaped before it ceases to present as a Shakespearean romance and begins to look more like *something else*? As my previous analyses of the Thanhouser *Cymbeline*'s cuts, additions and narrative emphases have demonstrated, a close examination of the film reveals an adaptation that shares few of those taxonomical ambiguities, metatheatrical excesses or incongruities of plotting so closely associated with Shakespeare's original play-text. I thus want to suggest that part of what made this resultant *Cymbeline* seem so 'singularly well-adapted to rendition in motion pictures' may well have been the fact that it bears little resemblance to a typical Shakespearean 'romance' *à la Pericles, The Tempest* or *The Winter's Tale*. Rather, the *something else* that has been created through *Cymbeline*'s 'fierce abridgement' is a typical Shakespearean romantic comedy.

Much of the 1913 film's narrowed, or perhaps transmuted, generic identity can be traced to its aforementioned stress on *Cymbeline*'s wager plot. The film's action follows the basic structural pattern of Shakespeare's other romantic comedies, unfolding in three more-or-less distinct stages: the hero and heroine fall in love; outside intervention and a grievous personal misunderstanding tear them apart; the circumstances that separated them are resolved and they are reunited. The wager plot of the 1913 *Cymbeline* is historicized, certainly, but issues of nationalism and the ultimate (if slightly perplexing) possibilities for peaceful coexistence between Britain and Rome that so strongly inform the political strand of the Shakespearean play are subverted in the film. Rather, the film's historical setting primarily serves as an opportunity for spectacle – an excuse to introduce sumptuous period costuming and elaborate military choreography. Resultantly, the lengthy battle scene between the Britons and Romans, given great prominence near the end of the film's second reel, is depoliticized to the extreme. Reduced in significance to a device that will reunite the various characters that have been personally separated from one another, its ultimate importance lies in that it offers Leonatus an apt opportunity to redeem his honour in the eyes of his formerly disapproving father-in-law.

In closing, I want to make the further suggestion that the 1913 film's appeal derives not merely from its broad resemblance to other Shakespearean romantic comedies but also from a more specific relationship that is cultivated between this 'fierce abridgement' and another familiar Shakespearean play, *Much Ado About Nothing*. The 1913 film's pared down version of the wager plot bears a striking and noteworthy resemblance to the Hero-and-Claudio storyline in *Much Ado About Nothing*. Like Claudio tricked into the belief that he has been erotically betrayed by Hero, Leonatus is similarly deceived about the sexual behaviour of his own female beloved. Both men's rash responses to these false rumours of infidelity are again in alignment: out of hand, they repudiate and unflinchingly denounce their innocent mates. Hero and Imogen, meanwhile, are exonerated only through eleventh-hour confessions – much to the seemingly-too-late distress of Claudio and Leonatus. Like Shakespeare's submissive Hero, who meekly accepts Claudio as her husband at the end of *Much Ado About Nothing*, Imogen, too, is unquestioning in her forgiveness of Leonatus's grave folly. These wider resemblances between *Cymbeline*'s wager plot and *Much Ado About Nothing*'s bed trick are conspicuously underscored for the film's audience in its final scene, where we see the previously mentioned title card confession of Iachimo: 'I belied a lady. The princess of this country'. The word choice in this title card has significant intertextual resonances, for Iachimo's vocabulary when he talks about his slandering of Imogen echoes language repeatedly used to characterize Hero's predicament in *Much Ado About Nothing*: 'my cousin is belied' (4.1.139); 'Hero is belied' (5.1.42); 'thou hast belied mine innocent child' (5.1.67); 'they have belied a lady' (5.1.193). To again cite Frye, it would seem that the 'singularly' cinematic *Cymbeline* of 1913 was 'Much Ado About Everything,' indeed.

Notes

1 *The Moving Picture World* (5 April 1913) as reproduced in Q. D. Bowers, *Thanhouser Films: An Encyclopedia and History, 1909–1918*, online version 2.0 (Portland: Thanhouser Company Film Preservation, 1997), n.p., www.thanhouser.org/tcocd (accessed March 2015).

2 This film has attracted little critical attention to date. The most sustained discussions appear in R. H. Ball, *Shakespeare on Silent Film: A Strange Eventful History* (New York: Routledge, 2013 [1968]); J. Buchanan, *Shakespeare on Film* (New York: Pearson Longman, 2005) and J. Buchanan, *Shakespeare on Silent Film: An Excellent Dumb Discourse* (Cambridge: Cambridge University Press, 2009).

3 Subsequent in-text citations to Shakespeare's works refer to the Cambridge edition but we have chosen to use the name 'Imogen' rather than Cambridge's 'Innogen'.

4 I borrow this phrasing from M. Billington, '*Cymbeline*: The Swan, Stratford', *The Guardian*, 8 August 2003, www.theguardian.com/stage/2003/aug/08/theatre (accessed March 2015).

5 Perhaps the most recent instance of the 'tragical-comical-historical-pastoral' joke appears in the introduction to J. Bate and E. Rasmussen (eds.), *Cymbeline* (New York: Modern Library, 2011), vii.

6 S. Orgel, 'Shakespeare Performed: *Cymbeline* at Santa Cruz', *Shakespeare Quarterly* 52.2 (2001), 277.

7 N. Frye, 'A Natural Perspective: The Development of Shakespearean Comedy and Romance', in T. Grande and G. Sherbert (eds.), *Writings on Shakespeare and the Renaissance* (Toronto: University of Toronto Press, 2010 [1965]), 168.

8 F. Kermode, *The Final Plays* (London: Longmans, Green and Co., 1963), 22.

9 A. Thorne, '"To Write and Read/Be Henceforth Treacherous": *Cymbeline* and the Problem of Interpretation', in J. Richards and J. Knowles (eds.), *Shakespeare's Late Plays: New Readings* (Edinburgh: Edinburgh University Press, 1999), 177.

10 This announcement is from *The Moving Picture World* [no date provided], as reproduced in Ball, *Shakespeare on Silent Film*, 68.

11 Buchanan, *Shakespeare on Film*, 43.

12 *The Moving Picture World* (12 March 1910) as reproduced in Bowers, *Thanhouser Films*.

13 Untitled advertisement, *The Billboard*, 28 May 1910, 25.

14 *Moving Picture News* (26 February 1910) as reproduced in Bowers, *Thanhouser Films*.

15 *The Moving Picture World* (11 June 1910) as reproduced in Bowers, *Thanhouser Films*; *The New York Dramatic Mirror* (4 June 1910) as reproduced in Bowers; and *The Moving Picture News* (21 May 1910) as reproduced in Bowers.

16 *The Moving Picture News* (21 May 1910) as reproduced in Bowers, *Thanhouser Films*; *The Nickelodeon* (1 June 1910) as reproduced in Bowers.

17 'Photoplays: Henderson Now IMP Director', *The Billboard*, 21 November 1914, 46. In 1912, Thanhouser sold the company which bore his name to a group headed by Charles J. Hite. However, after Hite's death in 1915, Thanhouser took charge of the company once again. This particular film was made during the founder's hiatus. See Bowers, *Thanhouser Films*, for a detailed history of the company.

18 'Photoplays', 46.

19 *The Moving Picture World* (5 April 1913) as reproduced in Bowers, *Thanhouser Films*.

20 *The New York Dramatic Mirror* (2 April 1913) as reproduced in Bowers, *Thanhouser Films*.

21 'Band Concerts at Air Dome', *The Daily Herald*, 7 May 1913, 8; untitled article, *Wilkes-Barre Times-Leader*, 23 April 1913, 18.

22 A useful point of contrast here is Moshinsky's later *Cymbeline* adaptation, which has aptly been called 'very much indoor Shakespeare': R. Warren, *Shakespeare in Performance: Cymbeline* (Manchester: Manchester University Press, 1989), 63.

23 Untitled advertisement, *The Billboard*, 29 March 1913, 53.

24 Buchanan, *Shakespeare on Film*, 43.

25 This is similar to the short note we are made privy to at 1.6.22–5 of Shakespeare's play when Iachimo introduces himself to his friend's wife.

26 Thorne, 'To Write and Read', 179.

27 Katherine Duncan-Jones, 'Sitting Pretty', *The Times Literary Supplement*, 22 July 1983, 773.

28 On the play's performance and reception history, see C. M. S. Alexander, '*Cymbeline*: The Afterlife', in C. M. S. Alexander (ed.), *The Cambridge Companion to Shakespeare's Last Plays* (Cambridge: Cambridge University Press, 2009), 135–54; and V. Wayne, '*Cymbeline*: Patriotism and Performance', in R. Dutton and J. E. Howard (eds.), *A Companion to Shakespeare's Works: The Poems, Problem Comedies, and Late Plays* (Oxford: Blackwell, 2003), 389–440. No doubt, the most famous of these reworkings is George Bernard Shaw's delightfully audacious rewriting of the final act in his *Cymbeline Refinished*, but Shaw's was certainly not the first attempt to 'fix' the play. In 1682, less than a century after *Cymbeline*'s original composition, it was rewritten by Thomas D'Urfey as *The Injured Princess or the Fatal Wager*. In 1759, William Hawkins's adaptation of the play renamed characters and reordered the plot so it would conform with the classical unities. Two years later, David Garrick's influential version made cuts and rearrangements which involved omitting Posthumus's imprisonment and dreams. J. P. Kemble published, in 1815, a version that reworked the play's opening scene for greater clarity. And Henry Irving's famed production at London's Lyceum Theatre in 1896 (the very version that inspired Shaw's irreverent rewriting) sought to simplify the plot by cutting the Shakespearean text to roughly three-quarters of its original length.

29 For Nevo's coinage of 'Imogenolatry', see R. Nevo, '*Cymbeline:* The Rescue of the King', in A. Thorne (ed.), *Shakespeare's Romances* (New York: Palgrave Macmillan, 2003), 91–116. I cite Swinburne's comments from A. C. Swinburne, *A Study of Shakespeare* (London: Chatto and Windus, 1880), 227.

30 A. Quiller-Couch, *Shakespeare's Workmanship* (Cambridge: Cambridge University Press, 1951 [1918]), 243–4.

31 *The Moving Picture World* (5 April 1913) as reproduced in Bowers, *Thanhouser Films*.

32 *The New York Dramatic Mirror* (6 December 1911) as reproduced in Bowers, *Thanhouser Films* and *The Morning Telegraph* (3 December 1911) as reproduced in Bowers.

WORKS CITED

Alexander, C. M. S., '*Cymbeline*: The Afterlife', in C. M. S. Alexander (ed.), *The Cambridge Companion to Shakespeare's Last Plays* (Cambridge: Cambridge University Press, 2009), 135–54.

Ball, R. H., *Shakespeare on Silent Film: A Strange Eventful History* (New York: Routledge, 2013 [1968]).

Bate, J. and E. Rasmussen (eds.), *William Shakespeare's* Cymbeline (New York: Modern Library, 2011).

Billington, M., '*Cymbeline*: The Swan, Stratford', *The Guardian*, 8 August 2003, n.p., http://www.theguardian.com/stage/2003/aug/08/theatre.

Bowers, Q. D., *Thanhouser Films: An Encyclopedia and History, 1909–1918*, online version 2.0 (Portland: Thanhouser Company Film Preservation, 1997), n.p., www.thanhouser.org/tcocd/.

Buchanan, J., *Shakespeare on Film* (New York: Pearson Longman, 2005).

Shakespeare on Silent Film: An Excellent Dumb Discourse (Cambridge: Cambridge University Press, 2009).

Duncan-Jones, K., 'Sitting Pretty', *The Times Literary Supplement* (22 July 1983), 773.

Frye, N., 'A Natural Perspective: The Development of Shakespearean Comedy and Romance', in T. Grande and G. Sherbert (eds.), *Writings on Shakespeare and the Renaissance* (Toronto: University of Toronto Press, 2010 [1965]), 127–225.

Kermode, F., *The Final Plays* (London: Longmans, Green and Co., 1963).

Nevo, R., '*Cymbeline*: The Rescue of the King', in A. Thorne (ed.), *Shakespeare's Romances* (New York: Palgrave Macmillan, 2003), 91–116.

Orgel, S., 'Shakespeare Performed: *Cymbeline* at Santa Cruz', *Shakespeare Quarterly* 52.2 (2001), 277–85.

Quiller-Couch, A., *Shakespeare's Workmanship* (Cambridge: Cambridge University Press, 1951 [1918]).

Swinburne, A. C., *A Study of Shakespeare* (London: Chatto and Windus, 1880).

Thorne, A., '"To Write and Read/Be Henceforth Treacherous": *Cymbeline* and the Problem of Interpretation', in J. Richards and J. Knowles (eds.), *Shakespeare's Late Plays: New Readings* (Edinburgh: Edinburgh University Press, 1999), 176–90.

Warren, R., *Shakespeare in Performance:* Cymbeline (Manchester: Manchester University Press, 1989).

Wayne, V., '*Cymbeline*: Patriotism and Performance', in R. Dutton and J. E. Howard (eds.), *A Companion to Shakespeare's Works: The Poems, Problem Comedies, and Late Plays* (Oxford: Blackwell, 2003), 389–440.

CHAPTER 3

Looking (at) Women in the BBC Pericles

Edel Semple

Although infamously described as a 'mouldy tale' by Ben Jonson, *Pericles, Prince of Tyre* was, nevertheless, a hugely popular play in its day.[1] Since then however, *Pericles* has had something of a chequered history. Omitted from the First Folio and critically neglected until recently, it is still rarely performed and infrequently taught. Indeed, as Paul Nelsen suggests, were it not for the BBC Shakespeare Series, which filmed and aired Shakespeare's entire canon from 1978 to 1985, *Pericles* may never have made it onto the screen.[2] Directed by David Jones, *Pericles* was the thirty-first play filmed in the Series and, to date, it remains the only film of the play ever produced.[3] However, along with other rarely performed plays, *Pericles* was deemed a surprising success of the Series. For instance, after beginning his review by enumerating the difficulties that *Pericles* presents to a director, Peter Kemp declared that Jones's version had successfully and 'triumphantly met' these challenges.[4] In a recent study of the film, Paul Nelsen proposes that 'Jones and his colleagues should be commended for generating an extraordinary video rendition of this particular play.'[5] Such praise suggests that the film fulfils the aims of the play's narrator, Gower, who wishes to 'glad [our] ear and please [our] eyes' (Prologue 4). And yet, despite the ratings success of the Shakespeare Series[6] and the popularity and uniqueness of the *Pericles* film, it remains relatively neglected in discussions of the play and in critical assessments of the Series.[7]

This chapter will examine the BBC *Pericles*, focusing on the representation of one source of pleasure – looking – and on a group that have often been the objects of such pleasure – women. In her study of Shakespeare's women on film, Carol Rutter argues that 'as film deprivileges Shakespeare's words, so it coincidentally redistributes the balance of power between men's and women's roles: not only are there more women in

My thanks to my colleagues and friends – Darragh Greene, Tom Birkett, Barry Monahan – and to all involved in the 'Shakespeare on Screen: The Romances' seminar at the Shakespeare 450 conference for their suggestions on an earlier draft of this chapter.

Shakespeare films than play-texts but they have much more to perform.'[8] The women of the BBC *Pericles* have much to perform and, as I will show, the film offers fresh and striking insights into each of the central female characters – Antiochus's Daughter, Thaisa, Marina, Dioniza, the Bawd, and the Goddess Diana – but also moves to balance the power between male and female roles. Throughout, I analyse the representation of women's roles (mother, daughter, virgin, wife, murderer, whore, goddess), the construction of gender and sexuality, the hierarchy of objectification and the ideological power of the gaze on the small screen. While the play frequently presents women as desirable objects of visual pleasure, the film repeatedly focuses on women's own looking. Taking this as a central interest, I argue that the film's portrayal of the female gaze is of a significance heretofore unrecognised, for, at various points, it acts as an expression of agency, character, desire, dependence and authority.

The first female character to appear on screen is King Antiochus's unnamed daughter, played by Edita Brychta. As Gower explains, Antiochus and the Daughter are engaged in an incestuous relationship. The film provides us with ocular proof of this as the pair enter a lush courtyard, hand in hand, and kiss on cue as Gower's voice-over tells us that Antiochus 'to incest [his daughter] did provoke' (Prologue 26).[9] The film's setting for Antioch is an enclosed garden – verdant greenery abounds, the earth is sandy, and the noise of cicadas gives the impression of a pleasant Mediterranean day. However, this setting is oppressive: the garden walls are high, soldiers stand at every door, the plants cast deep shadows and, mounted on a wall, the skulls of dead princes oversee the action. As petrified onlookers, the skulls serve to present the Daughter, whom Pericles seeks as his bride, as a kind of gorgon; to look upon her is to die.[10] Furthermore, while the mounted skulls are revealed to Pericles as a warning – solve Antiochus's riddle or die – they also prefigure his powerlessness; having gazed upon the Daughter but failed to see her true nature, the princes are now lifeless and eyeless, and thus stand for eternity as symbols of an inanimate, defective spectatorship. Such imagery, coupled with Gower's introduction, makes it blatantly clear that, when Pericles enters, he has arrived in a corrupt, post-lapsarian Paradise. Through costuming, the film suggests that the Daughter is a product of this landscape. Attired 'like the spring' in a shimmering green gown and wearing a headdress of silver leaves, she is presented as both an alluring and fertile potential spouse and as the snake in the Edenic garden. Costume designer Colin Lavers saw a symbolic connection between the Daughter's appearance, the garden setting and the concealed corruption at the heart of Antioch's ruling family: 'the incest is veiled, the plants are a veil, and the girl's costume is revealing but not quite revealing!'.[11] Remarking further on the Daughter's gown, through which we catch glimpses of her skin, Lavers noted, 'You're never quite sure how much you see of her'.[12] This comment might be said to aptly sum up the audience's experience of the character of the Daughter as a whole.

The emblem of Antioch is a portcullis and it appears in different guises throughout the scene. Wearing a wine-coloured gown with black leather trim, Antiochus's menacing demeanour is enhanced by the black portcullis that hangs on a chain about his neck.[13] The image of a portcullis appears again when we first catch sight of his daughter, who has been summoned by him. Pericles directs our gaze – 'See where she comes' (1.1.13) – as she slowly passes by a barred window in a medium shot. In Franco Zeffirelli's *Romeo and Juliet* (1968), Paris and the audience first see Juliet as she passes before an open window. In *Pericles*, as in Zeffirelli's film, the window is used to frame the woman as the focus of the men's discussion and as an object of desire. However, the window grid also separates her from Pericles and the viewer; the Daughter is forbidden and dangerous. In his framing here, Jones also perhaps draws on Zeffirelli's depiction of Lady Capulet in order to hint at the Daughter's corruption. Soon after we see Juliet, the camera zooms in on her mother passing a window. Conversely though, whereas Juliet is shown running and laughing – the epitome of joyous youth and attractive girlishness – the sour-faced, static, and silent Lady Capulet is presented as an example of one of the 'marred' mothers referred to by Lord Capulet. Similarly, Antiochus's Daughter is presented as an example of an ideal femininity that has been tragically tainted; she is an instrument that has been 'played upon before [her] time' (1.1.85) and, as Pericles later learns, she is thus a 'glorious casket stored with ill' (1.1.78).

Although the Daughter is present throughout this scene, she initially seems like something of a Petrarchan mistress: she stands aloof, immobile, and her contributions are limited. For instance, as Antiochus and Pericles speak to one another, she bestows a brief smile on her off-screen father, but her face is blank as she gazes at Pericles. She remains motionless and impassive as Pericles rhapsodises about her virtues (in an aside) and Antiochus openly praises her delectable qualities. Even when the Daughter does speak to wish her suitor well, her voice and expression are largely emotionless. Pericles is denied any reading of the princess; gazing at her illegible face, he instead constructs her through his own passionate projections. In this way, the film highlights for the audience the loud silences of the Daughter: she is more spoken about than spoken to and, in the play-text, she is assigned only two lines. However, as I suggest later, through the gaze of the camera, the film forms an extra-textual narrative where the Daughter's

Figure 3.1.   King Antiochus (John Woodvine) embraces his daughter (Edita Brychta), as imagined by Pericles in the BBC 1983 production. All rights reserved.

silence and unreadability become intentional acts of self-fashioning and self-expression.[14]

When Pericles deciphers the riddle and learns of the couple's incestuous relationship, the camera becomes subjective. With a series of jump cuts and jerky headshots, we see in Pericles' mind's eye the pair luxuriate in a kiss, before the Daughter smiles up at Antiochus and rests her head on his chest. Staring smugly at Pericles, Antiochus and his Daughter seem to mock him with their superior knowledge and transgressive love; their self-assured gaze frames him as their helpless dupe (see Figure 3.1).

The jump cuts and the unsettling musical motif key this as Pericles' tortured fantasy but it is a fantasy that the audience has already seen and knows to be true. On the one hand, this sequence encourages the audience to identify with Pericles and understand his subsequent disgust and decision to flee.[15] However, although problematic, this fantasy also adds to the character of the Daughter; she willingly engages in the relationship and she expresses pleasure and defiance as she directly gazes at Pericles.

At the close of this scene, as the Daughter is led away by Antiochus, she turns to stare blankly back at Pericles. Here, the female gaze appears as illegible; nothing can be read from the princess and Pericles must rely on his interpretation of the riddle and his imagination for proof of her guilt. However, the Daughter is not devoid of emotion, thought or agency. Rather, she deliberately withholds herself from Pericles; he is denied access to, and knowledge of, her true self, as she reserves this for her father alone. Our final view of the lovers shows Antiochus, anxious at Pericles' knowledge, rush to his concerned Daughter, who throws her arms open wide. The camera zooms in to an intimate close-up of Antiochus's back and the Daughter's face as they cling desperately to one another. In this moment, which does not appear in the play, the Daughter enacts the roles outlined in the riddle; she is all at once 'mother, wife [and] child' (1.1.70). In public, her silence and passivity define her as a dutiful daughter, but in private she is free to define herself and express the multiple identities that she occupies. In the play, by contrast, Antiochus's Daughter is a flat, undeveloped, and noticeably unnamed character that functions as a cipher and stock type (she is a symbol of immorality; as object of desire, she is a foil to Pericles' destined, ideal wife Thaisa; as corrupt child, she is a foil to his chaste daughter Marina). On screen, however, through a manipulation of the gaze – a manipulation not possible on stage – the Daughter is empowered. She has a measure of inwardness and, through visual means, this most silent of women says something about herself, her relationships and desires.

With Pericles' arrival at the court of Pentapolis, the new location and the mores of the monarch are signalled through the set and costuming. A trumpet sounds as the camera pans across the open, cream pavilion that dominates the set and we see in passing soldiers and courtiers in tunics of ivory, beige and tan. There is no darkness here, literal or moral. The atmosphere is convivial and inviting as we encounter the second father-daughter pairing of the play – King Simonides and Thaisa (Juliet Stevenson) – who clearly enjoy a happy relationship (see Figure 3.2).

Throughout the pageant of the knights, who have assembled to mark Thaisa's birthday with a tournament, the camerawork and Stevenson's performance make it patently obvious that Thaisa is her own woman. Unlike Antiochus's Daughter, Thaisa's gaze is not limited to her father or suitor; rather, her eyes follow her interests and she looks at everyone and everything in this scene. When Simonides describes her as 'Beauty's child' (2.2.6) and as Nature's marvel made 'For men to see, and seeing wonder at' (2.2.7), Thaisa looks bemused; she takes her father's precepts and praise with a pinch of salt. She obediently attends to Simonides' pronouncements on the divine authority of princes as well but, at his conclusion, glances away

Figure 3.2. Thaisa (Juliet Stevenson) and her father King Simonides (Patrick Allen) in the 1983 BBC *Pericles*.

with a wry smile and lick of her lips. Although she is dutiful, she is neither submissive nor uncritical.

As one by one the knights present themselves to Thaisa, the film attends to her responses. Each of the knights enters with his back to the camera. Thaisa, in the centre of the frame, faces them to read their mottos; the men are objects for her gaze. Although the camera is trained on Thaisa, she is far from being a mere object to be looked at; rather, she is a subject who looks, who looks for and with pleasure, and in particular who actively looks back at those who gaze upon her.[16] Thaisa and Pericles' falling in love at first sight, then, is accepted by the audience not simply because this is a romance play or because Thaisa is the 'right' fairy-tale princess but because it is presented as a fitting match of two subjects; the pair silently gaze at one another, equal in their looking and their attraction. During the tournament, which takes place off-screen, the camera focuses on Thaisa and Simonides who give rapt attention to the action. At the cries of 'The mean knight!' (2.2.49), Thaisa jumps up, smiles, and glances back at her father to share her joy and excitement at Pericles' success, before returning to gaze

Figure 3.3.   Thaisa (Juliet Stevenson) and Pericles (Mike Gwilym), with King Simonides
(Patrick Allen) in the background in the 1983 BBC *Pericles*. All rights reserved.

delightedly at the triumphant prince off-screen. In contrast to Antiochus's
Daughter then, Thaisa's father is not her sole source of pleasure; her gaze
marks her as an independent, self-aware and desiring individual actively
engaging with her world. Following the banquet, it comes as no surprise
to the audience that Thaisa has sworn to marry Pericles or 'never more to
view nor day nor light' (2.5.16). Although Simonides tests the couple by
pretending to be displeased at this turn of events, Thaisa cannot take her
eyes from Pericles and they hold hands at her instigation; resembling two
teenagers caught kissing, the couple only separate when Simonides walks
between them. With the good news that Simonides wishes them to wed, the
scene ends on a tight shot of Thaisa and Pericles in profile, with Simonides
in soft focus exiting in the background (see Figure 3.3). Thus, while the
benevolent paternal figure oversees and blesses the union, he is shown to
be, healthily, exterior to it and the couple's autonomous, reciprocal plea-
sured looking affirms that this is a marriage of equals and a marriage of
their choosing.

   After giving birth at sea to their daughter Marina, Thaisa apparently dies
and Pericles is forced to cast her body overboard. Her caulked coffin washes
up at Ephesus and here she is revived by the healer Cerimon. Whereas in
the play Thaisa shows signs of life within a short space of time – a mere
ten lines of speech – the film stretches out the revival. Over two and a half

minutes, during which time the only sound is music, we watch Cerimon strive to reanimate the young princess by massaging her face and limbs. Although Nelsen proposes that the drawing out of the scene 'attenuates the action of reviving Thaisa',[17] the lengthening of, and the camera's lingering on, Thaisa's recovery is purposive. A range of shots is used in the scene to convey that, in this death-like state, Thaisa has become a passive object of wonder. In long and medium shots, Cerimon, his servants and his friends crowd around the coffin, peering in at its occupant; in close-ups, their concern for their patient is revealed and, in reaction shots, the servants look to Cerimon for guidance. Thaisa is shown motionless, vulnerable, in over-the-shoulder shots, and her body is fragmented while, in close-ups, Cerimon rubs her face and hands. Here, the depiction of Thaisa and treatment of her as a corpse are akin to the monumentalising of other Shakespearean female characters, as described by Valerie Traub.[18] In Traub's analysis, the threat of female agency and erotic power posed by women such as Ophelia and Hermione is contained as they are rendered static and cold, becoming reified objects, such as a corpse (Ophelia) or a statue (Hermione). Lying motionless in her coffin, Thaisa is a frozen object, a 'block' in Cerimon's words and, as such she connotes 'to-be-looked-at-ness'.[19] Upon her awakening, however, this position is contested. At first we see Thaisa look up at the avuncular Cerimon but the camera then becomes subjective as one by one we see each of the spectators' faces from her point of view. This has two effects. Firstly, Thaisa's agency is restored as she questions the men and coolly returns their gaze. Secondly, the reaction shots of the spectators' faces – some gape at Thaisa, some stare anxiously – make the audience acutely aware of what it means to be gazed at and to spectate, and how the gaze can construct the object being viewed. What Rutter suggests about the multiplicity of onlookers in Baz Luhrmann's 1996 *Romeo+Juliet* is helpful here; in looking at the spectators, Luhrmann's film '[offers] an interrogation: how do we look, and how do we relate to the images we look at?'[20] Similarly, Thaisa looks at the lookers and our understanding of the gaze is laid bare for examination.

For the remainder of the play, much of the attention shifts to the fortunes of Thaisa and Pericles' daughter, Marina. If Pericles can be described as a 'hero [who] is in search of a father', then Marina can be said to be a hero in search of a mother.[21] The play gives us two women who are to fill the maternal gap left by Thaisa; however, until Marina is reunited with her father, she only suffers at the hands of these surrogate parents. The first foster mother we meet is Dioniza (Annette Crosbie), wife to the Tharsian governor Cleon. The role of Dioniza is 'a part with touches of Lady

Macbeth, touches of the Wicked Queen in any fairy-tale' and, in her performance of this *mater horribilis*, Crosbie drew on female stereotypes popular from TV: Dioniza is 'an antecedent of Joan Collins in [the American soap opera] *Dynasty*' and is like an 'archetypal Jewish mum'.[22] Crosbie relished the more 'outrageous' aspects of the role and she read Dioniza as an ambitious and uncompromising woman who was 'obviously stronger than [her husband]'.[23] Following Thaisa's death, Pericles leaves the infant Marina to be raised by the Tharsian couple. As Pericles hands his infant daughter over to her new foster mother, the baby begins to cry. As Nelsen observes, this may be an expression of the baby's sorrow at being separated from her father but it may also foreshadow Dioniza's ill intentions towards the teenaged Marina.[24] Unable to pacify the baby, Dioniza quickly passes her to the nurse; this action suggests that, for all her cooing, smiling, and promises of care, Dioniza is more comfortable with someone else doing the dirty work. This proves to be a sign of things to come as, when we next see Dioniza, she is urging the assassin Leonine to kill her now teenaged charge. On the surface, then, Crosbie's Dioniza is charming and ingratiating but beneath this façade is a calculating, determined intellect; with ease, she bends those around her – the reluctant assassin, her hesitant, fidgety husband and the naïve Marina – to her steely will. This inner strength is further in evidence when Dioniza informs her husband of Marina's (supposed) 'slaughter'. As Cleon complains of the seriousness and unnaturalness of the crime, a hint of a smile plays on Dioniza's lips and she toys with her gown, bored by his moralizing. As she explains her actions, Dioniza is self-satisfied, calm and commanding; in a tight shot she looks at Cleon with disdain and is dismissive of his fretting, bluntly accusing him of cowardice. The only slip in her nonchalant demeanour comes when she must smother a smirk at the mention of her poisoning of Leonine; apparently this is a clever crime she is proud of, but one that Cleon is too dim to appreciate. When she fully turns on Cleon, Crosbie's Dioniza emerges as much more than another Lady Macbeth or a fairy-tale's wicked stepmother. Enraged, Dioniza accuses Cleon of neglecting their biological 'sole daughter' (4.3.3) Philoten (4.0.30); her energetic fury confirms for the audience that she is a fiercely protective mother for whom the murder of Marina was simply the logical act of a loving parent.[25] As she exits, Dioniza warmly pats Cleon's hand and reassures him that all will be well because 'I know, you'll do as I advise' (4.3.50). Delivered in a tone that suggests 'mother knows best,' these parting words serve to affirm Dioniza's intellectual superiority and her mastery of the codes of femininity. Cleon does indeed conceal the murder and

Dioniza's performance of maternal benevolence fools even Pericles when he returns to claim his daughter.

Writing on the family in *Pericles*, Suzanne Gossett suggests that the uniting theme of the two halves of the play is that of parents loving children 'too well [and] not loving well enough'.[26] The BBC film illuminates this link by having Marina's second foster family, the keepers of a Mitylene brothel, figure as parents with immoral designs on their children. Whereas the 'wicked Dioniza' (4.4.33) sought to end Marina's life, it is Marina's virginity that is endangered by her second surrogate mother, the Bawd. Having been kidnapped from Tarsus, Marina is sold into prostitution; with only her wits for protection, she must defend herself against the brothel-keepers and customers alike. In Peter Kemp's estimation, Lila Kaye's fleshy 'hennaed, hissing Bawd' was instrumental in conveying the menace inherent in these sordid scenes.[27] Throughout Marina's time in the brothel, the Bawd endeavours to 'instruct her . . . [so that] she may not be raw in her entertainment' (4.2.42–3) of the clientele. The Bawd's efforts to mould Marina to her view of the world are not simply driven by profit, for the film makes it quite clear that she herself desires Marina as a sexual object.[28] This fervent erotic interest in Marina establishes the Bawd as a female counterpart to Antiochus; and so the film comes full circle. The set for the brothel scene also recalls the oppressive atmosphere of Antioch. The brothel is a gloomy, seedy space and its features create a sense of confinement; set designer Don Taylor 'used hanging, beaded curtains that look like prison bars, windows are grilled, murals are suggestive of the erotic wall paintings at Pompeii, and there is a lot of saturated colour'.[29] Like Antiochus's Daughter, Kaye's corpulent, predatory and overbearing Bawd is a product of her environment.

In her dealings with Marina, the Bawd frequently gazes at her and revels in scanning her body; whereas the pimp Boult itemised Marina's charms so he could go and stir up business, the Bawd's eyes catalogue Marina's qualities for her own pleasure. Sitting behind Marina, the Bawd operates like a Faustian devil, whispering at the young virgin's shoulder of the profit she will reap and the lovers she will enjoy. The Bawd's suggestive words and the lingering looks finally come to a head when she fondles Marina. Ironically, as the Bawd speaks of how Marina is now dependent on men for her living and sexual pleasure – 'men must you feed, men [must] stir you up' (4.2.73)[30] – she attempts to excite Marina by groping her from her groin to her breasts. At this moment, the Bawd seems to present women as an alternative to the men she describes (the brothel's patrons); it is possible, she implies, that women could provide for Marina and please her sexually. However, the Bawd's assault on Marina and the young woman's horrified response formulates women as simply another, more dangerous variety of predator; the brothel's men are at least honest in their desire but the Bawd conceals her lust under a veneer of maternal care.

As Peter Kemp noted in his review of the production, Marina could form something of a stumbling block for a modern audience; she is 'ethereally pure', a model of virtue with an eloquence that can apparently charm even assassins and the hardened patrons of the brothel.[31] In the BBC film, Amanda Redman's performance as the sixteen-year-old Marina lends this exceptional character credibility. This is evinced most strongly in the brothel scenes. In the 'fetid enclosure' of the brothel, the power dynamics of the relationship between the Bawd, the Pander,[32] their servant Boult and Marina are played out through the female gaze. When Marina enters the brothel, she sits on a faded ottoman and the Bawd wolfishly stalks her from behind. When the Bawd sits at Marina's back, a series of two shots capture both the Bawd's attempts to make the young virgin amenable and Marina's growing unease. Marina's response is to try to establish a protective distance from the moral pollution, embodied by the Bawd, by directing her gaze elsewhere and then by '[stopping her] ears' (4.2.64). Later, the meeting of Marina and the governor Lysimachus, a regular customer of the brothel, is similarly staged. Like the Bawd, Lysimachus sits behind Marina and assumes the position of a powerful, predatory figure. At several points, Marina faces away from him and looks off camera when she speaks; she rejects his interpretation of her as a 'creature of sale' (4.5.73) and eventually confronts him with the harsh reality that while he has political power, she has moral authority. Under the force of Marina's moving rhetoric, Lysimachus reforms. The change in their relationship is demonstrated by a reversal in their physical positions; having led Marina gently back to the seat, Lysimachus now sits on her right and the couple face each other in a medium shot.[33] At Lysimachus's exit, close-ups show the pair exchanging meaningful glances and Marina looks longingly after the converted governor. The performances and camerawork, then, compound the work of the dialogue which Jones added to this scene; thereby we are provided with 'a credible and substantial basis for accepting and endorsing the subsequent betrothal of Marina and Lysimachus'.[34]

In the climactic recognition scene, the use of close-ups creates a sense of intimacy and specialness as Marina and Pericles are finally reunited.[35] Sent to heal Pericles' melancholy-induced inertia, Marina declares that she has 'n'er before/Invited eyes, but have been gazed on like a comet' (5.1.80–1). Against the darkened interior of the ship, the lighting on Marina's face and her radiant white gown do in fact make her appear like a divine or celestial figure. We are thus primed for the moment when father and daughter recognise one another and for the arrival of the Goddess Diana, which follows soon after. Despite her luminous appearance though, Marina is not the spectacle in the cabin; rather, in his prone and bedraggled state, Pericles is the object of everyone's gaze. Near-catatonic, he is simultaneously revealed to Lysimachus and the audience as a pitiful oddity ('May we not see him?' – 'Behold him' [5.1.29–31]). Marina's energetic attempts to revive her 'kingly patient' (5.1.67) mark her out as the active, autonomous subject who is responsible for forwarding the narrative.[36] Her vitality is in marked contrast to Pericles' immobility; she moves about the cabin and she is, by turns, sharp and gentle, mocking, commanding and threatening. In the film, it is her energy and her story that ultimately restores Pericles; she is the life-giving force that 'begetst him that did [her] beget' (5.1.190).

Following the reunion with his daughter, Pericles hears the music of the spheres and, fatigued, is put to rest by his followers. As he slumbers, Diana (Elayne Sharling), the virgin goddess who was known in the early modern period as the protectress of chastity and childbirth, appears and instructs the prince to visit her temple in Ephesus. This is not the first time we have seen Diana however: at several points in the film, 'Jones inconspicuously composes covert allusions to the goddess Diana into his shots'.[37] Diana first appears in the guise of a Tharsian citizen; dressed in rags and sitting on the ground, with maternal care she cradles a famine victim, an elderly woman, on her lap. As Pericles promises succour to the needy Cleon and Dioniza, Diana pays keen attention and then turns to gaze pensively into the distance. In Mitylene, she walks past Boult who is busily harassing a potential customer. Diana stares at the pimp – she sees his work and does not approve – and he seems transfixed. Forgetting the customer, Boult gazes after her until she turns a corner; her beauty, divinity or, perhaps, her radiant virginity has mesmerised him. When Diana is gone, Boult shrugs at a whore who is ensconced in the brothel window; the pair are disappointed at losing a potential new employee or, perhaps, puzzled by Diana's disapproval of their profession. As Nelsen notes, 'first-time viewers would not recognize the connection' and this directorial decision may be based on a practical need to people the scenes but, by having Diana witness Pericles' charity and faith, 'Jones establishes rationalization for the goddess's subsequent benevolent interventions'.[38] Subtly but significantly, then, the BBC *Pericles* presents the goddess as an all-seeing, omniscient, and omnipresent authority who secretly influences the lives of mortals. While Gower is in the film's foreground narrating the action and guiding the audience, Diana is the power behind its happy ending; we often see her as a silent observer but it is her knowledge and active intervention that guide Pericles to the 'Great miracle' (5.3.55), the resurrection and reunification of his whole family.

Arriving at Ephesus, Pericles performs Diana's 'just command' (5.3.1) and he and Marina are reunited with Thaisa. Although this meeting is 'sketchy and more rapid' than the reunion of father and daughter and has been read by critics as 'experimental, or erroneous',[39] the staging in the BBC film deliberately marks and celebrates the two heterosexual unions as the most desirable of endings. Long shots show Pericles and Thaisa hand in hand, and in the background stand Marina and Lysimachus arm in arm. Marina kneels before her mother, but she quickly returns to Lysimachus's embrace. Although we have followed the fortunes of one family, by focusing on two distinct couples the film looks forward to the growth and joy of two families, one restored and one newly formed. Patience in the face of suffering is rewarded by familial expansion.

While the play may bear Pericles' name, the BBC *Pericles* presents us with a series of women who propel the narrative. In different ways, each of the female characters is a linchpin of this winding, episodic tale. Whereas the language of looking in the play often presents women as spectacles and objects of visual pleasure, in the film the women are not simply recipients of the gaze; rather, they are in their own right agents of the look and are clearly framed as such. The women refuse to look, refuse to look away, look longingly, look where they want, look for pleasure, look to criticise, look with and as authorities and look back at those who turn their gaze upon them. They spectate, ogle, glare, observe and scrutinise. In doing so, they develop their different characters, roles and desires and, above all, open up both the play and the film to new readings. The women, in short, provide us with one good reason why the BBC *Pericles* is worth a second look.

Notes

1 B. Jonson, 'Ode to Himself', in D. Bevington *et al.* (eds.), *The Cambridge Edition of the Works of Ben Jonson*, VI (Cambridge: Cambridge University Press, 2012), 311.

2 P. Nelsen, 'Shot from the Canon: The BBC Video of *Pericles*', in D. Skeele (ed.), *Pericles: Critical Essays* (New York: Garland, 2000), 297.

3 Like *Titus Andronicus*, *Timon of Athens* and *Henry VIII*, *Pericles* had never been televised before. *Pericles* was filmed in the BBC studios in June 1983 and aired in the US and the UK in 1984.

4 P. Kemp, 'Between Crest and Trough', *Times Literary Supplement*, 21 December 1984, 1476.

5 Nelsen, 'Shot from the Canon', 322.

6 In her in-depth study of the making of the Series, Susan Willis notes that each play typically drew in one to three million viewers in the United Kingdom; in America, where the Series was broadcast on PBS, one play could garner an audience of four or five million. The viewership was further expanded by worldwide sales; by 1987, fifty-three other countries had bought rights to the Series and, in a commercially lucrative move, the plays were made available on video (and now DVD). S. Willis, *The BBC Shakespeare Plays: Making the Televised Canon* (Chapel Hill: University of North Carolina Press, 1991), 40.

7 Nelsen's exploration of the film is the obvious exception. Stephen Purcell has recently suggested that the subject of Shakespeare on television has often suffered from critical neglect. See S. Purcell, 'Shakespeare on Television', in M. T. Burnett *et al.* (eds.), *The Edinburgh Companion to Shakespeare and the Arts* (Edinburgh: Edinburgh University Press, 2011), 522.

8 C. Rutter, 'Looking at Shakespeare's Women on Film', in R. Jackson (ed.), *The Cambridge Companion to Shakespeare on Film* (Cambridge: Cambridge University Press, 2000), 247.

9 For a discussion of the changes and additions made to the text of *Pericles* for the film, see Nelsen, 'Shot from the Canon'.

10 The Daughter's hairstyle also references Medusa: a silver garland holds up much of her hair, but several plaited strands hang down like serpents.

11 *The BBC TV Shakespeare: Pericles* (London: British Broadcasting Corporation, 1984), 19.

12 *Ibid.*

13 Later, Antiochus's servant Thaliard wears a similar chain. Elsewhere in the film, chains mark out various characters; for instance, Cerimon wears a crescent moon and Cleon dons an embossed square.

14 I borrow the idea of extra-textual narratives from Rutter's chapter. Rutter suggests that, in reading Shakespeare's women on film, it is vital to attend to 'what the camera records *between the lines* and *instead of the lines*,' and that in film 'meanings are going to reside in the extra-textual narratives the camera constructs by its looking' ('Looking', 242). Emphasis in original.

15 The fantasy may also act as a kind of ocular proof of the incest for Pericles and for the audience.

16 I draw on Laura Mulvey's influential arguments here. See L. Mulvey, 'Visual Pleasure and Narrative Cinema', in G. Mast *et al.* (eds.), *Film Theory and Criticism* (Oxford: Oxford University Press, 1992), 746–57; L. Mulvey, 'Afterthoughts on "Visual Pleasure and Narrative Cinema" inspired by *Duel in the Sun*', in C. Penley (ed.), *Feminism and Film Theory* (London: Routledge, 1988), 69–79.

17 Nelsen, 'Shot from the Canon', 317.

18 V. Traub, *Desire and Anxiety: Circulations of Sexuality in Shakespearean Drama* (London: Routledge, 1992), 25–49.

19 Mulvey, 'Visual Pleasure', 750.

20 Rutter, 'Looking', 259.

21 S. Gossett, '"You not your child well loving": Text and Family Structure in Pericles', in R. Dutton and J. E. Howard (eds.), *A Companion to Shakespeare's*

Works: The Poems, Problem Comedies, Late Plays (Oxford: Blackwell, 2005), 353.

22 *The BBC TV Shakespeare: Pericles*, 24. In its recurring attention to the female point of view, heightened emotions, familial crises and socio-sexual pressures, the BBC *Pericles* draws on elements of melodrama.

23 *The BBC TV Shakespeare: Pericles*, 24.

24 Nelsen, 'Shot from the Canon', 306.

25 See also Gossett's recent re-evaluation of Dioniza and the family in the play ('"You not your child"').

26 Gossett, '"You not your child"', 353.

27 Kemp, 'Between Crest and Trough', 1476.

28 In her recent Arden edition of the play, Suzanne Gossett remarks that, in several lines, the Bawd hints at her sexual attraction to Marina. See William Shakespeare, *Pericles*, S. Gossett, ed. (London: Arden Shakespeare, 2004), 330.

29 *The BBC TV Shakespeare: Pericles*, 20.

30 *The BBC TV Shakespeare: Pericles* adds 'must' (see BBC 4.2.91).

31 Kemp, 'Between Crest and Trough', 1476.

32 Willis, *The BBC Shakespeare Plays*, 195.

33 For a discussion of the additions to the script at this point, see Nelsen, 'Shot from the Canon', 311–15. Although the additions, as Nelsen notes, endow Marina with more verbal power, it is a pity that Jones and his cast did not treat this 'gap' in the received text as an opportunity. Marina's power is as much visual and performative as it is verbal and the medium of TV could have been fruitfully used to *show* Marina's abilities and Lysimachus's conversion rather than explain them via dialogue drawn from George Wilkins's prose text, *The painfull aduentures of Pericles prince of Tyre* (London: T. Purfoot, 1608).

34 Nelsen, 'Shot from the Canon', 314.

35 Nelsen observes that the limited use of close-ups up to this point means that they are used to great effect in this scene ('Shot from the Canon', 319–20).

36 I am thinking here of Mulvey's theories as put forward in 'Visual Pleasure' and of Linda Williams' arguments on women and monsters, spectacle and narrative, in the horror film. L. Williams, 'When the Woman Looks', in Gerald Mast *et al.* (ed.), *Film Theory and Criticism* (Oxford: Oxford University Press, 1992), 561–77.

37 Nelsen, 'Shot from the Canon', 306.

38 *Ibid.*

39 Gossett, '"You not your child"', 359.

WORKS CITED

BBC TV Shakespeare: Pericles (London: British Broadcasting Corporation, 1984).

Gossett, S. (ed.), *William Shakespeare's* Pericles (London: Arden Shakespeare, 2004).

Gossett, S., '"You not your child well loving": Text and Family Structure in *Pericles*', in R. Dutton and J. E. Howard (eds.), *A Companion to Shakespeare's Works: The Poems, Problem Comedies, Late Plays* (Oxford: Blackwell, 2005), 348–364.

Jonson, B., 'Ode to Himself', in D. Bevington *et al.* (eds.), *The Cambridge Edition of the Works of Ben Jonson*, VI (Cambridge: Cambridge University Press, 2012), 310–13.

Kemp, P., 'Between Crest and Trough', *Times Literary Supplement*, 21 December 1984, 1476.

Mulvey, L., 'Afterthoughts on "Visual Pleasure and Narrative Cinema" inspired by *Duel in the Sun*', in C. Penley (ed.), *Feminism and Film Theory* (London: Routledge, 1988), 69–79.

'Visual Pleasure and Narrative Cinema', in G. Mast *et al.* (eds.), *Film Theory and Criticism* (Oxford: Oxford University Press, 1992), 746–57.

Nelsen, P., 'Shot from the Canon: The BBC Video of *Pericles*', in D. Skeele (ed.), *Pericles: Critical Essays* (New York: Garland, 2000), 297–324.

Purcell, S., 'Shakespeare on Television', in M. T. Burnett *et al.* (eds.), *The Edinburgh Companion to Shakespeare and the Arts* (Edinburgh: Edinburgh University Press, 2011), 522–40.

Rutter, C., 'Looking at Shakespeare's Women on Film', in R. Jackson (ed.), *The Cambridge Companion to Shakespeare on Film* (Cambridge: Cambridge University Press, 2000), 245–66.

Traub, V., *Desire and Anxiety: Circulations of Sexuality in Shakespearean Drama* (London: Routledge, 1992), 25–49.

Williams, L., 'When the Woman Looks', in Gerald Mast *et al.* (ed.), *Film Theory and Criticism* (Oxford: Oxford University Press, 1992), 561–77.

Willis, S., *The BBC Shakespeare Plays: Making the Televised Canon* (Chapel Hill: University of North Carolina Press, 1991).

Wilkins, G., *The painfull aduentures of Pericles prince of Tyre Being the true history of the play of Pericles, as it was lately presented by the worthy and ancient poet Iohn Gower* (London: T. Purfoot, 1608).

CHAPTER 4

Scenes from Cymbeline and Early Television Studio Drama

John Wyver

Broadcasts of scenes from William Shakespeare's *Cymbeline* in 1937 and 1956 were among the earliest British television productions of Shakespeare.[1] On both occasions the selections included the 'wooing scene' of Act 1 scene 6 and Act 2 scene 2, known as the 'trunk scene'. Transmitted from a television studio with a small number of electronic cameras which were mixed live, the excerpts were taken from contemporary theatrical productions, in 1937 from André van Gyseghem's staging at the Embassy Theatre (London) and in 1956 from the production by Michael Benthall at the Old Vic. Neither broadcast was recorded but, for both of these 'lost' productions, the BBC Written Archives Centre (WAC) at Caversham preserves detailed camera scripts and other documentation. Jason Jacobs has demonstrated convincingly how this written archive of 'studio plans, camera scripts, memos, etc [can be] invaluable in the process of reconstructing the *visual* sense of early television drama. Other primary sources include[d] schedules, reviews, and criticism'.[2] Uniquely for Shakespeare on British television, the two *Scenes from Cymbeline* camera scripts detail a pre-war and a post-war treatment of the same written texts by studio directors (respectively, Royston Morley and Michael Elliott) nearly twenty years apart. This article considers the 1937 and 1956 camera scripts in order to outline the development of the language of television studio drama. Shot lengths, camera movements and framings – all of which are significantly more complex in the 1956 script – are explored as determinants of the available meanings of Shakespeare's dramatic poetry. An additional comparison is facilitated by the extant studio production of *Cymbeline* in 1982, directed by Elijah Moshinsky for *The BBC Television Shakespeare*.

Televising *Cymbeline* in 1937

Short scenes from Shakespeare's plays were televised on a number of occasions in the months after the start, in November 1936, of BBC Television's regular service from Alexandra Palace. The first presentation was a scene each from *As You Like It* and *Henry V* on 5 February 1937. Margaretta Scott played Rosalind in the former, while in the latter the wooing of Katharine by Henry was acted out by Yvonne Arnaud and Henry Oscar. What might be regarded as the first 'full-length' BBC Shakespeare production was a 67-minute adaptation of *Othello*, broadcast in December 1937. After scenes had been televised the previous month from eight other Shakespeare plays including *Julius Caesar*, *A Midsummer Night's Dream* and *Romeo and Juliet*, *Cymbeline* was perhaps a less obvious choice of play for the new medium's audience. Between Henry Irving's 1896 revival with Ellen Terry and post-World War II productions at Stratford, there were few distinguished performances of the drama; as Martin Butler notes, 'In the early twentieth century, expectations about the play were at their lowest'.[3] What critics have characterized as its decentred narrative structure,[4] however, perhaps made the play more suitable than others by Shakespeare as a source of standalone excerpts.

In November 1937 André van Gyseghem staged *Cymbeline* at London's Embassy Theatre, at the time a successful repertory house run by producer Ronald Adam. Van Gyseghem had been an actor with the Embassy's company and then a director there for four years until October 1934. His 1937 staging of *Cymbeline* was notable as being the first to use George Bernard Shaw's variation for Act 5, which had been written by the playwright for the Memorial Theatre at Stratford but not been played there; the interest of Shaw's script (which was not to feature in the scenes chosen for television) dominated the anonymous review of the production in *The Times*. The writer commented that the performance as a whole was 'intrinsically interesting' but that it 'left the impression that the actors were saving themselves up for Shaw at the expense of Shakespeare'.[5] A notice in *The Sunday Times*, however, included a more detailed response to the contributions of the cast:

> Mr George Hayes as Iachimo admirably suggested the 'slight thing of Italy'... Miss Olga Lindo, since she comes of player's stock, had no difficulty in giving flesh and blood to the shadowy Queen... Miss Joyce Bland began with a composite portrait of Imogen, half by Mary Anderson and half by Sybil Thorndike, the whole being like some Staffordshire potter's notion of a French actress in Racine, all drapery, frontal stare, and tragic nose.[6]

By the time *Cymbeline* took to the Embassy stage, the BBC television service had been on air for just over a year but there was as yet no long-term drama planning. The service was broadcasting for one hour in the afternoon and two each evening (although not on Sundays) and could be seen by perhaps 5,000 viewers within a radius of around ten miles from the north London transmitter. Talks and variety shows sat alongside three or four short dramas each week, many of the latter, like *Scenes from Cymbeline*, being drawn opportunistically from those productions in London's theatres that could be coaxed to the studios. On 29 November 1937, thirteen days after their theatre opening, nine actors from the Embassy company assembled at Alexandra Palace for rehearsals from 10 a.m. Later in the day they performed scenes from their production for roughly thirty minutes at 3.30 p.m. and then, as a live 'repeat', at 9.30 p.m. The whole television service was broadcast from two identical studios, each 21 metres by 9 metres; for elaborate productions (of which these *Cymbeline* scenes was one) both studios were utilized and linked through a single control room. As with all studio-based television until early 1953, the transmissions were live and no recording was made. Just one trace of a response to the television broadcast has so far been uncovered, in a round-up newspaper review of television broadcasts across a week, which noted simply that 'a high standard of production was maintained'.[7]

According to the camera script, the presentation begins with a music cue from a 78rpm twelve-inch disc of the London Symphony Orchestra playing Rimsky-Korsakov's *Cortège des Nobles*.[8] The announcer speaks over the simple caption 'Cymbeline': 'Now we are to see scenes from André van Gyseghem's production of *Cymbeline* from the Embassy Theatre (by permission of Ronald Adam)'. With the caption still on screen, the minor actors are introduced by name before a mix takes the viewer to a shot of one actor accompanied by an explanatory voice-over – 'Iachimo is played by George Hayes' and then another mix to a shot of three characters: 'The Queen by Olga Lindo, Posthumus by Geoffrey Toon and Imogen by Joyce Bland'. The next mix takes the shot to a further caption – 'The Palace Garden' – and then the television image returns to the previous three-shot. On a cue from the cameraman, the Queen begins to speak. Each of these mixes at this time would have taken approximately three to four seconds to complete; instantaneous cuts in live drama were not possible until after World War II. The first scene is drawn from Act I scene I and runs from the entry of the Queen, Posthumus and Imogen at line 79 through to the end of the scene – a total of 134 lines. Throughout, the text in the camera script follows almost exactly the First Folio text with no cuts. Act I scene 3 is then played in full. Both of these 'Palace Garden' scenes were acted in Studio A in front of a minimal setting. The scenes were covered by just two fixed-lens cameras, both of which were mounted on dollies which facilitated movement forward and backward, taking the shot closer or further away from the actors but with movement only on a central axis and not from side to side. In the first of these scenes, which may have lasted perhaps six minutes, there were just four shot changes mixing from one camera to the other; the second scene, which would have run for between two and three minutes, was played in a single shot. As a caption informed the viewer, the scene shifted to 'Philario's House in Rome' for Act 1 scene 4, the 124 lines of which were also given in full. The transmission also changed to Studio B, where cameras 3 (fixed in place on an 'iron man' mounting and also doing duty for the captions) and 4 (on a dolly) covered what was more than five minutes of drama with just two shot changes. Almost the whole of the scene, which involves four speaking parts and two non-speaking, was played to camera 4.

The following two scenes, taken from Act 1 scene 6 and Act 2 scene 2, are both located by the script in 'Imogen's bedroom,' even though, as Martin Butler notes, the setting for the former 'is a private room in Innogen's personal apartments, though the space is less intimate than the bedchamber of 2.2'.[9] The setting back in Studio A included four flats, arch-pieces to suggest a window and a door, a bed with pilasters, a low pedestal with two candles and a special trunk supplied by the Embassy Theatre. Act 1 scene 6 of *Cymbeline* begins with Imogen, alone, unhappy at the banishment to Rome of her husband Leonatus by 'A father cruel and a stepdame false' (1.6.1). Iachimo is announced – in the original text and in the 1937 script – by the servant Pisanio (although, in the 1956 scenes, he is announced by Imogen's maid). Iachimo brings news from Rome but he has really come to seduce Imogen, having made a bet with Leonatus that he will do so. There follows a lengthy exchange between the two main characters that lasts for 223 lines. Although tempted by Iachimo's charm, Imogen resists his wiles but, as a kindness to this supposed friend of her husband, she agrees to store his trunk overnight in her bedroom. This 'wooing scene' would have taken perhaps twelve minutes to act but it was planned with only two mixes. In the script the shot changes only briefly to camera 2 and presumably to a closer shot, as Iachimo attempts to kiss Imogen at line 139, which Imogen resists with a call to her servant Pisanio. After just nine lines, the shot then returns to the main camera, after Imogen has spoken of her absent husband and forcefully rejected Iachimo's advances; it remains on camera 1 to the close of the scene. Although this is not indicated, it is highly unlikely that the shot from camera 1 would have been static for all of the 214 lines which it was used to cover. It is possible, too, that the studio director improvised on the night and included other shots – but the fact that the camera script features only one change indicates the expectations of studio drama just over a year after the opening of Alexandra Palace.

During the scene transition to 2.2, in addition to the repetition of the caption, the script specifies a brief superimposition of a camera-1 shot of the trunk onto a wider shot of the setting from camera 2. This establishes the centrality and the mystery of the trunk. The subsequent 'trunk scene,' in which Imogen retires to bed and Iachimo emerges from the trunk to stare lasciviously at her sleeping body and to steal her bracelet, plays across just 53 lines and would have lasted for something over three minutes on screen.

As scripted, the action of the scene begins on camera 2. After twelve lines the script indicates a mix to camera 1 for Iachimo emerging from the trunk. After just two lines the shot mixes to camera 2 for most of Iachimo's speech before returning to camera 1 as he goes back to the trunk at the close. In one quarter of the length of the previous scene, there are four shot changes, two more than in the whole of the wooing exchange, which clearly underlines the greater intimacy and intensity of the action. The final scene played the first 192 lines of Act 2 scene 4, which might have lasted a further six minutes or more. The timings, of course, are approximate but if the presentation did indeed play its total of 790 lines in thirty minutes (recognising that productions at this time very often over-ran) – an average of 26 lines per minute, not allowing for breaks or music – the verse-speaking would have been almost impossibly fast. By contrast, the visual rhythm of the shots and mixes would have seemed, at least as judged by later standards, funereally slow. There are just 25 shot changes specified during the whole half-hour, less than one each minute, and half of these are mixes to and from captions.

Cymbeline on Screen in 1956

Nearly twenty years later, on 30 October 1956, the BBC televised another half-hour of scenes from *Cymbeline*. Following a wartime hiatus, the television service returned in the summer of 1946 and regularly presented full-length productions of Shakespeare from the studios as well as continuing on occasions to show excerpts. The last scene of Jean Meyer's Comédie-Française production of *Othello* was broadcast in French in March 1950, at a time when the company was visiting London, and scenes from Anthony Quayle's Stratford 1951 production of *Henry IV Part One* were shown as part of the *For the Children* slot.

After post-war presentations of *Cymbeline* by the Stratford Memorial Theatre in 1946 and 1949, the play was produced in 1956 at London's Old

Vic by Michael Benthall, who had taken on the role of artistic director of the theatre company three years before. By the time he came to stage *Cymbeline* he was part-way through a five-year plan to stage all of Shakespeare's plays, an initiative that had been warmly welcomed by audiences and critics. The production opened in the theatre near Waterloo on 11 September 1956, and the following day the anonymous theatre critic for *The Times* contributed an ambivalent notice:

> Mr Michael Benthall is probably right . . . to assume that when it comes to *Cymbeline* we shall prefer speed to colour and verisimilitude. More or less dispensing with scenery, he sets the action going in a high dark cavern as quickly as the actors can speak their lines . . . Mr Derek Godfrey, as Iachimo, alone reaches distinction: he is effective in his encounter with Imogen and the bedroom trick is played with a great sense of the Italian's delight in his own audacious finesse . . . Miss Barbara Jefford gives a somewhat hard reading of a woman who has all the gifts.[10]

The Old Vic's official record of the season later noted that 'the response by press and public was sadly disappointing . . . *Cymbeline* was withdrawn on December 8th after thirty-two performances, yet of all the season's plays it was the most enchanting and the one in which the company first showed its true quality'.[11] The idea of presenting part of the production was discussed at the BBC in August, when Assistant to Controller of Programmes Cecil Madden wrote to Head of Drama Michael Barry, 'Have we fixed a Sunday night for *Cymbeline*?'[12] Madden initially envisaged an outside broadcast (OB) of the whole or perhaps just part of a Sunday evening performance. Such outside broadcasts of extracts from theatrical productions were common at this time and were seen by theatre managements as effective publicity to attract the ticket-buying public. But the plan changed, perhaps because of the difficulty of securing an OB camera unit over a weekend when they were often committed to sporting events. Within a fortnight Madden was exploring a weekday slot for a studio presentation.[13] Head of Drama Michael Barry attended a dress rehearsal of *Cymbeline* on 10 September. On the following day, he sent a memo to senior BBC colleagues noting that he had met with Michael Benthall and the Old Vic's publicity manager Patrick Ide:

> They are both anxious for the company to be seen on television. Their new company is young and promising . . . My feeling is confirmed that we should take the opportunity of developing a liaison with the Old Vic.

While such a 'liaison' might have been important for the Old Vic, there is no mention of the television presentation of the scenes in the Old Vic's book that documented this year of the Shakespeare cycle.[14] The BBC had previously presented Act I of an Old Vic production of *The Two Gentlemen of Verona* from the theatre in July 1952 as well as a studio re-staging of scenes from the theatre's 1955 *Julius Caesar*, another production in Michael Benthall's five-year presentation of all of the plays. In his memo, Barry further suggested, seemingly without any recognition of the 1937 studio production, that it would be possible to present an excerpt from *Cymbeline* of about 30 minutes of two two-handed scenes between Iachimo and Imogen. These scenes, he suggested, 'are comprehensible in themselves with the briefest introduction, and are strongly acted and exciting to watch'.[15] After some discussions about a date, which had to be on an evening when the Old Vic company were playing *Timon of Athens*, so freeing up actor Barbara Jefford, it was decided that the scenes from *Cymbeline* would be broadcast live at 10.15 p.m. on Tuesday 30 October. Derek Godfrey, however, had to come to the studio for the broadcast after he had finished playing in *Timon*, arriving only at 9.30 p.m. Costumes, wigs and the required chest were hired from the Old Vic at a total cost of £25, and television producer Michael Elliott was attached to the broadcast. It was also agreed that Dame Sybil Thorndike, who had famously played Imogen at the Old Vic in 1918, should provide an introduction.

In contrast to the minimal preparations in 1937, these televised scenes from *Cymbeline* were rehearsed on several days prior to the broadcast. Michael Elliott worked with the actors for three half-days at the Old Vic from 25 October. Just before this, the script for Dame Sybil's introduction was written by Michael Barry after he had spoken with her.[16] From a total budget of 250 pounds and six shillings (not including the studio time and crew), Dame Sybil took home a fee of 52 pounds and ten shillings – over ten pounds more than each of the two stars. Having been only lukewarm in *The Manchester Guardian* about the Old Vic production on stage,[17] the critic Philip Hope-Wallace also wrote – this time for *The Listener* – about the television presentation:

> The voice of Dame Sybil Thorndike declaiming the threnody from *Cymbeline* lingers in memory . . . It was the sort of introduction which mishandled could have ruined the ensuing scenes, which in the event came up, I thought, a lot better than they had when I saw them on the stage. For this, credit must go to Michael Elliott who kept Imogen and Iachimo just near enough to engage our attention fully without thrusting them down our throats.[18]

As with all other pre-war programmes, there is no record of the audience's response to the 1937 broadcast. But for 1956 there is a detailed Audience Research Report, which recorded a Reaction Index figure of 61.

[This was] close to the figure (63) for a performance of Act I of *The Two Gentlemen of Verona* (which was, however, televised direct from the stage of the Old Vic theatre) in Week 29, 1952 . . . [The excerpt] made a strong appeal to well over half of the sample. These viewers enjoyed the acting (and particularly Derek Godfrey's performance as Iachimo) very much, and thought the presentation of the bedchamber scene 'entrancingly done', with the action made very dramatic by close-up camerawork and an 'effectively simple set'. Criticism from this group consisted mainly of regret that the play could not be broadcast in full.[19]

By October 1956, studio drama had developed significantly from the practices of 1937. The BBC had purchased a former film studio in west London in 1949, opening the new Lime Grove studios in 1950. Drama production had moved here from Alexandra Palace and it was from Studio D that the *Cymbeline* extracts were broadcast. The spaces were significantly larger than at Alexandra Palace, with Studio D, which was located on the fourth floor, measuring approximately 27 metres by 21 metres. Through the late 1950s, this was the BBC's main studio for drama transmissions and was to be the stage from which the first episode of *Doctor Who* was transmitted in November 1963. At the time of the *Cymbeline* transmission, the four cameras in the studio had recently been upgraded to CPS Emitron Mk3s and now had turret lenses, facilitating a choice of three shot sizes. They were also significantly more mobile than the pre-war cameras. For *Cymbeline*, one was mounted on a Mole Richardson crane, permitting the camera to be raised above head-height and to be manoeuvred over the actors. Two other cameras were on motorized 'Vintens' which facilitated rapid movement around the studio floor in all directions.[20]

The text of the two scenes played both in 1937 and in 1956 is much the same, although ten lines in Act 1 scene 6 were cut from the later production. But, as recorded in the camera script, the visual language on screen is far more complex. In the wooing exchange there are now 31 scripted shot changes, while in the shorter trunk scene there are 18. Almost all of these are now hard cuts. The change can be recognized in the treatment of Iachimo's introduction to Imogen, all of which in 1937 was presented as just part of the lengthy first shot from camera 1. Imogen's maid Helen says that Iachimo has come from Rome, after which there is a shot without dialogue described in the script in this way [abbreviations are explained in added square brackets]:

Deep 3-sh [*shot with three people in frame*] across IACHIMO LFG [*left foreground*] to HELEN/IMOGEN
Hold as IMOGEN walks twds cam [*towards camera*]

HELEN crosses out of frame r [*right*]
2-sh IACHIMO/IMOGEN.[21]

Before Iachimo speaks, the screen cuts to a medium-shot of him and, as he presents the letter from Leonatus, the script reads 'Pan him right to IMOGEN. 2-sh IACHIMO/IMOGEN'. As Imogen responds, there is a cut to a third camera, which presents a medium close-up of her. There is then another dialogue-free shot:

2-sh IACHIMO/IMOGEN
Hold 2-sh as IMOGEN walks into RFG [*right foreground*]
IACHIMO crosses to r of frame
Hold 2-sh

There have been four changes of shot so far for just five lines of dialogue and it is clear that, rather than the scene being simply played out in front of the lens, the shots and the cuts between them are actively contributing to the construction of the narrative and to the revelation of the relationships between the characters.

The instructions in the 1956 camera script are sufficiently detailed to allow a visual reconstruction of the scenes. For the most part it is clear that shots present the person who is speaking or very often both the speaker and the person being addressed in a two shot. But occasionally there are variations. Midway through the wooing, Iachimo declares his passion for Imogen, with the following words:

Had I this cheek
To bathe my lips upon; this hand, whose touch,
Whose every touch, would force the feeler's soul
To th'oath of loyalty; this object which
Takes prisoner the wild motion of my eye... (1.6.99–103)

At 'object', the shot, which has been a close two shot of both figures, cuts to a close-up of Imogen and remains focused solely on her and her reactions for the remaining ten lines of Iachimo's speech. This approach appears to have echoed the effect that stage director Michael Benthall sought in the theatre, as is detailed by Mary Clarke's description that it:

was played by the two characters alone in the small area of the lighted stage. The method was a revealing one: the reaction of each character to the other's every word was almost spotlit for the audience.[22]

A handwritten note in the archive file indicates that the scene played for 11 minutes and 5 seconds, with 31 changes of camera shot, compared to just 2 shot changes in 1937. As a consequence, the average shot length (ASL) in 1956 was just over 20 seconds, which was a significantly slower visual pace than contemporary feature films. David Bordwell has estimated that, between 1930 and 1960, the ASL in Hollywood films 'hovered between 8 and 11 seconds'.[23] The capabilities of technology, the expectations of audiences, and the importance attached by producers to the spoken word rather than the image – and perhaps especially so in presentations of Shakespeare – are among the factors that may account for this difference.

'To th'trunk again . . . ' (2.2.47)

At the end of the wooing scene, after Imogen has agreed to look after Iachimo's trunk, the action, as detailed in the camera script, is enhanced by the use of the studio crane. In a two shot (on camera 2), Imogen says to Iachimo, 'You're very welcome' (1.6.210) and walks away from the camera as the shot is held. Cut then to a dialogue-free medium close-up (camera 3) of Iachimo, quickly followed by another cut to camera 1. This is how the script then describes the screen image:

> Very high long shot of floor pattern
> Iachimo left of frame
> Hold shot as he moves away from cam.
> Two servants enter left of frame with trunk. 3-sh
> Crane down fast and track in to let trunk pass in bottom foreground of frame.
> Hold Iachimo centre
> Servants and trunk leave frame r.
> As soon as they leave frame
> TRACK IN fast to CU [close-up] Iachimo
> LOSE FOCUS

The focus on the trunk which was rendered in 1937 with a simple superimposition is achieved here with a more elaborate sequence of crane and tracking moves. These were followed in the broadcast by further comments from Dame Sybil, who spoke both of the unfolding narrative of the play and the Old Vic staging:

> Now several hours pass, so you must imagine the servants with the heavy trunk making their way through the tall columned corridors echoing in the flickering lamplight to Imogen's bedroom. Michael Benthall, the producer of the production at the Old Vic, as at the production at Shakespeare's Globe, uses no scenery because he deliberately wants you to give all your attention to the players.

Following this 'interval', the transmission returned to an out-of-focus shot
of the trunk which came into focus before the camera tracked past to a
medium close-up (MCU) of Imogen. Iachimo's subsequent soliloquy in
the text spoken over the sleeping Imogen (2.2.11–51) has been described
as an 'astonishing, voyeuristic episode . . . which can be both gripping and
unsettling to participate in'.[24] Mary Clarke recorded a description of the
scene on the stage:

> After Imogen had fallen asleep there was a moment of complete stillness and
> then, without a sound, a panel in the front of the trunk slipped down and
> a hand emerged from inside. Very slowly and cautiously Iachimo released
> the catch and then raised the lid of the trunk, his lively dark eyes quickly
> surveying the chamber before he stepped out and stretched his cramped
> limbs. He then approached the bed and as he moved round it, breathing
> softly his incomparable description of the sleeping Imogen, she stirred in
> her sleep and let fall her right arm over the side of the bed.[25]

Television producer Michael Elliott used the resources of his studio set-up
to bring additional drama to the scene. The script describes the elaborate
shot in which Iachimo slips the bolt from the inside and emerges from the
trunk (which was pictured in a production still reproduced in *The Listener*):

> High MCU [medium close-up] IMOGEN craned left.
> Pan right to trunk
> Crane r and down and pan l to
> pivot round trunk.
> End shot with trunk bottom RFG [right foreground] and
> IMOGEN LBG [left background]. Crane up as IACHIMO
> comes out of trunk to hold 2-sh.

As the scene unfolds in the script, on several occasions the camera pans
down from Iachimo's face to the prone Imogen and then back up to him.
There is the strong suggestion here of his symbolic violation, as there is in
the frequent use of high two shots of the pair (from camera 1 on the crane).
The script also indicates that a technique of shooting in to a mirror and
then inverting the picture electronically was also employed so as to achieve
a greater distance above the two characters. Imogen's prone body is also
fragmented by the camera as, at two moments, the script indicates that
only her arm is featured in the left of frame which otherwise shows first
the kneeling Iachimo and then him lying beside the bed. There is also a
brief close-up of the bracelet on Imogen's arm. At the close of the scene, the
opening crane shot is repeated as Iachimo returns to the trunk and slides the
bolt to lock himself in. This section of the script ends with the instruction,

'LOSE FOCUS'. As noted, there are 18 scripted shot changes in perhaps 11 minutes and 25 seconds of screen time, giving an ASL of 38 seconds, again underlining the intimacy and intensity of the scene. Yet one camera shot remains focused on Iachimo, with a single pan down to Imogen and back up, for the eleven lines (and more than a minute of playing time) from 'On her left breast/A mole cinque-spotted...' (2.2.37–8) to 'To th'trunk again, and shut the spring of it' (2.2.47). To a significantly greater extent than in the 1937 version, it would seem that the cameras contribute to the way in which 'the audience... is forced to confront its own complicity in Iachimo's deed. His gaze is ours'.[26] Certainly Philip Hope-Wallace was impressed, as he wrote, 'The trunk scene is unfailing: Derek Godfrey in his ruminations and Barbara Jefford in her slumber filled imagination fully. It was among the most successful brief screenings of Shakespeare that I can recall'.[27] And at least one member of the television audience described the bedchamber scene as 'entrancingly done'.[28]

When Elijah Moshinsky came in 1982 to direct *Cymbeline* in the studio for *The BBC Television Shakespeare* he reverted to a less complex visual language for the wooing and trunk scenes. The former, which is cut short by nine lines at the close of the scene, is played with just nine changes of camera shot and the trunk scene has only seven. There is no special focus on the trunk before Imogen (played by Helen Mirren) gets into bed while Iachimo (Robert Lindsay) appears naked at least to the waist, enhancing the threateningly invasive and fetishistic quality of the encounter.

For the first shot of Iachimo's appearance, Imogen is brightly lit in the background while he is a dark silhouette nearer to the camera. His leering closeness to Imogen as he clambers onto the bed, together with his play with the bracelet, caressing it off Imogen's arm before sliding his own hand slowly into it, leaves little doubt about the meaning of the scene. Yet there is perhaps not the same sense as there would appear to have been in 1956 of aligning the camera's (and thus the viewer's) gaze with Iachimo's. And his final line, spoken as he listens to a clock striking, 'One, two, three: time, time!' (2.2.51) is delivered while he is still on the bed and we do not see him returning to the trunk.

The analysis of the screen grammar of early studio drama is still very much in its infancy, especially when compared with the rich work of scholars working on early film such as David Bordwell, Janet Staiger and Kristin Thompson,[29] Barry Salt, Ben Brewster and Lea Jacobs, and many others. But questions can begin to be asked here as a focus for further research. Expressed crudely, in the study of early film, a key shift has been identified in the years around 1910 from a 'tableau' style dominated by lengthy long-shots to one in which editing, close-ups, cross-cutting and scene dis-section were developed to construct a film's narrative. This initial study of the camera scripts of the 1937 and 1956 television scenes from *Cymbeline* would seem to suggest that between these two dates a comparable shift can be identified in the development of the screen language of multi-camera studio recording. The simplicity of the camera plot for the 1982 produc-tion should, however, warn against any simple sense of a teleological pro-gression of this visual language. Clearly, too, television developed in social and cultural contexts quite distinct from the cinema of the early twentieth century, with quite different production technologies and a completely dif-ferent relationship with audiences. The similarities and differences suggest excitingly productive paths for future research, especially since the tech-niques and visual grammar of multi-camera studio production of drama are being developed again in live cinema broadcasts of theatre stagings by *NT Live*, *RSC Live from Stratford-upon-Avon* and others.

Notes

1 *Cymbeline* had been filmed by the American independent Thanhouser Film Company in 1913; see J. Buchanan, *Shakespeare on Film* (Abingdon: Routledge, 2005), 43–4.

2 J. Jacobs, *The Intimate Screen: Early British Television Drama* (Oxford: Oxford University Press, 2000), 4.

3 M. Butler, *The New Cambridge Shakespeare: Cymbeline* (Cambridge: Cam-bridge University Press, 2005), 6.

4 In the Introduction to *The New Cambridge Shakespeare: Cymbeline*, Butler identifies the 'remarkably decentred' design of the play, suggesting also that its 'fractures appeal to post-modern tastes for fictions that reveal their engineering and question the terms of their own mimesis' (2).

5 Anonymous, 'Shakespeare and Mr Shaw', *The Times*, 17 November 1937, 14.

6 Anonymous, *The Sunday Times*, 'Cymbeline', 21 November 1937, 6.

7 'E. H. R.', *The Observer*, 'Television', 5 December 1937, 31.

8 Both the 28-page camera script and the 4-page 'cue script,' which details the music elements that were included, are preserved in WAC T5/121.

9 Butler, *Cymbeline*, 104; both Butler and Bate and Rasmussen (*Cymbeline*, ed. J. Bate and E. Rasmussen, *The RSC Shakespeare* [London: Macmillan, 2007]) use the First Folio spelling of Innogen, although the more accepted Imogen is used here.

10 Anonymous, 'Old Vic: *Cymbeline*', *The Times*, 12 September 1956, 3.

11 M. Clarke, *Shakespeare at the Old Vic 1956–7* (London: Hamish Hamilton, 1957), n.p.

12 Cecil Madden, Memo to Michael Barry, 27 August 1956, WAC T5/121.

13 Cecil Madden, Memo, 10 September 1956, WAC T5/121.

14 Clarke, *Shakespeare at the Old Vic*.
15 M. Barry, Memo, 'The Old Vic', 11 September 1956, WAC T5/121.
16 M. Elliott, Letter to Sybil Thorndike, 22 October 1956, WAC T5/121.
17 'The Old Vic last night put on *Cymbeline* – not well, but not without merit here and there'. P. Hope-Wallace, 'The misfortunes of Imogen', *The Manchester Guardian*, 12 September 1956, 5.
18 P. Hope-Wallace, 'Drama: The heat of the sun', *The Listener*, 8 November 1956, 768.
19 Audience Research Report, *Cymbeline*, VR/56/571, WAC T5/121.
20 Floor plans and images of Lime Grove Studio D can be found at www .tvstudiohistory.co.uk/old%20bbc%20studios.htm#lime (accessed 10 February 2014).
21 The 12-page camera script together with production memos and other documentation is preserved in WAC T5/121.
22 Clarke, *Shakespeare at the Old Vic*.
23 D. Bordwell, *The Way Hollywood Tells It: Story and Style in the Movies* (Berkeley and Los Angeles: University of California Press, 2006), 121.
24 T. Tanner, *Prefaces to Shakespeare* (London: Belkamp Press, 2010), 740.
25 Clarke, *Shakespeare at the Old Vic*.
26 Bate and Rasmussen (eds.), *Cymbeline*, 2240.
27 Hope-Wallace, 'The heat of the sun', 768.
28 Audience Research Report, *Cymbeline*, VR/56/571, WAC T5/121.
29 D. Bordwell, J. Staiger and K. Thompson, *The Classical Hollywood Cinema: Film Style & Mode of Production to 1960* (London: Routledge & Kegan Paul, 1985); B. Salt, *Film Style and Technology: History and Analysis* (London: Starword, 1983); B. Brewster and L. Jacobs, *Theatre to Cinema: Stage Pictorialism and the Early Feature Film* (Oxford: Oxford University Press, 1977). For a pioneering approach to shot analysis in television, see J. G. Butler, *Television Style* (New York: Routledge, 2010).

WORKS CITED

Bate, J. and E. Rasmussen (eds.), *The RSC Shakespeare:* Cymbeline (London: Macmillan, 2007).
Bordwell, D., *The Way Hollywood Tells It: Story and Style in the Movies* (Berkeley and Los Angeles: University of California Press, 2006).
Bordwell, D., J. Staiger and K. Thompson, *The Classical Hollywood Cinema: Film Style & Mode of Production to 1960* (London: Routledge & Kegan Paul, 1985).
Brewster, B. and L. Jacobs, *Theatre to Cinema: Stage Pictorialism and the Early Feature Film* (Oxford: Oxford University Press, 1977).
Buchanan, J., *Shakespeare on Film* (Abingdon: Routledge, 2005).
Butler, J. G., *Television Style* (New York: Routledge, 2010).
Butler, M., The New Cambridge Shakespeare: *Cymbeline* (Cambridge: Cambridge University Press, 2005).

Clarke, M., *Shakespeare at the Old Vic 1956–1957* (London: Hamish Hamilton, 1957).

Jacobs, J., *The Intimate Screen: Early British Television Drama* (Oxford: Oxford University Press, 2000).

Salt, B., *Film Style and Technology: History and Analysis* (London: Starword, 1983).

Tanner, T., *Prefaces to Shakespeare* (London: Belkamp Press, 2010).

CHAPTER 5

Romance for Television
The BBC Cymbeline

Robert S. White

Although the BBC/Time Life 'Complete Works', made for television in the 1980s, is often maligned by critics, some productions have been praised. After the replacement of the initial executive director Cedric Messina by the more radical Jonathan Miller, the generally conservative and educationally pious aims of 'authenticity' and the myth of 'faithfulness' were modified, and directors were encouraged to present their own unique versions of Shakespeare's plays.[1] Amongst those which, by common consent, have succeeded in artistic terms, are especially Elijah Moshinsky's *A Midsummer Night's Dream* (1981), *All's Well That Ends Well* (1981), *Cymbeline* (1982), *Coriolanus* (1984) and *Love's Labour's Lost* (1985).[1] His *Cymbeline* is the only widely available TV representation of a play which is studied less often than others and lacks a particularly rich theatre history, even though, when it has been performed on stage, it has usually been successful. Rather incredibly, Moshinsky's is also the only complete, filmed English-language adaptation of the play, since there have been no others until Michael Almereyda's in 2015. However, television drama is different in kind from cinema and the way that Moshinsky handles the different medium, quietly but effectively, contributes his own unique interpretation of the play. He has allowed the small-screen medium, with all its limitations, to reveal aspects of *Cymbeline* that might not readily emerge from a stage production, a critic's reading or a lavishly funded box office film. Although these Shakespeare productions have been Moshinsky's only forays into drama, he is no stranger to either film or television, since, like Miller, his main profession over a distinguished career has been directing opera on stage and screen; he well understands the dynamics of 'making new' accessible adaptations of older works for a modern audience. *Cymbeline* shows that he could work adroitly in the necessarily low budget and relatively modest medium of television drama. More than thirty years later, it still shows that the potential of Shakespeare's well-worn texts, intrinsically plural and multi-vocal, can be realised in infinitely new ways. Perhaps surprisingly, none of his Shakespeare productions is operatic in style or intention but instead textually focused and generally understated, without arias and divas, and the music is discreetly and purposefully used. Instead of music, the main art-form Moshinsky chooses to reference, especially in the *Dream* and *All's Well*, is pictorial art.[2]

It is fairly clear that film and television drama are radically different from live theatre but it is less often acknowledged that they also differ from each other, as John Wilders, Shakespeare Adviser to the BBC series, insisted.[3] Cinema and television are often seen as more or less the same medium, with some refinements based on the fact that reception is different between collective audiences in large, darkened cinemas, and families watching (or not watching, just 'having on') a small screen in the privacy of their living rooms. This may be less true now than in the 1980s, since films often begin with sponsorship from television stations like Channel 4 in England and are later released in cinemas, on television and on video. However, three or four decades ago the media were even more sharply different, with radically different genealogies. Film was originally seen as a proletariat entertainment shown in music halls and nickelodeons. Despite arthouse and independent film movements, its mass, populist basis remained relevant.[3] With its silent roots, film is also, both historically and technically, a primarily visual medium; up to the 1930s, it was exclusively visual. There were intercut captions to guide the audience in understanding the plot, but often they were added to give a pretentious air of 'high culture,' carrying the cultural capital of the printed word, in the case of Shakespearean adaptation. Still today, even in avant-garde films, it is arguable that priority is given to the visual over the linguistic, licensing cuts of up to 50 per cent of the text in Shakespeare plays.

For institutional reasons, television in Britain evolved from sound radio and, in particular, BBC television drama grew from public educational radio. Its early brief was to educate rather than entertain: public broadcasting, which is not exclusively popular music, at least in Britain and Australia, is still expected to cater for minority audiences and ratings are lower than commercial outlets. The connection with radio, while explained by the historical accident of public ownership rather than intrinsic generic links, has important consequences. It may seem obvious but is worth emphasizing that radio drama, unlike stage and filmed varieties, exists solely in sound and has no visual component except what the mind's eye can supply through verbal description, inflected tone and evocative language. In the early days of television, budgets were tightly restricted by using actors employed by the corporations whose voices were already recognisable from radio drama and many of the presentation conventions were adapted from radio techniques. Sound effects can suggest the scene – seagulls, clattering hooves – whose justification lies in cues found in the text itself.

Paradoxically, radio relies on Shakespeare's language being itself full of 'speaking pictures,' rich in pictorial and metaphorical effects. Dialogue is obviously the strength of radio drama; tone and mood must be verbally transmitted and cannot be reinforced or undercut by facial expressions or gestures. The voice is everything. Most of these factors are omnipresent in television drama well into the 1990s: they are discernible in the whole enterprise of the BBC Shakespeare, whose publicised aim was to present the complete texts as written on the page. Among the most mediocre productions, a recurrent fault is the kind of literal-mindedness that comes from a training in radio – *telling* what is being *shown*. Since both media are played in the home, it cannot be taken for granted that the audience's concentration is captive to the image, as it is in the environment of film and stage. Certainly radio and probably television are, in many if not most households, just 'on' and the family may be doing other things than consciously 'watching' or even listening. Music can survive the challenge of an audience only partially engaged but if a drama production is to have any impact it must draw attention to itself, perhaps with effects which are, strictly speaking, unnecessary. Television must be more aural than one would expect in a medium we think of as being visual, and it must continually be giving enough information to satisfy somebody who is coming and going. Silence is leaden, a fact which advertisers for television know well. In fact, effects of true silence are probably impossible to achieve on radio and television since the audience would immediately suspect there is something mechanically wrong and start turning the volume up. For these and many other reasons, television and radio may in practice be more similar than we would expect, both having less in common with film and the stage. Even though television directors were steeped in film and rapidly absorbed filmic techniques, the different historical origins of commercial film and public corporation radio broadcasting are significant to the finished product.

Speaking of his experience in directing *All's Well* and no doubt true of *Cymbeline* too, Moshinsky has described the limitations imposed by working for a bureaucratic institution with 'impossible schedules: the group were allowed only four weeks' rehearsal and five or six days of filming'.[4] By fiat, each play had to be set in either Shakespeare's time or the specific period which the play was depicting, since the series was made with school and educational audiences as its market. Filming had to be done in a studio where budgeting control could not fluctuate with the weather

and light, while set-making, costuming, lighting and make-up were done
by salaried BBC employees who had no specific artistic expertise in Shakespeare or even drama but were contracted to a kind of distinctive studio system. Constant re-takes, common in film production, could not be afforded.
Moshinsky says the 'holy writ' was faithfulness to the written text, although
he, with Miller's tacit approval, was the first 'discreetly' to make cuts in
order to alter 'the rhythms of scenes which seemed fractionally too long for
television, to make the performance more forceful,' a freedom which any
stage or film director would unquestioningly expect.[5] Ironically, he was crit-
icised at the time for his cuts, which were regarded by some as tantamount
to the eighteenth-century rewritings of Shakespeare's texts.[6] Finally, even
when the production had been completed, transmission was at the mercy
of the Corporation, which could, as in the case of Moshinsky's *Dream*,
divide the play into two parts by inserting the evening news in which it
was announced Russia was invading Poland. Because of strict timetables
of studio usage (the lights would be turned off on the dot at 5 p.m.), and
financial restraints on use of filming materials, repeated takes were frowned
upon, to the extent that usually just one take had to suffice. At every stage
of the process, then, television directors were limited by production and
transmission circumstances, despite the relative independence granted by
Miller in the later offerings of the Shakespeare series, an autonomy border-
ing on *auteurism*.

   One genuine advantage offered by working for the BBC in the 1980s
was the choice of some established and emerging stars amongst the BBC
contract actors. Moshinsky could cast Helen Mirren as Titania in *A Midsummer Night's Dream* and as Imogen in *Cymbeline* (1982), since she had
already made the transition from the Royal Shakespeare Company to the
BBC's very successful and politically provocative series 'Play for Today'
(1970–84).[7] He cast Alan Howard in *Coriolanus* (1984); the aging but still
radiantly expressive Celia Johnson in *All's Well That Ends Well*, alongside
Michael Hordern and Ian Charleson; while in *Love's Labour's Lost* he chose
as Rosaline Jenny Agutter, who had been in one of the BBC's 'Plays of the
Month,' *The Wild Duck* (1971) and was well known to television audiences
as Roberta ('Bobbie') in the BBC's *The Railway Children* (1968).

   Even more positively, Moshinsky advanced some considered theories on
the potential strengths of television as a medium for Shakespeare plays;
here we move towards the intrinsic uniqueness of his *Cymbeline*. In casting, Moshinsky chose his actors with their faces and voices in mind and,
to some extent, their *personae* derived from other well-known roles they
played. 'If you are doing films for television, the primary element is still

the actor's face,' he says, which can carry 'psychological allusiveness' and express feelings. If star quality and superficial bodily perfection are not the dominating criteria, older actors can come into their own, especially in Moshinsky's *All's Well* where the cast includes actors from different generations. Age differences can arguably be more subtly realised on television than on the stage, where often a bent back and a white beard denote age, rather than natural lining of the face which cannot be seen from the back rows. 'It was her face that told you the story of the Countess as much as her performance,' said Moshinsky of Celia Johnson in *All's Well*.

Issues of age and youth, of faces and voices, are just as important for the production of *Cymbeline*, although here the acting styles are more significant than actual age differences. Richard Johnson as king, at 55, was not exactly elderly and he had a track record playing the rakish Bulldog Drummond in *Deadlier than the Male* (1967) and *Some Girls Do* (1969), but here he is made to appear and behave as a much older man, careworn and haggard – no wonder, the production seems to suggest implicitly, with his family decimated and dysfunctional and with the full weight of Augustus Caesar's Roman Empire bearing down upon Britain. (The king bears the shame of Rome's 'yoke' over England [3.1.49] and, for Elizabethan audiences the reference would obliquely be to the Rome of the Pope, just as Iachimo represents the perceived evils of contemporary Italians rather than ancient Romans.)[8] Claire Bloom at 53 was virtually the same age as Johnson and yet, as the Queen, she is deliberately presented as considerably younger than her husband and full of the glamour of the social *arriviste* who has married upwards, as well as the menace of the wicked stepmother of fairy tales who wishes her own foolish son Cloten (Paul Jesson) to be king.

At the other end of the age scale are two stars who were in reality not especially young, Helen Mirren (then 35) and Michael Pennington (39), but they were associated with the 'young' medium of television and particular darlings of the BBC's prestigious 'Play of the Month' series. Mirren was interviewed by a seriously politically incorrect Michael Parkinson in 1975 (of which, more anon) and, by 1982, she had still not lost the reputation and aura of youthful, frankly expressed sexuality that epitomised the post-1960s' age. Robert Lindsay (33) as Iachimo was already a well-known Shakespearean stage actor but his common persona in movies of the time was as a cheerful but somewhat shady cockney character; he was especially associated with sitcoms such as Thames's *Get Some In!*, the comedy *Citizen Smith* (1977–80) and a starring role as a clownish boxer in the BBC's *Seconds Out* (1981–2). Again, there were financial and industrial reasons behind such casting decisions, since the younger actors were regularly contracted by the BBC, but Moshinsky uses them to further characterisation and, in particular, he concentrates on their facial gestures and expressions in the intimate medium of television.

A special quality which Moshinsky theorizes as a strength of television, stemming from facial close-ups, is the capacity for an emotional subtlety that is only rarely achievable on stage and differently on the 'big screen'.[9] As he developed his television style, he 'discovered that the characters had to become more dense in their psychology. The production of the voice and the speaking had to be extraordinarily subtle to succeed, because basically you are always working in close-up, in a space more intimate than this studio'. For Moshinsky, 'enormous consequences developed from playing *All's Well That Ends Well* on television, because suddenly it became a very intimate play'. 'Mood-laden' is the word he uses, and it is appropriate for his *Cymbeline* as well.[10] For once, the actor is liberated from a stage requirement to project and to exude physical energy, since a different discipline asserts itself. In order to gain plausibility from the lines in a medium requiring 'realism' in close-up, the actors in their delivery have to concentrate on the thought processes driving the lines rather than their musical qualities, and this contributes to a pervasive atmosphere allowing us to identify powerful emotional strands in the play. Moshinsky's valuing of the close-up for intimate revelation is based on the inheritance from radio, with its prioritising of the voice as the vehicle for emotion and mood, in direct relationship with each individual listener. He also exploited the special quality of television in dwelling on one face at a time, preventing spectators from allowing their eyes from wandering as they would when watching a stage and even the large cinema screen. Here again, radio is an influence, since it can make soliloquies and monologues seem more plausibly 'inward' than any visual medium; Moshinsky recognises the link: 'Television does gain with soliloquies and monologues, where the character is looking inward and considering what to do next'.[11] The assertion of 'inwardness' would be contested these days by theatre practitioners and performance critics, since the dominant twentieth-century understanding of the soliloquy as a kind of overheard stream of consciousness no longer prevails and they are seen more as direct address to the stage audience. But in television it does seem still valid to accept that 'talking heads' are a central part of the medium itself and that what Moshinsky in the previous quotation calls 'intimacy' generated is a special quality, once again shared by the parent medium, radio. Gary Waller puts clearly what is understood by Moshinsky:

> However, television does have an enormous strength – its intimacy. The pri-
> mary reality of television drama – and here it is somewhat unlike film – is not
> spectacle, but the intimacy with which it records human emotions . . . The
> television actor expresses himself not, as on the stage, in body movements,
> but in facial change . . . we [viewers] become the privileged participant [sic]
> in a voyeuristic revelation.[12]

However, when he came to work in television, Moshinsky, unlike Cedric
Messina, did also fully realise the importance of the visual component,
though it caused him much thought to define what kind of visual impression was appropriate to the small screen. He argued that 'cardboard sets
in studios' undermine television Shakespeare since the audience 'is watching a screen, not a space'. Television staging, 'without theoretical support'
meant asking whether we are indeed 'looking at an actor in space.' Modern staging theory, focusing on the actor in space, was irrelevant. There
was, he said, a 'difficulty which I couldn't solve' with the 'flat screen and
the two-dimensional picture' of television, so he made the production at
times like a set of *tableaux vivants*: 'I found myself,' he acknowledged, 'cutting out entrances and exits, since on stage, 'an actor making an entrance
seemed very false and theatrical, because the eye had become accustomed
to looking at a two-dimensional image.'[9] The slightly disconcerting but
again partly purposeful effect is a steady and gradual alternation between
sustained stasis and slow movement of the camera pulling in to close-
ups, which might be seen as focusing intensely on the individual characters' response in an emotionally charged moment and drawing the viewer
into the mind's workings with a steady, rhythmic pacing. Roger Warren
describes one especially effective example (see Figure 5.1):

> There is one superb visual effect in the production when, at the start of I.vi,
> the camera moves slowly across a Jacobean long gallery illuminated by tall
> windows towards Innogen's solitary figure sitting absolutely motionless, lost
> in thought. The shot perfectly captures her sense of isolation at a court ruled
> by 'a father cruel and a stepdame false', and separated from her banished
> husband (I.vi.1–3). The sense of stillness is prolonged because, as the camera
> nears her face, it reveals that this too is motionless: the lines are spoken in
> 'voice-over', and accompanied by a broad cello melody, to romantic effect.[13]

As Warren suggests here, and not surprisingly for this particular director,
Moshinsky uses music to telling effect throughout, most often in sombre
snatches, from stringed instruments such as lutes, violins and cellos, suggesting a generally baroque ambience, heightening subtle shades of emotion and making the moments of silence still more powerfully expressive
by contrast.

Figure 5.1. Isolation and stillness in a corrupt court in the 1982 BBC *Cymbeline*.
All rights reserved.

All these aspects of Moshinsky's approach are exemplified in the lengthy
and potentially convoluted second scene in Act 4, with all its apparent
improbabilities and narrative shifts. Shakespeare's scene presents in one
long, overlapping sequence the series of events in and outside the cave of
Belarius and his two 'found' sons, Guiderius and Arviragus, beginning with
Imogen's sickness, the men's departure from her to hunt, she swallowing
the drug given by Pisanio which causes death-like sleep; then Guiderius's
slaying and beheading of Cloten dressed in Posthumus's clothes and its
aftermath. The decapitated corpse is left beside the prone Imogen while
the head is thrown into the stream. Imogen awakens and assumes from
the clothing that the body is Posthumus's, and she is found mourning over
it by a group of Romans including a soothsayer. Even described in such
bald summary, the scene is chaotic in its narrative complexity and improbable coincidences. No doubt it was a theatrical *coup* of economy created
by Shakespeare on his own stage but it is fiendishly difficult to present in
modern terms, without losing the audience in either confusion or risible
disbelief. However, laughter seems rarely a response and the possible confusion can be given a more positive, ethical and emotional note in the light

of the vehement but misdirected amalgam of grief and passion expressed by the heroine faced with such a strange and potentially necrophiliac situation. The emphasis can be placed on Imogen's violently engaged feelings, rather than on the incongruity and the corpse of the ridiculous Cloten. There may also be a sardonically disturbing implication that love itself can be so dependent on externals like clothing.

Moshinsky's solutions are interesting to trace in his attempt to make the events somehow credible and clear on the small screen. He firmly turns his back on any possible laughter as response, presenting the scene instead with intense seriousness. In order to clarify the action, the events are separated out into sequential episodes and re-ordered. The main effect achieved and presumably intended is to focus attention centrally on the emotional experiences of Imogen, while showing the discreteness of the events leading to the slaying of the Queen's foolish son, Cloten, in a way that avoids tangling the narrative with its disparate and coincidental ordering in the original. A strong atmosphere is established initially with close-ups of Imogen, Belarius, Guiderius and Arviragus in the cave, a flickering fire in the background, intensifying their relationships and warm feelings. This is followed by a cut to the bleakly snow-clad countryside outside the cave (wholly an illusion created in the studio) where Cloten brags of his status before Guiderius. The fight is brief and its violence conveyed not in direct observation but by suggestion, through a sudden image of falcons (repeated elsewhere between scenes, a glimpse of the natural world which is necessarily otherwise absent) and overlaid sound of jangling, discordant stringed instruments, followed immediately by the sight of the bloody, severed head and Belarius's shocked 'What hast thou done?' (4.2.116). A rather doleful looking, shaggy hound looks on impassively, while the lighting suggests evening sun on the snow. To transition into the next scene (now not one longer scene but two shorter ones in Moshinsky's adaptation) we hear, in the words of Shakespeare's stage direction, 'solemn music' (4.2.184), which takes us back into the cave and the apparently dead Imogen (as an economy enabled by the medium, she is not carried out of the cave, as in Shakespeare's presentation). Belarius's repeated word 'melancholy' (4.2.202–7) establishes the mood and the camera then picks up the literalness of Shakespeare's words in describing the woman's precise and strangely serene pose:

> ARVIRAGUS: [...]
> Thus smiling, as some fly had tickled slumber,
> Not as death's dart, being laughed at; his right cheek
> Reposing on a cushion.
> GUIDERIUS: Where?
> ARVIRAGUS: O'th'floor,

> His arms thus leagued. I thought he slept, and put
> My clouted brogues from off my feet, whose rudeness
> Answered my steps too loud. (4.2.209–14)[14]

Shakespeare's hint has been observed and actualised, that the scene is eerily quiet and very clearly focused on Imogen's body and the dawning emotions. Rhythm and pacing are important here, as the action has been slowed down after the rapid fight. Moshinsky now cuts some fifty lines, perhaps judging that they would inappropriately slow down the pace in the wrong sense, with explanations, and risk distraction from the sombreness. To maintain the mood, he jumps instead straight to the beautiful elegies sung over the body of 'Fidele' by Guiderius and Arviragus ('Fear no more the heat o' the sun' [4.2.257]). In this segment we detect Moshinsky the opera director, orchestrating music and song to reinforce atmosphere.

The television version now once again makes a distinct transition into a new scene, rather than running on as the text does. A moment of darkness with Imogen's delirious 'Yes, sir, to Milford Haven, which is the way?' (4.2.290) marks her awakening to find herself beside a lighted candle and Cloten's body which she gradually becomes aware of, thinking it is Posthumus. At this stage the camera moves into and then out of an intense close-up of Mirren. We do not see the body at all as she feels over its contours, so that it is her feelings that are foregrounded entirely rather than the bizarre image. An even more intimate close-up, the camera still unobtrusively moving slowly and out, focuses entirely on her face alone in her distress and as she smears blood on it. Mirren's characteristically light and expressive voice registers subtle shifts of feelings. There is now another cut, as though to another scene, and the Roman soothsayer reads an enigmatic (and ultimately incorrect) prophecy concerning the war between Rome and Britain. Despite – or rather because of – his cuts and rearrangements of this long, complicated and challenging scene, Moshinsky has arguably simplified and enhanced the staging effects. By shifting the perspective away from the events themselves and concentrating on the emotional intensity and play of feelings, the adaptation has avoided any hint of inappropriate but tempting comic effects, in ways that genuinely use the medium of televisual methods for serious and affective ends, rather than simply presenting a sequence of 'filmed events'.

Watching 'a screen, not a space,' causes problems when creating a visual setting if the venue is a cramped studio space. In his *Dream*, Moshinsky tends to use Jane Howell's solution in the *Henry VI* plays in the BBC production, allowing the audience to see simply a studio, without disguising the artifice. He sets the *Dream* partly in a forest, making the problems of studio filming quite acute, as they are in the Milford Haven scenes in *Cymbeline*. In the latter, Moshinsky uses elegantly minimalist means to establish changes of scene without this time making explicit the illusion (he was gratified when I asked him in correspondence if the snow scenes in Milford Haven were shot *en plein air*: answer? They weren't). The 'outdoors' location in Milford Haven is starkly simple but suggestive in its snowy whiteness, contrasting the domestic warmth of the cave on one hand and the politically charged claustrophobia of the court on the other. As elsewhere, Moshinsky tends to make a virtue out of a technical problem and work with the medium rather than resisting it, in order to direct attention to the fluctuating emotions, often registered most clearly on faces, without scenic distractions.

The other way in which Moshinsky deals with the problem of working with something that he sees as 'more like a picture, a photograph or a painting' is to bring right to the foreground iconic paintings from history. The paintings are the most immediately striking aspect of some of Moshinsky's productions for the BBC Shakespeare. Reasons are not too hard to fathom. First, it is a cunning ploy to create a historical context of his own choice without breaking the BBC's 'holy writ' of period settings as a historically distancing device. Secondly, some of the most effective television programmes in the 1960s and 1970s, such as Kenneth Clark's *Civilisation*, were being televised with great success. *Civilisation* itself was first broadcast in 1969 and, coincidentally, was repeated in the very week that *Cymbeline* was screened. According to the *Radio Times* of that week (see Figure 5.2), Shakespeare's play was on BBC2 at 7.15 p.m. on Sunday 10 July 1983, while part 3 of *Civilisation* was on the following Friday, also on BBC2. Such programmes were in the cultural realm of the BBC Shakespeare series itself, scholarly and educational contributions to art history, a genre acknowledged as something the medium could 'do' extremely well. The camera could rove a painting like the viewer's eye, picking up details, tracing patterns and enhancing visual rhythms. Conversely, the painting could be made to move and live, to the extent that the different two-dimensional aspects were complementary. What television could add, of course, was movement within the screen or picture and so, like Pygmalion, Moshinsky allows his images slowly to come to life, having first attuned us to thinking of the image as a flat surface. Effects of realism would then be as effective as Hermione's statue 'coming to life' in *The Winter's Tale*. In *Cymbeline*, paintings in the background from the Renaissance, particularly Rembrandt and Dutch realists, highlight the opulence of the British

Figure 5.2.   Pre-publicity – 'Virtue under siege' in the 1982 BBC *Cymbeline*. All
rights reserved.

royal court, here placed in Jacobean times and without any attempt to be
true to the period of Augustus Caesar and Cymbeline, but they also reflect
ominously and thematically on the action.[15]

The casting of Helen Mirren as Imogen was clearly an important choice.
Interviews with Moshinsky and Mirren confirm that her star billing was

a conscious challenge to the prevailing view, stemming from Victorian times and through Harley Granville-Barker, that Imogen is too good to be true, a virtuous 'fairy-tale princess, a puppet, too ethereal, too much the symbol of female virtue; or what female virtue was once supposed to be'.[16] 'What,' the interviewer asked Moshinsky, 'is Helen Mirren doing in the part? . . . ' 'Voluptuous,' 'sensual,' 'earthy,' are the sort of words bandied about whenever she is discussed. For better or worse, the particular kind of star quality had been invested in Mirren, not only through some of her earlier roles but also by a notorious Parkinson interview recorded in 1975, which was widely seen because of the programme's popularity; judging from the audience's knowing laughter, it struck a chord in the popular imagination. Even for its time, it was complacently misogynistic. Parkinson introduces Mirren by quoting a critic speaking of her 'sluttish eroticism'. He patronisingly describes her as '*in quotes* "a serious actress"' (my emphasis), a qualification which she spiritedly challenges. But then he proceeds salaciously to focus his questions (and his eyes) on what he coyly describes as Mirren's 'equipment' and asking whether the sight of her breasts might 'detract from her performance'. The result (which can now be seen on YouTube)[17] represents an unnervingly close anticipation of Iachimo's employment of the 'male gaze' in the bedchamber scene as he uncovers and inspects Imogen's breasts for signs of identification. Moreover, Mirren's own responses, by turns embarrassed, frank, intelligent, mildly outraged and at times drily indifferent, anticipate her presentation of Imogen. This character offers an actor an unusually wide spectrum of interpretations. Like Hermia, Desdemona and Cordelia, she demonstrates active decisiveness by defying her father in her marriage choice, while the male disguise she dons links her to more vulnerable and guarded women like Julia in *The Two Gentlemen of Verona* and Viola in *Twelfth Night*. Rosalind (*As You Like It*) comes to mind as one who in disguise expresses her sexual choices forthrightly, although Imogen's situation offers her less freedom. Even though she shares some other facets with Helena in her pursuit of Bertram in *All's Well That Ends Well*, the roles are reversed since Posthumus is below her royal rank. Like Isabella in *Measure for Measure*, there is evidence of 'saintliness' in that Imogen has chosen not yet to consummate the marriage and she strongly repulses Cloten's attentions. It is an unusually wide range of possibilities that faces a director and the actor in how they will portray the character.

Moshinsky explained that, although the casting of Helen Mirren might have surprised some, it was a deliberate provocation to provide a new way of understanding the character and the play: 'I wanted an actress of great sexual voltage'. He asserts in the interview that *Cymbeline* is about 'the corruption of the good' and is at one level of action 'like a series of night-mares . . . a totally bizarre dream'. Imogen is 'not the symbol of all that is untouched: she is capable of being sullied'. Crucial to this realisation is the scene in which Iachimo spies on, and conspicuously fondles, the sleep-ing woman – apparently a simple confrontation of good and evil but in Moshinsky's view, 'more complex than that . . . Both seduction scene and bedroom scene [Shakespeare] has imbued with sexuality. In the bedroom scene of a particularly threatening and nightmarish sort'. He explains that an interpretation of a potentially corruptible Imogen was arrived at by Mir-ren herself in rehearsal, since she recognised aspects that linked up with another role she had played (on stage), Isabella in *Measure for Measure* deal-ing with her attempted seduction by Angelo:

> It's very clear that the character is susceptible and is almost seduced and that makes her feel enormously uneasy about herself. She's not a good person in a world of evil. The moment when she has to struggle she comes to understand something very uneasy about herself.[18]

This is a debatable interpretation of Imogen's role since it is difficult to sus-tain a reading of her as being 'almost seduced' – if she is 'capable of being sullied' there is little evidence of it being because of 'a potential for cor-ruptibility' but because she is treated by others as a sex object, a position which she resists as firmly as Mirren resists Parkinson, but with the same helpless and almost innocent entrapment in other people's assumptions. However, the decision to clarify her sexual presence is one that at least res-cues Imogen from Victorian sentimentality; moreover, Mirren's reputation for erotic danger in televisual drama at the time results in a new and com-plex resonance (see Figure 5.3).

The scene under consideration is 1.6, in which Iachimo introduces him-self to Imogen. On a reading, there may not be enough textual evidence to construct this psychological interpretation from her response to his surrep-titious attempt to besmirch Posthumus's good name. Imogen characteristi-cally demands straight answers instead of his coded messages (like Angelo's in *Measure for Measure*): 'Deliver with more openness your answers/To my demands' (1.6.88). Admittedly Iachimo himself is, first in asides and then more openly, suggestive in his rhetoric and, after claiming her husband has been 'vaulting variable ramps' (1.6.134) in Italy, he offers himself as a vehicle for her revenge, attempting to force a kiss on Imogen. Her reply shows at least a dawning awareness of being implicated in a world of sexual betrayal and intrigue that must have been well beyond her experience as

Figure 5.3.   Iachimo paws Imogen; the audience pores over both in the BBC 1982
Cymbeline.

a loving wife, the words italicized suggesting that she has internalized the
full impact of the suggestions:

> IACHIMO: [. . .] revenge it.
> I dedicate myself to your sweet pleasure,
> More noble than that runagate to your bed,
> And will continue fast to your affection,
> Still close as sure.
> INNOGEN: What ho, Pisanio!
> IACHIMO: Let me my service tender on your lips.
> INNOGEN: Away, I do condemn mine ears that have
> So long attended thee. If thou wert honourable
> Thou wouldst have told this tale for virtue, not
> *For such an end thou seek'st, as base* as strange.
> Thou wrong'st a gentleman who is as far
> From thy report as thou from honour, and
> *Solicits* here a lady that disdains
> Thee and the devil alike. What ho, Pisanio!
> The king my father shall be made acquainted
> Of thy *assault.* If he shall think it fit
> A *saucy* stranger in his court to mart
> As in a *Romish stew,* and to expound
> His *beastly* mind to us, he hath a court
> He little cares for, and a daughter who
> He not respects at all. What ho, Pisanio! [my italics] (1.7.135–55)

Again, the comparison with Isabella in *Measure for Measure* might be instructive. After Imogen indignantly repulses him, Iachimo pretends to be merely testing her and recants his calumny of her husband, begging pardon, which she grants. It is not entirely easy to see this moment as a crisis in which Imogen doubts her own sexuality, though she certainly does understand the full emotional impact of the attempted act of soliciting. Mirren, speaking almost thirty years after the production, reflects on the reading and reveals how she came to it. Speaking of the extreme difficulty of playing the tonally strange scene in which Imogen wakes beside the headless body of Cloten, thinking it is Posthumus's corpse, she describes how she created her own 'secret story,' what it meant to her without caring about what critics think: 'My internal energy is telling that story . . . with Imogen it was about learning about love as much as anything, learning all the fault-lines in love and how you repair them'.[19]

Moshinsky's summation is this:

> I thought of the play as being neurotic and exploratory and it seemed to me it needed an actress like that. Helen can act enormously complex sexual emotions at war with each other particularly well. She can take this character and make it undergo a crisis.

The bedroom scene itself, in which Iachimo removes Imogen's bracelet, is understandably described by Moshinsky as the enactment of 'a rape,' but more than this, he suggests that the woman herself is 'made to feel soiled': 'Iachimo's evil depends on having made the other person guilty'. This is perhaps harder to sustain since Imogen is sound asleep throughout and the only thing she notices is – tellingly – the bracelet which has been slipped off her arm by Iachimo. She is a completely unwitting and vulnerable object of the male gaze, not only from Iachimo but from the prying camera as well, whose recent parallel might be the strange Australian film, *Sleeping Beauty* directed by Julia Leigh (2011). Here more than anywhere Waller's suggestion that the television viewer is 'the privileged participant in a voyeuristic revelation' becomes disturbingly true. It is an exceptionally uncomfortable scene in Shakespeare and Moshinsky heightens rather than evades the likeness to physical rape denoted by Iachimo himself in his references to Tarquin and the story of Cytherea (2.2.12–14), as well as in the reference to the book she has been reading, 'The tale of Tereus' with 'the leaf . . . turned down/Where Philomel gave up' (2.2.45–6). There is no real need for Iachimo to be half naked or to lie on Imogen, except to emphasize these aspects; his lines are whispered salaciously in a way that would be impossible for a stage audience to hear: 'O sleep, thou ape of death . . .'

(2.2.31), 'Though this a heavenly angel, hell is here' (2.2.50). Nothing is left to the imagination since the camera is close enough to show in close detail the man detaching the 'slippery' bracelet (2.2.34); the camera colludes in inviting us to inspect the telltale mole beneath the sleeping woman's breast. We might agree that the two scenes taken together are explicit in their sexual content and the proximity of the bodies in the bedroom scene is more physical, erotic and intimate than anything else in Shakespeare, except perhaps the murder of the equally innocent Desdemona. It is enough for us probably to agree with Moshinsky that at least, in his version, *Cymbeline* is not a fairy-tale romance but 'psychologically enormously intense and analytical in its revelation of very dark motives. The play deals with two things: evil – it's a very dark play, it deals with evil at great depth – and moral ambiguity'.[20]

The greatest challenge to directors of *Cymbeline* lies in handling the multiple disclosures of the ending. Here perhaps Moshinsky's choice, at first sight, is surprising, since he leaves this section largely intact while he has cut – sometimes drastically – earlier, more intense scenes. From the intervention of Jupiter when Posthumus is in prison, the steady cataloguing of identity disclosures seems irremediably located in the world of romance literature – and not to modern taste. Many directors cut much of the action and hasten to the end so as not to try the audience's patience. Moshinsky, however, although he changes the order to some extent, retains almost all the dialogue and tends to trust Shakespeare's leisurely presentation. The Jupiter scene is a turning point; however creaky as a stage device it might appear to us, it is a simple solution to an inextricably tangled set of narrative problems – all the consequences are anticipated but we are required to wonder *how* the predictions will come true (bookended later with the soothsayer's explanation). The dream quality of romance and what Hazlitt called 'the logic of passion'[21] overriding plot concerns seem to be the heart of Shakespeare's preoccupation here, since his other plays suggest he could certainly have been quicker in giving closure if he had wanted.

There is a sense of miracle compounded on miracle and a recognition that what is needed morally at this point is not simply narrative revelations but full acknowledgement of innocence and exposure of guilt; in this sense Posthumus must slowly and steadily be washed clean of his own culpable suspicions of Imogen. This process, as we see in *The Winter's Tale*, takes time – if not sixteen years in this case, at least a lot of stage time. Pisanio, like a chorus, sententiously observes, 'All other doubts, by time let them be cleared' (4.3.45), and he recognises that personal agency is not always effective: 'Fortune brings in some boats that are not steered' (4.3.46). Given such a full treatment, the effect of wonder – ''Tis still a dream,' (5.3.208) says Posthumus and 'the action of my life is like it' (5.3.212) – is comparable to the 'lawful' magic of the awakening of the 'statue' of Hermione (*The Winter's Tale*, 5.3.111), in this case, 'The same dead thing alive' (5.4.123), to which a character may well say: 'strike me/To death with *mortal* joy' [my italics] (5.4.234–5). It is not magic or supernatural intervention that is required for the romance ending but time and the human qualities of patience (befitting one named 'Fidele' and also a Pisanio who is 'beaten for loyalty' [5.4.344]) and, above all, forgiveness. For Shakespeare it is this quality above all others that seems at least to define the resolution to human problems and ideally to resolve moral conflicts with finality: 'Pardon's the word to all' (5.4.422).

Notes

1 For a general summary of the BBC's Shakespeare enterprises, see S. Green-halgh's introductory chapter, 'UK Television', in R. Burt (ed.), *Shakespeares After Shakespeare: An Encyclopedia of the Bard in Mass Media and Popular Culture* (Westport, CT: Greenwood Press, 2007), 2 vols, vol. 2, 651–74; see 660–5 for survey of the BBC series in particular.

2 Early paragraphs in this chapter summarize some material already published in my essay, 'All's Well as Television: The 1980 Moshinsky Production', in Gary Waller (ed.), *All's Well That Ends Well: New Critical Essays* (New York: Routledge, 2007), 234–46. I am grateful to the editor for giving his permission.

3 J. Wilders, 'Shakespeare with No Audience', in R. S. White *et al.* (ed.), *Shakespeare: Readers, Audiences, Players* (Nedlands: University of Western Australia Press, 1998), 56–63. See also G. K. Hunter, 'The BBC *All's Well That Ends Well*', in J. C. Bulman and H. R. Coursen (eds.), *Shakespeare on Television: An Anthology of Essays and Reviews* (Hanover: University Press of New England, 1988), 185–7, esp. 186.

4 E. Moshinsky and J. Elsom, 'Does Shakespeare Write Better for Television?', in J. Elsom (ed.), *Is Shakespeare Still Our Contemporary?* (London: Routledge, 1989), 123.

5 *Ibid.*

6 G. P. Jones, 'Nahum Tate is Alive and Well: Elijah Moshinsky's BBC Shakespeare Productions', in J. C. Bulman and H. R. Coursen (eds.), *Shakespeare on Television: An Anthology of Essays and Reviews* (Hanover: University Press of New England, 1988), 192–9.

7 See L. Cooke, *British Television Drama: A History* (London: British Film Institute, 2003) and the summary in the British Film Institute's website at www.screenonline.org.uk/tv/id/454719/index.html (accessed 12 January 2015).

8 A possible criticism of the production is that there may be insufficient visual differentiation between English and Roman clothes which sometimes leads to confusion – although part of this effect may be in the play itself since Posthumus changes national allegiances himself.

9 The historical importance of the close-up in film adapting stage plays is highlighted by K. S. Rothwell in *Early Shakespeare Films: How the Spurned Spawned Art* (Stratford-upon-Avon: International Shakespeare Association, 2000).

10 Moshinsky, 'Shakespeare', 123; 117.

11 *Ibid.*, 117.

12 G. F. Waller, 'Decentring the Bard: the BBC Shakespeare and Some Implications for Criticism and Teaching', in J. C. Bulman and H. R. Coursen (eds.), *Shakespeare on Television: An Anthology of Essays and Reviews* (Hanover: University Press of New England, 1988), 22; 23.

13 R. Warren, *Cymbeline: Shakespeare in Performance* (Manchester: Manchester University Press, 1989), 63.

14 All quotes follow the Cambridge University Press edition; however, *Cymbeline*, James Nosworthy, ed. (London: Methuen, The Arden Shakespeare, 1969) may be the edition used in the production. Throughout the chapter, we have used the more commonly known name 'Imogen' even though the Cambridge edition uses 'Innogen'.

15 For analysis focused on the use of iconic pictorial art in the production of *All's Well*, see T. Murray, 'Camera Obscura Ideological: From Vermeer to Video in *All's Well That Ends Well*', in *Drama Trauma: Spectres of Race and Sexuality in Performance, Video and Art* (London: Routledge, 1997), 189–216.

16 The following quotations come from an interview with Moshinsky by Henry Fenwick, 'Mirren's Imogen', published in the *Radio Times*, 9–15 July 1983, 4–5.

17 www.youtube.com/watch?v=jWxRUDjjXN8 (accessed 29 April 2015).

18 Interview in *Radio Times*, 4.

19 Interview on DVD box-set, *Helen Mirren at the BBC* (BBC Worldwide, 2008).

20 Interview, *Radio Times*, 4.

21 William Hazlitt, *Hazlitt's Criticism of Shakespeare*, ed. R. S. White (Lewiston: Edwin Mellen Press, 1996), 146.

WORKS CITED

Cooke, L., *British Television Drama: A History* (London: British Film Institute, 2003).

Greenhalgh, S., 'UK Television', in R. Burt (ed.), *Shakespeares After Shakespeare: An Encyclopedia of the Bard in Mass Media and Popular Culture* (Westport, CT: Greenwood Press, 2007), 2 vols, vol. 2, 651–732.

Hazlitt, William, *Hazlitt's Criticism of Shakespeare*, ed. R. S. White (Lewiston: Edwin Mellen Press, 1996).

Hunter, G. K., 'The BBC *All's Well That Ends Well*', in J. C. Bulman and H. R. Coursen (eds.), *Shakespeare on Television: An Anthology of Essays and Reviews* (Hanover: University Press of New England, 1988), 185–7.

Jones, G. P., 'Nahum Tate is Alive and Well: Elijah Moshinsky's BBC Shakespeare Productions', in J. C. Bulman and H. R. Coursen (eds.), *Shakespeare on Television: An Anthology of Essays and Reviews* (Hanover: University Press of New England, 1988), 192–9.

Moshinsky E. and J. Elsom, 'Does Shakespeare Write Better for Television?', in J. Elsom (ed.), *Is Shakespeare Still Our Contemporary?* (London: Routledge, 1989), 114–39.

Moshinsky, E., Interview with Henry Fenwick, *Radio Times*, 9–15 July 1983, 4–5.

Murray, T., *Drama Trauma: Spectres of Race and Sexuality in Performance, Video and Art* (London: Routledge, 1997).

Rothwell, K. S., *Early Shakespeare Films: How the Spurned Spawned Art* (Stratford-upon-Avon: International Shakespeare Association, 2000).

Waller, G. F., 'Decentring the Bard: the BBC Shakespeare and Some Implications for Criticism and Teaching', in J. C. Bulman and H. R. Coursen (eds.), *Shakespeare on Television: An Anthology of Essays and Reviews* (Hanover: University Press of New England, 1988), 18–30.

Warren, R., *Cymbeline: Shakespeare in Performance* (Manchester: Manchester University Press, 1989).

White, R. S., '*All's Well* as Television: The 1980 Moshinsky Production', in Gary Waller (ed.), *All's Well That Ends Well: New Critical Essays* (New York: Routledge, 2007), 234–46.

Wilders, J. 'Shakespeare with No Audience', in R. S. White *et al.* (ed.), *Shakespeare: Readers, Audiences, Players* (Nedlands: University of Western Australia Press, 1998), 56–63.

CHAPTER 6

The Winter's Tale
Comparing the Polish Television Theatre and the BBC Versions

Jacek Fabiszak

Shakespeare's romances or tragicomedies do constitute a quite homogenous group of plays. They are characterised by a number of features, some typical of the (adventurous) romance, either of Hellenistic or Medieval and Renaissance origin, some typical of the new dramatic genre popularized in England by John Fletcher and his older and more experienced colleague, William Shakespeare. In this chapter I look at two television versions of *The Winter's Tale* arguing that the peculiarities of both this work and the dramatic genre it is classified with are the main factors that affected the televising of this romance in a similar way in two different countries and in different years – in a Polish series of television broadcasts branded 'television theatre' in 1977 and in the BBC/Time-Life production directed by Jane Howell in 1981. The two screen versions do not refer to or acknowledge each other, neither explicitly nor implicitly, yet the correspondences between them are surprising. They both attempt to render 'televisually' the nonrealistic nature of the play, while reflecting on the way television realism might work.

1.   Shakespeare's Romances/Tragicomedies

As Charles Boyce observes:

> [a]ll of the romances share a number of themes, to greater or lesser degree. The theme of separation and reunion of family members is highly important . . . The related idea of exile also features in the romances, with the banished characters . . . restored to their rightful homes at play's end. Another theme, jealousy, is prominent [too] . . . Most significant, the romances all speak to the need for patience in adversity and the importance of providence in human affairs.

91

> Compared with earlier plays, realistic characterisation in the romances is
> weak; instead, the characters' symbolic meaning is more pronounced. The
> plots of these plays are episodic and offer improbable events in exotic
> locales . . . Seemingly magical developments arise . . . and supernatural beings
> appear. These developments are elaborately represented, and all of the
> romances rely heavily on spectacular scenic effects.[1]

Boyce first of all emphasizes the major themes of the romances, which
are mainly derived from Shakespeare's most immediate sources – prose
romances composed by Greene or Lodge.[2] According to Stanley Wells,
these themes help characterize the generic nature of the romances: '[i]f
the literary genre of romance can be defined . . . it is not by formal characteristics. Rather perhaps is it a matter of certain recurrent motifs'.[3] These
motifs or themes function like large-scale *topoi*: their significance is such
that it can only be shown by means of the most general and universal. Boyce
rightly stresses the symbolism of the characters, which has also been noted
by Wells, who finds the figures 'larger than life size'[4] and whose actions are
driven by most fundamental passions such as love, hatred, jealousy, forgiveness, and so on. The workings of these passions are often finally controlled
by Providence and/or supernatural forces. Furthermore, romances present
another ubiquitous aspect of human life: family bonds, which are put to
the most severe tests.

Boyce then voices another vital feature that is so characteristic of the
romances: their lack of realism – which, again, results from the assumed
symbolism of the message. The setting is usually a far, far away country, quite fantastical in the eyes of the Jacobean audience, an environment
where even the most improbable can happen. H. W. Fawkner[5] draws our
attention to the miraculous nature of at least some of the late works, calling
Pericles, *The Winter's Tale* and *Cymbeline* miracle-centred plays. Wells saw
the romances's 'delight in the marvellous; [which] quite often . . . involves
the supernatural . . . All is unrealistic; the logic of cause and effect is ignored,
and chance or fortune governs all.'[6] The lack of logic in the construction
of the plot is linked with its episodic nature. Regarding the symbolic and
universal message that the romances are supposed to convey, the spiritual
effect and the fantastic and spectacular elements of the represented world,
the plays are similar to fairy tales and, as such, rely on a specific, simplified
and yet universal scheme.

Despite Wells's claim that it is difficult to find formal features that would
characterize the romances, one can try to locate them in the definition of
'tragicomedy'. Boyce notes that '[e]ach [romance] is a tragicomedy, in the
broadest sense of the term: elements of tragedy find their resolution in the

traditional happy ending of comedy'.[7] Similarly Zbierski, reminding us of the Italian origin of this dramatic genre, claims that the late plays are in fact tragedies which Shakespeare 'unconvincingly directed towards comedy's happy ending'.[8] The artificiality of the structure reflects the fantastic and unrealistic storyline. Combined together, the form and the contents constitute a most interesting example of *theatrical* decorum: even more powerfully than Shakespeare's comedies, tragedies or history plays, tragicomedies/romances explore the motif of theatrical illusion and magic as well as the kind of theatrical realism offered by the Elizabethan/Jacobean stage conventions.

The title of *The Winter's Tale* already suggests a fairy-tale-like story; according to Ernest Schanzer, '[i]n the popular usage of his [Shakespeare's] day, "a winter's tale" meant a fantastic tale, especially a ghost story'.[9] Not only does this drama display the typical motifs of the romances – separation of a father and daughter, mother and daughter, husband and wife; unmotivated yet powerful jealousy leading to a triple tragedy (the real death of Mamillius, alleged death of Hermione and presumed death of Perdita), which is redeemed by unprecedented patience and penitence. It also contains the motif of hidden identity of the princess Perdita, who – as an infant – miraculously survived the storm and a bear's attack on the fantastic Bohemian shore. Perdita's is not the only marvel or miracle in the play: Hermione's living in hiding for sixteen years is certainly another example. A pseudo-miracle is the culminating moment in *The Winter's Tale* when the alleged statue of Hermione turns live at Paulina's pseudo-magical command and the family is almost complete again (symbolically, the place of Hermione and Leontes' son, Mamillius, is filled by their son-in-law-to-be, Florizel).

The play has spectacular scenes of different sorts – ranging from Hermione's trial in 3.2 or Autolycus's 'shows' in Act 4, to the storm and the famous indication of Antigonus's death in the 'Exit, pursued by a bear' stage direction (very spectacular and theatrical, indeed), to the statue of Hermione becoming alive. The statue was allegedly sculpted by 'that rare Italian master Giulio Romano' (5.2.82–3) who 'would beguile nature of her custom' (5.2.84). S. J. Freedberg reminds us that Giulio Romano was famous for his 'pseudo-tapestries... [which were known to have] aggressive excavation of a depth of space and, in the figures, a plasticity of nearly violent insistence. In contradiction of the look of tapestries, the figures... suggest an almost tangible existence'.[10] When one contrasts Romano's reputation of sculpting realistic figures with the conventions and, indeed, the possibilities of illusion that the Shakespearean stage offered, one realizes that such an artistic feat was not possible (it is for this reason that the spectator is prepared for this spectacle by the Third Gentleman's description of the statue and his reference to the fame of the Italian artist). The scene only underscores the highly conventional and artificial representation of the fictional world.

One more non-realistic element of the play should be mentioned: the structure of the play, especially its division into two parts separated from each other by the temporal gap of sixteen years. Shakespeare introduces (4.1) the choric character of Time who accounts for what has happened since Hermione's trial until Perdita's reaching the age of sixteen as a shepherd's daughter. This device obviously breaks the theatrical illusion, unashamedly exploiting the metatheatrical nature of Shakespearean stage.

2.   The BBC/Time-Life Shakespeare Series

Shakespeare and television have enjoyed a rather difficult, at times stormy relationship. As Anthony Davies observed, with reference to critical approaches to television Shakespeare:

> Until the mid-1980s the predominant thrust in critical writing about televised Shakespeare was directed at performance, and television's achievement was measured by the extent to which it managed or failed to promote the sense of *theatrical* experience. It has been during the last six years [the first half of the 1980s] that there has emerged sustained probing, and vigorous discussion about such issues as the nature of the television audience, the nature of the television idiom, and the relation of artistic to realistic presentation in the medium.[11]

Davies's reservations had earlier been echoed in a question posed by Stanley Wells: 'Do we want good television drama or pure Shakespeare?'[12] Both scholars point to the necessity of adapting Shakespeare to television in such a way as to produce television works of art rather than 'archaeological Shakespeare'. This concern is also visible in the ways in which Shakespeare's plays were treated in an unprecedented attempt to put the Bard on the tube with the BBC/Time-Life Shakespeare series (1978–85). The ideas and strategies on how to accommodate Shakespeare onto the small screen are generally associated with the three producers (Cedric Messina, Jonathan Miller and Shaun Sutton), each of whom had his own vision of what to do with Shakespeare on television. Michèle Willems identifies three ways of televising Shakespeare in the series – naturalistic, pictorial and stylized. The first type is associated with the producer Cedric Messina:

> Without denying the attractiveness of many realistic productions or the visual pleasure they can produce, it must be said that the naturalistic approach often aggravates the tensions between the two media [i.e., the verbal and the visual] instead of solving them. What happens in effect is that each mode of communication imposes its own prevalent signs, which often vie for the spectator's attention without supporting each other. Shakespeare's idiom is transported wholesale on television. The message is dense, polyvocal; layers of significance qualify and enrich the basic narration. Now naturalism, instead of trying to find ways to transpose this complex language, retaliates by superimposing its own favourite representational idiom.[13]

Willems thus dismisses the highly realistic approach to Shakespeare, pointing to issues of signification – the intricacies of the verbal plane are lost in the lushness of the visual frame. Another problem that this conflict between word and picture raises is 'the clash between the conventional mode and the representational mode'.[14] The conventions of Shakespeare's theatre do not work well on naturalistic television if the set and camerawork attempt to create a complete illusion of reality, which is achievable in the case of the cinema. The television studio can hardly compete with the cinematic studio or set on location in their ability to render a scene realistically.

A solution was 'pictorial' style (or, to be precise, 'verbal-pictorial'), preferred by the producer Jonathan Miller, 'initiated by . . . [his] passion for Renaissance painting and supported by his intimate knowledge of it'.[15] Miller's idea was to stylize represented events, especially in the case of the plays the action of which was located in historical times from the Elizabethan perspective. This approach favoured conventionality and artificiality. According to Susan Willis, '[f]or Miller, Shakespeare production is both denotative and connotative, both narrative and reflexive. It *is* art, is *composed* of art, and is to some extent *about* art'.[16]

Jonathan Miller also granted artistic freedom to the directors he invited on the production of the series. One of the directors was Jane Howell; both Michèle Willems and Neil Taylor found her style so significant and idiosyncratic that they singled it out as a separate category of televising Shakespeare. Willems finds Howell's approach most successful: 'The metonymic mode of expression brings television much nearer to the theatre.[17] Given the obligation to use a basically unabridged, unmodified text, it appears that an approach where the visual element is used as functional or suggestive is preferable to one in which it is referential or decorative'.[18] Howell's treatment of the medium can be compared to working in the theatre – critics have noted that she preferred working with the same group of actors ('operating as an *ensemble*'[19]) and using the technical staff as proxy audience.[20] Another element of Howell's 'theatricality' and conventionality is her deployment of a 'permanent set'; as Taylor observes, 'Howell achieved *two sets*, the *known* permanent set, and the *framed* set [framed by the camera]'.[21] The result was a 'set [which] called attention to itself *as a set*'.[22] This effect of patent artificiality, further reinforced by the doubling of parts and characters' recognition of the presence of the camera on the set, contributes to alienation practice[23] whereby the viewer is constantly reminded of watching a *television* drama.[24]

The reason why Howell decided to adopt such a strategy is twofold. On the one hand, she fully recognized the possibilities and shortcomings of the medium she was working with. On the other, a logical corollary of such an assumption was fine-tuning Shakespearean text, so heavily steeped in specific Elizabethan theatrical conventions, to the television of the turn of the 1970s. Although 'television Shakespeare' may sound like an oxymoron, one needs to consider different types of realism/illusionism created on the big and small screens and different tenses that the two media deploy. Film is supposed to produce a complete illusion of reality and narrates a story that is finished (like a novel, in the past tense). Television achieves a reality effect in different ways: being a live medium, it does not weave 'illusion' but is supposed (ideally) to objectively show the world in front of the camera lens. The tense of television show is thus the present (like the tense of a theatrical production). Television is an intimate medium, which – among others – implies closeness rather than distance.[25] As a result, it is difficult to hide the tricks of the trade; furthermore, since among the most televisual broadcasts one finds 'talking heads'[26] or reportage, there is no need to hide editorial tricks, as they, too, constitute formal elements of television communication. Such qualities of the television show can also be identified in a television genre known in Poland as 'television theatre.'

3.   Television Theatre in Poland

The fact that the poetics of television theatre in Poland relies on similar assumptions is linked with the very beginnings of the genre. The tradition of television theatre (in Polish, *teatr telewizji*) goes back more than sixty years. It can be compared with the British 'Armchair Theatre' or with the French 'dramatiques' and is an equivalent of television drama. It has not, however, been gradually replaced by television film or filmed stage productions in the way it happened in many other national television corporations. The present-day television theatre is becoming more and more filmic (shooting on location, more dynamic editing), while attempting to go back to its roots: viewers have a chance to watch live broadcasts of studio-located productions (these proved to be immensely popular and, for a while, revived the genre on Polish television).[27]

Television theatre has enjoyed in Poland a canonical status and its premiere shows, especially those based on classical texts (such as those by Shakespeare), are considered major events in the television week, being advertised high and low well before their airing. Television theatre and Shakespeare in particular may be compared to the iconic status of the BBC Shakespeare series. Russell Jackson writes about the shift in the treatment of the series when it was reissued in the DVD format;[28] major television theatre productions in Poland were also published as 'The Golden Hundred Television Theatre Productions' ('Złota Setka Teatru Telewizji').

Jerzy Limon underscores the exceptionality and autonomy of television theatre, differentiating it both from theatre and film, although it is 'split...between filmic narrative and theatrical *mimesis*'.[29] He finds

> [t]he art of television theatre fundamentally non-illusionistic; it conventionally shows the represented world...not as a record of something that came into being in the real world but as a filmically modelled artistic composition which resembles a stage production, one – however – that, in this form, could not be created in the theatre.[30]

Limon thus stresses the conventionality and artifice of television theatre, in which so much is left to the spectators' imagination and in which the 'theatrical' substance is negotiated by means of the camera, thus becoming an example of an extended ekphrasis.[31] In a sense, one could risk saying that a television theatre production can be treated as a *report* about a performance resembling a staging of a play. This is the nature of television – reporting about events – and the character of television realism.

Another defining feature of television theatre is its treatment of the space. The argument is that television theatre rests on the logic of the TV studio. The studio, similarly to a theatrical stage, is considered open to be moulded according to the requirements of a particular stage/set design. In a way, it is amorphous; its final form – in the theatre – is an outcome of stage design (often symbolic in nature) seen through the spectator's perspective. In the case of television theatre, the space is given its shape by the set design (rather symbolic, too) and camera lens (the viewer's perspective). In both cases (stage and television theatre), the look of the space is complemented by elements that do not belong to the represented world of fiction: in the former, these would include the wings or the lighting grid; in the latter, the lights, cameras or microphones.[32] Whereas a theatre goer does *see* those elements when watching a performance, a television viewer may be given a glimpse of, say, a camera, although in the majority of productions s/he remains unaware of these parts of the space.

   Limon puts some constraints onto television theatre space since what the TV screen shows is not part of the real space or reality extending beyond the confines of the screen (which is generally the case in films).[33] Furthermore, the space of a teleplay is not infinitely open physically (it is, after all, limited by the walls of the studio), but it is open psychologically: emphasis is given to spoken lines or natural language and to the character, whose psychological states are also highlighted by means of specific shots, especially close-ups of their faces.

4.   Zofia Mrozowska's *Zimowa opowieść*[34] and Jane Howell's *The Winter's Tale*

Zofia Mrozowska and Jane Howell treat television art in similar terms: both employ meta-televisual devices; both are sensitive to the peculiarities of television drama; both carefully avoid turning it into a film or filmed theatre. Both directors, independent of each other, apply this approach to their adaptations of Shakespeare's romance/tragicomedy. It is important to notice that Howell's vision of television drama and Shakespeare is a result of her attempts to find a most appropriate manner of putting the Bard on the tube, whereas Mrozowska's production is a consequence of her working within a specific, well-established television genre[35] and then fine-tuning a Shakespeare play to its requirements. The starting point for Mrozowska (unlike Howell) was the fact that the production was a performance of students from the Warsaw theatrical academy, who prepared the production under Mrozowska's (their professor's) supervision. In other words, the teleplay was supposed to help them showcase their professional skills, which would account for the enormous focus on the characters.[36] At the same time, one cannot help but notice Howell's remark about the significance of acting on television in general and in *The Winter's Tale* in particular: 'What needs to be [realistic on TV] – what has to be real – is the actor's performance, but what's around that need not be realistic at all'.[37]

   Mrozowska and Howell offer a similar *mise-en-scène*. Both sets are unrealistic and visibly located in the television studio. They help distance the viewer from the story and emphasize the fairy-tale nature of the play's fantastic and far-away location – Sicily and Bohemia with a seashore. Moreover, both sets remain the same when the action moves from Sicily to

Bohemia and back. Shakespeare does differentiate the settings for Sicily and Bohemia: in the former, the action is located in the court, in the latter in the country. Such a differentiation is visible only in Howell's production, mainly in the use of colours.

Ryszard Grajewski's set in Mrozowska's production is ultimately bare: what one watches is the open space of the television studio; the background is composed of simple screens resembling theatrical wings. The central position of the space is occupied by a plain wooden platform. The set's simplicity is further underscored by the use of monochromatic colouring in the production – that of sepia, which symbolises nostalgia and the past (a *mise-en-scène* equivalent of a 'winter's tale'). Costumes are very simple, sepia-coloured too and rather similar to each other, although it is mainly by means of costuming and properties that changes in location are signalled. As a result, when action moves to the sea, Leontes' throne from the trial scene (a chair) is turned around by a Mariner (in short trousers and with a bandana on his head) and transformed into a ship; the idyllic location of the Bohemian countryside is marked by the Shepherds wearing straw hats and holding long staffs, and so on. The changes in location are thus symbolic and highlight artifice,[38] which is so much in tune with the nature of the romances in general and *The Winter's Tale* in particular. New places can also be indicated by means of lighting – the storm on the seashore is signalled not only by the chair-turned-ship that the Mariner tosses but also by blinking lights (a trick used by Howell too). Symbolism in the representation of setting and action can become even more abstract: in the scene when Hermione gives birth to Perdita, Hermione (Grażyna Szapołowska), seconded by two ladies-in-waiting, is half lying on the platform and pretends to be in labour. When Perdita is eventually delivered, the Ladies gesticulate as if they were holding an infant and giving her to Hermione who cuddles her in her arms – in fact, she is cuddling air. When Perdita is later presented to Leontes (Marcin Troński-Szalawski), she has the form of a gray bundle, without a doll, let alone a live child, in it. The same kind of symbolic convention is applied to the presentation of Mamillius played by an adult actor (Michał Anioł, who also doubles the parts of Florizel and Time),[39] dressed only in a long, white shirt (when the actor doubles the other roles, he wears a different costume).

Don Homfray's set in Howell's production is highly artificial and conventional, too. It consists of huge wedges and a backdrop. Alleys between the wedges allow actors to get on and off the set, functioning similarly to the screens/wings in Mrozowska's production. Susan Willis notes Howell's propensity for using a 'stark setting': 'a theatre set such as Shakespeare's, by which she means one that *suggests* rather than duplicates'.[40] As a result, '[t]he actual physical construction of the set [was] a flat area surrounded by wedge-shaped ramps with exits and entrances cut through them',[41] which was anti-illusionistic, leaving the viewers no doubt that they were watching the space of a television studio.

A major difference between the two productions is the use of colours – Howell's is a most colourful teleplay and the colouring is applied to both set and costumes. The British director employs colours to indicate the change in locations and the passage of time. As Willis observes,

> [u]sing one set, however, does not mean the setting is static or unchanging. In all six of her productions, a number of design variations are wrought on the basic circular unit: in *Winter's Tale* it is color and textural changes as the huge wedges go from Sicilia's winter white to gray and stony for Bohemia's coasts, golden for Bohemian fields, and a creeping spring-green verge back in Sicilia.[42]

Seasonal changes were also signalled by a single tree on the set, a kind of radical synecdoche that is very Elizabethan in essence. Homfray explains the static/dynamic nature of the set in a more philosophical way:

> Jane felt that one of the themes of the play is that life is always the same and that it depends on how you open yourself to it, what you do to it, that makes you see it differently. The landscape of life . . . is seen in a certain way; but if a different action is taken, a different choice is made, then the landscape changes. So we felt that the set should always be the same place but always seen slightly differently.[43]

Willis draws our attention to the changes in the texture of the wedges which are especially visible when they stand for the Bohemian coast, as if they were covered with pebbles (props looking like huge pebbles also litter the floor of the studio).

Similar to the set, the costumes are colourful and they change with the locations and seasons. They are, unlike in Mrozowska's production, rather realistic, yet stylised at the same time. According to the designer John Peacock, 'the play can be set in any period. Jane didn't particularly want any period; she knew the *feel* that she wanted . . . and she wanted costumes that might be [in] detailed close up but from a distance looked like shapes'.[44] Consequently, costumes played a symbolic role in the production and, similarly to Mrozowska's production and the conventions of the romance, they were meant to be timeless and universal in that they were stylised in the Renaissance fashion, associated with Shakespeare. Howell herself wanted the costumes to be first realistic and then emblematic; when discussing

Leontes' (Jeremy Kemp's) clothing, she remarked, 'I don't suppose anyone will notice, but gradually in the first half Leontes does wear more and
more fur and by the trail [*sic*, should be "trial"] scene he looks more and
more debased and animal-like'.[45] By means of dress, Leontes symbolically
turns into a bear-like figure, of which we are also reminded by Joan Lord
Hall.[46]

Universality of costuming in the productions also consists in their referencing various periods and cultures. As Elizabeth Schafer notes, 'The
costumes enhanced . . . seasonal change as the heavy, quasi-Tudor hats and
robes of freezing Sicily were left for the spring world of Perdita, who was
dressed as the Botticelli Primavera'.[47] The critic's observation is corrobo-
rated by the director's idea: 'The period I suppose I dressed the play in was
early 1600s, but it went backwards and forwards quite a bit, so it's impossible to say any specific period. Perdita was pure Botticelli . . . The peasants
were Bruegel'.[48] The eclectic nature of costumes, despite their detailed realism, again emphasizes the production's romance-like artificiality.

The two most spectacular scenes of the play – 'Exit, pursued by a bear'
and Hermione's statue becoming alive – are also very stagey and metatelevi-
sual. Incidentally, in Mrozowska's production, the role of the bear is played
by Troński-Szalawski who also stands for Leontes, thus literally implement-
ing Howell's idea of Leontes' gradually resembling a bear and 'the bear
[being] the long arm of Leontes'.[49] The actor is dressed in a long and bulky
fur coat and gradually eats up Antigonus (Stanisław Górka) by acrobatically
pushing the character under the fur coat. The scene is comic in its artifice
and theatricality; the comedy is additionally enhanced as the bear starts in
Polish and then switches to English, and makes allusions to contemporane-
ous Polish delicacies (naturally, the text is here non-Shakespearean). Howell's rendering of this scene is more serious, yet remains artificial. Its seriousness consists in that Antigonus's (Cyril Lukham's) perspective is taken over
by the camera lens which is about to be swallowed by a gaping jaw with
rows of sharp teeth. The artifice and, to a degree, comedy of the scene, are
displayed in the figure of the bear impersonated by an actor who has put
on a bear's costume (which is more realistic than a fur coat, though). Both
Mrozowska and Howell attempted to render this most intriguing scene in
a very theatrical fashion, relying on clearly marked conventions rather than
on realistic effects.

Likewise, they avoid a spectacular final scene. Both directors decide to
be consistent and, instead of dazzling the viewers visually, they focus on the
power of words. The viewer is instantly aware that it is the real Hermione –
and not a statue – that Paulina uncovers in front of Leontes. Mrozowska

resorts to a trick in order to differentiate between a potential statue and a human character: we see Hermione on a dais (the platform) with her back to the camera and to other characters; yet, we have no doubt that this is the same actress who played the part before, which is confirmed when she turns around. She is, indeed, dressed in the same way as in the first part of the play. Although Howell has Hermione (Anna Calder-Marshall) dress differently than in the previous scenes – the costume (especially the serious matron-like mobcap) may symbolize the character's maturity –, the immovable, yet clearly breathing, Hermione looks exactly like the wife Leontes used to know. The lack of movement, contrasted with the heaving breast, is highly artificial and draws the viewers' attention to the theatrical convention employed by Howell.

Televisual conventions are, in turn, evoked in the camera use, especially in letting characters recognize the presence of the camera on the set and address it directly. Susan Willis notes this phenomenon in Howell's production:

> *Winter's Tale* also displays her use of the camera, which is not just there invisibly to record movement and dialogue, but which is consciously an eye, a perceiver that some characters, especially Autolycus, address, raise an eyebrow toward, or glance at knowingly. Howell...giv[es] the camera the role of confidant in these productions, a technological adaptation of an age-old theatrical tradition. Howell says she likes seeing faces on television and direct address to camera, as her productions reveal.[50]

Interestingly enough, neither director favours a single character; thus, several figures can command the attention of the viewers and control the events. The first character to be allowed to deliver his aside to the camera (as direct camera address becomes a conventional televisual equivalent of an aside) is Leontes, commenting on Polixenes and Hermione's 'paddling palms and pinching fingers' (1.2.114). As Schafer observes, 'Howell chose to follow Jeremy Kemp as Leontes in close-up, with him whispering intently to the camera: sometimes only part of Leontes' face was in shot while Hermione and Polixenes were visible together in the background. This close-up work was untheatrical'.[51] It may be untheatrical but it illustrates the Shakespearean lines in a televisual way, showing the innocent play between Hermione and Polixens 'poisoned' and 'made corrupt' by Leontes' words; Leontes also desperately seeks support for his sick suspicions and the only people he turns to are the viewers. Joan Lord Hall reminds us of one more typically televisual technique employed when characters address the camera: 'This production uses television's specialty, the tight shot, to define character or persona more sharply. All the soliloquies and asides of Leontes are pitched directly at the camera'.[52]

Other instances of employing the direct address would include two other obvious candidates: the choric figure of Time and Autolycus, the master of (histrionic) ceremony in the second part of the play. Schafer comments on Autolycus's addresses in Howell's production: 'Autolycus [Rikki Fulton], often played close-up to the camera, taking the audience into his confidence, but he was also able to be knowingly theatrical at the same time, laughing at the absurdity of it all',[53] thus reminding us that the direct camera addresses were framed in a close-up, so that the viewer has absolutely no doubt that it is s/he who is the recipient of the speeches. Other, less towering characters approach the camera as well. Thus, in the same production, Antigonus expresses his anxiety and fear on the Bohemian shore straight into the viewer's eyes, whereas in Mrozowska's teleplay, Camillo, commenting on Leontes' jealousy and plans to have Polixenes murdered, turns to the viewer. It is in this production, too, that when Hermione defies Leontes' accusations for the first time, she addresses the camera as if asking the viewer to be her witness. Such devices, obvious as they are, serve the purpose of breaking the illusion of reality; furthermore, they follow the 'realism' of the medium as the TV viewer is used to newscasters, reporters, interviewers and interviewees seeking the camera eye and speaking to it directly.

The fact that the directors of both productions are women may have affected the treatment of feminist issues in the play. Shakespeare in general in the last plays emphasizes the role of female characters, especially in the solutions of the complicated plots;[54] furthermore, in the majority of the romances, there is one female figure who helps restore the order at the end of the play, usually the (absent) mother and daughter – in *Pericles* it is Thaïsa and Marina; in *Cymbeline* it is the Queen (an evil substitute of the absent mother) and Perdita; in *The Tempest* it is 'Prospero's wife'[55] and Miranda. In *The Winter's Tale*, Shakespeare introduces even more significant female characters – not only Hermione and Perdita, but also Paulina. In the productions under scrutiny, their importance is particularly emphasized. Mrozowska inserts a scene missing in the play – the birth of Perdita in prison (already referenced earlier), which highlights a special bond between mother and daughter and the joys of motherhood. Howell, too, noticed the special position of female figures, for instance Hermione. Joan Lord Hall observes that '[t]he slow coming to life of the statue accentuates Hermione's majesty and dignity. It also highlights her warmth – she "hangs" about her husband's "neck" and is ecstatic at having found Perdita – and her graciousness, for when she gazes beseechingly at Leontes, she reveals not a trace of resentment. Warmth, dignity, and grace define Anna Calder-Marshall's portrayal of Hermione throughout'.[56] As a result, both directors underscore the influence of female sensitivity on a patriarchal world. The latter is powerfully evoked in Howell's production by, among others, Leontes' costume and towering posture and, in the trial scene, by the loneliness of Hermione – as Lord Hall called her 'a diminutive figure in the midst of a large assembly'.[57] In Mrozowska's production, patriarchy is underlined by the men's constant surveillance of women.

The initial assumption of this chapter was Limon's observation that '[i]n many ways, the play itself shows us the process of text interpretation ... the play seems to prompt us how it should be interpreted'.[58] The analysis demands that I modify this original hypothesis by expanding and complementing it. As the two remarkably similar approaches to televising *The Winter's Tale* demonstrate, it is not only the play but also the medium in which it is adapted that suggests how it should be read and accommodated within that medium. Zofia Mrozowska had it perhaps easier than Jane Howell, as she did not need to 'invent' television art since it had been there developing as television theatre for well over twenty years before the shooting of the production. However, she was capable of fully deploying the artistic possibilities offered by television theatre in her bravura rendering of a Shakespeare play in general and a romance in particular. Jane Howell, in the opinion of many critics, most successfully combined the outdated Shakespearean text and its dramatic and theatrical conventions with the limits and opportunities she found in television. She realized that television cannot compete with cinema, that the nature of its realism is different from that of the film; she was also aware that television is no longer theatre, as the final artistic outcome is organized and given the ultimate shape by the camera. The result was a production which relies on television conventions and television only, although it is indebted to theatre and cinema alike. One may argue that the fact that she was shooting a romance – with its fantastic world described in a language that is both archaic and artificial – was decisive in her formal choices. It certainly affected her thinking about Shakespeare on the tube.

Notes

1 C. Boyce, *Encyclopedia of Shakespeare. A–Z of his Life and Works* (New York, Oxford: A Roundtable Press Book, 1990), 555.

2 For a discussion of the origins of the romances with reference to Shakespeare's oeuvre see Stanley Wells's essay 'Shakespeare and Romance', in D. J. Palmer

(ed.), *Shakespeare's Later Comedies* (Harmondsworth: Penguin Books, 1971), 118–124.

3 *Ibid.*, 117.

4 *Ibid.*

5 H. W. Fawkner, *Shakespeare's Miracle Plays*. Pericles, Cymbeline *and* The Winter's Tale (Rutherford, Madison, Teaneck: Fairleigh Dickinson University Press, 1992).

6 Wells, 'Shakespeare and Romance', 117.

7 Boyce, *Encyclopedia*, 555.

8 H. Zbierski, *William Shakespeare* (Warszawa: Wiedza Powszechna, 1988), 483–4. All quotations from Zbierski and other sources in Polish are translated by the author.

9 E. Schanzer (ed.), *The Winter's Tale*. The New Penguin Shakespeare (Harmondsworth: Penguin Books, 1969), 7.

10 C. Hoy, 'Jacobean Tragedy and the Mannerist Style', *Shakespeare Survey* 26 (1973), 65.

11 A. Davies, 'Shakespeare and the Media of Film, Radio and Television: A Retrospect', *Shakespeare Survey* 39 (1987), 8–9.

12 S. Wells, 'Television Shakespeare', *Shakespeare Quarterly* 33:3 (1982), 266.

13 M. Willems, 'Verbal-Visual, Verbal-Pictorial or Textual-Televisual? Reflections on the BBC Shakespeare Series', *Shakespeare Survey* 39 (1987), 95–6.

14 *Ibid.*, 97.

15 *Ibid.*, 99.

16 S. Willis, *The BBC Shakespeare Plays: Making the Televised Canon* (Chapel Hill, London: The University of North Carolina Press, 1991), 105.

17 A similar observation has been made by Stephen Purcell who remarked about successful televised Shakespeare: 'It is striking that the most effective of the "straight" television Shakespeares tend to be those that emphasise their own theatrical qualities' (528) and 'Television Shakespeares seem to respond well to metaphorical rather than realistic staging' (529). He also specifically commented on Howell's productions, noting that 'Self-advertising theatrical techniques are used throughout' and 'Long takes on a moving camera allow actors to turn to the TV audience for asides and then back into the scene in one fluid movement' (529). S. Purcell, 'Shakespeare on Television', in M. T. Burnett, A. Streete and R. Wray (eds.), *The Edinburgh Companion to Shakespeare and the Arts* (Edinburgh: Edinburgh University Press, 2011), 522–40.

18 M. Willems, 'Verbal-Visual', 100.

19 G. Holderness, *Visual Shakespeare: Essays in Film and Television* (Hatfield: University of Herfordshire Press, 2002), 21.

20 N. Taylor, 'Two Types of Television', *Shakespeare Survey* 39 (1987), 106–7.

21 *Ibid.*, 107.

22 *Ibid.*, 106.

23 As Graham Holderness put it, '[a]ll these devices are defamiliarising, estranging, "alienating"; they induce the kind of alert and vigilant curiosity sought by Brecht's "epic" theatre.' (G. Holderness, 'Radical Potentiality and Institutional

Closure: Shakespeare in Film and Television', in J. Dollimore and A. Sinfield (eds.), *Political Shakespeare: New Essays in Cultural Materialism* (Manchester: Manchester University Press, 1985), 198.

24 This is a general remark, which is applicable to action situated both in the space of the television studio and indoor or outdoor location.

25 It must be noted, however, that today television fiction is rather unlike other nonfiction television shows, as it comes close to being more filmic than televisual, which implies a change of tense. In the case of Shakespeare on television, one should mention such productions as *The Hollow Crown* (2012), whose filmic quality is highlighted by John Wyver. See his essay '"All the Trimmings?": The Transfer of Theatre to Television in Adaptations of Shakespeare Stagings', *Adaptation* 7:2 (1994), 115–16.

26 This highlights the significance of the verbal plane on television.

27 John Wyver suggests that we approach Shakespeare on TV as 'mediated theatre' and claims that filmed theatre (even productions filmed in a TV studio) is an example of doubled adaptation – from Shakespeare's page to stage/set and from stage/set to screen (105). Wyver talks about 'restaging' Shakespeare in a TV studio (a term most appropriate to Mrozowska's production), 'translating' theatrical productions via a television studio or 'studio remounting' (111–12).

28 R. Jackson, '*The BBC* All's Well That Ends Well', in S. Hatchuel and N. Vienne-Guerrin (eds.), *Shakespeare on Screen. Television Shakespeare: Essays in Honour of Michèle Willems* (Rouen: Publications des Universités de Rouen et du Havre, 2008), 132–33.

29 J. Limon, *Obroty przestrzeni [Revolutions of space]* (Gdańsk: słowo/obraz terytoria, 2008), 21.

30 *Ibid.*, 19.

31 J. Limon, *Trzy teatry [Three theatres]* (Gdańsk: słowo/obraz terytoria, 2004), 144.

32 When watching some stills from television theatre productions, one cannot fail to notice the microphone which, attached to a crane, hovers above the actors' heads (its presence, though, is carefully edited in the final version). Employing the logic of the space of television theatre, the microphone is an inherent part of the set, which the viewer ignores, although s/he is aware of it.

33 Limon, *Trzy teatry*, 92; 127.

34 I use the English original title of the play, *The Winter's Tale*, instead of the Polish translation throughout the rest of the chapter.

35 For a more in-depth scrutiny of Mrozowska's teleplay as an example of a television theatre production, see J. Fabiszak, *Polish Televised Shakespeares: A Study of Shakespeare Productions within the Television Theatre Format* (Poznań: Motivex, 2005).

36 A critic observed that a viewer can see 'a whole range of acting tasks, from a pompous monologue to nearly dumb show and Commedia dell'Arte'. K. T. Toeplitz, 'Giełda' ['Exchange'] *Teatr* 14 (1977), 13.

37 H. Fenwick, 'The Production', in *The BBC Shakespeare:* The Winter's Tale (London: British Broadcasting Corporation), 18.

38 Noted by Toeplitz, 'Giełda', who called the production 'naïve and simple', which actually reflects the conventions of the romances.
39 The doubling of parts obviously adds to the sense of artificiality and estrangement and is concordant with Elizabethan conventions.
40 Willis, *BBC Shakespeare*, 165.
41 Fenwick, 'The Production', 21.
42 Willis, *BBC Shakespeare*, 166.
43 Fenwick, 'The Production', 21.
44 *Ibid.*, 21–2.
45 *Ibid.*, 23.
46 J. Lord Hall, *The Winter's Tale: A Guide to the Play* (Westport, CT, London: Greenwood Press, 2005), 183.
47 E. Schafer, *Ms-Directing Shakespeare. Women direct Shakespeare* (New York: St. Martin's Press, 2000 [1998]), 105.
48 Fenwick, 'The Production', 22.
49 *Ibid.*, 23.
50 Willis, *BBC Shakespeare*, 169.
51 Schafer, *op. cit.*, 104.
52 Lord Hall, *op. cit.*, 180.
53 *Ibid.*
54 In *Pericles* it is Marina who pulls her father out of his stupor and is instrumental in bringing the family together (with the help of another female figure – the goddess Diana). In *Cymbeline* Imogen's actions are indispensable for the reconciliation with her jealous husband, Posthumus, and with her weak father, king Cymbeline. In *The Tempest* Prospero's plans to return to Milan and ensure peaceful rule depend on Miranda and her relationship with Ferdinand, over which the magus has hardly any control.
55 As Stephen Orgel's now classic essay is titled. Orgel's 'Prospero's wife' draws our attention to the conspicuous absence of women in *The Tempest*, with only one reference to Miranda's mother and the girl's memory of, not her mother, but women attending on her. See S. Orgel, 'Prospero's Wife', in M. W. Ferguson, M. Quilligan, and N. Vickers (eds.), *Rewriting the Renaissance: The Discourse of Sexual Difference in Early Modern Europe* (Chicago: University of Chicago Press, 1986), 50–64.
56 Lord Hall, *op. cit.*, 184.
57 *Ibid.*, 185.
58 J. Limon (1999), 115.

WORKS CITED

Boyce, C., *Encyclopedia of Shakespeare. A–Z of his Life and Works* (New York, Oxford: A Roundtable Press Book, 1990).
Davies, A., 'Shakespeare and the Media of Film, Radio and Television: A Retrospect', *Shakespeare Survey* 39 (1987), 1–11.

Fabiszak, J., *Polish Televised Shakespeares. A Study of Shakespeare Productions within the Television Theatre Format* (Poznań: Motivex, 2005).

Fawkner, H. W., *Shakespeare's Miracle Plays:* Pericles, Cymbeline *and* The Winter's Tale (Rutherford, Madison, Teaneck: Fairleigh Dickinson University Press, 1992).

Fenwick, H., 'The Production', in *The BBC Shakespeare: The Winter's Tale* (London: British Broadcasting Corporation, 1981), 17–27.

Holderness, G., 'Radical Potentiality and Institutional Closure: Shakespeare in Film and Television', in J. Dollimore, and A. Sinfield (eds.), *Political Shakespeare: New Essays in Cultural Materialism* (Manchester: Manchester University Press, 1985), 182–201.

Visual Shakespeare: Essays in Film and Television (Hatfield: University of Herfordshire Press, 2002).

Hoy, C., 'Jacobean Tragedy and the Mannerist Style', *Shakespeare Survey* 26 (1973), 49–67.

Jackson, R., 'The BBC *All's Well That Ends Well*', in S. Hatchuel and N. Vienne-Guerrin (eds.), *Shakespeare on Screen. Television Shakespeare: Essays in Honour of Michèle Willems* (Rouen: Publications des Universités de Rouen et du Havre, 2008), 127–45.

Limon, J., 'Thomas Kyd's *The Spanish Tragedy*: A play about a play', in J. Świdziński and J. Fabiszak (eds.), *Studia nad literaturami europejskimi. Księga poświęcona pamięci Profesora dr. hab. Henryka Zbierskiego [Studies in European Literatures. Essays in Memory of Professor Henryk Zbierski]* (Poznań: Motivex, 1999), 115–25.

Trzy teatry [Three theatres] (Gdańsk: słowo/obraz terytoria, 2004).

Obroty przestrzeni [Revolutions of space] (Gdańsk: słowo/obraz terytoria, 2008).

Lord Hall, J., *The Winter's Tale: A Guide to the Play* (Westport, CT, London: Greenwood Press, 2005).

Orgel, S., 'Prospero's Wife', in M. W. Ferguson, M. Quilligan, and N. Vickers (eds.), *Rewriting the Renaissance: The Discourse of Sexual Difference in Early Modern Europe* (Chicago: University of Chicago Press, 1986), 50–64.

Purcell, S., 'Shakespeare on Television', in M. T. Burnett, A. Streete and R. Wray (eds.), *The Edinburgh Companion to Shakespeare and the Arts* (Edinburgh: Edinburgh University Press, 2011), 522–40.

Schafer, E., *Ms-Directing Shakespeare. Women Direct Shakespeare* (New York: St. Martin's Press, 2000 [1998]).

Schanzer, E. (ed.), *The Winter's Tale*. The New Penguin Shakespeare (Harmondsworth: Penguin Books, 1969).

Taylor, N., 'Two Types of Television', *Shakespeare Survey* 39 (1987), 103–11.

Toeplitz, K. T., 'Giełda' ['Exchange'], *Teatr* 14 (1977), 13.

Wells, S., 'Shakespeare and Romance', in D. J. Palmer, (ed.), *Shakespeare's Later Comedies* (Harmondsworth: Penguin Books, 1971), 117–42.

'Television Shakespeare', *Shakespeare Quarterly* 33.3 (1982), 261–77.

Willems, M., 'Verbal-Visual, Verbal-Pictorial or Textual-Televisual? Reflections on the BBC Shakespeare Series', *Shakespeare Survey* 39 (1987), 91–102.

Willis, S., *The BBC Shakespeare Plays: Making the Televised Canon* (Chapel Hill, London: The University of North Carolina Press, 1991).

Wyver, J., '"All the Trimmings?": The Transfer of Theatre to Television in Adaptations of Shakespeare Stagings', *Adaptation* 7.2 (2014), 104–20.

Zbierski, H., *William Shakespeare* (Warszawa: Wiedza Powszechna, 1988).

CHAPTER 7

The Winter's Tale's *Spectral Endings*
Death, Dance and Doubling

Judith Buchanan

It is a truism to say that the endings of plays matter, and even that they matter in ways disproportionate to their playing time in relation to the performance as a whole. The ending can resolve or problematize, bring peace or withhold it, generically conform or generically confound, remember alternative conclusions or suppress them, deliver the 'promised end' or refuse to. While true of any Shakespeare play, the endings of the late plays carry a particular force for the ways in which they reframe and generically respin the material that precedes them. Moreover, to borrow Kermode's phrase, it is 'the sense of an ending' as *in prospect*, a place where the playing will find rest (or at least stop) that gives piquancy and purpose to all the preceding sequential moments of the play.[1] They are delightful because they defer the end, and bearable because an end is nonetheless assured.

More acutely than in any other cluster of plays, a set of alternative endings – referenced, remembered, eschewed, averted, suppressed – haunt the endings of Shakespeare's romances. These deflected endings function as key structuring absences in how the drama then unfolds: called to mind by incidental detail only to be dismissed by the play's actual ending which then plays out partly through an assertion of what it is not, through establishing its distinction from the alternatives it has rejected. But, as is the wont of the most emphatically asserted absences, despite their explicit banishment from the narrative, each, like the Derridean *trace*, 'makes its necessity felt' even in its own eviction.[2]

This intricate tapestry of conjured, remembered and rejected narratives embedded in the ending of *The Winter's Tale* offers a particular sort of invitation – and licence – to productions to find the stories that can be told from within and behind the surface narrative. In effect, these suppressions and negations invite productions to exhume the buried and place the recovered in sight of the audience, even if in order then to reject it. Of central interest in this regard will be Christopher Wheeldon's 2014 ballet of *The Winter's Tale*, composed by Joby Talbot and designed by Bob Crowley for

The Royal Ballet at Covent Garden and then directed for the screen by Ross MacGibbon. First broadcast by live relay into cinemas in April 2014, it was commercially released on Opus Arte DVD in the United Kingdom in early 2015. Later, I seek out the endings embraced and those eschewed in this beautiful production, to ask how both the presences and the absences it performs give expression to the potent suggestiveness of the Shakespeare drama it inherits and rethinks.

In order to bring the consideration about performed endings into best relief, I attend first to the end of the Shakespeare play itself. The serial suppression and rejection of alternative endings embedded there, only semi-acknowledged, proves insufficient to constitute their complete expurgation from the fabric of the scene – or, crucially, from our experience of it. It is for this reason that the alternative and averted endings bear attention. I take in turn the three endings *manqués* of prime interest here.

i) Paulina's Faux Ending: Averted

Shortly before the play's closing *coup de théâtre*, Paulina teases Leontes with the possibility that she might halt the exquisite drama then in train. 'Shall I draw the curtain?' she asks (5.3.83). Should she withdraw sight of the statue? If the suffering it induces is too great, she continues, Leontes might even like to step back and '[q]uit presently the chapel' (5.3.86) where the statue is on show. The ending Paulina has planned must, as she knows, come at a cost: Leontes, she provocatively speculates, might therefore prefer to be spared any further potential suffering.

In giving Leontes the option of declining the ending she has choreographed, Paulina also thereby invites him to assume some elected agency in its actual outworking. In context, the explicit agreement to proceed is no small thing for him to give; his current equilibrium has, after all, been hard won through long years of suffering. Would he like to be excused the possibility of endangering this? No, says Leontes; it may indeed 'afflict [him] farther' (5.3.74), but let the drama play out. In rejecting Paulina's offer to retreat, Leontes rewrites his own generic allegiances, refusing his place in the protracted, un-end-stopped version of *Othello* in which he had previously found himself. By choosing to remain open to what might yet transpire, Leontes thereby makes provision for, and renders himself amenable to, a tragicomic ending.[3] And it is this articulated willingness to risk further emotional trial that allows the play to find its way back from the absoluteness of loss. The play's generic complexity and generic permissiveness are, therefore, chosen from within as well as determined from without. 'Do,

Paulina', responds Leontes (5.3.75) to the question about whether or not to proceed, and the play, remembering the more timid and less risky ending that might have been, rewards him for his willingness to feel.

ii)   Greene's Ending: Sanitized

Given the number of close parallels between Shakespeare's *The Winter's Tale* and Robert Greene's prose romance *Pandosto, The Triumph of Time* (1588),[4] the moments of departure of the one from the other are the more noticeable.[5] The key differences become focused in the ending of each: in the Greene prose romance, the slandered wife remains dead, the king's encounter with his daughter is marked by incestuous desire and the king finally kills himself in 'a tragical stratagem';[6] whereas, in Shakespeare, the king does not die, his encounter with his daughter remains chaste, and his wife, daughter and 'brother-king' are all finally restored to him.

In turning away from the non-concessionary character of Greene's ending, however, Shakespeare's narrative cannot entirely forget the darkness of its prose source. In, for example, Paulina's rebuke to Leontes about his way of looking at Perdita: 'Sir, my liege,/Your eye hath too much youth in't' (5.1.223–4), that disquieting memory is invoked. And even though swiftly then banished through Paulina's crisp intervention, once referenced, it cannot be entirely erased from the landscape of the play's ending.

Its shadow contributes to the sense of human messiness that must be forcibly contained, and to the range of things that must be repressed or remain unsaid for the 'happy' ending to hold. The glancing presence of Greene at the end of *The Winter's Tale* adds piquancy to anxieties about *the ending that might have been*, weight to the anxieties that remain and, concomitantly, additional dimension to the joy nonetheless discovered in the ending, given the considerable impediments that threatened to obstruct it.

iii)   Ovid's Ending: Healed

When his wife is restored to Leontes at the end of the play, Paulina counsels him explicitly about the terms on which Hermione has been brought back:

> . . . Do not shun her
> Until you see her die again, for then
> You kill her double. (5.3.105–7)

The prospect of dying again and being killed double offers a refracted, but audible, echo of Ovid's account of Orpheus and Eurydice from *Metamorphoses* Book X (lines 1–85)[7] – and one which would have been quickly identifiable to the educated sections of the play's first audiences.[8] Eurydice, it will be recalled, dies once (of a snake bite) and her grieving husband Orpheus goes down to the Underworld to plead for her life. His articulacy, musicianship and devotion charm the gods: the Furies weep and even the stony heart of Pluto is moved. A deal is struck. Eurydice can be restored to Orpheus on condition that he does not once turn his eyes to look at her on the journey back out of the Underworld; if he does, she will be lost again. That is, he must prove his love for his wife by, in effect, feigning neglect of her. When nearly back to their own world, Orpheus loses his discipline and turns to gaze upon his wife. In line with the contract, she slips back to the Underworld, 'dying a second time' ('iterum moriens', l. 60) and Orpheus is plunged into deep grief by 'the double death of his wife' ('gemina nece coniugis', l. 64).[9]

The Shakespearean phrases 'die again' and 'kill her double' (5.3.106, 107), closely capturing 'iterum moriens' and 'gemina nece' as they do,[10] summon the Ovidian tale of the much-loved wife who dies twice as a shadow memory within the end of *The Winter's Tale*. But the Ovidian story is invoked by Shakespeare less as pattern than foil. Eurydice being claimed back by death through a 'gemina nece' is narratively cruel: the 'mistake' that causes it (a husband's concern for the welfare of his wife) should have been commended not punished. Shakespeare sees the pitilessness of the story and conjures it (as he does Greene) to subvert it – and in some manner even to speak back to it with a newly charged humanity. Whereas, therefore, Orpheus is instructed specifically to shun his wife as a savagely conceived test of his devotion, Paulina's brief to Leontes about how to prevent his wife dying a second death is, equally specifically, 'Do *not* shun her' (5.3.105, my emphasis). The Shakespearean instruction – to keep his spousal eye fixed firmly *on* his wife – is, in fact, consciously anti-Ovidian, an undoing of the harshness of the source tale. The rewritten dynamics of Orpheus's story in Shakespeare perhaps even expose something in the original tale that craves gentler treatment.[11] In both conjuring and resisting its Ovidian *doppelgänger*, the restoration of Hermione at the end of *The Winter's Tale* thus emerges as the more miraculous and the more affecting for being legibly a revisionist response to Eurydice's story, radically underpinned by compassion.

So it is that the spectres of alternative endings are held in a state of poised, conscious acknowledgement at the end of *The Winter's Tale*. The option of turning away from an engagement with further pain (Paulina's offer to Leontes), the intensity of the husband's guilty mortification that must lead to death (through Greene) and the unsparing double death of the wife (through Ovid): for those with a passing knowledge of the other tales inhabiting Shakespeare's appropriative consciousness in *The Winter's Tale*, these things cannot but inform a reading of the final scene. But what happens to such structuring absences in performance? Having inherited a play-text busy with suggestions of endings that then *are not*, how might this intricate network of ellipses and suppressions, of things unsaid and things unshown, then find form in performance?

Christopher Wheeldon's 2014 ballet of *The Winter's Tale* at the Royal Opera House, Covent Garden, broke new narrative ground in the history of Shakespearean ballet and was a landmark production in The Royal Ballet's programme of commissions.[12] On 28 April 2014, Ross MacGibbon's live film of the production from Covent Garden, on a seven-camera shoot, was transmitted into cinemas around the world. I saw the ballet once on stage in a very full Royal Opera House and once on screen in a near-empty multiplex auditorium in York. I found the production powerful on both occasions, but in their difference as mediated events they made for strikingly distinct experiences, and in ways that bear analysis. The fierce intelligence of the Wheeldon choreography and interpretive vision, the deeply affecting performances of Edward Watson (the most harrowing Leontes I have seen in any medium) and of Lauren Cuthbertson (the most emotionally intelligent Hermione) and MacGibbon's thoughtful capture and re-visioning of the production for the screen will be of interest here, with a particular concentration on the final scene.

In the context of predominantly enthusiastic reviews of the production ('consistently inventive'; 'a clarity of intention and shape'; 'profoundly disquieting, and ever inviting of understanding'; 'a visual triumph, potent, evocative, eye-delighting'),[13] this final scene met with some scepticism. Luke Jennings of *The Observer* thought it 'disappointingly rushed', found that the statue's awakening 'falls flat' and judged that 'in the revival of Hermione, Wheeldon is inconsistent'; *The Guardian*'s Judith Mackrell suggested that 'Wheeldon strains to find choreography to match the piercing drama of the simple stage direction "Hermione comes down"'; *The Independent*'s Zoë Anderson that Wheeldon's final 'pas de deux can't match the magic of its source'.[14] This disappointment in the final scene seems to me significantly misplaced. The choreography conspicuously takes its time – much more so than the Shakespeare play – as it psychologically investigates and emotionally intuits how a husband and wife, reunited after sixteen years, might find a way of being in each other's presence despite the extent of the pain inflicted on one by the other when last they met. Watson and Cuthbertson are awkward, mortified, exploratory, nostalgic, tentative, hopeful, embarrassed, desirous, generous, believing, disbelieving, earnest, rueful, moved and finally quietly, soberly joyful and the choreography understands and expresses all this. Their *pas de deux* – tormented, embarrassed and redemptive as it is – asks invested questions of Shakespeare's final scene in ways that take seriously the import of Paulina's suggestion that the ending might bring 'affliction' (5.3.76) as well as joy. To counter the critics' sense that the ending falls short in relation to its source, here I pay attention to the choreography, performances and finally the specifics of the filming. I start, however, with the crucial intervention made by the set.

There is a visual *coup* built into the set design at the end of the Wheeldon *Winter's Tale*. When the statue is unveiled, it is discovered to be not just of Hermione but also of her young son Mamillius (see Figure 7.1). Unveiled, they stand in petrified stillness together awaiting the admiration of their onlookers and the magical intervention of the end of the drama. It is to this double statue that Leontes is drawn; from it that Hermione descends as 'stone no more' (5.3.99); in the presence of the remaining statue of their

Figure 7.1.   Paulina (Zenaida Yanowsky) shows Leontes (Edward Watson) the double statue in Wheeldon's 2014 ballet of *The Winter's Tale*.

Figure 7.2.   Leontes (Edward Watson) and Hermione (Lauren Cuthbertson) reach
cautiously for each other in the presence of their son's statue in Wheeldon's 2014 ballet of
The Winter's Tale. All rights reserved.

son that Leontes and Hermione must find a (dance) vocabulary through
which to reconnect (see Figure 7.2); and to that remaining statue of the
boy that Leontes returns in the final moments of the ballet in the heart-
breaking, vain hope of witnessing a second miraculous resurrection (see
Figure 7.3).

As an additional piece of stage furniture, the Mamillius statue is a relatively simple interpolation into the scene: as a piece of interpretive business,
however, it has significant consequences for the production as a whole,
and consequences that became not only more conspicuous but, as I will
argue later, different in kind for the film version. In order to understand
the startling and varied effects of the double statue in this production across
media, however, we need first to understand the ontology and power of the
single statue that the play and its performance history tutor us to expect.

Of the many things that Hermione's statue constitutes in the world
of *The Winter's Tale*, at first glance it stands most obviously as a point
of obdurate resistance to the realm of the living. In its apparent act of
stony memorializing, it hyperbolically expresses the deathly silence and
stillness that the brutality of Leontes' jealousy has wished upon his wife.
Implicitly, the Shakespearean character had wanted Hermione deprived of
speech (because, after all, 'Is whispering nothing?' [1.2.281]), and robbed
of the capacity to act (to prevent any further possible paddling of palms,

Figure 7.3.   Leontes (Edward Watson) returns to the statue of Mamillius in hope of a second miracle in Wheeldon's 2014 ballet of *The Winter's Tale*.

pinching of fingers or 'horsing foot on foot' [1.2.285]): the Shakespearean statue gives form, in precise and unforgiving terms, to the deferred out-working of these misogynist desires to still and to silence. So it is that the woman accused in Shakespeare of being 'slippery' (1.2.270) is replaced with a figure apparently epitomizing fixity. Part of what the Hermione statue represents, therefore, is an embodied accusation to Leontes about the very fate his own condemnatory misreading of his wife has implicitly wished upon her.

But as audiences of *The Winter's Tale* in any medium know, intuitively if not yet actually, the statue is not the end of the drama: rather it is the engine for the play's quiet but vital conclusion. In dramatic context, there-fore, despite the wrinkles on the statue of the queen that illustratively map the painful *durée* of time past, the statue of Hermione stands as much as a promise of what might be as an ossified ruing of what once was. Our deep-seated, shared knowledge of the fable in which a statue comes to life collaborates with our understanding of how stories work structurally, how art functions psychically and with the further 'amazement' promised by Paulina (5.3.87) to imbue the Hermione statue with a deep and tingle-inducing sense of *expectation*.

As represented on film, the expectational impulse in response to the statue is, if anything, enhanced. In early cinema, paintings came to life and statues moved with striking regularity. In fact, so nearly conventionalized was it in the early years of the medium for filmed paintings, drawings and statues to shed the inertia of still art and participate in the animate world, that, for a short period, any privileging attention given to a work of art within a film would be sufficient to generate the expectation that at some point it would then self-transform into 'living' form. Films that narrated a transmediating act of this sort (still art to moving pictures) were sufficiently numerous in this period to constitute, in effect, a genre in their own right. Early films that featured a painting or statue coming to life included: *Pygmalion and Galatea* (1898), *The Mysterious Portrait* (1899), *The Haunted Picture Gallery* (1899), *An Artist's Dream* (1899), *The Artist's Dream* (1899), *The Spirit of His Forefathers* (1900), *The Artist's Dilemma* (1901) and *A Modern Galatea* (1904). That moving the artistically still should have proved so popular and become such a regular feature of the cinematic repertoire so early in the medium's exploration of its own identity should not surprise; the subject, after all, allegorizes the animating force of cinema itself, a medium which converts the still into the moving as the very spring of its being.[15]

In the earliest days of the film industry, moving picture shows even began with a still image projected onto the screen that then erupted into life once the projectionist started cranking. In July 1896, for example, Maxim Gorky famously reported his early encounter with the touring Lumière show in the following terms:

> When the lights go out in the room..., there suddenly appears on the screen a large gray picture, *A Street in Paris* – shadows of a bad engraving. As you gaze at it, you see carriages, buildings and people in various poses, all frozen into immobility... [Y]ou anticipate nothing new in this all too familiar scene, for you have seen pictures of Paris streets more than once. But suddenly a strange flicker passes through the screen and the picture stirs to life. Carriages coming from somewhere in the perspective of the picture are moving straight at you, into the darkness in which you sit.[16]

The wonder of Gorky's 'But suddenly' moment finds an equivalent in many reports of early film shows. The medium's gasp-worthy properties might even have found their most lucid and emblematic expression in that one magical instant, the moment that referenced the still image and then left it behind so decisively in favour of the new world of animation.

The statue of Hermione as seen on film inherits this frisson of expectation that the artistically still has historically communicated in the cinema. This medium-specific history heightens the anticipatory charge of the promise immanent in the Hermione statue, a charge already encouraged by the play and consolidated by its stage performance history. The version of stillness that this Shakespearean statue performs on stage, and more particularly yet on screen, is, therefore, of the most provocative, unstable and expectant character – kin, in fact, to the tense and pregnant projected stillness craving Gorky's 'But suddenly' moment of disruptive magic-making. So it is that the Hermione statue is read more as part of a temporal trajectory than a destination, constituting an ontological challenge to the blocky permanence of statuary as usually understood. In its celebration of the moment of poised anacrusis that anticipates vitality, therefore, Hermione's statue understands and, in contemporary performance, can harness the force of the cinematic. In fact, in the statue's will to self-animate, and its subsequent rejection of its own reification, the Shakespearean 'she stirs' moment metaphorically enacts the eruptive kinesis of cinema itself.

How, then, does the interpolated Mamillius statue in the Wheeldon production contribute to this frisson-laden landscape of instability and expectation? In summary, it stands in massy opposition to it, introduced as if from the prosaic extra-dramatic world to de-fabularize the meaning and function of statuary. Even without any transformational magic, however, given the pain that the memory of Mamillius's death brings to the play, the embodied reminder of that in statue form cannot but constitute a complex addition to the scene. Mamillius was the much-loved boy whose tale about sprites and goblins was prematurely broken off, never to be finished. His death is scarcely subsequently spoken of in the play but his absence from the ending is conspicuous. However miraculous the reconstituting of the rest of this fractured family (Leontes, Hermione and Perdita) may be, in his absence that reconstituted family unit cannot but telegraph its incompleteness.

Bob Crowley's design for the Wheeldon ballet takes the over-conspicuous absence of Mamillius at the end of the play, and converts it into an over-conspicuous presence in unsparingly stark and arresting form. The introduction of a material reminder of his death changes the dynamics of the scene. The Mamillius statue obstinately articulates the thing that in Shakespeare remains unspoken and the principal effect of this is the unrelenting mortification of Leontes.

When Hermione demonstrates the startling difference between stone and flesh by descending, Leontes and she then take it in turns to be the more embarrassed and unnerved in the presence of the other. Shakespeare's 'resurrected' Hermione is slow to find her way back to language – 'If she pertain to life, let her speak too', says Camillo by way of encouragement

Figure 7.4.   Leontes' (Edward Watson) foetal collapse in the presence of the wife he
has wronged (Lauren Cuthbertson) in Wheeldon's 2014 ballet of *The Winter's Tale*.

(5.3.113) – and in fact she says nothing to Leontes in the final scene (what
could she say at any speed to the man who has robbed her of daughter,
marriage, respect and liberty for sixteen years, and of her son forever?). In
the ballet production, in interpretive extension of her silence to Leontes,
it becomes clear that she cannot initially return the gaze of the husband
who has wronged her. With quiet dignity she looks away, or closes her
eyes, as his hands explore her face, neck, shoulders, arms with childlike
wonder. But as soon as self-consciousness catches up with this Leontes, it
is then he who cannot either take or give the gaze, stricken as he then is
by his unworthiness to look upon the woman he has wronged. Embarrassed, he collapses at her feet, curling foetally around her ankles by way
of instinctive, primal apology (see Figure 7.4). This is a long way from the
Shakespearean Leontes who, with Hermione restored to him, has the emotional wherewithal and self-possession to move humorously into marriage-
brokering mode ('O peace, Paulina!/Thou shouldst a husband take by my
consent' [5.3.135–6]), in what feels in context almost like an emotionally
jarring meta-joke about the generic exigencies for multiple couplings to
confirm a quasi-comic ending. Although Shakespeare's Leontes does issue
an apology to Hermione and Polixenes at the end of the Shakespeare play

('Both your pardons/That e'er I put between your holy looks/My ill suspicion' [5.3.147–9]), the measured tone and temperate dimensions of this apology strike an odd note at such a moment, given the extremity, duration and, in the case of Mamillius and Antigonus, irreversibility of the consequences of that 'ill suspicion' (5.3.149). Wheeldon's adaptation of the scene suggests, firstly, an intense interest in what Hermione's silence to Leontes might be imagined to be masking and, secondly, a preference for a Leontes who finds the searing intensity of the moment far harder to inhabit than the hearty, self-possessed words of his Shakespearean counterpart might suggest.

So it is that Cuthbertson's Hermione, sensing the extent of Leontes' distress in her presence, then partially assumes the burden of finding a way back for them both as they begin to reach yearningly for invested ways of connecting that don't yet require them to meet each other's gaze. It is too early for anything so personally exposing but other ways of relating can be found: he stretches out backwards in search of her hand, and she cautiously allows herself to touch the back of his head (see Figure 7.2); back-to-back, they strain away from each other while tilting their heads back to retain a connection; he carries her on his back in an intimacy of would-be togetherness that still spares them the requirement to look directly on each other (see Figure 7.5). And in these elaborately gaze-avoiding modes of relating, they incrementally relearn a confidence in connecting with each other physically. Within the narrative fiction of the ballet, in dancing with each other each is dancing with a body that s/he had known well but has learned to *unknow* across many painful years of separation. Their complex

Figure 7.5.   Leontes (Edward Watson) and Hermione (Lauren Cuthbertson) long to connect, even in their sustained inability to look at one another, and then find an inventive range of intimacies without meeting each other's gaze in Wheeldon's 2014 ballet of *The Winter's Tale*.

and evolving *pas de deux* gently charts the stages of reacquainting themselves with the contours, familiarity and consolation of that partner both known and unknown. And through the unorthodox and cautious asymmetries of their dance, we see them beginning to dare to trust once again.

In their marriage, before Leontes' polluting jealousy had intervened to spoil everything, Watson's Leontes and Cuthbertson's Hermione had developed a private love language, expressed through a distinct series of reciprocally exchanged and complementary gestures, clearly codified as intensely intimate (see Figure 7.6). When wrongly accused earlier in the production, Hermione had movingly tried to resummon the intimate liturgy, to remind Leontes of the 'them' that he was throwing away; at that stage this had only provoked in Leontes a savagely mocking parody of her movements. But now, after their tentative dance of compromised trust but desperately desired connection has developed into a more expansive dance of recovery, hope and shared lyricism, Hermione once again steels herself to reach for their own private communicative mode. Accompanied by a privileging climactic sting in the score to mark the significance of the moment, she bravely assumes the posture of her opening line in their antiphonal gestural conversation, hoping this time that he will feel able to reassume his role in this exchange. But so overcome is he at the sight of her willingness to re-engage in this ritual, despite its now-tainted history, that he crumples in a heap of self-accusation. Sensing the impediment, she steps in to fortify him, physically manoeuvring his arms as she wills him to take part in a renewed version of the love exchange that they historically shared (see Figure 7.6). It is an intervention that speaks poignantly of unconditional acceptance. And it is the more powerful for taking place directly beneath the monument to their dead son, in the very shadow of which Hermione is determinedly choosing to believe in a future. Touched by her belief in him, he allows his arms to be manipulated to express those things that he cannot now presume to articulate without her generous intervention. Having recovered their own communicative channel, infused as this is with a proper sense of history, Hermione and Leontes are then finally released to dance face-to-face. Their newfound freedom allows for a much more fluid and recognizable range of steps drawn from a classical dance repertoire, including a series of beautiful, travelling pirouettes performed in joyous unison. Without making light of the hurt, guilt and grief still appropriately present within this ending, this is a couple whose story of mutual rediscovery has been persuasively and affectingly dramatized through a six-minute *pas de deux* of the not-quite and the nearly and then of the reclaimed, performed with a telling hesitancy and an uninhibited passion illuminatingly attuned

Figure 7.6.   Leontes (Edward Watson) and Hermione's (Lauren Cuthbertson) private love language from Act I. In the final act, Hermione empowers Leontes to participate in their language of old in Wheeldon's 2014 ballet of *The Winter's Tale*.

to both the intensely burdened and the intensely joyful imperatives of the Shakespearean dramatic moment.

As viewed by audiences in the Royal Opera House, the entirety of this scene was played in the presence of the Mamillius statue. Presiding over

Figure 7.7.   The statue of Mamillius acts as a reminder that this partially reconstituted family can never be complete in Wheeldon's 2014 ballet of *The Winter's Tale*. All rights reserved.

all reunions, the statue gave sobering context to the intensity, emotional awkwardness and transporting beauty of the dance of marital restoration and to the return of Perdita: it served as an ever-present reminder of the price paid for these moments of joy. And in a near-mordant take on a family portrait, the statue was even compositionally included in the reconstituted familial grouping as a reminder of what had been lost (see Figure 7.7).

In the live relay transmission (and resulting DVD), however, the statue's role in this final scene was strikingly revised. The relationship with the set into which viewers of the relay were invited was, inevitably perhaps, more intricate than that which had been on offer for Royal Opera House audiences. The crucial difference was determined by what was included in the shot and the sequencing of the edit. In the live relay, the statue was sometimes fully visible in shot; at other times, the camera followed the Hermione-Leontes *pas de deux* into areas of the stage that then excluded the statue from the frame, or the sequence would cut in to focal lengths that had the same exclusionary effect. And when that happened, the relay audience was temporarily allowed to become exclusively absorbed in the nascent joy of a couple being restored to each other, as if unburdened by all the other things pressing upon their past, present and future. The shot composition allowed the poetic intensity of the dance and the re-emerging relationship of trust it dramatized to claim the audience's undiluted concentration and emotional energy. But at such moments, with our focused attention on this assured, the movement of the dance would then travel back into visual alignment with the plinth, or the shot would cede to a panoptic view of the stage that included renewed sight of the statue, having the effect of then jolting the audience back into recalling the death of Mamillius. In this way, the spectatorial pleasure that had temporarily been on offer through the exquisitely danced drama of a marriage being gingerly and passionately put back together would pall painfully as the irrevocable loss of the much-loved son heaved back into literal and metaphorical view.

In an interview with Ross MacGibbon, director of the live relay production, I asked what had determined shot choices for the scene, and specifically what had determined when the statue was and was not in shot. He responded thus:

> I always want to convey the emotional resonance of a scene as accurately as possible, but sometimes the choreography just doesn't play well to camera from certain angles. This depends largely on the architecture of the choreography on the body; so, for example, if a section of the *pas de deux* looks much better aesthetically from the front camera right, then that will be the predominant angle. There were times where the statue was excluded deliberately, but there were also times when the statue just had to take care of itself. In a film studio, we could have moved the statue in and out of shot to intensify/diminish the emotional impact as we wished, but with fixed cameras in an auditorium, that isn't possible.[17]

MacGibbon's commission was to create a film that was properly attentive to, and in step with, Wheeldon's theatrical vision for the ballet. The style of filming for *The Winter's Tale* is, as a result, as narratively clear and as cinematically self-effacing as possible.[18] That said, it is no surprise that a consciousness of the statue's absence or presence in shot and its potential to 'intensify/diminish the emotional impact' specifically informed production thinking for the shoot. Given the statue's prominent positioning on stage, practical and aesthetic considerations were clearly the principal determinants of frame compositions: choosing the angle from which the shapes made by the dancers' bodies would be best showcased was paramount and the result is some pleasingly intimate proximities to memorable and well-displayed performance moments.

But it was also true that, in playing by turns with the statue's visibility and invisibility, the multi-camera shoot could do what the open stage of the live performance could not. So although MacGibbon's compositional preferences and edited sequencing of the scene were primarily driven by a desire sensitively to capture the contours of the dance and adeptly to map the progress of the stage-choreographed story, nevertheless those shot choices and editorial discriminations could never be entirely neutral in enacting this commission: in mediating the tale, they could not but make an interpretive intervention on the way in which the scene was then read. In particular, the film's fluidly alternating, if near-insouciant ('the statue just had to take care of itself'), exclusion and inclusion of the plinth from shot had a considerable impact on how the scene was experienced: by turns licensing its audiences to forget the Mamillius statue and the deep, ongoing sadness it represented, and issuing the jarring reminder both of the statue and its import. These repeating cycles of pleasurable forgetting and pleasure-dispelling remembering generated an emotional roller coaster of a viewing experience. And the adrenalin-rich effect of this disquieting oscillation between joy curbed and joy released was, as it happens, not only different from the architecturally more stable experience of the scene as experienced by audiences at Covent Garden (for whom the statue's joy-muting presence was a constant); it was also, I suggest, more closely connected to the tonally mixed allegiances at the end of the Shakespeare play. The tonal dynamics in Shakespeare's final scene are, after all, protean, allowing for plenty of looking away from the sadness and even for some quietly charged excitement alongside the pained sobriety: it is for these emotional returns, in fact, that we are required to 'awake [our] faith' (5.3.95).

When Shakespeare alluded to, but then significantly revised, Greene's *Pandosto* and Ovid's tale of Eurydice's double death at the end of *The Winter's Tale*, he was consciously rejecting alternative endings that would, had they held sway, have added pain to the drama: the expulsion, or transformation, of those narratives helps steer the ending towards the joy, such as it is, that it knows at its close, such as this is. Working in the Shakespearean tradition of both embracing and rejecting alternatives, Wheeldon introduced his own alternative ending to the drama. In the closing moments of his production, Leontes returned to the statue of Mamillius, and stretched out his hand once again, earnestly hoping for a reprise of the earlier miracle (see Figure 7.3). If one statue could come alive, why not two? In context, Leontes' reasoning was as understandable as it was misplaced. But it also inadvertently caught the impulse to invert Ovid that is evident in Shakespeare through Paulina's anti-Ovidian instruction to Leontes *not* to 'shun' his wife lest he 'kill her double' (5.3.105, 107). Through Leontes' fantasy of the imagined return of both wife and son, in the Wheeldon production, the Ovidian double death was, in effect, reconfigured as the dream of a double rebirth.

If fulfilled, the interpolated business would have decisively changed the generic hue of the drama's ending. But this statue was imbued with none of that heady anticipatory charge that attaches to Hermione's statue and constituted no destabilizing challenge to what a statue is; with unsparing banality, it was just a statue, impervious to its capacity to generate false hope and unresponsive to the fabular expectations invested in it. With a little shake of the head, Paulina drew an uncomprehending Leontes sadly away from both the statue and the dream, commissioning him instead to focus on the living. There was in this production no brisk and hearty requirement that Paulina should marry for jollity, convenience and neat endings. Spared that disempowering indignity, Yanowsky's Paulina was instead given the privilege of the production's closing tableau. Her own purpose amongst the living now apparently played out, she herself turned back to the statue of the dead boy, sinking quietly into an attenuated pigeon pose before it, her restless, sinuously winding arms stretched out in second, bowing her head in resignation towards this memorial of things gone as the curtain fell.

Gordon McMullan reminds us that tragicomedy depends upon 'the conscious redeployment of earlier modes'.[19] In the accommodations of the form, the conventions and impulses of comedy are drawn in and problematized; those of tragedy drawn in and eased. There is no formulaic balance to the transformative elision thereby created and Early Modern tragicomedies work to different tonal preferences from each other in this respect.

Both Shakespeare and Wheeldon assert the balance of their own generic allegiances within the permissive terms of tragicomedy partly through clarifying the stories they are not telling. While, for example, the close of the Shakespeare play's relationship to comic impulse is compromised in comparison with that of Shakespeare's early comedies, its rejection of Greene's 'tragical stratagem', refusal of Ovid's 'gemina nece' and explicit diversion from the narrative patterning of *Othello* articulates the clear will to temper tragedy.

In line with his Shakespearean source, Wheeldon's engagement with alternative endings also became a channel through which generic sensibility was expressed. However, the principal alternative ending with which Wheeldon flirted – the possible resurrection of Mamillius – was one that, if realised, would have added joy not pain to the drama. Toying with, and then decisively eschewing, this possibility could not, therefore, but deepen the note of regret on which the production ended. Whereas Shakespeare advertised by reference and rejection the ways in which the story he was telling was not 'tragical' (and his tale gained buoyancy through the foils

thereby offered), the story that Wheeldon's production was emphatically
not telling at its close was, more heartrendingly, essentially a 'comical' one.
In allowing space for the fantasy of *what might have been* but then dis-
pelling it, Wheeldon affectingly positioned his *Winter's Tale* adaptation at
the most freighted end of tragicomic possibility.

In Shakespeare's *The Winter's Tale*, Mamillius is the would-be narrator
of the tale and the play even self-consciously derives its title from his storytelling preferences. For their 1914 three-reel film *The Winter's Tale* (*Una
Tragedia alla Corte di Sicilia*),[20] Italian production company Milano-Film[21]
cut Mamillius completely, inserting instead an implied external narrator
in the form of Shakespeare himself. The film was, therefore, book-ended
with a shot of the playwright reading to his friends (see Figure 7.8). In
the context of a wordless telling of the tale, this is a striking intervention,
apparently anchoring the drama in a worded form even as its own performance codes all but dispensed with the need for words, and in a configured
Shakespearean authority even as its own dramatization of the play diverged
creatively from that authority.

Figure 7.8.   In the prefatory sequence to Negroni's 1914 *The Winter's Tale*, an animated
Shakespeare begins his reading of the tale. In the film's coda, Shakespeare completes the
tale, but one listener has fallen asleep. All rights reserved.

However, there is also a mini-joke built into this framing sequence.
Although in the opening shot Shakespeare's friends look animated, by the
story's close, one of them has conspicuously fallen asleep (see Figure 7.8).
Even when recounted by Shakespeare himself, a word-based reading of *The
Winter's Tale* is not, the sequence impishly implies, the best means of guar-
anteeing the sustained interest of an audience. What therefore presents initially as the film's desire for validation not only through authorial, but also
specifically through textual association, is self-subvertingly and impishly
then revealed as an implicit assertion of the potential tedium of words in

comparison with performed action. A spectator for the film can therefore look upon that snoozing listener with wry amusement, feeling privileged to have been exposed instead to the film's visualized performance that has by then unspooled before her.

Although separated from the Milano silent film by a hundred years, the 2014 Wheeldon ballet draws powerfully upon the same implicit relative values communicated in Milano's book-ending sequence.[22] As both productions, in fact, beautifully adduce, wordless performance forms can be a source both of communicative authority and of wonder beyond words producing, as the first gentleman in the play reports of the Leontes-Camillo reunion, 'speech in their dumbness, language in their very gesture' (5.2.11–12). In response to Watson's athletic angularities and eloquent contortions, Cuthbertson's elegance, strength and compassion, Talbot's soaring, celebratory figures, temporal, clock-like chimings and passages of wearied, unbearable grief, Wheeldon's emotionally pointed and narratively compelling choreography and MacGibbon's thoughtful re-envisaging for the screen, there is certainly no temptation to join Milano's on-screen audience member and sleep: as a possible extra-dramatic ending amidst a rich field of intra-dramatic options in this respect, that one too is pleasingly averted.

Notes

1 F. Kermode, *The Sense of an Ending* (Oxford: Oxford University Press, 1966; repr. 2000).

2 J. Derrida, *Of Grammatology*, trans. Gayatri Chakravorty Spivak (Baltimore, MD and London: Johns Hopkins University Press, 1976), 61.

3 On the stimulating problems of taxonomy and nomenclature in relation to Shakespeare's 'late plays'/'romances'/'tragicomedies', see G. McMullan, '"The Neutral Term"?: Shakespearean Tragicomedy and the Idea of the "Late Play"', in S. Mukherji and R. Lyne (eds.), *Early Modern Tragicomedy* (Cambridge: Boydel and Brewer, 2007), 115–32.

4 The popularity of Greene, *Pandosto, The Triumph of Time* (London: Thomas Orwin, 1588), may be gauged from the number of times it was reprinted ahead of the writing of *The Winter's Tale*: 1592, 1595, 1607, 1609.

5 On Shakespeare's sources for *The Winter's Tale*, including Greene's romance, see G. Bullough (ed.), *Narrative and Dramatic Sources of Shakespeare*, vol. VIII, Romances (London: Routledge & Kegan Paul, 1975), 113–233.

6 Greene, *Pandosto* (1588), sigs. F4r–G4r (G4r).

7 On the glancing allusion to Orpheus and Eurydice at the end of *The Winter's Tale*, see A. D. Nuttall, '*The Winter's Tale*: Ovid Transformed', in A. B. Taylor (ed.), *Shakespeare's Ovid: The Metamorphoses in the Plays and Poems* (Cambridge: Cambridge University Press, 2000), 137.

8 As a late play, *The Winter's Tale* will have had a performance life at the Blackfriars, in addition to the one we know it had at the Globe (where Simon Forman saw it performed on 15 May 1611). The Blackfriars attracted a more consistently educated clientele than the Globe. Plays in all periods of Shakespeare's writing career appeal to the recognition of classical reference; those written in this late period trust to that recognition with greater assurance and include such allusions with greater economy, confident that audiences can catch nuanced and unglossed classical reference at speed.

9 For the Latin text, I use the Loeb edition: *Metamorphoses*, vol. II: Books IX–XV (Cambridge, MA: Harvard University Press, 1916), 64–71.

10 Shakespeare would have known Ovid's *Metamorphoses* in both Latin and English. We know (from Prospero's farewell to magic speech in *The Tempest*) that he was familiar with Arthur Golding's popular English translation (first published 1567; further editions 1575, 1587, 1603, 1612). Golding renders the Eurydice phrases of crucial interest to Shakespeare as 'dying now the second tyme' (l.64) and 'the double dying of his wyfe' (l.69). Golding, *The XV Bookes of P. Ovidius Naso, entytuled Metamorphosis* (London: Willyam Seres [1567]), sig. R4r.

11 The draw to temper the pain at the end of this Ovidian story has been felt by others too. In Christoph Willibald Gluck's 1762 opera *Orfeo ed Euridice* (original libretto by Ranieri de Calzabigi), for example, Eurydice, having slipped back to the Underworld in line with the Ovidian pattern, is then allowed a glorious resurrection to enable the opera to end happily.

12 It was the first three-act ballet based on Shakespeare to be premiered at the Royal Ballet since Kenneth MacMillan's 1965 *Romeo and Juliet* and only the second full-length story ballet on any subject commissioned by the Royal Ballet since 1995.

13 First two quotations are from S. Crompton, review of *The Winter's Tale*, *The Telegraph*, 11 April 2014, 25; latter two from Clement Crisp, review of *The Winter's Tale*, *Financial Times*, 14 April 2014, Arts Section, 13.

14 Jennings, review, *The Observer*, 13 April 2014, The New Review section, 30; Mackrell, review, *The Guardian*, 11 April 2014, 56; Anderson, review, *The Independent*, 11 April 2014, 44.

15 On the relationship of the still art object to the moving image in early cinema, see N. Mowll Mathews, 'Art and Film: Interactions', in M. and C. Musser (eds.), *Moving Pictures: American Art and Early Film 1880–1910* (Manchester, VT: Hudson Hills Press, 2005), 145–58; and J. Buchanan, '"Un Cinéma Impur": Framing Film in the Early Film Industry', in S. Allen and L. Hubner (eds.), *Framing Film: Cinema and the Visual Arts* (Bristol: Intellect, 2012), 238–60.

16 Gorky's review of the pioneering Lumière programme, seen at the Nizhny-Novgorod Annual Fair, 'The Kingdom of Shadows', was published in Russian in the local newspaper, *Nizhegorodski listok*, 4 July 1896. Cited from Gorky, 'In the Kingdom of Shadows' (1896), in C. Harding and S. Popple (eds.), *In the*

Kingdom of Shadows: A Companion to Early Cinema (London: Cygnus Arts; Teaneck, NJ: Fairleigh Dickinson University Press, 1996), 5–6 (5).

17 R. MacGibbon, interviewed by author (6 May 2015).

18 While the camera work here does little to draw attention to itself, that is not the case in all MacGibbon-directed live relays. In his 2014 filming of Carrie Cracknell's National Theatre *Medea* with Helen McCrory in the title role, for example, the camera work is significantly more visible, including through zooms and conspicuous camera movement across planes of action, to give attentive colour to key speeches.

19 McMullan, '"The Neutral Term"?', 117.

20 The 1919 re-issue of the original 1914 print of the film, directed by Baldassare Negroni, is now commercially available, with English intertitles, on the British Film Institute DVD *Play On! Shakespeare on Silent Film*. A Buchanan expert voice-over commentary to the film is included as a DVD extra.

21 On the significance of Milano, see Rafaelle de Berti and Giorgio Bertellini, 'Milano Films: The Exemplary History of a Film Company of the 1910s', *Film History* v.12, n.3 (2000), 276–87.

22 While less than obvious stablemates (not least in the time gap between them), the paucity of other wordless productions of this play suggests the alignment. Three other films of *The Winter's Tale* were made in the silent era: by Edison (1909), Cines (1910) and Thanhouser (1910). Of these, the Edison and Cines are presumed lost; the Thanhouser survives but its final scene is missing. It is available to view free online through the Thanhouser website, with a Buchanan voice-over commentary, at: thanhouser.org/films/winter_tale.htm. I can find no record of any prior ballet of *The Winter's Tale*.

WORKS CITED

Anderson, Z., review of *The Winter's Tale*, directed by Christopher Wheeldon, The Royal Ballet, Royal Opera House at Covent Garden, *The Independent*, 11 April 2014, 44.

Buchanan, J., '"Un Cinéma Impur": Framing Film in the Early Film Industry', in S. Allen and L. Hubner (eds.), *Framing Film: Cinema and the Visual Arts* (Bristol: Intellect, 2012), 238–260.

Bullough, G. (ed.), *Narrative and Dramatic Sources of Shakespeare*, vol. VIII, *Romances* (London: Routledge & Kegan Paul, 1975).

Crisp, C., review of *The Winter's Tale*, directed by Christopher Wheeldon, The Royal Ballet, Royal Opera House at Covent Garden, *Financial Times*, 14 April 2014, Arts Section, 13.

Crompton, S., review of *The Winter's Tale*, directed by Christopher Wheeldon, The Royal Ballet, Royal Opera House at Covent Garden, *The Telegraph*, 11 April 2014, 25.

de Berti, R. and Bertellini, G., 'Milano Films: The Exemplary History of a Film Company of the 1910s', *Film History* 12.3 (2000), 276–87.

Derrida, J., *Of Grammatology*, trans. Gayatri Chakravorty Spivak (Baltimore, MD and London: Johns Hopkins University Press, 1976).

Gluck, C. W., *Orfeo ed Euridice*, 1762 opera (original libretto by Ranieri de Calzabigi).

Golding, A. (trans.), *The XV Bookes of P. Ovidius Naso, entytuled Metamorphosis* (London: Willyam Seres [1567]).

Gorky, M., review of the Lumière programme at the Nizhny-Novgorod Annual Fair, 'The Kingdom of Shadows', *Nizhegorodski listok*, 4 July 1896, reprinted in C. Harding and S. Popple (eds.), *In the Kingdom of Shadows: A Companion to Early Cinema* (London: Cygnus Arts; Teaneck, NJ: Fairleigh Dickinson University Press, 1996), 5–6.

Greene, R., *Pandosto, The Triumph of Time* (London: Thomas Orwin, 1588).

Jennings, L., review of *The Winter's Tale*, directed by Christopher Wheeldon, The Royal Ballet, Royal Opera House at Covent Garden, *The Observer*, 13 April 2014, The New Review section, 30.

Kermode, F., *The Sense of an Ending* (Oxford: Oxford University Press, 1966; repr. 2000).

Mackrell, J., review of *The Winter's Tale*, directed by Christopher Wheeldon, The Royal Ballet, Royal Opera House at Covent Garden, *The Guardian*, 11 April 2014, 56.

McMullan, Gordon, '"The Neutral Term"?: Shakespearean Tragicomedy and the Idea of the "Late Play"', in S. Mukherji and R. Lyne (eds.), *Early Modern Tragicomedy* (Cambridge: Boydel and Brewer, 2007), 115–32.

Mowll Mathews, N., 'Art and Film: Interactions', in M. and C. Musser (eds.), *Moving Pictures: American Art and Early Film 1880–1910* (Manchester, VT: Hudson Hills Press, 2005), 145–158.

Nuttall, A. D., '*The Winter's Tale*: Ovid Transformed', in A. B. Taylor (ed.), *Shakespeare's Ovid: The Metamorphoses in the Plays and Poems* (Cambridge: Cambridge University Press, 2000), 135–49.

Ovid, *Metamorphoses*, 2 vols, trans. F. Justus Miller, rev. G. P. Goold (Cambridge, MA: Harvard University Press, 1916).

CHAPTER 8

Shakespeare's Puppets
The Tempest *and* The Winter's Tale *in the* Animated Tales

Maddalena Pennacchia

When writing about Shakespeare's romances, Northrop Frye famously defined them as 'popular plays', meaning that they meet 'the audience response at its most fundamental level'.[1] More interestingly yet, Frye stated that 'there's a close affinity between the romances and the most primitive (and therefore most enduring) forms of drama, like the puppet show', further explaining his opinion in terms of a 'scaling down of characters'.[2] For example, according to the Canadian critic, the titanic size of Othello's jealousy is considerably dwindled in Leontes' performance. In addition to this, dramatic circumstances do not seem to occur for plausible reasons in the romances, where characters move instead in a world of magic and classical myth:

> If you watch a good puppet show for very long you almost get to feeling [sic] that the puppets are convinced that they're producing all the sounds and movements themselves, even though you can see that they're not. In the romances, where the incidents aren't very believable anyway, the sense of puppet behavior extends so widely that it seems natural to include a god or goddess as the string puller.[3]

Frye's analogy between romances and puppet shows is particularly intriguing when one happens to consider two remarkable adaptations for children of *The Tempest* (1992) and *The Winter's Tale* (1994), both directed by Stanislav Sokolov for the television series of the *Animated Tales from Shakespeare*. In these adaptations the performers are handcrafted puppets that appear to move thanks to an extremely refined stop-motion technique, beautifully mastered by Sokolov, one of the most talented Russian film directors in the field of animation.[4] Before going further in the

I would like to thank Victoria Bladen and Peter Smith who responded with insightful remarks to the paper I delivered for the 'Shakespeare on Screen – The Romances' seminar, convened by Sarah Hatchuel and Nathalie Vienne-Guerrin at the 'Shakespeare 450 Congress' in Paris (April 2014). I treasured their questions and suggestions.

analysis, however, a few words will serve to introduce the *Animated Tales from Shakespeare*, a television project launched at the beginning of 1990s by S4C, the Welsh language TV channel, in collaboration with the Russian Soyuzmultfilms, the prestigious state-run cartoon and animation studio established in Moscow in 1936.[5]

From its inception, the project had a clear didactic aim, in imitation of Charles and Mary Lamb's *Tales from Shakespeare* (1807); it addressed a global audience, preferably made up of children but also of people who needed to be introduced to Shakespeare in their adult age. The first series of six adaptations was broadcast by the BBC in 1992 and was followed, two years later, in 1994, by a second series of six further adaptations; thus, only twelve adaptations out of Shakespeare's thirty-six Folio plays were produced. The making of the *Animated Tales* was, indeed, a brave collaboration between East and West in the name of Shakespeare: the plays were at first drastically abridged by British writer Leon Garfield, the celebrated author of *Shakespeare Stories* (1985), who only kept those lines that, in his opinion, were capable of driving the story forward, while also introducing a narrator (who in the film turns into a voice-over) in order to fill in any information gaps; the scripts (which were afterwards published separately) were recorded in the Welsh studios by actors mainly trained at the Royal Shakespeare Company and subsequently sent to the Russian visual artists who worked to create images that could match the 30-minute audio-tracks. The Russian artists had leeway to make slight changes in the scripts when they thought it necessary to strengthen their own take on the story, either cutting out more words or, in some cases, using different lines from those chosen by Garfield. The correspondence between scripts and films is therefore far from identical. By way of example, the importance of the Russian origin of Hermione, who is the daughter of the Emperor of Russia (3.2.117), is understandably given unusual emphasis in the adaptation of *The Winter's Tale* (1994). While, in Garfield's version of the romance in *Shakespeare Stories II* (1994), no hint is made to this piece of information, in the adaptation and its published script, Garfield's *Shakespeare: The Animated Tales* (2002), Hermione speaks all the lines referring to her father in the sequence of the trial: 'The Emperor of Russia was my father/O, that he were alive, and here beholding/His daughter's trial! that he did but see/The flatness of my misery – yet with eyes/Of pity, not revenge' (3.2.117–21). In addition to this, the camera shows for a few seconds the detail of her necklace and its medallion, that is a miniature likeness of the Russian Emperor, her father. According to Daryl Palmer, the conjuring of the Russian Emperor in the play is not only to be related to the presence of the bear onstage but generally understood as a reminder of the legendary ferociousness of Ivan IV.[6] Interestingly, in the animation the features of Hermione's father seem precisely to be drawn on Ivan IV's, thus almost offering a sort of visual rendering of such interpretations.

The *Animated Tales* enjoyed great success; they were soon translated into several languages and broadcast all over the world. They also rapidly became a series of twelve separate videotape cassettes, thus turning from a transient televised message into products to be used and watched at will in private homes; they were afterwards copied from analogue to digital recording in 2005. The whole series has since been made available as a DVD set entitled *Shakespeare: The Animated Tales*, which offers interactive menus with subtitles, a *Shakespeare Timeline* file and two documentaries, *The Making of the Animated Tales* and the *Shakespeare Schools Festival*.[7] The DVD set presents the series as the definitive canon of Shakespeare for children by grouping the plays into three separate discs not according to their chronological order of production or their different artistic techniques, but rather imitating the Folio's well-known division in Comedies, Histories and Tragedies. The series displays a variety of animation techniques, from traditional painting on celluloid to more experimental modes – such as a highly artistic oil painting on glass – to stop-motion animation of puppets.

Soyuzmultifilm has owned a very efficient puppet division since 1954 that is considered a flagship of the studio; this may have led to the decision to put on no fewer than four puppet adaptations of Shakespeare out of the twelve animations in the television series. Namely, *The Tempest* directed by Stanislav Sokolov and *Twelfth Night* directed by Mariya Muat in the first series (1992); *The Winter's Tale*, directed by Sokolov, as well as *The Taming of the Shrew* directed by Aida Zyablikova in the second series (1994). Despite the specific approaches to Shakespeare chosen by each director, the Soyuzmultifilm's puppets all look stylistically very similar; in other words, they are immediately recognizable as artefacts of the Russian Studio: they are sophisticated 9-inch doll-like puppets, fit to represent high-rank characters, with delicate and naturalistic features and richly embroidered, laced clothes. Their exquisite workmanship brings back to mind the 'marionette' tradition of court culture.[8]

For the sake of clarity, let us specify that when a puppet is worn on the hand, it should be called a *burattino*; conversely when it is pulled by strings, it is referred to as a *marionetta*. The 'marionette theatre', according to Birgit Beumer, was brought to Russia only in the eighteenth century, under the Empress Anna Ivanovna (1730–40) who also imported the *commedia dell'arte* with its masks to the Russian court. Marionettes were thus part of court culture, whereas handheld and glove finger puppets were part of folk traditions and had their place among the people.[9]

The distinction between a *burattino* and a *marionetta* is also meaningful, as Susan Young makes clear, with respect to the kind of relationship that each type of performing object entertains with the performer's body:

> The relationship between a *burattinaio* and the *burattino* is very close and immediate because the *burattino* becomes an extension of the body of its animator and usually speaks with his voice. The *marionetta* however is separated physically from its operator by the length of the strings, and psychologically by the slight delay in the action as it is transmitted and by the fact that it is often someone other than the *marionettista* who gives voice to the *marionette*.[10]

The traditional difference between *marionette* and handheld puppets should, therefore, be understood both in terms of class distinctions and of the different relationship that the two forms create between puppets and puppeteers.

It is, indeed, the 'puppeteer theme' that Northrop Frye discerns as characteristic of both *The Tempest* and *The Winter's Tale*.[11] Textual evidence that Prospero sees himself as a puppeteer is to be found in the play-text and precisely in the abjurement monologue, when the sorcerer conjures up his magical servants for the last time addressing them as 'demi-puppets' (5.1.36). Because the text legitimizes the analogy between Prospero and a puppeteer, we may push the argument further and suppose that Shakespeare may have been inspired to compare Prospero to a puppeteer because he actually attended puppet shows in London. According to Frances K. Barasch, this might have been the case; in her essay on the topic, she states that the first testimony of the presence of Italian *marionettisti* and *burattinai* in Elizabethan London can be traced back to the 1573 Privy council minutes of July 14. The account records the summary of a letter addressed to the Mayor by 'certain Italian plaiers' who asked for permission 'to make shewe of an instrument of strainge motiones within the Citie';[12] after carefully examining a number of occurrences of the words 'puppet', 'interpreter' and 'motions' in Shakespeare's plays, Barasch can safely state that 'Shakespeare's allusions to "motions," comic "devices," and "puppets," along with Italian settings, phrases, and commedia theatergrams, suggest themselves as evidence of a continuous presence of Italian puppet theatre in England since the 1570s'.[13] It is not therefore outlandish to believe that aesthetic patterns of a centuries-old popular entertainment like the puppet show might have left a trace in Shakespeare's text; a trace that can be excitingly reactivated in new readings, performances and adaptations.

In fact, as I see it, the Shakespearean text is endowed with an extraordinary intermedial energy, ready to be released and circulated again at each new reading, performance and adaptation. Born between stage and page at a time when oral and written culture were not yet separated by an insurmountable divide – a situation that, with due difference, is present also in the digital age[14] – the Shakespearean text is charged with the power not only of many literary genres (i.e. forms that have to do with the written letter, the *litera* and its favourite medium, the printed book) but also of non-literary entertainments (including performing and visual arts), either popular or aristocratic (bear-baiting, puppet shows, magic illusions, courtly and popular dances, ballads and songs and also painting, sculpture and so forth), each referring to a specific medium; in other words, Shakespeare's writing (with its peculiar '*litera*-ry' quality) is not only 'unstable',[15] but does seem to possess an 'intermedial predisposition' and, consequently, an unusual aptitude for adaptation that has always enabled it to bear up with ease the crossing of arts and media boundaries.[16]

It may be no accident therefore that *The Tempest* inspired a critically celebrated Italian adaptation by Eugenio Monti Colla for the 'marionette theatre' in 1985.[17] The adaptation was performed for the first time at the Teatro Goldoni, in Venice, for the 'Biennale di Venezia' by the legendary Italian Puppet Company of 'Carlo Colla e Figli' ('Carlo Colla & Sons'). The Collas put on a show that has since made history: their astonishing *marionette* performed the play to the sound of the recorded voice of the much acclaimed Neapolitan actor and playwright, Eduardo De Filippo.[18] De Filippo had not only produced a creative translation of the play into Neapolitan dialect in 1983; he had also recorded, before dying, a dramatic reading of the translation, in which he played all the characters with the exclusion of Miranda. That recording – painstakingly edited by De Filippo's son, Luca – was used as the 'soundtrack' of the Collas' production. The fact that 'Prospero's voice' plays all the roles in that production inevitably strengthens the metatheatrical idea that every action onstage is determined by Prospero's will; conversely, it also suggests that those actions may be taking place in his mind only (a lonely man on a deserted island, prey to his own unleashed imagination). It is interesting to notice that this theatrical device can be found again at work, but turned into a film technique, in Peter Greenaway's *Prospero's Books* (1991), where John Gielgud's voice often intrusively adds itself onto the other actors' voices, speaking over their lines (see, on this topic, Victoria Bladen's and Russell Jackson's chapters in this volume).

Differently from the Collas' adaptation, however, Soyuzmultfilm's is a re-mediation of puppet theatre into cinema through the stop-motion animation technique, one of the most fascinating forms of film illusionism. Here is a telling description by the famous practitioner Barry J. C. Purves who writes about stop motion in terms of a 'magic show':

> Having watched dozens of magic shows, there is one inescapable moment essential to every trick: there has to be a moment of misdirection, and it's in this split second that the mechanics of the trick happens unseen...For animators, that moment of misdirection is...a black frame that does not register with the audience, and allows the animator, acting as both magician and glamorous assistant, to step in and tinker with the puppets, rearranging everything before stepping out again, as if nothing had happened. The audience hasn't seen us, but they see the trick. The puppet appears to have moved.[19]

Mariya Muat, who directed *Twelfth Night* for the *Animated Tales from Shakespeare*, interestingly explains her work at Soyuzmultfilm's puppet division:

> The puppets are built around a flexible metal skeleton which we can manipulate in any way we like. We move the puppets frame by frame. During filming, we take a shot of the puppet, move it, take another shot, and so on. When you play this back at twenty-four frames per second, you get realistic movement.[20]

It is only through the medium specificity of cinema, therefore, that the film puppeteer creates the illusion of movement; his/hers is a magical art that animates stringless puppets as if they were alive. The physical relationship between puppet and puppeteer is now hidden by and inside the camerawork: no strings are visible unless the film director wants them to be seen as a quote of the remediated medium.[21] In *The Tempest*, for example, Ariel's wires can often be distinctly seen, even though the flying puppet appears to be diaphanous on screen thanks to a fade in and fade out superimposition technique; the visible wires device emphasizes the puppet's link to its puppeteer, or, to put it differently, the sprite's slavery relationship to its wizard master.

Laurie Osborne has rightly drawn attention to the fact that in Sokolov's *Tempest* 'the puppets and their carefully manipulated movements enabled an exploration of Prospero's magical abilities to control stillness and motion'.[22] To further expand this brilliant intuition, we may add that stop-motion animation calls attention to the way cinema works, that is, its ability in creating movement out of photographic stillness through the manipulation of time, thus blurring the boundaries between animate and inanimate bodies. If the absolute control of movement that cinema exerts on all kinds of bodies through its mastery over time is highlighted in the animated *Tempest* and *Winter's Tale*, however, this can happen only because that issue is already there in the original text. *The Tempest* is very much concerned with the function of time in the theatre[23] and, as always happens with well-made adaptations, the animated romances bring to the fore such a concern by remediating it.

Magic as one of the most important themes in the two plays is often represented as an obsession with the power to dominate human bodies through a cunning management of theatrical time. In the animated *Tempest*, this dynamic becomes evident, for example, when Ferdinand tries to react to the magician's accusation that he is a usurper and is stopped still by him; the dramatic interaction between the two characters draws our attention to Ferdinand being a puppet whose movements are determined from the outside (as in the stop-motion technique) and Prospero being a puppet who participates in a superior diegetic level, thus representing onstage the function of the puppeteer.

Prospero, the mighty enchanter who is in control of the narrative is not the only character empowered with such a gift. In *The Winter's Tale*, Paulina acts as Prospero's female counterpart: she is, indeed, a powerful woman who knows more than the other characters do and, at the end of the play, puts on a 'magic' show to reanimate the supposedly dead queen through the medium of music. It is King Leontes who orientates the audience towards seeing her as a 'mankind witch' (2.3.67) and a 'hag' (2.3.107) when she stubbornly presents him with his newly born daughter. And it is King Leontes, again, who confirms his former opinion, although in a positive light, when she brings his wife (or her replica), back to life: 'If this be magic, let it be an art/Lawful as eating' (5.3.110–11). In contrast to the drastic textual cuts, these lines are all preserved in the animated *Winter's Tale*, thus acquiring greater relevance and meaning. More explicitly than in *The Tempest*, magic is identified in *The Winter's Tale* with the art of provoking astonishment through a 'prestige', or trick of the eye, which seems to control time by stopping it and making it flow again at will. Intriguingly, in order to make time flow again, both Paulina and Prospero need the aid of music, the most time-based of all arts. The lines 'Music, awake her, strike!' in *The Winter's Tale* (5.3.98) and 'when I have required/Some heavenly music . . . /I'll break my staff' in *The Tempest* (5.1.51–4) are duly kept in the shortened scripts of the animated romances.

The control over time that is exerted by Paulina, as a witch, and Prospero, as a sorcerer, should also be linked to the control over the natural cycle of death and rebirth which is made more explicit in *The Winter's*

Tale through the scene of Hermione's 'resurrection'. According to Jane Bottoms, what impairs these adaptations is precisely a lack of time – for time is needed by the audience in order to develop a correct sense of the characters' psychological depth and complexity:

> what human drama requires is time, and time is precisely what the *Animated Tales* lack. Their essential feature is length – 26 minutes of playing time ... What is lost is depth and human complexity, something that requires time to build.[24]

As far as the animated romances are concerned, however, the already cited 'primitive' form of this specific genre benefits from the extreme compression of the time of performance; this very compression offers us an opportunity to immediately perceive the cyclic pattern that structures the plays. This may be considered as a specific achievement of the Welsh-Russian production – especially when we think that one of its explicit aims is to prepare the viewer for a more thorough and deep experience of the original play-texts.

More to the point, Frye noticed that the romances are organised as diptychs with the topical scene of the tempest usually operating as a temporal hinge between 'before' and 'after'. This is particularly evident in *The Winter's Tale* where the first and the second part of the play stand against each other with opposite myths and genres: winter vs spring, death vs resurrection, old age vs youth, tragedy vs comedy. Such a structure is endorsed in the play by the appearance onstage of the (male) personification of Time announcing the passing of sixteen years (4.1.5–6). In the Welsh-Russian adaptation, the diptych structure is visually enhanced by a representation of Time as a winged female character, shown to avoid repetition of represent/ representation (see above) as a fantastical creature midway between a Christian angel and a classical goddess, who soars over a spring pastoral landscape thus leading the viewer into the setting of the 'regeneration'. Similarly, in the animated *Tempest*, the 'primitive' structure that is hidden in the play comes to be highlighted. Twelve years have passed from the events that happened in Milan and Miranda has turned fifteen; but while in the original text a lengthy narration of those events is made by Prospero to his daughter soon after the tempest (1.2.36–187), in the adaptation, the story of what happened in Milan is moved to the beginning when a voice-over narrator (who is not Prospero) briefly explains the tragic fate of the 'Duke of Milan' (1.2.58); only after the explanation has begun can the scene of the tempest take place and the 'regeneration' start.

The theme of resurrection and spring is related in the romances to younger generations and in particular to daughters, whose healing function has been studied by a number of critics.[25] In Sokolov's adaptations, however, the role of young female characters is greatly downplayed; the number of lines they are actually assigned in the animated romances is inferior even to that in Garfield's scripts, which had, in their turn, already been drastically cut if compared to the narrative versions in *Shakespeare Stories I* and *II*, in a process of progressive oversimplification.[26] It follows that these young women, to which a feminized Ariel should be added, appear as selfless doll-like puppets, never stirred by the faintest glimpse of self-awareness or instinctive rebellion as they are in the Shakespearean plays. Interestingly, even though adult female characters are given enough dramatic space in the adaptation of *The Winter's Tale*, a misogynistic vision seems to surface there – women are Janus-faced creatures, showing themselves either as patient white-clad Madonna (Hermione) or shrewd red-haired Witch (Paulina).

Such a distorted vision of femininity is surely Leontes' own in the original play, and the adaptation cleverly stresses such a crucial point by making the hallucinatory state of the king visible in a scene where malignant sprites circle his head, tormenting him with flames and driving him to a fit of violent madness against his daughter. In line with this approach, the adaptation gives considerable importance to a pair of eyeglasses (that are not mentioned in the play-text) and may symbolically hint, in the animation, at the issue of visual disturbances.[27] As a prop that characterizes the figure of the faithful courtier, Antigonus, the eyeglasses are broken when he is chased and devoured by the bear; they are retrieved by the clowns who treasure them together with the baby's dowry and finally they are presented many years later as evidence of Perdita's noble origins. Paulina receives them soon after the resurrection scene. Only then, when the King's correct perspective is finally restored, can the broken eyeglasses be wrapped in a handkerchief and put away forever.

One final reflection may be devoted to Frye's observation that if '*The Tempest* has a human puppeteer in Prospero . . . [i]n the *Winter's Tale* the question "Who's pulling the strings?" is more difficult to answer; but it still seems to be relevant'. In fact, 'it is Apollo, the Greek god of music and poetry, who seems to "direct" the actions "from above"'.[28] These acute remarks invite us to think further on aspects of control and agency in the two play-texts and their adaptations. If we consider Prospero as a kind of puppeteer, we are compelled to ask ourselves what it means for Prospero himself to be represented as a puppet. Comparatively, we cannot but wonder what is the role of Apollo with respect to Paulina. Answers to these questions can only be tentative at the end of this chapter, and yet I would like to suggest that if 'Shakespeare's plays are centrally, repeatedly concerned with the production and containment of subversion and disorder', as Stephen Greenblatt famously writes,[29] this is all the more true for the romances, where the containment of subversion, I think, takes – metatheatrically speaking – the form of a 'script' directing as 'from above' the dramatic destiny of all characters. The '*litera*' of the script appears onstage in both romances in the form of props capable of signifying 'writing': Prospero's 'book' (5.1.57) in *The Tempest* and Apollo's 'sealed-up oracle' (3.2.125) in *The Winter's Tale*.[30] The animated romances do not fail to spot the crucial importance of these objects and give them visual emphasis, thus proving once again an extraordinary ability to preserve momentous elements of the plays even while editing out a sizeable chunk of text.

Notes

1 N. Frye, 'Shakespeare's Romances: *The Winter's Tale*', in R. Sandler (ed.), *Northrop Frye on Shakespeare* (New Haven and London: Yale University Press, 1986), 154.

2 Frye, 'Shakespeare's Romances', 155.

3 *Ibid.*

4 Stanislav Sokolov, Chair of Animation and Computer Graphics at the prestigious *Gerasimov Institute of Cinematography* (VGIK) in Moscow, is the director of many famous animation films. He is currently working on an ambitious project called *Gofmaniada*, based on Hoffman's tales, to be finished, as it seems, in the near future.

5 I have more broadly dealt with this topic in 'Shakespeare for Beginners: *The Animated Tales* from Shakespeare and the Case Study of *Julius Caesar*', in A. Müller (ed.), *Adapting Canonical Texts in Children's Literature* (London and New York: Bloomsbury Academic, 2013), 59–75.

6 See D. W. Palmer, 'Jacobean Muscovites: Winter, Tyranny, and Knowledge in *The Winter's Tale*', *Shakespeare Quarterly* 46.3 (1995), 323–39.

7 With respect to the important changes that have been brought about by digital home video, see R. Burt and L. E. Boose (eds.), *Shakespeare the Movie, II: Popularizing the Plays on Film, TV, Video, and DVD* (London and New York: Routledge, 2003), 1–13.

8 It was probably to this kind of 'marionette theatre' that the task of adapting literary classics for didactic aims was mostly assigned in Eastern Europe, as Pyotr Bogatyrev – the expert in folk theatre who participated in the Moscow Linguistic School and the Prague Linguistic Circle together with Roman Jakobson – makes clear. In an important article of 1923 that was translated from Russian

into English in 1999 and is considered by many as a cornerstone of the performing object theory, he writes: '[p]uppet theatre in Czechoslovakia is used as a pedagogical tool. More often than not children experience their first contact with native literature and folktales in schools by means of puppet theatre . . . In one Czech middle school, *Elektra* and *Hamlet* were staged in the puppet theatre. For the production of *Elektra*, an exact replica of a Greek stage was built. The performance was directed by one of Czechoslovakia's best scholars of classical theatre, University Professor [Josef] Král. The students themselves operated the puppets and spoke their lines. It is not uncommon for elementary school children to participate in puppet theatre productions'. P. Bogatyrev, M. Minnick, 'Czech Puppet Theatre and Russian Folk Theatre', *TDR* 43.3 (1999), 98.

9 See B. Beumers, *Pop Culture Russia! Media, Arts and Lifestyle* (Santa Barbara, CA: ABC Clio, 2005), 160.

10 See S. Young, *Shakespeare Manipulated: The Use of the Dramatic Works of Shakespeare in* Teatro di Figura *in Italy* (Cranbury, NJ and London: Associated University Press, 1996), 16.

11 Frye, 'Shakespeare's Romances', 155.

12 Quoted in F. K. Barasch, 'Shakespeare and the Puppet Sphere', *English Literary Renaissance* 34 (2004), 162.

13 *Ibid.*, 167.

14 See, for instance, R. Neil and J. Sawday (eds.), *The Renaissance Computer: Knowledge Technology in the First Age of Print* (London and New York: Routledge, 2000).

15 On the instability of Shakespeare's text, see, obviously, E. A. J. Honigmann, *The Stability of Shakespeare's Text* (London: Edward Arnold, 1965).

16 See M. Pennacchia, *Shakespeare intermediale. I drammi romani* (Spoleto: Editoria e Spettacolo, 2012), 13–51.

17 A fascination with puppets also inspired Pier Paolo Pasolini's short film *Che cosa sono le nuvole* in 1967. See, for instance, S. Massai, 'Subjection and Redemption in Pasolini's *Othello*', in S. Massai (ed.). *Worldwide Shakespeares: Local Appropriations in Film and Performance* (London and New York: Routledge, 2005), 95–103.

18 Eduardo De Filippo is one of the acknowledged great authors of 1900 Italian theatre. For his relationship with Shakespeare's plays, see A. Lombardo, *Eduardo e Shakespeare* (Roma: Bulzoni, 2004). For a study of his translation of *The Tempest* into Neapolitan dialect, see S. de Filippis, 'Shakespeare ed Eduardo: scrittura e riscrittura della *Tempesta*', in A. Lombardo (ed.), *Shakespeare e il Novecento* (Roma: Bulzoni, 2002), 187–206.

19 B. J. C. Purves, *Stop Motion: Passion, Process and Performance* (Amsterdam: Focal Press, 2008), 3.

20 The interview is included in the 'Making of' documentary of the DVD set.

21 Interestingly, even though the appearance of Soyuzmultfilm's puppets recalls the aristocratic tradition of *marionetta*, there is also much hands-on practice in

the stop-motion technique that makes it also akin to the art of *burattini*. The manipulation of puppets in the stop-motion animation technique is described by practitioners in terms of a sensual physical proximity. On this, see Purves, *Stop Motion*, 207–10.

22 See L. Osborne, 'Mixing Media and Animating Shakespeare Tales', in R. Burt and L. E. Boose (eds.), *Shakespeare the Movie, II: Popularizing the Plays on Film, TV, Video, and DVD* (London and New York: Routledge, 2003), 144.

23 Prospero's obsession with time has been recently reconsidered in S. Bigliazzi and L. Calvi (eds.), *Revisiting 'The Tempest': The Capacity to Signify* (Houndmills, Basingstoke and New York: Palgrave Macmillan, 2014), see in particular A. Serpieri's and S. Bigliazzi's chapters in Part II, 95–136.

24 J. Bottom, 'Speech, Image, Action: Animating Tales from Shakespeare', *Children's Literature in Education* 32.1 (2001), 9–10.

25 See, for instance, M. De Sapio Garbero, *Il bene ritrovato. Le figlie di Shakespeare dal* King Lear *ai Romances* (Roma: Bulzoni, 2005).

26 L. Garfield, *Shakespeare: The Animated Tales* (London: Egmont Books, 2002).

27 For a fascinating interpretation of *The Winter's Tale* in the context of early modern anatomical studies of the eye and debates on optics and Renaissance perspective, see M. Del Sapio Garbero, 'A Spider in the Eye/I: The Hallucinatory Staging of the Self in Shakespeare's *The Winter's Tale*', in U. Berns (ed.), *Solo Performances: Staging the Early Modern Self in England* (Amsterdam and New York: Rodopi, 2010), 133–55.

28 Frye, 'Shakespeare's Romances', 155.

29 See S. Greenblatt, *Shakespearean Negotiations: The Circulation of Social Energy in Renaissance England* (Berkeley and Los Angeles: University of California Press, 1988), 40.

30 In *Cymbeline*, a similar prop, Jupiter's tablet, takes on an equally decisive role for the plot. In my reading of the play, the apparition of the tablet, that the God puts in Posthumus's hands in Act 5, marks the precise moment when the play is miraculously turned from 'tragedy' into 'comedy'. The shift happens as a result of the insistent requests made by the 'audience' (the ghosts) to the 'playwright' (Jupiter); in other words, giving way to the ghosts' unrelenting supplications, Jupiter decides to 'change' Posthumus's 'destiny,' literally re-writing the happy ending on the tablet that will become, later on, the key to the denouement of the whole play. See Pennacchia, *Shakespeare Intermediale*, 135–7.

WORKS CITED

Barasch, F. K., 'Shakespeare and the Puppet Sphere', *English Literary Renaissance* 34 (2004), 157–75.

Beumers, B., *Pop Culture Russia! Media, Arts and Lifestyle* (Santa Barbara, CA: ABC Clio, 2005).

Bigliazzi, S. and L. Calvi (eds.), *Revisiting 'The Tempest': The Capacity to Signify* (Houndmills, Basingstoke and New York: Palgrave Macmillan, 2014).

Burt, R. and L. E. Boose (eds.), *Shakespeare the Movie, II: Popularizing the Plays on Film, TV, Video, and DVD* (London and New York: Routledge, 2003).

Bogatyrev, P., Minnick, M., 'Czech Puppet Theatre and Russian Folk Theatre', *TDR* 43.3 (1999), 97–114.

Bottoms, J., 'Speech, Image, Action: Animating Tales from Shakespeare', *Children's Literature in Education* 32.1 (2001), 3–15.

de Filippis, S. 'Shakespeare ed Eduardo: scrittura e riscrittura della *Tempesta*', in A. Lombardo (ed.), *Shakespeare e il Novecento* (Roma: Bulzoni, 2002), 187–206.

Del Sapio Garbero, M., 'A Spider in the Eye/I: The Hallucinatory Staging of the Self in Shakespeare's *The Winter's Tale*', in U. Berns (ed.), *Solo Performances: Staging the Early Modern Self in England* (Amsterdam and New York: Rodopi, 2010), 133–55.

Il bene ritrovato. Le figlie di Shakespeare dal King Lear *ai* Romances (Roma: Bulzoni, 2005).

Frye, N., 'Shakespeare's Romances: *The Winter's Tale*', in R. Sandler (ed.), *Northrop Frye on Shakespeare* (New Haven and London: Yale University Press, 1986), 154–70.

Garfield, L., *Shakespeare Stories* (London: Puffin, 1997 [1985]).

Shakespeare Stories II (London: Puffin, 1998 [1994]).

Shakespeare: The Animated Tales (London: Egmont Books, 2002).

Greenblatt, S., *Shakespearean Negotiations: The Circulation of Social Energy in Renaissance England* (Berkeley and Los Angeles: University of California Press, 1988).

Honigmann, E. A. J., *The Stability of Shakespeare's Text* (London: Edward Arnold, 1965).

Lombardo, A., *Eduardo e Shakespeare* (Roma: Bulzoni, 2004).

Massai, S. 'Subjection and Redemption in Pasolini's *Othello*', in S. Massai (ed.), *Worldwide Shakespeares. Local Appropriations in Film and Performance* (London and New York: Routledge, 2005), 95–103.

Neil, R. and J. Sawday (eds.), *The Renaissance Computer: Knowledge Technology in the First Age of Print* (London and New York: Routledge, 2000).

Osborne, L., 'Mixing Media and Animating Shakespeare Tales', in R. Burt and L. E. Boose (eds.), *Shakespeare, the Movie, II: Popularizing the Plays on Film, TV, Video, and DVD* (London and New York: Routledge, 2003), 140–53.

Palmer, D. W., 'Jacobean Muscovites: Winter, Tyranny, and Knowledge in *The Winter's Tale*', *Shakespeare Quarterly* 46.3 (1995), 323–39.

Pennacchia, M., 'Shakespeare for Beginners: *The Animated Tales* from Shakespeare and the Case Study of *Julius Caesar*', in A. Müller (ed.), *Adapting Canonical Texts in Children's Literature* (London and New York: Bloomsbury, 2013), 59–75.

Shakespeare Intermediale. I Drammi Romani (Spoleto: Editoria e spettacolo, 2012).

Purves, B. J. C., *Stop Motion: Passion, Process and Performance* (Amsterdam: Focal Press, 2008).

Young, S., *Shakespeare Manipulated: The Use of the Dramatic Works of Shakespeare in Teatro di Figura in Italy* (Cranbury, NJ and London: Associated University Press, 1996.

CHAPTER 9

'Something Rich and Strange'
Jarman's Defamiliarisation of The Tempest

Peter J. Smith

The Tempest is a strange play and this strangeness resides in many forms.[1]
In spite of its being the last single-authored play that Shakespeare wrote,
it is the first play in the posthumously edited collection of his works, a
position of prominence noted by the glimpse of the blank pages at the
beginning of the last of *Prospero's Books* (1991): '*Thirty-Six Plays*. This is
a thick printed volume of plays dated 1623. All thirty-six plays are there
save one – the first. It is called *The Tempest*'.[2] In spite of Peter Greenaway's
apparent confidence in the play's canonical primacy, its foremost location
in Heminges and Condell's collection of Shakespeare's works serves only to
baffle its recent editors: 'Why *The Tempest* was given pride of place in the
Folio of 1623 is one of the book's minor mysteries'.[3] I will suggest in what
follows that while Greenaway's baroque and visually extravagant cinematic
version relies upon the conventional, not to mention, sentimental view of
the play as Shakespeare/Prospero/Gielgud's benevolent swansong, Derek
Jarman's 1979 adaptation with its youthful, acerbic and frequently cruel
Prospero, acknowledges the *strangenesses* of Shakespeare's play in order to
defamiliarize a complacent 'realist' tradition and undermine the comfortable assumptions about the Romances as being plays of forgiveness, resignation and restoration.[4] In spite of Jarman's protestation that 'The concept
of forgiveness in *The Tempest* attracted me', his film, while it ends in a splen-
didly camp troupe of horny horn-piping sailor-boys, does not attempt to
avoid the play's darker tones.[5]

I want to focus on just two of the play's unusual features – the portrayal of the protagonist and the masque – before considering the manner in which Jarman's film serves to portray them, warts and all. Unlike
Greenaway's epicurean or Julie Taymor's (2010) illusionist versions, Jarman's refusal to smooth out the play's roughnesses makes it, oddly, closer
to Shakespeare's work than might first appear.

Prospero

Shakespeare's play is set on a distant desert island governed over by a magician whose servants include a fairy and a monster. The strangeness of its *dramatis personae* barely masks the fact that, in narrative terms, not very much happens. Instead of intricacies of plot we have extravagant special effects which, in David Lindley's opinion, compel 'many modern reviewers [to] argue that *The Tempest* is more dramatic poem than play'.[6] Jarman's fidelity to Shakespeare's play is, in part, the film's sense that everything and nothing has changed by the end; nobody has suffered physical harm but through Jarman/Prospero's magical illusions, a drama of the psyche has been presented, a drama in which a young couple fall in love, a king repents his previous political iniquities and two ambitious courtiers are forced to confront their wicked past. Central to both these unfolding stories, and Jarman's realisation of them, is the figure of the magician himself, unsettled and unsettling, strange and estranged.

The magician is able to command the forces of nature: 'I have bedimmed/The noontide sun, called forth the mutinous winds,/And 'twixt the green sea and the azured vault/Set roaring war' (5.1.41–4). His own daughter is timidly aware of his capacity to stage tempests and threaten the lives of the ill-fated sailors who find themselves storm-tossed by his power: 'If by your art, my dearest father, you have/Put the wild waters in this roar, allay them' (1.2.1–2). Miranda seems to comprehend not only the callousness of Prospero's artificial tempest but also the moral implications of interfering with the forces of nature.

Now we have seen sailors victimized by artificial storms earlier in Shakespeare's theatrical career: because the sailor's wife refused to give the First Witch chestnuts to munch, the witch has promised to stage a storm upon which 'Though his bark cannot be lost,/Yet it shall be tempest-tossed' (*Macbeth*, 1.3.23–4). Both *Macbeth* and *The Tempest* open with foul weather – as Macbeth's very first words make clear, the day is miserable: 'So foul and fair a day I have not seen' (1.3.36). In *The Tempest*, Gonzalo talks of 'foul weather' and Antonio concedes it is 'Very foul' (2.1.138–9). In both plays the weather is indicative of a 'breach in nature' (*Macbeth*, 2.3.106) as the usurping Antonio and the invading Norway respectively challenge the rightful Duke of Milan and King of Scotland.

Jarman's take on this sinister atmosphere is implicit in his crepuscular settings. The beach scenes (filmed outside Bamburgh Castle) literally have the blues as camera gels darken and flatten natural colour into a sapphire gloom. Even Ferdinand's naked flesh is a frigid blue, while Ariel's white boiler suit takes on a bluish tint. Jarman's insistence on anti-illusionism is clear: 'The blue filters worked. I was desperately anxious that the exteriors should not look real, and chose the dunes at Bamburgh for their lack of features'.[7]

The interior shots appear to be lit only by open fires and candles and take us back to the chiaroscuro of Jarman's favourite painter, Caravaggio. The mysterious layout of Stoneleigh Abbey – one room opening onto another – the invasion of nature, dead leaves, dead butterflies, crawling spiders and squeaking rats, imbues the ruined mansion with a sense of valediction, reminiscent of Larkin's evocative phrase 'out on the end of an event'.[8] Lisa Hopkins underlines the importance of the house itself which 'becomes virtually a character in its own right' while Colin McCabe calls it 'an imperial monument'.[9] Though Jarman's film predates the interest in post-colonial readings of *The Tempest*, Virginia Mason Vaughan nonetheless finds in Stoneleigh Abbey the suggestion of 'the fruits, as well as the decay, of British colonialism'.[10] While Russell Jackson asserts that the 'post-colonial dimension of the play...is wholly absent in Jarman's film' in respect of the characterisation of Caliban who, although 'described in the opening credits as "a savage and deformed slave"...is really nothing of the kind', it is certainly the case that Jarman's troubled and violent Prospero is at least incipiently colonial.[11] At the very least, he has moved a long way from the Gandalfesque benevolence attributed to the magus by Frank Kermode's 1954 Arden edition of the play, the dramatic personification of which is Michael Hordern's Prospero for the BBC Shakespeare production, directed by John Gorrie and released in the same year as Jarman's version: 'Hordern's Prospero looks like an absent-minded professor who has forgotten his notes'.[12]

Kate Chedgzoy proposes that the ruined country house is a 'sardonic and critical contribution to the tradition of the stately home as microcosm of the national culture'.[13] Whether or not we choose to read the mansion's decay as a comment on the privations of Jim Callaghan's 'Winter of Discontent' (a suitably Shakespearean description of the film's immediate context), Jarman's adaptation is, for the most part, one of mourning, dedicated to the director's recently deceased mother.[14] Michael O'Pray describes it poignantly as a 'dream of a lost community'.[15]

In an interview with John Cartwright, shot the year before he died, Jarman fondly remembered arriving at Stoneleigh to begin shooting *The Tempest*. He notes the association of Shakespeare's play and the wedding of James I's daughter, Elizabeth, to Frederick, the Elector Palatine. Jarman suggests that she was married in the hall of Stoneleigh (in fact she was married at Whitehall) and he goes on to identify a picture there as her portrait:

> The day we got there we sort of thought, well this is serendipity – look, there she is, in the front hall, so maybe she'll look on us benevolently and we had a very wonderful time filming there. It was the middle of the winter; it was quite *magical*, the place was covered in snow.[16]

Stoneleigh Abbey has a sorcerous resonance for Jarman – a curious mixture of coincidence and historical precedent and, as we will see, his faith in the occult is an important aspect of his filmic style.

The title of our play derives from the word *tempestas*, Latin for 'the weather' and, in demonstrating his capacity to subdue nature, Prospero is, like the witches before him, acting in a profoundly unnatural way.[17] Even his friend, the kindly old Gonzalo is terrified: 'All torment, trouble, wonder, and amazement/Inhabits here. Some heavenly power guide us/Out of this fearful country!' (5.1.104–6). But Prospero is not merely guilty of usurping the role of what Gonzalo refers to as 'heavenly power' in his command over the elements. As his speech goes on to make explicit, his magic is even more sinister: 'Graves at my command/Have waked their sleepers, oped, and let 'em forth/By my so potent art' (5.1.48–50). That is, like the eternally and justly damned Doctor Faustus, Prospero is a necromancer, setting out and managing to speak with the dead. Faustus remarks on the limited climatic powers of earthly rulers: neither emperors nor kings are able to 'raise the wind or rend the clouds' (A: 1.1.61).[18] Aware of the inadequacies of potentates and bored by his Humanist erudition, Faustus longs for the power over life and death and the magus draws his circle within which he invokes the appearance of Mephistopheles. As Prospero draws his version of the magic circle (spectacularly realized as a wall of flame in Taymor's film), he too utters a spell:

> Ye elves of hills, brooks, standing lakes, and groves,
> And ye that on the sands with printless foot
> Do chase the ebbing Neptune, and do fly him
> When he comes back... (5.1.33–6)

Prospero summons not a devil from Hell, but a group which includes one who is no less diabolical to him: 'For you, most wicked sir, whom to call brother/Would even infect my mouth...' (5.1.130–1). What is commonly romanticized as one of Shakespeare's final plays, full of forgiveness and resolution, actually portrays a protagonist who is not unlike the witches in *Macbeth* or Marlowe's damnable magician.[19]

Jarman's fascination with the preternatural is well documented. Rowland Wymer insists that both Jarman and Heathcote Williams, who plays Prospero, 'were seriously interested in the Renaissance occult philosophy which influenced the play. They *believed* in the magic.'[20] Andrew Moor reads this sorcerous fascination in terms of gay politics: Jarman's reading of gay subculture is 'a cabbalistic activity which rests upon an alternative, esoteric language, known to an inner circle of preferred initiates. It is worth stressing that for Jarman, this subculture amounts metaphorically to a form of magic'.[21]

The early modern magician, Dr John Dee, was in many ways a model for the director's realisation of the play's protagonist. Dee's vision of an English dystopia had vexed the Virgin Queen in the earlier film, *Jubilee*, of 1978 – Jarman's apocalyptic reaction to the pomp of Elizabeth II's silver jubilee the previous year. But according to the designer of *The Tempest*, Yolanda Sonnabend, the figure of the magician was more than simply a narrative presence; it was also a form of self-identification: 'the presiding magus', she writes, 'was Derek [. . .] Derek was our Prospero'.[22]

Williams was himself a member of the Magic Circle and Jarman's own copy of Cornelius Agrippa's *De Occulta Philosophia* (1631) is one of Prospero's key hand properties. In Jarman's film, Prospero's study is daubed with magic characters, zodiacal symbols and recondite emblems. His wizard's staff is surmounted by Dee's Hieroglyphic Monad as well as a glass lens which allows an anachronistic dumbshow vision of a pre-exile Prospero with a tiny Miranda (played by Jarman's own niece, Kate Temple) in a *tableau vivant* – a cross between the device that will punctuate the later film, *Caravaggio* (1986), and the posed formality of a Victorian family daguerreotype.

Jarman writes of how he 'cut away the [play's] deadwood' (he was of course as well known for his horticultural as his cinematic innovations) but then needed to restore the play's wonder: 'The theatrical magic had to be replaced'.[23] Jarman considered filmmaking itself to be a 'potent art' while the enigmatic symbiosis between magic, the surreal and cinema goes all the way back to the sci-fi fantasies of the prolific and pioneering Georges Méliès, whose many films specialized in the creative deformation of time and space. For Jarman, such cinemagic creativity was both buoyant and enchanted and was directly inspired by a series of early modern Prosperos: 'Film is the wedding of light and matter – an alchemical conjunction. My readings in the Renaissance magi – Dee, Bruno, Paracelsus, Fludd and Cornelius Agrippa – helped to *conjure* the film of *The Tempest*'.[24] Magic merges with myth in Jarman's own version of the Faustus/Prospero arena: 'Setting up a film like this you form a magic circle, like King Arthur. Once the circle is complete it is impossible, fatal, to attempt to break it'.[25] It is noteworthy that the lines in which Shakespeare's Prospero abjures his rough magic, breaks his staff and buries his book do not appear in Jarman's film.[26]

But, in spite of such conjuration, Jarman is reluctant to realize the magic's efficacy. The play's now-you-see-it-now-you-don't banquet is cut. Ariel (Karl Johnson) appears not as a harpy but is prosaically elevated by standing on a mantelpiece. The chasing dogs (computer-generated, flaming mastiffs in Taymor's version) are simply Ariel and Prospero making woofing noises, while the sudden appearance of the rocking horse's head infantilizes their barking and stresses the fact that it is nothing more than a schoolboy prank. In Jarman's version, Ariel suddenly vanishes (twice) not by virtue of magic spells but by self-conscious, Mélièsque film trickery. In fact, while the film makes much of the effort with which Prospero studies arcane books and papers, there is very little to show for it. It is as though Prospero's solipsistic bibliophilia – which cost him his dukedom in the first place – has not been exorcized by his exile. While Chedgzoy argues that 'Jarman's *Tempest* emerges from the conjunction of magic and power', the film portrays a far from superhuman Prospero whose idea of pinching Caliban with cramps is to stamp on his hand – no mysterious magus but an irritated and spiteful playground bully.[27] McCabe's ingenious reading of Prospero as a personification of the ominous workings of the Elizabethan secret service is thus greatly exaggerated. Indeed, as McCabe later concedes, there is an 'absence of any real public political sphere in *The Tempest*'.[28] The violence of Prospero is neither magically orchestrated nor state-sponsored but rather personal, opportunistic and always spiteful.

From the opening sequence with Prospero's heavy breathing and restless sleeping, this is a portrait not of an ascendant magician but of one struggling to assert control. Wymer writes, 'The repeated cries of "We split! We split!" enact a nightmare of psychic disintegration rather than showing Prospero as in full magical control of the storm scene'.[29] For Kenneth S. Rothwell, the disintegration is as much that of the filmmaker as his protagonist, and demonstrates 'self-referentially Jarman's own split from conventional movie making'.[30] The waves are both driving Prospero's sighs and being driven by them. Chantal Zabus and Kevin A. Dwyer point to Prospero's being 'near demented and out-of-control' and, noting the 'half-empty wine bottles and glasses', they wonder if he 'may have taken to drink'.[31] What in the play is merely intimidation is realized in Jarman's film. In the play, Prospero terrifies Ariel with the prospect of being pegged into the entrails of an oak tree (1.2.295–6) and the servant is quickly brought to heel. But Jarman's vicious magician actually carries out this threat, pinioning Ariel behind a glass screen, his features crushed claustrophobically against it. Opportunistic sadism is clearly something this Prospero relishes. We see him roughly chaining Ferdinand's feet, cackling with sadistic laughter, and later, he stands over the sleeping prince with a raised axe, pondering the possibility of killing him on the spot. The assassination of a sleeping enemy is something the play assigns to the cowardly Sebastian and Antonio. The fact that Jarman's film also puts Prospero in that role serves to undermine his heroic status.

In an uncanny anticipation of *Prospero's Books*, Jarman's early draft of *The Tempest* had 'a mad Prospero, rightly imprisoned by his brother [and who] played all the parts'.[32] The final version has roles taken by different actors, of course, but Jarman's initial theory of Prospero's insanity, albeit transmuted into paranoia, still haunts the film. As Judith Buchanan writes, 'Heathcote Williams' Prospero is prey no longer to the delusions of the mad, but to the vexed fantasies of the terrified'.[33] As he vengefully approaches the exiles, he thrusts his staff before him, his head filling the frame, and almost looks directly into the camera: 'cure thy brains,/Now useless, boiled within thy skull' (5.1.59–60). It is as though his rage is directed at us. Williams, in an interview following the release of the film, described Prospero as 'a psychopath in a sensory deprived chamber'.[34]

The Masque

There emerges then a paradoxical relationship between Jarman's faith in the magic of filmmaking and the anxious impotence of his magician. Moreover, in its determination to underline such ambiguities, Jarman's film replicates the play's most disturbing feature: its capacity to foreground strangeness. The inexplicable nature of the events within *The Tempest* is something that the characters continually remark upon. The expression that resonates throughout the play, the key term which appears in the title of this essay, is *strange*.

While not every one of these instances makes it to Jarman's final cut, their cumulative effect is something that registers in his adaptation. As the Boatswain notes the newly restored condition of the previously wrecked ship, Alonso opines, 'These are not natural events, they strengthen/From strange to stranger' (5.1.227–8). Prospero tells Miranda that the proximity of his enemies to their island is down to 'accident most strange' (1.2.178). In the same way that she then falls into a sleep at the command of Prospero (186), so Alonso and Gonzalo are instantly overcome with exhaustion.

Sebastian remarks, 'What a strange drowsiness possesses them?' (2.1.194). Later in the same scene, as they are woken by Ariel in order to fore-stall the murderous conspiracy of the courtiers; Gonzalo muses that 'I heard a humming,/And that a strange one too' (315–16). Prospero concedes that Ferdinand has successfully remained untempted by Miranda's sexual charms: 'thou/Hast strangely stood the test' (4.1.6–7) and the magician compliments his supernatural assistants for their 'good life/And observa-tion strange' (3.3.86–7) while only eight lines later Gonzalo asks Alonso 'why stand you/In this strange stare?' (94–5). While the Boatswain notes the 'strange and several noises/Of roaring, shrieking, howling' (5.1.232–3) as he and the crew were confined below decks, Alonso draws attention to the bizarre landscape around them in a way which utilizes our key term while insisting that it is opposed to the natural scheme of things: 'This is as strange a maze as e'er men trod,/And there is in this business more than nature/Was ever conduct of' (242–4). Without hesitation, Prospero responds, attempting to allay these anxieties: 'Sir, my liege,/Do not infest your mind with beating on/The strangeness of this business' (245–7). While Prospero might succeed in fobbing Alonso off, the audience is intrigued by 'The strangeness of this business'. In *The Tempest* the inclusion of the word *strange* in three stage directions demonstrates that it is not just the Boatswain, Alonso, Gonzalo, Ferdinand, Francisco, Sebastian or Prospero (all of whom use the word) who regard the events on this desert island as peculiar – the playwright (if the stage directions are authorial), the scrivener (if, as is more likely the case, they are not) also drew attention to it.[35]

In 3.3 Ariel stages a magic banquet which effortlessly appears for the courtiers. The feast is heralded by the playing of '*Solemn and strange music, and [enter] Prospero on the top, invisible*' (SD following 3.3.17). Those involved in setting out the banquet are no ordinary waiters: '*Enter several strange shapes, bringing in a banquet, and dance about it with gentle actions of salutations, and inviting the king, etc. to eat, they depart*' (SD following 19). The music is '*strange*' and the banquet's bearers are '*strange*'. Moreover, the resonance of such a term is clear when we note that within twenty-one lines Francisco remarks that 'They vanished strangely' (40) – the word still echoing and requiring pronouncement by one of the otherwise almost silent lords in order that the audience may sit up and take notice of it. Fur-thermore, the appearance of the term *strange* is very specific and suggests that the effects being called for by the stage directions are unlike anything else seen heretofore in the public theatre.[36] This strange magical theatrical-ity is, of course, that made feasible to the King's Men by their move into the Blackfriars with its state-of-the-art lighting and sound facilities. Theatre historians have long been aware of the ways in which Shakespeare utilized cutting-edge technology in his late plays, mimicking the innovations and special effects of the Jacobean court masque.[37]

Given his obsession with magical illusion, it is no surprise to hear Jarman stressing the importance of this genre. In doing so he appears to be attempting to resurrect a kind of fantasy which subverts the apparent orthodoxies of realist representation: 'The masque . . . seems to have been lost, not only in the English theatre (Lindsay Kemp is in exile) but also in everyday life – it's such a vital element and so distrusted by chapel and Eng. Lit. *The Tempest* is a masque; what it lacks in the theatre productions I've seen, is a sense of fun. . . . Whatever is buried in the play, the surface must glitter and entertain'.[38] Note in passing Jarman's anti-chapel innovation of making Sebastian (Neil Cunningham) a cardinal who blesses Antonio (Richard Warwick) with a sign of the cross just before the attempted assassination of the sleeping Alonso (Peter Bull). Lindsay Kemp, who had so memorably performed an orgiastic dance at the opening of *Sebastiane* (1976), had left for the Continent in 1979 while the oppressions of Thatcherism stifled Jarman's 'sense of fun'.[39] In this light, Jarman's investment in the masque may be read as an act of political reaction, a symptom of what Pascale Aebischer describes as a 'disenchantment with the repressive politics of the present'.[40] But this fondness for the masque was also, evidently a lifelong obsession, as much an aesthetic pleasure as a political protest. Sonnabend describes the 'reflected light and magic' of parties she attended when she and Jarman were students together: 'In my mind I recall this masque-like levity'.[41] And she goes on to compare the costuming of Elisabeth Welch, singer of the film's *Stormy Weather*, to 'an Inigo Jones creation filtered through the movies' (see Figure 9.1).[42]

The masque in *The Tempest* is not, in conventional terms, a masque at all. David Norbrook insists on 'the ways in which [the] spectacle is *unlike* a court masque. [Prospero's] masque really is insubstantial, because as prince in exile he does not have any actors, musicians, and set-designers'.[43] Instead of the crowds of dignitaries in the Banqueting House jostling for position nearest the enthroned monarch, the onstage audience of this masque numbers just two – Ferdinand and Miranda – who crouch downstage, keeping as mum and as inconspicuous as possible.

The script of Shakespeare's masque is strangely discordant in various subtle ways. It mentions the river banks which are 'pionèd and twillèd' (4.1.64), that is, excavated and reinforced against flooding which suggests a cussedness in nature rather than its blithe cooperation.[44] Within the next few lines we hear of 'cold nymphs', 'chaste crowns', 'the dismissèd bachelor'

Figure 9.1. Elisabeth Welch singing 'Stormy Weather' in Jarman's 1979 *The Tempest*. All
rights reserved.

who is 'lass-lorn' and the vineyard which has been cut back (66–8). The
seashore is 'sterile and rocky-hard' (69) and Ceres' acres are not tended
but overgrown with bushes or 'unshrubbed' (81) – that is, infertile. The
'sun-burned sickle-men of August weary' (134) personify the exhausting
labour necessary to coax nature into giving up her foison. In the opinion of
Ernest B. Gilman, these are elements 'that reveal either the frigid extremes
of Prospero's mind, or glimpses of a harsher world that cannot quite be
exorcised'.[45]

Clearly the single most discordant element of Prospero's masque is its
ending – no tripping the light fantastic here in buoyant and elaborate revels,
rather a clunking and sudden destruction. The stage directions read:

> *Enter certain reapers, properly habited. They join with the nymphs, in a graceful
> dance, towards the end whereof Prospero starts suddenly and speaks, [. . .]. To
> a strange hollow and confused noise, [the spirits] heavily vanish* (SD following
> 138 and 143).

Rather than melting into air, Prospero's masque is clamourously demol-
ished. In this way, Shakespeare inverts the usual anti-masque/masque structure. Notice the reappearance of our key term – 'a *strange* . . . noise' – the

word seems to connote neither the mysteries of magic nor the arcane harmonies of neoplatonic abstractions but the shock of a memory which serves to disrupt the current entertainment: 'I had forgot that foul conspiracy/Of the beast Caliban and his confederates/Against my life' (139–41). In Shakespeare's play, Prospero's masque relies upon his faulty memory. In that way, it flourishes on the condition of its sponsor being forgetful and infirm. As soon as he remembers the conspiracy, the masque is done for. Rather than illustrate the invulnerability of Jacobean monarchy then, Prospero's masque demonstrates the perilousness of his authority.

Jarman's take on the masque reinforces the play's ambiguous attitude towards the tyrannical magus. To begin with, Prospero is neither author nor director of the masque as he is in Shakespeare's play. Here, the masque is introduced by a grinning Ariel who, in white tuxedo, acts as a welcoming master of ceremonies, precipitating a shower of marital confetti by dropping his hand, having gestured us towards the naval larks behind him. For Simon Ryle, the carnival festivity of the dancing sailors defies Prospero's authority: it is a 'rapturous and disharmonic anti-masque that Prospero would silence'.[46] It is the stunning brightness and full colour luxury of the scene which marks it out dramatically in contrast to the world of Prospero's dark deliberations. Maggie Taylor describes the dance as 'a human wave of happiness, which transforms Shakespeare's theme of reason into a celebration of the body, community and sexual freedom'.[47] The recklessly leaping sailors (the choreographer was the fortuitously named Stuart Hopps) constitute a joyful parody of Busby Berkeley synchrony and *HMS Pinafore* silliness.[48] Indeed, we might take the sequence as typifying what David Hawkes has identified throughout Jarman's work as the 'burning desire to undermine the normative sexuality assumed by the classical Hollywood cinema'.[49] The masque's campness does serve to undermine the heteronormative marriage it is designed to commemorate but the passionate denunciation (Hawkes's 'burning desire') is here altogether more cordial, the absence of Prospero's controlling presence allowing an atmosphere which is both sexually permissive and patriarchally unconstrained.

The slight untidiness of the dancing (at one point there is a near-miss between two vaulting sailors that looks quite unrehearsed) imbues the sequence with a spontaneous irreverence which is miles away from the formal revels of the Jacobean masque. For this reason, William Pencak's description of the sequence is wholly inaccurate, overestimating, as it does, the polish of the choreography: 'This precision dancing is art for people who like military parades and Vegas shows'.[50] The exactitude, order and symbolic harmony of the traditional masque is here replaced by a fervent and extemporaneous frivolity. Indeed, Buchanan suggests that, in their re-enactment of Caliban's daft prancing on the beach, the sailors' joyous cavorting defies Prospero's command: 'It is thus in an idealised form of Caliban's, not of Prospero's, image that the world is made anew'.[51] Jim Ellis shares this sense of optimism at the film's closure, emphasizing the inclusiveness of its audience: 'the masque is staged not just for Ferdinand and Miranda but, rather, for the whole community assembled at the end of the film (which now includes Caliban and the other rebels, who react with pleasure to the spectacle) . . . The film at this moment engulfs the viewer in an intensely pleasurable spectacle'.[52] The character missing is of course, Prospero, and the film ends with his complete isolation, *sans* Ariel, *sans* Miranda and without his even having adopted the 'thing of darkness' (5.1.274), Caliban.

Writing of the closing dance sequence, Douglas M. Lanier remarks on the way that the play's canonical status is challenged by the film: 'Jarman's approach critiques the politics of mainstream Shakespearean productions through camp, disrupting the play's status as an icon of straight high culture'.[53] It is this act of disruption or defamiliarisation, in respect of its stark characterisation of Prospero as well as its wholesale appropriation of the final masque sequence which makes Jarman's version of *The Tempest* both rich and strange.

Notes

1 Having written my introduction, I read David Lindley's *The Tempest: Shakespeare at Stratford* (Surrey: Thomas Nelson, 2003). His opening sentence: '*The Tempest* is in many ways a very odd play', 1. Earlier versions of the present chapter were delivered as conference papers in London and Paris in 2014 and I am grateful to the following for discussions at those events: Pascale Aebischer, Sarah Hatchuel, Gordon McMullan, Stéphanie Mercier and Nathalie Vienne-Guerrin. Neil Allan advised me on *Prospero's Books*. Deborah Cartmell, Kinga Földváry, Russell Jackson and David Salter all read earlier drafts and made some very useful suggestions.

2 P. Greenaway, Prospero's Books: *A Film of Shakespeare's* The Tempest (London: Chatto & Windus, 1991), 25.

3 *The Tempest*, edited by A. T. Vaughan and V. M. Vaughan, The Arden Shakespeare third series (London: Thomas Nelson, 1999), 124. By way of explanation, John Jowett proposes, 'Its status as one of Shakespeare's last plays and its courtliness of tone are two possible reasons why it was singled out in this way'. ('Varieties of Collaboration in Shakespeare's Problem Plays and Late Plays', in R. Dutton and J. E. Howard (eds.), *A Companion to Shakespeare's Works*, 4 vols (Oxford: Blackwell, 2003), vol. 4, 122).

4 For a thoughtful analysis of the Shakespeare/Prospero/Gielgud superimposition, see G. McMullan, *Shakespeare and the Idea of Late Writing: Authorship in the Proximity of Death* (Cambridge: Cambridge University Press, 2007), 331–7.

5 D. Jarman, *Dancing Ledge* (London: Quartet Books, 1984), 202.

6 Lindley, *Tempest*, 11.

7 Jarman, *Ledge*, 203.

8 P. Larkin, *The Whitsun Weddings* (London: Faber, 1974), 22.

9 L. Hopkins, *Screen Adaptations: Shakespeare's* The Tempest*: The Relationship between Text and Film* (London: Methuen Drama, 2008), 88. C. McCabe, 'A Post-National European Cinema: A Consideration of Derek Jarman's *The Tempest* and *Edward II*, in D. Petrie (ed.), *Screening Europe: Image and Identity in Contemporary European Cinema*, (London: British Film Institute, 1992), 13.

10 V. M. Vaughan, *The Tempest: Shakespeare in Performance* (Manchester: Manchester University Press, 2011), 180.

11 R. Jackson, *Shakespeare and the English-Speaking Cinema* (Oxford: Oxford University Press, 2014), 62.

12 *The Tempest*, edited by F. Kermode (London: Methuen, 1954); Vaughan, *The Tempest*, 177.

13 K. Chedgzoy, *Shakespeare's Queer Children: Sexual Politics and Contemporary Culture* (Manchester: Manchester University Press, 1995), 199.

14 The 'Winter of Discontent' refers to the winter of 1978–79 during which the Prime Minister, James Callaghan, attempted to control inflation by imposing public-sector pay control. This led to a series of strikes, most notably the gravediggers of Liverpool. There is a moving account of the death of Jarman's mother in Jarman's *Dancing Ledge*, 183–5. Rowland Wymer cites a particularly interesting observation of Jarman on Thatcher and *The Tempest* which was deleted from his published work: 'I would hate to equate the Tempest [sic] full of forgiveness and maturity with the politics of Thatcher's infantile regime', *Derek Jarman* (Manchester: Manchester University Press, 2005), 71.

15 M. O'Pray, *Derek Jarman: Dreams of England* (London: British Film Institute, 1996), 116.

16 The interview is available as an extra feature on the DVD of Jarman's *Tempest*. My emphasis.

17 In 1610 the King's Men had staged *The Alchemist*, Ben Jonson's parody of wizardry. It is likely that the company's leading actor, Richard Burbage, played not only Subtle but Shakespeare's Prospero.

18 *Doctor Faustus*, in M. T. Burnett (ed.), *The Complete Plays – Christopher Marlowe* (London: Everyman, 1999).

19 In 1875 Edward Dowden wrote of the similarity between Prospero and Shakespeare: 'The temper of Prosper, the grave harmony of his character, his self-mastery, his calm validity of will, his sensitiveness to wrong, his unfaltering justice, and, with these, a certain abandonment, a remoteness from the common joys and sorrows of the world,' are characteristic of Shakspeare as discovered to us in all his latest plays.' Quoted in Vaughan and Vaughan (eds.), *The Tempest*, 88. An illustration of the tenacity of this myth is illustrated by

Katherine Duncan-Jones's explanation of the placing of the play in F1: 'Immediate encounter with *The Tempest* served to remind readers in 1623 of Shakespeare's last prominent appearances on stage, as a great practitioner of white magic who feels himself to be near the end both of his powers and his life.' *Shakespeare: Upstart Crow to Sweet Swan, 1592–1623* (London: Methuen, 2011), 258.

20 Wymer, *Jarman*, 76, his emphasis.

21 A. Moor, 'Spirit and Matter: Romantic Mythologies in the Films of Derek Jarman', in D. Alderson and L. Anderson (eds.), *Territories of Desire in Queer Culture* (Manchester: Manchester University Press, 2000), 62.

22 Y. Sonnabend, 'The "Fabric of this Vision": Designing *The Tempest* with Derek Jarman', in R. Wollen (ed.), *Derek Jarman: A Portrait* (London: Thames and Hudson, 1996), 79.

23 Jarman, *Ledge*, 188.

24 *Ibid.* My emphasis.

25 *Ibid.*, 197.

26 Wymer writes, 'shortly after Jarman's HIV positive diagnosis in 1986, he deliberately broke Prospero's wand', *Jarman*, 80.

27 Chedgzoy, *Shakespeare's Queer Children*, 198.

28 McCabe, 'A Post-National European Cinema', 14.

29 Wymer, *Jarman*, 77.

30 K. S. Rothwell, *A History of Shakespeare on Screen*, 2nd edition (Cambridge: Cambridge University Press, 2004), 196. Rothwell notes elsewhere in the same study how Jarman's work 'heroically but forlornly ran against the grain of commercial movie making' (195).

31 C. Zabus and K. A. Dwyer, '"I'll be wise hereafter": Caliban in Postmodern British Cinema', in N. Lie and T. D'haen (eds.), *Constellation Caliban: Figurations of a Character* (Amsterdam: Rodopi, 1997), 277. Jarman records how a presumably inebriated Williams demanded to be entertained: 'One night at dinner he says, "I've been entertaining you lot far too long – if no one entertains me within one minute I'm going to piss all over you." Then he jumps on the long refectory table and starts to pee a cider torrent. We dive for cover.' *Ledge*, 194.

32 Jarman, *Ledge*, 183. Jarman's disdain for Greenaway was pronounced. Nick Stanley writes, 'Peter Greenaway was a particular target, possibly because he was so successful in getting funding and also, Jarman felt, because he reinforced traditional class relationships.' 'Derek Jarman: An Art Educator for our Times?', *Journal of Art and Design Education* 26 (2007), 110.

33 J. Buchanan, *Shakespeare on Film* (Harlow: Pearson Longman, 2005), 164.

34 Cited in Sian Barber, *The British Film Industry in the 1970s: Capital, Culture and Creativity* (Houndmills: Palgrave, 2013), 172.

35 Received opinion is that the stage directions are the additions of Ralph Crane. John Jowett notes that they are 'literary' rather than theatrical. He continues: stage directions 'are characteristically restricted in function and formulaic in expression. The word-range of the directions in *The Tempest* is

remarkably great, and includes over fifty words which do not occur else-where in the stage directions of Shakespeare's plays.' ('New Created Creatures: Ralph Crane and the Stage Directions in *The Tempest*', *Shakespeare Survey* 36 [1983], 110–11.) Vaughan and Vaughan contend that the authorship of the stage directions is less important than their accuracy: 'Whether *The Tempest*'s stage directions were written by Shakespeare or a prompter, or were interpolated later by Crane, they represent the earliest evidence we have of how the play was staged by the King's Men.' Vaughan and Vaughan (eds.), *The Tempest*, 130.

36 On this stage direction specifically, see Jowett, 'New Created Creatures', 112–14. He notes how '"*Strange*" is a key word in *The Tempest* but here could have been taken from its nearby occurence in the text, just five lines below the direction' (113).

37 See S. Orgel's Oxford edition, especially 43–50, and D. Bevington, '*The Tempest* and the Jacobean Court Masque', in D. Bevington and P. Holbrook (eds.), *The Politics of the Stuart Court Masque* (Cambridge: Cambridge University Press, 1998), 218–43.

38 Jarman, *Ledge*, 203.

39 Stanley has written of Jarman's 'personal passionate hatred for Margaret Thatcher' ('An Art Educator', 109). It is important to note that this hatred predates the introduction of the homophobic Section 28 (1988). *Ledge* was published in 1984 (see Wymer, *Jarman*, 110). In a powerful opinion piece for *The Guardian* (24 January 2014), Neil Bartlett describes the position of Jarman's work in a post-Thatcher culture: 'But now – ding dong, the witch is dead. Clause 28 is (mostly) forgotten, the flea markets are shiny with rede-velopment, the derelict warehouses have all acquired penthouses, and Dave [Cameron] and Boris [Johnson] and the Evening Standard compete to see who can go the most moist-eyed with sincerity at the prospect of gay marriage.' See www.theguardian.com/film/2014/jan/24/celebrating-derek-jarman-20-years-death (accessed 30 May 2015).

40 P. Aebischer, 'Early Modern Drama on Screen: A Jarman Anniversary Issue', *Shakespeare Bulletin* 29 (2001), 495.

41 Sonnabend, 'Designing', 77.

42 Sonnabend, 'Designing', 78. Shakespeare certainly had ample opportunity to witness these remarkable theatrical spectaculars: by the year of *The Tempest*'s first performance, Whitehall had seen eleven court masques. Shakespeare's membership of a company directly under the patronage of James, the King's Men, would have made his performance in one or more of them not unlikely. Yet although masques and entertainments were penned by many of the play-wrights with whom Shakespeare was familiar – Ben Jonson, Francis Beaumont, George Chapman, Thomas Dekker, Samuel Daniel and Thomas Campion – there is no freestanding Shakespearean masque.

43 D. Norbrook, '"What Cares these Roarers for the Name of King?": Language and Utopia in *The Tempest*', in K. Ryan (ed.), *Shakespeare: The Last Plays* (London: Longman, 1999), 262. My emphasis.

44 Wells *et al.* have 'peonied' here rather than Orgel's 'pionèd'. S. Wells and G. Taylor (eds.), William Shakespeare's *Complete Works* (Oxford: Clarendon Press, 1988).

45 E. B. Gilman, '"All Eyes": Prospero's Inverted Masque', *Renaissance Quarterly* 33 (1980), 224.

46 S. Ryle, *Shakespeare, Cinema and Desire: Adaptation and Other Futures of Shakespeare's Language* (Houndmills: Palgrave Macmillan, 2014), 206.

47 M. Taylor, 'Memory, Magic and the Musical in Derek Jarman's *The Tempest* and *Edward II*', in B. Marshall and R. Stilwell (eds.), *Musicals: Hollywood and Beyond* (Exeter: Intellect Books, 2000), 158.

48 D. Harris and M. Jackson, 'Stormy Weather: Derek Jarman's *The Tempest*', *Literature/Film Quarterly* 25 (1997), 95.

49 D. Hawkes, '"The Shadow of this Time": The Renaissance Cinema of Derek Jarman', in C. Lippard (ed.), *By Angels Driven: The Films of Derek Jarman* (Trowbridge: Flicks Books, 1996), 103.

50 W. Pencak, *The Films of Derek Jarman* (Jefferson, NC: McFarland, 2002), 106.

51 Buchanan, *Shakespeare on Film*, 165.

52 J. Ellis, 'Conjuring *The Tempest*: Derek Jarman and the Spectacle of Redemption', *GLQ* 7 (2001), 265–84, 276.

53 D. M. Lanier, 'Drowning the Book: *Prospero's Books* and the Textual Shakespeare', in R. Shaughnessy (ed.), *Shakespeare on Film* (Houndmills: Macmillan, 1998), 182.

WORKS CITED

Aebischer, P., 'Early Modern Drama on Screen: A Jarman Anniversary Issue', *Shakespeare Bulletin* 29 (2001), 495–503.

Aebischer, P. and K. Prince (eds.), *Performing Early Modern Drama Today* (Cambridge: Cambridge University Press, 2012).

Barber, S., *The British Film Industry in the 1970s: Capital, Culture and Creativity* (Houndmills: Palgrave, 2013).

Bartlett, N., 'Celebrating Derek Jarman 20 years after his death', *Guardian*, 24 January 2014. www.theguardian.com/film/2014/jan/24/celebrating-derek-jarman-20-years-death

Bevington, D., '*The Tempest* and the Jacobean Court Masque', in D. Bevington and P. Holbrook (eds.), *The Politics of the Stuart Court Masque* (Cambridge: Cambridge University Press, 1998), 218–43.

Buchanan, J., *Shakespeare on Film* (Harlow: Pearson Longman, 2005).

Burnett, M. T., *The Complete Plays – Christopher Marlowe* (London: Everyman, 1999).

Chedgzoy, Kate, *Shakespeare's Queer Children: Sexual Politics and Contemporary Culture* (Manchester: Manchester University Press, 1995).

Duncan-Jones, K., *Shakespeare: Upstart Crow to Sweet Swan, 1592–1623* (London: Methuen, 2011).

Ellis, J., 'Conjuring *The Tempest*: Derek Jarman and the Spectacle of Redemption', *GLQ* 7 (2001), 265–84.

Gilman, E. B., '"All Eyes": Prospero's Inverted Masque', *Renaissance Quarterly* 33 (1980), 214–30.

Greenaway, P., Prospero's Books: *A Film of Shakespeare's* The Tempest (London: Chatto & Windus, 1991).

Harris, D. and M. Jackson, 'Stormy Weather: Derek Jarman's *The Tempest*', *Literature/Film Quarterly* 25 (1997), 90–8.

Hawkes, D., '"The Shadow of this Time": The Renaissance Cinema of Derek Jarman', in C. Lippard (ed.), *By Angels Driven: The Films of Derek Jarman* (Trowbridge: Flicks Books, 1996), 103–16.

Hopkins, L., *Screen Adaptations: Shakespeare's* The Tempest: *The Relationship between Text and Film* (London: Methuen, 2008).

Jackson, R., *Shakespeare and the English-Speaking Cinema* (Oxford: Oxford University Press, 2014).

Jarman, D., *Dancing Ledge* (London: Quartet Books, 1984).

Jowett, J., 'New Created Creatures: Ralph Crane and the Stage Directions in *The Tempest*', *Shakespeare Survey* 36 (1983), 107–20.

'Varieties of Collaboration in Shakespeare's Problem Plays and Late Plays', in R. Dutton and J. E. Howard (eds.), *A Companion to Shakespeare's Works*, 4 vols (Oxford: Blackwell, 2003), vol. 4, 106–28.

Kermode, F. (ed.), *William Shakespeare's* The Tempest (London: Methuen, 1954).

Lanier, D. M., 'Drowning the Book: *Prospero's Books* and the Textual Shakespeare', in R. Shaughnessy (ed.), *Shakespeare on Film*, (Houndmills: Macmillan, 1998), 173–95.

Larkin, P., *The Whitsun Weddings* (London: Faber, 1974).

Lindley, D., *The Tempest: Shakespeare at Stratford* (Surrey: Thomas Nelson, 2003).

McCabe, C., 'A Post-National European Cinema: A Consideration of Derek Jarman's *The Tempest* and *Edward II*', in D. Petrie (ed.), *Screening Europe: Image and Identity in Contemporary European Cinema* (London: British Film Institute, 1992), 9–18.

McMullan, G., *Shakespeare and the Idea of Late Writing: Authorship in the Proximity of Death* (Cambridge: Cambridge University Press, 2007).

Moor, A., 'Spirit and Matter: Romantic Mythologies in the Films of Derek Jarman', in D. Alderson and L. Anderson (eds.), *Territories of Desire in Queer Culture* (Manchester: Manchester University Press, 2000), 49–67.

Norbrook, D., '"What Cares these Roarers for the Name of King?": Language and Utopia in *The Tempest*', in K. Ryan (ed.), *Shakespeare: The Last Plays* (London: Longman, 1999), 245–78.

O'Pray, M., *Derek Jarman: Dreams of England* (London: British Film Institute, 1996).

Orgel, S. (ed.), *William Shakespeare's* The Tempest (Oxford: Oxford University Press, 1994).

Pencak, W., *The Films of Derek Jarman* (Jefferson, NC: McFarland, 2002).

Rothwell, K. S., *A History of Shakespeare on Screen*, 2nd edition (Cambridge: Cambridge University Press, 2004).

Ryle, S., *Shakespeare, Cinema and Desire: Adaptation and Other Futures of Shakespeare's Language* (Houndmills: Palgrave Macmillan, 2014).

Sonnabend, Y., 'The "Fabric of this Vision": Designing *The Tempest* with Derek Jarman', in R. Wollen (ed.), *Derek Jarman: A Portrait* (London: Thames and Hudson, 1996), 77–9.

Stanley, N., 'Derek Jarman: An Art Educator for our Times?', *Journal of Art and Design Education* 26 (2007), 108–18.

Taylor, M., 'Memory, Magic and the Musical in Derek Jarman's *The Tempest* and *Edward II*', in B. Marshall and R. Stilwell (eds.), *Musicals: Hollywood and Beyond* (Exeter: Intellect Books, 2000), 157–62.

Vaughan A. T. and V. M. Vaughan (eds.), *William Shakespeare's The Tempest*, The Arden Shakespeare third series (London: Thomas Nelson, 1999).

Vaughan, V. M., The Tempest: *Shakespeare in Performance* (Manchester: Manchester University Press, 2011).

Wells, S. and G. Taylor (eds.), *William Shakespeare's Complete Works* (Oxford: Clarendon Press, 1988).

Wymer, R., *Derek Jarman* (Manchester: Manchester University Press, 2005).

Zabus, C. and K. A. Dwyer, '"I'll be wise hereafter": Caliban in Postmodern British Cinema', in N. Lie and T. D'haen (eds.), *Constellation Caliban: Figurations of a Character* (Amsterdam: Rodopi, 1997), 271–89.

CHAPTER 10

The Absent Masque in Three Films of The Tempest

Russell Jackson

'These Things are but Toyes, to come amongst such Serious Observations', wrote Sir Francis Bacon in 'Of Maskes and Triumphs', in his *Essayes or Counsels, Civill and Morall*, adding that 'yet, since Princes will have such Toyes, it is better they should be Graced with Elegance, then Daubed with Cost.' This seems like a warning directors of *The Tempest* should take to heart: daub with cost at your peril.[1] In 1973 Peter Hall directed the play for the National Theatre, then still housed at the Old Vic. The elaborate flying effects and movable scenery were inspired by Hall's recent Glyndbourne production of Francesco Cavalli's opera *La Calisto*. The result was generally agreed to be an overloading of the play. Michael Billington commented that 'it is a fallacy to argue that because *The Tempest* contains elements of Jacobean masque, the whole play is nothing but an Inigo Jones spectacular'. The production's 'weakness' was that 'one [could] discuss it only in terms of its images: not in terms of the triumph of virtue over vengeance or the ultimate superiority of life-giving Nature over artificial Nurture'.[2] Criticism of the production seemed to revisit the terms of Ben Jonson's 'Expostulation' with his colleague Inigo Jones and disgust at the prevalence in masques of 'mythology there painted on split deal':

> Oh, to make boards to speak! There is a task!
> Painting and carpentry are the soul of masque.[3]

As well as harking back to the controversies of the 1600s, Billington's review is representative of a long history of debate about the play and its kinship with the courtly medium. Of the three full-length feature films of the play, two stand out as exemplifying the ways in which the terms of this debate have been inherited by the new medium. This essay discusses this aspect of the films by Derek Jarman (1980) and Peter Greenaway (*Prospero's Books*, 1991), with a briefer consideration of Julie Taymor's 2010 version. It will be argued that an engagement with the masque/play relationship is central to the work of the first two film directors, but plays a less significant

role in that of the third. Comparison is made with two theatre productions, Giorgio Strehler's for the Piccolo Teatro, Milan (1978), and Daniel
Mesguich's 1999 Comédie-Française production.[4] Both directors handled
the play's other moments of spectacle with virtuosity – arguably excessive
in Mesguich's case – but neither used the text of the masque presented by
Prospero to Ferdinand and Miranda as a 'vanity of [his] art' (4.1.41) as it
appears in the 1623 Folio.

The three films respond in markedly different ways to the masque, a
point at which the courtly genre's combination of the arts of song, poetry
and spectacle would seem to lend themselves to the new visual media of
film and TV. The play's own masque has seemed, though, to prove problematic as an event in the narrative, while the medium it draws on, lacking
resonance with modern audiences, has occasioned some embarrassment.
None of the films delivers the scene as it appears in the play's script, whatever standard of 'faithfulness' to an 'original' we apply: it seems to have
resisted being repurposed for the cinema. At the same time, aspects of the
court masque have chimed with the intentions of the film's directors, with
markedly different results.

Before turning to the films, it is appropriate to consider *The Tempest's*
relationship with the masque genre. This perspective in theatrical history
is reflected in the way – as Diana Harris and MacDonald Jackson suggest –
both Jarman's and Greenaway's versions dwell, 'in their vastly different
idioms... on the original script's obsession with the interaction between
life, art, dream, and play, subtly shifting through different planes of reality and representation'.[5] These two films might be said to complement in
method and ambitions both the play itself and the masque form that it
both courts and departs from.

Discussing the post-Restoration adaptation of *A Midsummer Night's
Dream* in *Musicking Shakespeare: A Conflict of Theatres* (2007), Daniel
Albright distinguishes between the masque, as represented by Ben Jonson
and Inigo Jones's *Masque of Oberon* (performed in 1611), and the comedy's
employment of the dramaturgy of Shakespeare's theatres:

> Metamorphosis is central to the aesthetic of both the Shakespeare play and
> the masque. But Shakespearean metamorphosis is balky, palimpsestic, a tis-
> sue of changes and of erasures of change provoked by the vicissitudes of
> sexual desire; masque-metamorphosis, on the other hand, is simply a shift-
> ing fringe of gorgeous inconsequentialities playing around the king.[6]

Albright cites Jonson's text for the song with which the Sylvans, accompa-
nying Oberon in his chariot, approach the king:

Melt earth to sea, sea flow to air,
And air fly into fire,
Whilst we in tunes to Arthur's chair
Bear Oberon's desire;
Than which there nothing can higher be
Save James, to whom it flies:
But he the wonder is of tongues, of ears, of eyes.[7]

The contrast between *A Midsummer Night's Dream* and *Oberon* is starker than that between Jonson's masques and *The Tempest*: Shakespeare's late play is more tightly constructed than the earlier comedy – indeed less consistently *comic* in its transformations – and it deals directly with matters of state and sovereignty. But, for all its relative simplicity of plot, it shares the 'balky' quality identified by Albright, refusing the unified movement towards confirmation that the court masques require. They execute a simplistic political and ethical intention with paradoxical sophistication and complexity. Nothing in *The Tempest* is quite so simple.

There is a sense of a masque-like movement from images of hellish chaos in the shipwreck and the vanishing banquet, to concord in the betrothal celebration and the frustration of two conspiracies on the island, and the resolution of one that took place twelve years before in Milan. The play includes music, song and dance, as well as the routing of comic characters like those in an anti-masque, but what in a masque would be simple is here made problematic. One of the 'anti-masque' figures, Caliban, has a claim to possession of territory that has been usurped; Ariel, the spirit who acts as the agent of the presiding magus, complains that he is being bound to work beyond the terms of his contract; and the one direct imitation of a masque is interrupted by Prospero's recollection of unfinished business. There is no appeal, either in words or in the organization of the playing space, to the all-resolving presence of a monarch. In Prospero's final speech a conventional plea for 'pardon' to the audience is combined with a reminder of the ultimate arbitration available only by prayer, 'Which pierces so, that it assaults/Mercy itself, and frees all faults' (Epilogue 17–18). Without this, his ending will be 'despair', a note not to be sounded at the end of a court masque. Stephen Orgel comments that the court masque

> attempted from the beginning to breach the barrier between the spectators and actors, so that in effect the viewer became part of the spectacle. The end toward which the masque moved was to destroy any sense of theater and to include the whole court in the mimesis – in a sense, what the spectator watched he ultimately became.[8]

The inclusiveness of the theatre's intimacy between audience and stage, invoked in Prospero's speech, is not of this order: the separation is confirmed even as the audience's 'pardon' is appealed for. The dancing of spectators in the 'revels' that ended a court masque was a continuation of its signification by other means, distinct from whatever dancing may have followed a play in the theatre.

The Tempest, then, includes elements associated with the court masque but not arranged so as to create its equivalent. Most of these no longer resonate with a modern audience, so that any dissonance apparent to listeners and spectators in the 1600s is no longer heard. The music and spectacle of the play continue to be effective, whether or not the means used correspond to those of its own time: new scores and new ways of rendering the visual effects can maintain the general sense of magic and wonder. In the 'most majestic vision . . . harmonious charmingly' (4.1.118–19), the appearance of Iris, Ceres and Juno and the graceful dance of the 'temperate nymphs' with the 'sun-burned sicklemen' (4.1.132–4) reinforce Prospero's insistence on premarital continence for the young couple. It has been pointed out that the general significance of this allegory, with its explicit exclusion of the potentially disruptive Venus and Cupid, would have been clear to a moderately well-informed audience, even if the specific connotations of the other deities were not.[9] Unlike the court masque, this affirmation of positive values is followed by a recurrence of the kind of excess (appetite, rancour, ambition) that it should vanquish: Prospero is reminded that he has to deal with 'that foul conspiracy/Of the beast Caliban and his confederates/Against [his] life' (4.1.139–41). Many subsequent stage productions claiming to deliver the play according to the published text have elaborated on the masque and the subsequent dance, but film versions have gone further in avoiding or modifying the episode's significance.[10] David Lindley observes that out of the sixteen Stratford-upon-Avon productions between 1947 and 2002 that he studied, only three had 'really found a satisfying means of persuading an audience of the importance of the masque', and of what he calls 'the most period-bound of all literary forms'.[11]

Derek Jarman: Dancing Sailors and 'Stormy Weather'

In *The Times*, Derek Jarman's film was welcomed by the paper's film critic as 'one of the most successful, authentic and truly poetic adaptations of Shakespeare: text and images are totally integrated, to afford interpretation, not mere illustration'.[12] This perceptive and detailed evaluation, though, was not to be the review that lingered in the critical consciousness. Unsurprisingly, given his eminence as a literary critic and influence as the New Arden editor of the play, the most famous (or notorious) response was Frank Kermode's savagely hostile review, published in the *Times Literary Supplement* under the headline 'Ideas Strangle Director'. Kermode centred his criticism on the speaking of the verse, admitting Heathcote Williams's Prospero as a lone exception to the general condemnation. As for the 'beautiful masque', wrote Kermode, 'it vanishes, apart from a fragment recited by Ariel and Miranda on a rocking horse, and is replaced by Elisabeth Welch's rendition of "Stormy Weather" – charming notions of a kind which it is the duty of good directors to strangle at birth'. Kermode concedes that 'Somehow [the film] does sustain a mood, for all the coarseness and perversity with which it makes its points as a movie, it has a dreamlike, underwater quality, cold, dimly magical'.[13]

Kermode's quarrel seems to be with the director as an intrusive authority as much as with the specifics of the film under review. He was correct in this respect with regard to Jarman's film: the ultimate legitimate authority in the director's filmed works is that of the artist himself, behind, in front of or around the camera. 'I am the most fortunate film-maker of my generation', he writes in *Modern Nature*, 'I've only ever done what I wanted. Now I just film my life, I'm a happy megalomaniac... Making films our way makes all others seem fabricated'.[14] Although he was sometimes bashful about taking credit for the collaborative work that had to be labelled 'Derek Jarman's film of...', Jarman could hardly disclaim his *auteur*ship – it was that of a master of ceremonies, described in the costume designer Yolanda Sonnabend's reminiscence of the filming of *The Tempest*: 'Like the dream of *The Tempest*, work and life were suspended. Derek, our Prospero, pulling the threads together, making us all willing conspirators in his vision. Some celestial harmony breathed on us for a while'.[15]

Explicitly in some films, by implication in others, Jarman posits a new society, with values that are paradoxically conservative – with that all-important lowercase 'c.' His indignation at the destruction of the authentic past and the 'true' English landscape makes Jarman read at times like a queer (or queerer) John Betjeman. 'In the short space of my lifetime', Jarman wrote, 'I've seen the destruction of the landscape through commercialization, a destruction so complete that fragments are preserved as if in a museum'.[16] A particular *bête noire* was the National Trust, and at times the indignation combines this process with the tastes and prejudices of 'heterosoc', the name Jarman gave to the heterosexual hegemony regarded as inimical to much that he valued in society and art:

Sissinghurst, that elegant Sodom in the garden of England, is 'heritized' in
the institutional hands of the National Trust. Its magic has fled in the vacant
eyes of tourists. If two boys kissed in the silver garden now, you can be sure
they'd be shown the door. The shades of the Sackville-Wests pursuing naked
guardsmen through the herbaceous borders return long after the last curious
coachload has departed the tea shoppe closed.[17]

The Eden here is a comically energetic version of a queer aristocratic landscape, as though the true aristocracy had been supplanted by the 'general
public', a case of *noblesse* not being allowed to *oblige*.

In one sense, then, Jarman is as much Gonzalo as Prospero, envisioning
an ideal 'commonwealth' and lamenting the loss of one that used to exist.
In his reflections on art and the past he often returns to the prospect of
alternative and authentic Edens. In his published journals, these are sometimes figured as an escape, while at others they are described in terms of a
way of making – in film and in other media: 'To keep myself occupied . . . I
took up my Super 8 camera, deciding to develop a parallel cinema based on
the home movie which would free me. A space where I could paint my garden'.[18] The home movies from Jarman's childhood used in *The Last of England* (1987) are a surprising appearance among the film's dominant imagery
of oppression and mayhem: 'The home movie is bedrock, it records the
landscape of leisure: the beach, the garden, the swimming pool. In all home
movies is a longing for paradise'.[19] Occasionally a vision of paradise might
be revealed where 'heterosoc' would fear to tread. On the derelict piers of
Manhattan in the 1970s, for example, 'You walked through a succession of
huge empty rooms, with young men often naked in the shafts of light which
fell through the windows. The piers had their own beauty; surrounded by
water, they were a secret island'.[20] Or it might be found by cruising for
sex on Hampstead Heath: 'Ours is a separate and parallel world, under the
stars. Here you can fade away into the dark'.[21] But these were special worlds
that for most of his lifetime were forced on queers (the word he came to
prefer, rejecting 'gay' as lacking combative force): 'No man is an island, but
each man created his own island to cope with prejudice and censure. The
time for politeness had to end'.[22]

Both indoor and outdoor refuges figure largely in Jarman's life and work:
'The images of the closed spaces in my films are an attempt to find a safe-
house. As early as the age of five I knew I wouldn't join'.[23] In *Kicking the
Pricks* he reflects on his interest in the magician John Dee, 'his preoccupation with secrets and ciphers', and asks of his own work: 'Why this obsession with the language of closed structures, the ritual of the closet and the
sanctuary?'[24] Dee, a presence – arguably the unseen presiding genius – in

The Tempest is the presenter of marvels in the future to Elizabeth I in Jarman's *Jubilee* (1978). The frame of that film's main narrative, beginning in a garden and ending on the cliffs near Dancing Ledge, represents a vision of the lost garden, with Elizabeth as the bewildered observer who possesses an authentic and acknowledged majesty that her tawdry inheritors can only ape.

In the final phase of his life, Jarman made what he once called his 'avant-garden' outside Prospect Cottage on the seafront at Dungeness, a paradoxical creation of a horticultural domain on a windswept, stony beach. The garden was a quasi-magical transformation of unpromising terrain. Like Gonzalo's optimistic account of the island in Shakespeare's *Tempest*, 'Though this island seem to be desert . . . /Uninhabitable, and almost inaccessible . . . /Yet . . . /It must needs be of subtle, tender, and delicate temperance' (2.1.34–42). The words of Ceres in the play's masque, it has been pointed out, complement Gonzalo's ideal world: 'Earth's increase, and foison plenty,/Barns and garners never empty' (4.1.110–11). Nevertheless, the main purpose of this masque did not accord with Jarman's world view: 'marriage-blessing' (4.1.106) would be an invitation to participate in the loathed 'heterosoc'.

The Tempest is unusual among Jarman's films, closer than many to the norms of commercial filmmaking in its linear narrative and many of its techniques, and based on a securely 'classic' text. It lacks the anger and confrontational vigour of *Sebastiane* (1976), *Jubilee* or *The Last of England*, in comparison with which it does not seem especially *queer* in the specific sense of gender and sexuality. Taking the word in its wider sense, it can be said to be determinedly queer. In particular, the images of the exercise of power, the sense of a closed (or, arguably, closeted) world, and the framing of it as a dream are queer in ways that go beyond eroticism. The kind of disorientation that marks Cocteau's *Testament d'Orphée* (a film in Jarman's personal pantheon) is present throughout the film: the opening sequence, with Prospero's disturbed sleep (the heavy breathing of deep sleep) and the blue-filtered footage of a storm at sea, is not explained until much later, rather than in the first exchanges between Prospero and his daughter. There are few clues as to the geography of the house in which the action is taking place, although there are a main staircase, backstairs passages and staircases, a kitchen (where Miranda finds the key to Ferdinand's shackles) and a number of panelled rooms. Prospero's study, with its cabbalistic signs chalked on the walls and floor and the paraphernalia of magic, is at once a refuge and a control room, but it is also haunted, albeit by invitation. When Ariel is summoned for the first time, his arrival is heralded by a tinkling chandelier and a key turning mysteriously in a lock. Prospero, in Heathcote Williams' quietly eloquent performance, seems to be subject to spirit disturbances to an extent not usual in other interpretations. One of Jarman's temporary childhood homes was reputed to be haunted. His accounts of it do not suggest that this was especially disturbing: 'The ghosts opened and closed the heavy oak doors, lifting the iron latches as they came and went'.[25] This kind of uncanny phenomenon, a ghostly distortion of the familiar, pervades *The Tempest*.

These instances of a 'so potent art' are not explicitly called up by Prospero but follow on from intense thought and the chalking up of symbols. More than in the play's full text, Ariel appears to divide responsibility with him. Ariel may stand waiting for orders but, with his enigmatic smile, he possesses a power that is wielded as confidently as that of his master. At the same time, his stillness, pallor and reticence, and the whiteness of his overalls seem appropriate to the containment of a spirit. Summoning him is not a matter to be taken lightly: on his first appearance, Prospero has to turn away from the flash of light as he arrives. It is Ariel, sitting on a rocking horse, who speaks the lines 'Honour, riches, marriage-blessing . . .' (4.1.106). Later Miranda repeats them to herself, standing on the horse, as though the idea has been implanted by him. In the absence of the masque itself they seem to exist independently of Prospero or of his 'so potent art.'

In the final scenes, Ariel's direct communication with the film's audience – he has often been seen in close-up, full-frame – is now confirmed, as, clad in an elegant white dinner jacket and black bow tie, it is he who invites the viewers, who share the point-of-view of the young couple and Prospero, into the ballroom, where sailors are happily dancing. This is very much Ariel's show. Once the young couple is enthroned, red petals rain as Elisabeth Welch makes her entrance – at once grand, commanding and genial – to sing 'Stormy Weather.' Rowland Wymer suggests that this is a 'playful breach of generic decorum' and 'a brief "camp" childish gesture of liberation in the face of the grimly adult destiny of heterosexual marriage'.[26] As such it may count as Jarman's refusal to celebrate an institution he detests, but this is the most truly *gay* scene in Jarman's film, in both senses of the word: it is light, bright and joyous. (On Jarman's engagement with the masque form and its aesthetics, and for a complementary view of the sequence, see Peter J. Smith's chapter in this volume.) Elisabeth Welch's costume is more like that of a masque goddess than anything seen elsewhere in the film; her performance is radiant and the crowd of young sailors, cavorting before she arrives, are spellbound by it, as are the members of the court who have already arrived. Ferdinand and Miranda, costumed as if for a fancy-dress ball, look on in appropriately appreciative amazement. Although the lyrics refer to the 'stormy weather', the blues that have set in now that the singer's man has left her, the dominant effect is one of resilience. Singing the blues is, after all, good for you, if it's done like this.

Suddenly the film cuts to the now deserted and dimly lit ballroom. Ariel is seen tentatively sitting on the throne Miranda occupied, shifting to sit on the steps of the dais as he becomes aware of Prospero in the foreground, apparently asleep. Ariel vanishes in the twinkling of a jump cut, as he ascends a staircase that leads out of the room. Prospero speaks: 'Our revels now are ended . . .' (4.1.148) in voice-over as if in his sleep – and 'sleep' is indeed the film's final word. Arguably the whole film may have been his dream, begun in the opening sequence and now about to continue beyond its on-screen conclusion. In any case, he does not now take responsibility for the film. Jarman's allusive, sometimes frankly teasing art, is that of a magus, often good humoured (as he appears in a number of genial and urbane interviews) but sometimes angry and acerbic, moving between painting, writing and filmmaking. The shots of himself in his studio in *The Last of England* recall the scenes of Prospero in his study, surrounded by the paraphernalia not simply of magic with its active interventions in the world and the head of Mausolus that the director had rescued from the cast room at the Slade School of Art, but with the monad, Dee's staff incorporating its optic means of seeing worlds beyond and behind 'reality.' One of Jarman's actions at Dungeness was the breaking of this talismanic possession: 'I took hold of it silently, shut my eyes for a moment, then smashed it'.[27] Tony Peake notes that in the unpublished diary entry this was prefaced with an explicit reference to Prospero.[28]

Prospero's Books: A Surplus of Signification

Jarman thought that the erasure of the authentic past was abetted by the scorned 'heritage films', soaking up resources that should be available for radical filmmakers, and complicit in the destructive process: 'Most English artists have put on the specs of Albion and see the present through an imaginary past'.[29] Included in his commination was not only the overtly patriotic *Chariots of Fire* (1981) but also the work of Peter Greenaway, whom he despised as a faux radical, part of the loathed institution of cinema, 'made by the cunning for the dimwitted'.[30] The claim that 'I don't make films. I make moving pictures' was partly a refusal to take part in conventional narrative cinema ('films') but also a statement of intent not far removed from that of Greenaway, whose success as a fashionable art-house *auteur* offended him.[31] 'If Gucci handbags were still in fashion', he wrote, 'Greenaway would carry his scripts in them'.[32] In many respects, though, the films of the two directors converge in image-making and in an obsession with the artist as maker. In 1974 Jarman had even contemplated a *Tempest* in which, as in Greenaway's film, Prospero should play all the parts, in accord with the view (suggested by Frances Yates) that Shakespeare was using secret texts 'to liberate himself from the known limits of man and to attempt a reconciliation'.[33] (Jarman's early plans for a film of the play are discussed in detail in Peter J. Smith's chapter in the present volume.) At the same time, 'heritage' lingers in Jarman's film, if only in the dilapidated country mansion and the period clothes. As Pascale Aebischer observes, 'The film invoke[s] the trappings of period drama in order to dismantle them before our eyes'.[34] Neither filmmaker in fact participates in the 'heritage cinema' as it is usually understood, a commercial genre privileging nostalgia, often in adaptations of canonical fictional texts and, its critics claim, essentially conservative in its ideology.[35] In another construction of the term, Greenaway does engage with 'heritage', but it is a bricolage of inherited symbols, artworks and imagery. Amy Lawrence identifies this as 'the usual postmodern shuffle through the rubble of Western culture'.[36]

Interviewed in *Sight and Sound* in May 1991, Greenaway described his interest in two Jacobean genres: the tragedy of revenge and the masque. The latter, 'basically an elite private entertainment, very much to do with symbols and emblems and allegories', was particularly important for him: 'anybody who has seen my cinema will know that metaphors and allegories fascinate me enormously'.[37] Greenaway's understanding of the masque suggests the emphasis proposed by Keith Sturgess in *Jacobean Private Theatre* (1987) which identifies the play's kinship with the masque form in terms of its presentation of a dream-like series of images rather than a forward-moving plot:

> Design, not narrative, is *The Tempest*'s major impulse and its structure is architectural, not dynamic . . . The audience is given a series of stage pictures which, like the visions in a dream, have a sharp-edged clarity and a sense of careful composition. They seem, again as in a dream, to be both emblematic and not readily accessible to simple interpretation. For the play moves in a masque-like way, proceeding by way of a series of counterpointed events that act like revelations of epiphanies.[38]

This seems to devalue not only the play, which does after all present a narrative, but also the masque genre, where an often tenuous but always intelligible action supports and complements sophisticated emblematic signification. Sturgess's perspective on the medium accords less with the visions of Jarman's film than those of Greenaway's *Prospero's Books*. Here the narrative is attenuated, often to the point of standstill, by the elaboration of imagery, constantly harking back to the written word or painted image, or the stasis of sculpture. Peter S. Donaldson connects the effects with the digital technology employed by the filmmaker: 'Subtler references [than the acts of writing and inscription] – should we call them metacomputational or metadigital? – help to explain the extraordinarily restrictive, stilted blocking and dancing style of *Prospero's Books*.' Donaldson interprets this as 'an attempt to make live performers on film look as much like computer animations as possible', a sign that 'Prospero is a double for Greenaway, the digital artist, as much as for Shakespeare the playwright'.[39] Jonathan Romney's review in *Sight and Sound* suggested that the film's presentation of Prospero, 'at once actor, author and director of his own script', was a reflection of 'Greenaway's own self-questioning aspirations to transcendental authorship'.[40] The director recalled in an interview that 'many years ago' he had written a script about the relationship between Ben Jonson and Inigo Jones. The need 'to fashion their opposing interests to make a coherent whole' was 'also the quandary of cinema'.[41] The published script shares a function of explication with Jonson's printed accounts of his masque texts, though here the functions of Jones and Jonson as devisers are fused in one person's creativity.[42] This script is *the* book of Greenaway's/*Prospero's Books*, with the additional purpose of indicating intentions that could not be executed. Merely *watching* the film can never be enough.

This relative devaluation of narrative form in favour of the articulation of symbolism on multiple levels has been fundamental to his cinema. Sometimes the narrative balances or even outweighs the symbolic freighting: this is certainly the case with *The Draughtsman's Contract* (1982), his nearest approach to a conventional 'heritage' film, and *The Cook, the Thief, his Wife, and her Lover* (1989), which partakes of the 'revenge tragedy' element. The achievement of *Prospero's Books* lies in its technical accomplishment and complexity, although the basic given – that Prospero/Gielgud thinks, writes and speaks the play – is in itself simple. The play's story is in fact related, but with a notable lack of forward momentum. From the beginning words, ideas and images are lingered over, repeated, mirrored and refashioned. Effectively, Greenaway (in Douglas M. Lanier's phrase) 'denarrativizes' the action.[43] With the exception of those in which water and waves feature, the books, supposedly Prospero's rescued library, often have nothing to do with 'imagery' if that is taken to refer to the poetic language itself. They represent rather the extensive furnishings of the Renaissance mage's mind. In some cases, their animated elements exceed the capabilities of any known book, so that they might even be said to include cinema in their pages.[44] There is an unidentified narrator to describe them, so that, unlike the authentic masques of the 1600s, this one has its learned commentary playing alongside it in image and words. The commentary, like the books we are shown, is not so much extra-diegetic as part of the diegesis. (One might even wonder how the distinction can be made in the film.) Romney, in his *Sight and Sound* review, observes that Greenaway 'obscures action while displaying it' and 'provides all the elements of spectacle but leaves the task of ordering them to the viewer.' To dismiss the film on this account would be to reject a major element of modernism in the arts – let alone post-modernism – but it does return us to the significance of the word 'of' in the film script's identification as '*a film of* Shakespeare's The Tempest'. This is a work that is 'of', interpreted as 'about' and 'derived from' as much as (or more than) 'delivering' the play. Moreover, before the availability of VHS or DVD copies, screenings in circumstances that excluded the ability to interrupt and pause the film meant that its complexities could be grasped only by repeated viewings.

One consequence of this is that the whole film is effectively a masque – mythology and cultural history painted on celluloid rather than split deal – so that even for a critic who applauds the overall achievement, the celebration of the betrothal seems both confusing and oddly beside the point. Amy Lawrence, in most respects an admirer of the director's work, notes that Prospero 'unleashes the masque when his power is confirmed', and accepts that 'unfortunately, for a modern audience', the 'utter lack of anxiety' of the masque genre 'translates into a lack of suspense'. This is because 'the already high level of spectacle throughout the film makes the endless parade of extras decidedly anticlimactic'.[45] Although Greenaway differs from Jarman in including the speeches of the three deities, the soundtrack rendition of Michael Nyman's setting of the lyrics sometimes makes them unintelligible. The profusion of attendant spirits, wielding symbolic objects or executing repeated and automaton-like movements and gestures, also gets in the way – literally, when Ceres sings some of her verses from the midst of what seems like a rush-hour crowd of naked and semi-naked figures. Miranda and Ferdinand are led to thrones facing a proscenium-like portico, from which Juno emerges to address them while spirits pass in front of the couple with what seem to be ornately fashioned wedding presents.

At moments, this section of the film invokes the theatre directly: curtains are drawn to reveal singers and action and there is a procession towards the camera that, to the irreverent eye, suggests the 'walk down' at the end of a traditional British Christmas pantomime. Within Jarman's aesthetic, such a resonance would have been intentional, a moment of self-conscious 'camp.' Greenaway eschews such vulgarity: nothing joyous or festive is allowed to invade the sacred space of the film; this is a *solemnization* of betrothal in the strictest sense. There has been no dance of nymphs and sicklemen, although the call for it is included. When Prospero remembers the conspiracy of Caliban and his associates, there is no reassuring 'Be cheerful, sir' (4.1.147) to Ferdinand. The director seems determined to prevent any possibility of cheerfulness breaking in. There is nothing *gay*, in the sense of 'joyous' in the performances by Prospero's spirits and nothing exciting in the 'queer' sense of the word either, for all the multitude of bared bosoms, buttocks and male genitalia on display. Although two of the spirits evoke fetishistic figures by Félicien Rops, there is no sign of anything remotely like an orgy breaking out in this out-of-hours museum. As Prospero assures the couple that 'these our actors/Were all spirits' (4.1.148–9), the latter fall to the ground and Prospero strides past them towards the camera bringing Miranda and Ferdinand with him. (The twenty-eight stages listed in the published script as 'the masque and its company begin to dissolve', are not executed.)[46] A curtain falls behind Prospero as he speaks the rest of the speech (152–63) and a blackout precedes the next scene in which, seated in his 'study', he contemplates his strategy. After the hounding of the would-be usurpers, Prospero's abjuration of his magic (5.1.33–57) is spoken as he walks the length of the library and a bell tolls ominously from 'the solemn curfew' (5.1.40) onwards.

Masque Avoided, Masque Overloaded, Masque Simplified: Julie Taymor, Daniel Mesguich and Giorgio Strehler

To very different effect, the films of both Jarman and Greenaway take the viewer towards the wilder shores of adaptation. Three other productions, one on film and two on stage, are chosen here to afford another perspective on the masque and its difficulties. In her 2010 film, Julie Taymor omits the text of the masque altogether, substituting what her published script describes as 'a thrilling spectacle of sea creatures and constellations' that 'dance together and explode like fireworks before the eyes of the young couple, melding sky and ocean in an animated alchemical chart'.[47] In her DVD commentary, the director appears to have no great respect for what is described as 'a trifle that [Prospera] puts on because she has the power and the magic'. The masque with its goddesses 'really has no meaning now' and

Prospera (Helen Mirren) consequently entertains the young couple with a 'combination of tantric images, alchemical images…a combination of the heavens and the seas'.[48] Although, as Victoria Bladen points out in the present volume, the alchemical references are consistent with Taymor's depiction of Prospera's work in her laboratory, it is hard to imagine that this vaguely New Age event will be more intelligible than Ceres, Iris and Juno to all but the adepts among the audience; the sense of the masque has been ignored altogether. (The message now seems to be that all you need is love.) This spectacle, whatever one thinks of it, does reflect a common quandary: what to do with the space provided for the masque if you want to do without it? Jarman's rejection of the original text at this point and his shifting of a masque-like entertainment to a later scene were at least combined with a desire to provide joyousness and magic without obscurity.

Greenaway's faith in the power of mythological imagery leads to a degree of confusion in the tale-telling aspect of his film. A stage production by Daniel Mesguich at the Comédie-Française in 1998 seemed determined to out-Greenaway Greenaway by a layering of a slightly different kind, quoting the plays that (it was claimed) had a bearing on the narrative from the wider range of Shakespearean 'écriture.' With its three Ariels, a mute double for Prospero and a set dominated by stacks of huge books, the staging all but overwhelmed the narrative. Mesguich's appetite for *bricolage* was evident in the snatches of *Romeo and Juliet* that were heard and in the substitution of a poem by Louis Aragon, 'Les poètes' (1960), for Prospero's epilogue. As for the masque, Mesguich replaced it with a cross-dressed enactment of Richard III's wooing of Lady Anne by Éric Génovèse (Caliban) and Catherine Salviat, the latter billed simply as '*la figure du masque*'. The text included in the programme states at the appropriate points 'here the "masque" begins' and 'here the "masque" ends', with quotation marks to signal scepticism about the business.[49] A programme note states that the original text seemed significant more by virtue of its function than by the letter of the text, which seemed dated and of doubtful authenticity. The substituted scene offered 'a cyclone of Shakespearean writing' in which the 'eye' of the storm was the 'symbolic and sinister union of two young people…over the corpse of a king, the corpse of a father'.[50] Mesguich's productions have often evinced a similar desire to blend texts together, draw parallels and, in some cases, literally pile books on the stage.[51] Here, as Ruth Morse observed in a review, the problem was that he had 'tried to make spectacle replace wonder'.[52] In the final moments, when Prospero changed into modern clothes and joined the audience to deliver Aragon's poem, we moved from Prospero's to Mesguich's books.

A simpler, more effective, and in the last analysis more radical, response was that of Giorgio Strehler in the 1978 staging at the Piccolo Teatro, Milan, that has come to be regarded (like Peter Brook's 1970 *Midsummer Night's Dream*) as a defining production in late twentieth-century theatre. Accounting for his need to revisit the play thirty years after his 1948 production in the Boboli Gardens in Florence, Strehler described its presence, secret but constant, in all his artistic enquiry into theatre and humanity in the intervening years: 'Here, at the heart of *The Tempest*, the man of the theatre finds himself face to face with the theatre in its ultimate essence. He touches, or so he thinks, the extreme limits of the theatre'.[53] One of those limits seems to have been marked by the masque. At a late stage, Strehler abandoned its text in favour of a simple and elegant demonstration of the effect of Prospero's authoritative instructions on premarital chastity. After a formal procession to the sand circle in the centre of the platform, with the father carrying a flaming torch and Miranda bearing two sheaves of wheat, a simple ceremony consisted in the transference of the sheaves to each of the couple while Prospero put out the torch by inverting it against the sand. Then, in response to his instructions to Ariel, a white cloth enveloped the platform and the couple lay down, head to head, parallel to the front of the stage and stretching out their arms to touch hands chastely above their heads. (This seems to be the action depicted in the video: in the stage performance, Ferdinand 'merely [stood] silhouetted against a golden cloud formation suggestive of a baroque theatre set'.)[54] When Prospero remembered the conspiracy, the cloth was pulled away. Like other directors, Strehler was concerned that the masque, if played as written, might seem superfluous after the earlier spectacular scenes, especially that of the banquet and Ariel's appearance as the Harpy.[55] Moreover, this revision, although it dispensed with the masque's text, connected the episode with Prospero's anxieties about his own situation, his feelings towards his daughter, and the serious business of ensuring the integrity of the marriage. The inserted ritual was in itself hymeneal, neither a fancy light show in the Taymor manner nor a cross-referencing of other works *à la* Mesguich.

In their responses to the play's masque-like aspects and, in particular, to Prospero's own masque, the productions discussed here reflect the difficulty that directors of this text have evinced in arriving at a balance between showing and telling. In that respect, the play itself may be said to anticipate the condition of cinema and its own responsibilities as well as opportunities: part of its own special quality lies in this challenge and in particular in Prospero's masque. The limits of the cinema, a medium with apparent ease in delivering 'cloud-capped towers' convincingly, seem to come into touch with the limits of theatre as Strehler apprehended them. Jarman and Strehler can be said to have incorporated the serious implications of this 'vanity of [Prospero's] art' (4.1.41) while omitting its actual text. Greenaway and Mesguich, by ingenious and overabundant overloading, vitiate the impact of this aspect of the play, while Taymor simply shies away from it. The question of the masque seems to put the directors on their mettle; paradoxically, rising to its challenge may not involve performing it to the letter. Gracing it with elegancy, as Bacon recommends, while making it intelligible to a modern audience and avoiding daubing it with cost, are no easy tasks. The spirit of Ben Jonson's 'expostulation' with Inigo Jones still haunts both theatre and film.

Notes

1 F. Bacon, 'Of Maskes and Triumphs', in M. Kiernan (ed.), *The Essayes or Counsells, Civill and Morall* (Oxford: Clarendon Press, 1985), 117.

2 M. Billington, *One Night Stands. A Critic's View of Modern British Theatre*, 2nd edition (London: Nick Hern Books, 2001), 48.

3 B. Jonson, 'An Expostulation with Inigo Jones' (49–50), in I. Donaldson (ed.), *Poems* (Oxford: Oxford University Press, 1975), 322.

4 For the former I draw on the DVD of the RAI broadcast, while the second I saw in the theatre myself.

5 D. Harris and M. Jackson, 'Stormy Weather: Derek Jarman's *The Tempest*', *Literature/Film Quarterly*, 25:2 (January 1997), 90.

6 D. Albright, *Musicking Shakespeare: A Conflict of Theatres* (Rochester, NY: University of Rochester Press, 2007), 237.

7 R. Hosley (ed.), Ben Jonson's *Oberon, The Fairy Prince. A Masque of Prince Henry's*, in T. J. B. Spencer and S. Wells (eds.), *A Book of Masques, in Honour of Allardyce Nicoll* (Cambridge: Cambridge University Press, 1967), 43–70 (59).

8 S. Orgel, *The Jonsonian Masque* (New York: Columbia University Press, 1981), 6–7.

9 V. M. Vaughan and A. T. Vaughan (eds.), *The Tempest*, revised edition (London: Bloomsbury/New Arden, 2011), 70–3. See also S. Orgel (ed.), *The Tempest* (Oxford: Oxford University Press, 1987), 47–50.

10 On the play's stage history, see C. Dymkowski, *Shakespeare in Production: The Tempest* (Cambridge: Cambridge University Press, 2000); D. Lindley, *Shakespeare at Stratford:* The Tempest (London: New Arden Shakespeare, 2003); and V. M. Vaughan, *Shakespeare in Performance:* The Tempest (Manchester: Manchester University Press, 2011).

11 Lindley, *Shakespeare at Stratford*, 213; 205.

12 D. Robinson, 'A "Tempest" full of magic and surprises', *The Times*, 2 May 1980.

13 F. Kermode, 'Ideas strangle director', *Times Literary Supplement*, 16 May 1980, 553.

14 D. Jarman, *Modern Nature* (London: Century 1991), 131.

15 Y. Sonnabend, '"The Fabric of this Vision": Designing *The Tempest* with Derek Jarman', in R. Wollen (ed.), *Derek Jarman: A Portrait* (London: Thames and Hudson, 1996), 79.

16 D. Jarman, *Kicking the Pricks* (London: Vintage, 1996), 136; 138.

17 Jarman, *Modern Nature*, 15.

18 *Kicking the Pricks*, 90.

19 *Ibid.*, 54.

20 *Ibid.*, 63.

21 *Ibid.*, 60.

22 D. Jarman, *At Your Own Risk: A Saint's Testament* (London: Hutchinson, 1992), 20.

23 *Kicking the Pricks*, 108.

24 *Ibid.*, 60.

25 Jarman, *Modern Nature*, 65.

26 R. Wymer, *Derek Jarman* (Manchester: Manchester University Press, 2005), 79.

27 Jarman, *Kicking the Pricks*, 181.

28 T. Peake, *Derek Jarman: A Biography* (Woodstock, NY: Overlook Press, 2000), 395.

29 D. Jarman, *Smiling in Slow Motion* (London: Century, 2000), 46.

30 Jarman, *Smiling in Slow Motion*, 325.

31 Peake, *Jarman*, 326.

32 Jarman, *Modern Nature*, 189.

33 Peake, 231.

34 P. Aebischer, *Screening Early Modern Drama: Beyond Shakespeare* (Cambridge: Cambridge University Press, 2013), 25.

35 A. Higson's *English Heritage, English Cinema: Costume Drama Since 1980* (Oxford: Oxford University Press, 2003) includes both *Prospero's Books* and Jarman's *The Tempest* among films that, are 'in their way, films with elements of costume drama,' but 'resist...visual historicism' and 'play with representation in a postmodernist fashion that challenges the realistic effect' (22).

36 A. Lawrence, *The Films of Peter Greenaway* (Cambridge: Cambridge University Press, 1997), 144.

37 A. Barker, 'A Tale of Two Magicians', *Sight and Sound*, 1 May 1991, 27.

38 K. Sturgess, *Jacobean Private Theatre* (London and New York: Routledge and Kegan Paul, 1987), 73; 79.

39 P. S. Donaldson, 'Shakespeare in the Age of Post-Mechanical Reproduction: Sexual and Electronic Magic in *Prospero's Books*', in R. Burt and L. E. Boose (eds.), *Shakespeare the Movie, II: Popularizing the Plays on Film, TV, Video, and DVD* (London and New York: Routledge, 2003), 107.

40 J. Romney, 'Prospero's Books,' *Sight and Sound*, 1 September 1991, 44–5 (45).

41 M. Rodgers, '*Prospero's Books* – Word and Spectacle. An Interview with Peter Greenaway', *Film Quarterly* 45:2 (Winter 1991–2), 11.

42 *Prospero's Books: A Film of Shakespeare's* The Tempest *by Peter Greenaway* (London: Chatto and Windus, 1991). Significantly, the title page and cover do not use italics or inverted commas to demarcate title, description and authorship.

43 D. M. Lanier, 'Drowning the Book: *Prospero's Books* and the Textual Shakespeare', in J. Bulman (ed.), *Shakespeare, Theory, and Performance* (London: Routledge, 1996), 195.

44 The meta-cinematic/meta-literary aspect of the film is explored by L. M. Hotchkiss, 'The Incorporation of Word as Image in Peter Greenaway's *Prospero's Books*', in L. S. Starks and C. Lehmann (eds.), *The Reel Shakespeare: Alternative Cinema and Theory* (Madison, Teaneck and London: Fairleigh Dickinson University Press/AUP, 2002), 95–117.

45 Lawrence, *Greenaway*, 16.

46 *Prospero's Books* (script), 145: 'montage' numbered as scene 83.4.

47 J. Taymor, *'The Tempest', adapted from the Play by William Shakespeare* (New York: Abrams, 2010), 137.

48 *Ibid.*

49 Programme/script, *'La Tempête' de William Shakespeare. Texte français de Xavier Maurel et Daniel Mesguich* (Paris: Comédie Française, 1998), 78–9.

50 *Ibid.*, 35.

51 On Mesguich's productions in general (but excluding his *Tempest*), see M. Carlson, 'Daniel Mesguich and Intertextual Shakespeare', in D. Kennedy (ed.), *Foreign Shakespeare: Contemporary Performance* (Cambridge: Cambridge University Press, 1993), 213–31; in the same volume, see D. Goy-Blanquet, 'Titus Resartus: Deborah Warner, Peter Stein and Daniel Mesguich have a cut at *Titus Andronicus*', 36–55.

52 R. Morse, 'This Insubstantial Pageant', *Times Literary Supplement*, 13 March 1998, 19.

53 G. Strehler, 'Appunti di regia della Tempesta del 1978 (seconda edizione)' at http://archivio.piccoloteatro.org/shakespeare/?tipo=6&ID=37&imm=1& contatore=0&real=0 (accessed 18 April 2015) ('Ma qui nel cuore della Tempesta l'uomo di teatro si trova davanti al teatro nella sua ultima essenza. Tocca o crede toccare gli estremi limiti del teatro.'). My translation.

54 Dymkowski, 287, quoting a *TLS* review by Roger Warren (9 March 1984). A DVD of the RAI broadcast of the production is included in the 4-DVD box set *Giorgio Strehler – Il Grande Teatro*, 1 (RAI/Eri, 2012).

55 On Strehler's decision to omit the masque's text, and his earlier consideration of the use of Bunraku-style puppets for the goddesses, see the correspondence between him and the translator, Agostino Lombardo in R. Colombo (ed.), *William Shakespeare, Agostino Lombardo e Giorgio Strehler: 'La Tempestà,' tradotta e messa in scena 1977–78. Un carteggio fra Strehler e Lombardo e due tradizioni inedite* (Roma: Donzelli, 2007), esp. 123–31. The production team's discussions of the masque are described in the rehearsal diary of the dramaturg Ettore Gaipa, edited by S. Casteghi, *Il metodo Strehler: Diari di prova della 'Tempestà' scritti da Ettore Gaipa* (Milan: Skira, 2012), 42; 81–2; 85–6. On

the background of the production, see P. Kleber, 'Theatrical continuities in Giorgio Strehler's *The Tempest*', in Kennedy, *Foreign Shakespeares*, 140–58 and David Hirst, *Giorgio Strehler* (Cambridge: Cambridge University Press, 1993), 83–9.

WORKS CITED

Aebischer, P., *Screening Early Modern Drama: Beyond Shakespeare* (Cambridge: Cambridge University Press, 2013).

Albright, D., *Musicking Shakespeare: A Conflict of Theatres* (Rochester, NY: University of Rochester Press, 2007).

Bacon, F., 'Of Maskes and Triumphs', in M. Kiernan (ed.), *The Essayes or Counsells, Civill and Morall* (Oxford: Clarendon Press, 1985), 117–18.

Barker, A., 'A Tale of Two Magicians,' *Sight and Sound*, 1 May 1991, 26–30.

Billington, M., *One Night Stands: A Critic's View of Modern British Theatre*, 2nd edition (London: Nick Hern Books, 2001).

Carlson, M., 'Daniel Mesguich and Intertextual Shakespeare', in D. Kennedy (ed.), *Foreign Shakespeare: Contemporary Performance* (Cambridge: Cambridge University Press, 1993), 213–31.

Casteghi, S., *Il metodo Strehler: Diari di prova della 'Tempestà' scritti da Ettore Gaipa* (Milan: Skira, 2012).

Colombo, R. (ed.), *William Shakespeare, Agostino Lombardo e Giorgio Strehler: 'La Tempestà,' tradotta e messa in scena 1977–78. Un carteggio fra Strehler e Lombardo e due tradizioni inedite* (Roma: Donzelli, 2007).

Donaldson, P. S., 'Shakespeare in the Age of Post-Mechanical Reproduction: Sexual and Electronic Magic in Prospero's Books', in R. Burt and L. E. Boose (eds.), *Shakespeare the Movie, II: Popularizing the Plays on Film, TV, Video and DVD* (London and New York: Routledge, 2003), 89–105.

Dymkowski, C., *Shakespeare in Production:* The Tempest (Cambridge: Cambridge University Press, 2000).

Goy-Blanquet, D., 'Titus Resartus: Deborah Warner, Peter Stein and Daniel Mesguich have a cut at *Titus Andronicus*', in D. Kennedy (ed.), *Foreign Shakespeare: Contemporary Performance* (Cambridge: Cambridge University Press, 1993), 36–55.

Greenaway, P., Prospero's Books. *A Film of Shakespeare's* The Tempest *by Peter Greenaway* (London: Chatto and Windus, 1991).

Harris, D. and M. Jackson, 'Stormy Weather: Derek Jarman's *The Tempest*', *Literature/Film Quarterly*, 25.2 (January 1997), 90–8.

Higson, A., *English Heritage, English Cinema: Costume Drama Since 1980* (Oxford: Oxford University Press, 2003).

Hosley, H. (ed.), Ben Jonson's *Oberon, The Fairy prince. A Masque of Prince Henry's*, in T. J. B. Spencer and S. Wells (eds.), *A Book of Masques, in Honour of Allardyce Nicoll* (Cambridge: Cambridge University Press, 1967), 43–70.

Hotchkiss, L. M., 'The Incorporation of Word as Image in Peter Greenaway's *Prospero's Books*', in L. S. Starks and C. Lehmann (eds.), *The Reel Shakespeare:*

Alternative Cinema and Theory (Madison, Teaneck and London: Fairleigh Dickinson University Press/AUP, 2002), 95–117.

Jarman, D., *At Your Own Risk: A Saint's Testament* (London: Hutchinson, 1992).

Kicking the Pricks (London: Vintage, 1996).

Modern Nature (London: Century, 1991).

Smiling in Slow Motion (London: Century, 2000).

Jonson, B., 'An Expostulation with Inigo Jones' (49–50), in I. Donaldson (ed.), *Poems* (Oxford: Oxford University Press, 1975), 319–24.

Kermode, F., 'Ideas strangle director,' *Times Literary Supplement*, 16 May 1980, 553.

Kleber, P., 'Theatrical continuities in Giorgio Strehler's *The Tempest*', in D. Kennedy (ed.), *Foreign Shakespeare: Contemporary Performance* (Cambridge: Cambridge University Press, 1993), 140–58.

Lawrence, A., *The Films of Peter Greenaway* (Cambridge: Cambridge University Press, 1997).

Lanier, D. M., 'Drowning the Book: *Prospero's Books* and the Textual Shakespeare', in J. Bulman (ed.), *Shakespeare, Theory, and Performance* (London: Routledge, 1996), 187–209.

Lindley, D., *Shakespeare at Stratford:* The Tempest (London: New Arden Shakespeare, 2003).

Morse, R., 'This Insubstantial Pageant', *Times Literary Supplement*, 13 March 1998, 19.

Orgel, S., *The Jonsonian Masque* (New York: Columbia University Press, 1981).

Orgel, S. (ed.), *The Tempest* (Oxford: Oxford University Press, 1987).

Peake, T., *Derek Jarman: A Biography* (Woodstock, NY: Overlook Press, 2000).

Robinson, D., 'A "Tempest" full of magic and surprises', *The Times*, 2 May 1980.

Rodgers, M., '*Prospero's Books* – Word and Spectacle: An Interview with Peter Greenaway', *Film Quarterly* 45.2 (Winter 1991–2), 11–19.

Romney, Jonathan, 'Prospero's Books,' *Sight and Sound*, 1 September 1991, 44–5.

Sonnabend, Y., '"The Fabric of this Vision": Designing *The Tempest* with Derek Jarman', in R. Wollen (ed.), *Derek Jarman: A Portrait* (London: Thames and Hudson, 1996), 77–9.

Sturgess, K., *Jacobean Private Theatre* (London and New York: Routledge and Kegan Paul, 1987).

Taymor, J., *'The Tempest', adapted from the Play by William Shakespeare* (New York: Abrams, 2010).

Vaughan V. M. and A. T. Vaughan, *Shakespeare's Caliban: A Cultural History* (Cambridge: Cambridge University Press, 1991).

Vaughan V. M., *Shakespeare in Performance:* The Tempest (Manchester: Manchester University Press, 2011).

Wymer, R., *Derek Jarman* (Manchester: Manchester University Press, 2005).

CHAPTER 11

Prospero's Books
Hyperreality and the Western Imagination
Randy Laist

The theme of ambiguous ontology runs throughout the works of Shakespeare but it is in *The Tempest* that this motif receives its fullest and most complex treatment. Throughout the drama, characters continually doubt their senses, question whether they are awake or dreaming and wonder whether the people they encounter are real or phantasmal. Prospero, our guide through the drama's ontological labyrinth, repeatedly warns us to avoid taking reality too literally, most notably in his 'cloud-capped towers' speech (4.1.152) and in his concluding address to the audience. The tradition in Shakespeare scholarship that conflates the playwright himself with the main character of his last self-authored play encourages us to see in Prospero's skepticism a hint to Shakespeare's own philosophy – simultaneously an aesthetic and an ontological one – in which theatrical representation and experiential reality share an underlying identity.

Unlike the many more conventional adaptations of *The Tempest*, Peter Greenaway's *Prospero's Books* (1991) focuses on the conceptual rather than the narrative structure of the play. While Greenaway's film does recapitulate the play's story from beginning to end, the central preoccupation that propels the production is the theme of what Jean Baudrillard and Umberto Eco famously called hyperreality, a condition of vertiginous indeterminacy between representation and reality.[1] John Gielgud plays a Prospero who is a textual, theatrical entity, bound in a Mobius-strip condition of being both character and author. The arrangement of the film around the volumes in Prospero's library emphasizes one of the play's most startling metaphors of hyperreality: that it is out of his books that Prospero has managed to conjure up the reality in which he lives. Moreover, the film as a whole, in its dense allusiveness to the history of European arts and sciences, implies that the consciousness of the Western imagination is itself embedded in an elaborate, hyperreal fantasy that has always been marooned on Prospero's island.

Commenting on the unique quality of *The Tempest*, Northrop Frye states that, while plays within plays are common throughout Shakespeare's works, 'In *The Tempest* the play and the play within the play have become the same thing: we're looking simultaneously at two plays, Shakespeare's and the dramatic structure being worked out by Prospero'.² Likewise, Frye observes, 'It's not uncommon for a play to depict one play in rehearsal and then have another story move across it . . . But for one play to be consistently both process and product is surely very unusual'.³ Frye's comments draw attention to the paradoxical nature of the reality staged in *The Tempest*: Prospero is presented as the magus responsible for devising all of the play's theatrical spectacles, yet, because of the density with which 'the play and the play within the play' have been woven together, Prospero himself is also depicted as a creature of this art of illusion, opening a vortex into an infinite regress of signification. Rather than a real magus weaving an illusory spectacle, the audience encounters an illusory magus weaving a spectacle with a fundamentally ambiguous ontology. This uncanny effect recalls Baudrillard's speculations regarding hyperreality as 'the generation of a real without origin or reality'⁴ and Eco's descriptions of hyperreal environments in which 'the distinction between Real Worlds and Possible Worlds has been definitively undermined'.⁵ Written in 1986, Frye's remarks on *The Tempest* were likely influenced by post-modern cultural theorists such as Baudrillard and Eco, and this post-modern philosophical climate in which Frye considered the 'unusual' relationship between reality and representation in *The Tempest* was the same one in which Greenaway conceptualized and produced *Prospero's Books*.

The casting of an iconic thespian in the role of Prospero is a time-honored cliché, but Greenaway's film one-ups the cliché by having Gielgud read the parts of the play's other characters as well. This dispersal of Gielgud's famous voice throughout the play's *dramatis personae* is one of the most prominent stylistic oddities in Greenaway's adaptation, and it has multiple effects on the overall impression of reality conveyed by the film. Most immediately, it underscores Greenaway's conflation of Prospero as a character in the play and as a writer of the play. Shakespeare anticipated post-modernism by several hundred years in *The Tempest*'s insinuation that the art practised by Prospero, the arrangement of his revenge and of Miranda and Ferdinand's relationship, is akin to the art practised by writers and directors of theatrical productions. With his hoard of spells, his familiarity with the backstage mechanisms of his performance space and the deft proficiency of his stage-manager, Ariel, Prospero is able to spellbind the people around him into rapt captivity and, in Hitchcock's phrase, to play them like an organ.[6] The parallelism established in the play between Prospero's magic and Shakespeare's artistry suggests that the condition of dreamlike befuddlement that overwhelms the visitors to Prospero's island also bewitches the play's audience. Shakespeare's fiction has the magical ability to escape the world of make-believe and enchant real human beings with its strange power to twist reality and illusion into an ambiguous third state that is both and neither. *Prospero's Books* builds on this theme by explicitly positioning Gielgud's Prospero as the writer of *The Tempest*, not only by depicting him writing the play's dialogue in flowing script, but also by having him read many of the other characters' lines. In the play's exposition scene, in which Prospero speaks to Miranda for the first time about the circumstances of how they came to be exiled, Gielgud reads Miranda's lines in unison with the actress who plays Miranda, emphasizing the extent to which Miranda is a passive partner in the father-daughter relationship. Throughout the dialogue, Miranda is actually shown to be asleep, as if the conversation were taking place in a dream. In the play, Prospero withholds and imparts information to Miranda in a way that reflects his use of knowledge as a source of power, and this power of information is followed by his more surreal but no less magical power to cause Miranda to fall asleep when Ariel arrives. Greenaway's decision to film Miranda as magically asleep during her first scene foregrounds Shakespeare's theme of sleep as an arena of ambiguous reality and establishes Prospero as an artist whose medium is dreams.

At other times, Gielgud's is the only voice delivering dialogue, as in the opening scene of both the movie and the play, the 'tempest' scene that gives the play its name. Whereas in the play this is an ensemble scene performed by at least five characters along with an unspecified number of mariners, Greenaway depicts Gielgud's Prospero alone in a bath *à la* David's Marat, and in a book-lined study, *à la* van Eyck's Saint Jerome, reading and writing all of the parts himself. Rather than capturing the tone of comic panic presented in the first scene of Shakespeare's play, Greenaway uses this first scene to establish the theme of gleeful illusion-weaving that the film will go on to elaborate. The first line of Shakespeare's play, 'Boatswain!' is presented not as the urgent appeal of a doomed ship's master, but as a curious phonological and graphological artifact, spoken and written multiple times as if for the purpose of accentuating the word's strangeness. As he repeats the word over and over again, Gielgud laughs exuberantly, delighting in the word as a simple pair of syllables, stripping the word of signification and giving it over to a kind of verbal music, a pronouncement of the power of the voice itself to create, to fill a room with sound, and to assert a human presence. As Gielgud splashes with childlike delight in the creative urge represented by the play's dialogue, a muse-like Ariel urinates in an endless stream, bringing together a number of images that connect the play's water imagery to the theme of free-flowing imaginative power.

Prospero is simultaneously a character in a play, the writer of the play, and an actor in the play. In his final monologue, Prospero's appeal to the audience for their applause is not so much a break with his character as a revelation that his character has been an elaborate, self-conscious performance. Indeed, the very source of Prospero's magic is precisely his ability to leap across ontological planes, to be simultaneously in the story (as a character), in control of the story (as a writer) and also in some third dimension that is neither fictional nor metafictional, but which is rooted in Prospero's recognition of the illusory nature of all of human perception (like an actor, who, being the embodiment of some writer's conception, is literally 'such stuff/As dreams are made on').

Greenaway seizes on this surprisingly contemporary-sounding effect in Shakespeare's play and extends the premise to encompass himself as the film's director. Indeed, Greenaway's 'voice' is just as pervasive in *Prospero's Books* as Gielgud's. In characteristic defiance of the popular culture's cinematic aesthetic, according to which a director is required to subordinate his or her artistic vision to the dictates of narrative, Greenaway's signature directorial effects are not only present in every frame of the film, but actually overwhelm Shakespeare's story to such an extent that an audience unfamiliar with Shakespeare's play (and with the various Romantic and post-modern commentaries on Shakespeare's play) would find it impossible to follow the story. The presence of Shakespeare's original text in Greenaway's film is both all-pervasive and illegible, like the overwritten text of a palimpsest. Greenaway's fondness for long, elaborate takes, dense arrangements of human figures and painterly allusiveness, along with his visual experimentation and deliberate narrative pacing, fills the film with the director's distinctive presence and refracts the signification of the film's central magus to refer not only to Gielgud, Shakespeare and Prospero, but to include Greenaway as well. In defiance of a realist ontology according to which real artists create illusory representations of reality, *Prospero's Books* depicts a hyperreal condition in which the art and the artist both inhabit a shifting landscape of ontological indeterminacy.

Of the many devices that Greenaway uses to make Shakespeare's play into his own film, the most conspicuous is the interpolation of the twenty-four eponymous books. Godard's famous dictum, articulated in *Le Petit Soldat* (1963), that 'cinema is truth at twenty-four frames per second' audaciously plays upon the manner in which image-making technology has become the ontological bedrock in post-modern society. The resonance of the quotation results from the sense in which Godard both asserts a realist faith in the possibility of truth, while simultaneously redefining this realist value by displacing it from the domain of direct experience into the domain of mediated images; the representations become the reality. In characteristic fashion, Greenaway's appropriation of Godard's remark as a structural principle for *Prospero's Books* not only applies the sentiment expressed in the quotation to the film itself (implying that this elaborately choreographed cinematic artifact is itself a statement of 'truth'), but also extends this idea to envelop not only cinematic representation, but literary representation as well. While there is a realistic sense in which cinema does tell the truth (it uses light to record the existence of physical objects), books, especially works of fantastic fiction such as Shakespeare's *The Tempest*, bear no direct relationship to any realist definition of 'truth.' The search to find what kind of 'truth' is embodied in a work of fantasy fiction cannot come to rest on anything as solid as a visual image; it continues to penetrate into an ontological labyrinth where truth consists not in what is visible or even in what is actual, but in moods, ideas, states of consciousness and dreams. Of course, there is a sense in which this psychological maze is the foundational truth of human existence, but to acknowledge as much is to abandon an Enlightenment faith in an objective reality in favor of a dreamscape of true lies.

Greenaway's Prospero inhabits just such a dreamscape. Greenaway's emphasis of Prospero's books as the source of the magus's power corresponds with Caliban's assessment in the play ('Remember/First to possess his books; for without them/He's but a sot' [3.2.83–5]), but it also represents a statement about the foundational role played by literacy in all Western cultural achievements. In Greenaway's film, Prospero has used the magic of his books to build a 'poor cell' (1.2.20) that is a dizzying collage of classical, renaissance, romantic and post-modern allusions and motifs. Like Crusoe, he has modeled his island exile after the cultural values of his native land. The magic power of his books, however, has allowed Greenaway's Prospero to create a reality that is like Renaissance Milan as it would be depicted in one of Umberto Eco's Californian wax museums,[7] with iconic images jumbled together, anachronisms abounding, scales magnified, and the whole panoply staged as an elaborate spectacle. Prospero's ability to conjure up such a world out of his twenty-four books reflects the 'real magic' of literacy to stock consciousness with imaginary contents, to transfer knowledge and techne across temporal and spatial distances and, ultimately, to transform reality itself into a reflection of the content of books. Green-away's script teases out a nuance that is present in Shakespeare's play, in which Prospero's style of book-magic exists in contrast with the nature magic of the witch Sycorax, whom Prospero has bested and displaced. The play's backstory suggests that the abstract knowledge represented by literacy has conquered the embodied knowledge of nature, and Greenaway depicts Prospero's island as one in which all natural forms have been subordinated to the artistry of the magus (Shakespeare/Prospero/Greenaway/Western Civilization).

As dense and busy as Greenaway's images tend to be, nothing is ever left to chance; every detail of the composition is always tightly controlled. Greenaway's images are painterly not only or even primarily in their direct or stylistic allusions to famous paintings, but more importantly because the ontology of his tableaux has more in common with oil painting than with photography due to Greenaway's rigorous dominion over every brushstroke that appears in his film. Every nuance in the world of the film is meticu-lously orchestrated by Greenaway/Prospero; it is a world of total mind, a phantastic mindscape that even reaches out to include other people. Pros-pero and Greenaway use their respective forms of magic to transform the island's resident spirits (in Prospero's case) and a large cast of film extras (in Greenaway's) into sprawling neoclassical tableaux.

In the introduction to his elaborate screenplay for the film, Greenaway explains that most of the architectural and painterly styles he borrows for the purposes of adorning his island exile "are historical or contemporary to [Prospero's] life, but being a magician he can also slip time and borrow and quote the future."[8] This is a roundabout way of saying that the world elaborately staged in *Prospero's Books* is not uniquely that of a seventeenth-century Milano, but is the world of a seventeenth-century Milano as seen through the imagination of a twentieth-century Renaissance man. Green-away, the real-world filmmaker, and Prospero, the fictional magus, col-laborate across ontological boundaries to build a fantasy world that turns the raw materials of light and time into a visionary landscape in which reality and representation coalesce into a third order of being: a hyperre-ality. The iconography of the imagery itself, drawing so heavily on alle-gorical and classical motifs, suggests the manner in which the history of Western art is itself a precession of signs that relies more heavily on recy-cling and reiteration than on invention. The Renaissance, conventionally understood to be the coming-of-age of Western Europe, is itself an elabo-rate project of reiterating the forms and philosophies of the classical world, famously rediscovered through key texts of ancient scholarship. European civilization, like Prospero's island, popped up out of pages of written text in the same way that the illustrations in *A Bestiary of Past, Present, and Future Animals* come to life and crawl out of the book, or the way that the buildings in *A Book of Architecture and Other Music* fold into shape as the book opens.

The final 'pop-up' structure revealed in the Book of Architecture sequence folds out into a three-dimensional replica of the staircase in the vestibule of Michelangelo's Laurentian library, and the film dissolves from a shot of this book-bound model into a magical-cinematic replica of these steps, with Prospero regally striding down them. Architecture, in which two-dimensional marks on a page refer to substantial physical objects in the world, provides a vivid synecdoche of the sense in which writing occupies a liminal status between imagination and reality, and the magical quality of all of the books in Prospero's library consists of variations on this concept. The book of motion moves; the book of anatomy bleeds; the pages of the book of earth are suffused with minerals, acids, and soils. The books in Prospero's library are not books in the modern sense of the word – the expression of the point of view of a particular author – they are 'books' in an abstract, mystical sense – the essence of the written word as an elemental disclosure, a bringing-forth of potent arcana. They represent a religion of literacy according to which the ultimate secrets of the universe are located not in the universe itself, but in the uncanny melding of the physical world and the imagination of an inscrutable bookmaker. At the same time, many of Prospero's magical books use fantastical imagery to evoke the surreal phenomenology of the act of reading. The flowing diagrams in the book of water suggest the fluidity of the reading mind, the way words on a page can stream into new configurations and significations upon repeated readings. The ability of the Book of Mirrors to show the reader to himself 'as he would be if he were a child, a woman, a monster, an idea, a text, or an angel' symbolizes the sense in which all books are reflective surfaces of this sort. *The Book of Universal Cosmographies*, likewise, presents a potent metaphor for the aspiration of certain texts – *The Bible*, *The Origin of Species*, or *Ulysses*, for example – 'to place all universal phenomena in one system'.[9] Each of Greenaway's interpolated volumes performs some variation on this theme of the interpenetration of the literary imagination and the physical world. The film's motif of calligraphy provides the most compelling expression of this theme. The ability of Prospero to write his story into existence is epitomized in the physical act of writing, a deed that transforms a mental operation into an objective presence in the world. The flip-art-style animation effects that appear in several of the film's book sequences advance this suggestion a step further by revealing the sense in which filmmaking is itself an extension of writing as an art that conjures dreams into realities.

On the scale of the narrative as a whole, Shakespeare's First Folio and Prospero's own manuscript of *The Tempest* are two of these magical volumes. As titles in Prospero's magical library, these real-world books are invested with the fantastical power that characterizes the rest of Prospero's books to manifest their contents in physical, perceptual form. The fact that we are watching the movie represents the magical instantiation of marks made on a page four hundred years ago. The characters of Shakespeare's play have 'popped up' out of the pages of these books to become images on a screen, archetypes in the collective consciousness and moons of Uranus (which have been named Ariel and Miranda – a dramatic example of Shakespeare's world bursting out into the real cosmos). At the same time, these intra-worldly hypostases of Shakespeare's characters slither back into the books, influencing their cultural signification. An entity like Prospero derives its meaning from a hybrid register that encompasses both the text and the world. Greenaway captures this effect through his portrayal of the magus as the author not only of the other characters around him, but also of the text that contains himself. In this sense, Greenaway's Prospero epitomizes the Baudrillardian definition of the hyperreal as a 'copy without an original', a perfect simulation that gives birth to itself through a precession of signs. Like the hand that illustrates itself in the M. C. Escher drawing, Prospero uses the magic of the written word to weave together reality and representation into a vertiginous ontological synthesis.

Although a book of art history is not specifically identified among Prospero's books, the movie clearly uses the language of art history to develop the sense in which Prospero both builds his three-dimensional world out of two-dimensional representations and in which he is himself constructed out of such representations. Not only is his island a collage of art historical allusions, but, when he relates his memory of his pre-exilic life to Miranda, the memory is represented as a similarly allusive collage. In particular, Prospero's memory of Milan blends together the famous tableau from Veronese's *The Wedding at Cana* with the style of dress associated with Dutch Golden Age painting. This sequence insinuates that not only is Prospero's island environment a pastiche of European iconography, but his memory and his identity also constitute a similar assemblage of cultural forms. The uncanny nature of Prospero's island, that is, seeps out onto the mainland, and all of Europe is reconstituted as a hyperreal phantasy. Moreover, since Prospero stands as a personification of the European mind itself, the insinuation that his memories rely so heavily on a bank of shared cultural representations suggests the extent to which Western subjectivity articulates itself out of its inheritance of literary and artistic models.

The most conspicuous interpolation in Prospero/Greenaway's recreation of Veronese's painting is the costuming of the revelers in elaborate ruffs reminiscent of the fashion depicted in Dutch paintings such as Frans Hals's *The Meager Company*, and the expansive ruffs associated with this style become detached from this context to become one of *Prospero's Books's* most distinct motifs. The ruffs worn in the film are exaggerated in a way that amplifies the already-exaggerated quality of this fashion accessory into a principle in itself. In Prospero's imagination, the cartwheel ruff of early modern fashion mutates into a symbol of European disembodiment. This interpretation of the seventeenth-century ruff had been memorably suggested several years earlier in Terry Gilliam's *The Adventures of Baron Munchausen* (1988), in which the ruff worn by Robin Williams's character acts as a flying saucer that detaches his head from his body and allows it to fly around in space. The enormous ruffs that encircle the heads of characters at various points throughout *Prospero's Books* have an identical effect of removing their heads from any bodily or environmental context. This effect has something in common with the sensibility of head-and-shoulders portrait-painting itself, and Greenaway implies that the fashion of elaborately starched and goffered neckwear coevolved with the art of oil painting as two facets of an underlying thrust toward abstraction and depersonalization that characterize the legacy of the early modern period.

While the reality engendered by Prospero's books is frequently rich and beautiful, it is also strewn with scenes of horror. During the long credit-sequence tracking shot that introduces us to the texture of Prospero's magic world, Prospero strides regally past the progeny of his craft, including figures drawn not only from Veronese and Botticelli, but also from Hieronymus Bosch and other visionary torture-scapes. For a minute or so during Prospero's tour of his domain, Michael Nyman's stirring score fades out, and, as Prospero walks majestically past a series of tableaux which advance from lightning-lit arrangements of classical figures associated with drowning to fire-lit images of 'John White' Indians, the soundtrack plays the ominous sounds of the thunder from the storm and the percussive sounds of mechanical clanking. Greenaway's camera travels just as indifferently as Prospero's person past the violence and orientalism that constitute the dark underbelly of the world they have brought into being. At the same time that the film celebrates and revels in its pageantry of extravagant spectacles, the very formality of the artist's tableaux, the fanatical precision and single-mindedness that is evidenced in their studied complexity, suggests a mania for power that we also see reflected in the less admirable traits of Prospero's personality. The same books that have made him a masterful technician and artist have also made him a control freak, a colonizer, and a crypto-fascist. The insinuation, understated in *The Tempest* but pronounced in *Prospero's Books*, is that the Western imagination itself is stranded in a hall of mirrors of its own invention, so dazzled by the Faustian power granted by its vast library of representations that it is unable to perceive the systemic oppression implicit in its structure.

The peremptory nature of this oppression is dramatized by the film's depictions of Caliban and Ariel. Caliban is introduced as the lone hold-out to Prospero's perfect mastery of his domain. His introduction into the story is accompanied by a montage depicting the effacement of books – with knives, urine, feces – in a graphic rejection of the values of literacy that constitute the key principle of Prospero's reign. In the startling phys-ical contortions of Michael Clark's movements, Caliban's body language constitutes a counterforce to the hyperlinguisticism of the world as it has been designed by Greenaway and Shakespeare. Caliban's fate, however, is summed up in one of his most famous lines: 'You taught me language, and my profit on't/Is, I know how to curse' (1.2.363–4). Caliban's inescapable dilemma is that, even in his very statements of resistance, he expresses his embeddedness within the colonizer's language, along with all of that language's attendant semantic and political structures. This tragic irony implicit in Caliban's character is memorably represented in the film when, during Caliban, Stephano and Trinculo's representation of their successful coup, Caliban appears crouched in a doglike posture dressed in nothing but a surreally outsized cartwheel ruff. The image exemplifies the futility of any rebellion on Caliban's part, not only or even primarily due to the power imbalance between he and Prospero, but more importantly because Caliban's entire identity and desire-structure are always already Prospero-ized in their being; even his ambition to usurp Prospero's reign demon-strates Caliban's enthrallment to Prospero's own decidedly Western brand of Faustian ambition. Like post-modern dissidents everywhere, Caliban is inextricably bound up in the culture that he would resist.

Ariel, the 'good' subaltern, seems to make out much better than Cal-iban. The Ariel we see in the film is a caprice of Prospero's; as with all of the island's spirits, he appears as a painterly allegorical figure in Prospero's human tableau. He embodies each of his four figurative avatars with the same dispatch and fidelity with which he carries out Prospero's commands throughout the film, fully aware, like Caliban, of the futility of challeng-ing the magus's complete authority. Ariel is just as enslaved by Prospero as

Caliban, and arguably more so, since his glimmerings of resistance are so understated. Nevertheless, Ariel is able to exert his own subjectivity within the story in a way that appears to disrupt Prospero's totalitarian grip on reality. Ariel's statement of pity on behalf of Prospero's victims introduces a new voice into the story. The four Ariels actually write the line into Prospero's book in their own handwriting, suggesting that they articulate a sensibility that comes into the world of the movie from outside Prospero's sphere of control. Ariel's statement of mercy is the first element in the entire film that does not trace its origin to Prospero's books; it is a message from the island 'itself,' from Ariel 'himself' – whoever or whatever he might be behind the allegorical façade – penetrating the hyperreal snow globe of Prospero's Western fantasy to touch the magician's heart and redirect his intentions. On the one hand, this detail suggests the existence of a deeper reality underneath the hyperreal veneer of mirroring simulacra. On the other hand, Prospero's ability to fold Ariel's perspective into the structure of his own drama reinforces his own power and dictatorial supremacy over his entire environment. He is able to reverse the momentum of his entire project from vengeance to mercy on a whim, even if Ariel himself is not manumitted any earlier than Prospero had always intended. Ultimately, the impression is that Prospero has co-opted Ariel's perspective into his own world view without fundamentally altering the overriding principle of his unrivaled mastery. Whether he condemns or forgives, Prospero's bibliotopia is a totalitarian state.

Shakespeare provides a simple, if nihilistic, solution to this dilemma of Western consciousness. Drown the books. The height of Prospero's accumulated wisdom is expressed in his conclusion that the ultimate lesson that he has learned from the books is that the books need to be destroyed. Prospero's renunciation of his power and his island kingdom and his decision to return to the bourgeois banality of the mainland recall such landmark statements of post-modern negation as William Gibson's self-erasing electronic poem *Agrippa* (1992) or the last chapter of Toni Morrison's *Beloved* (1987). This rejection of the books is of a piece with Prospero's decision to pardon his usurpers; both decisions rely on a rupture with history, a commitment to present realities rather than to the representations forged in the past. Greenaway's film identifies Prospero's decision to forgive the conspirators as a turning point in the narrative. Once released from the grip of Prospero's grudge, Alonso, Ferdinand, and the others finally speak in their own voices, rather than being overvoiced by Gielgud. Even Caliban gets a reprieve, suggesting that an integral part of Prospero's enlightenment is his determination to release control over others in order to allow them to express their own perspectives and independent identities. In this gesture, the film seems to be making a definitive break with the hyperreal ontology of its preceding scenes. Rather than a reality entirely determined by an orbital, solipsistic representation of a representation, the emergence of other voices suggests a path back to a consensual, social reality that is a collective enterprise. This emerging social realism, however, is quickly extinguished when Prospero, having destroyed his books, turns to the audience to deliver his final monologue in which he reestablishes the sense that everything that has happened over the course of the story, up to and including the part where other people spoke in their own voices, has all been an effect of his artistry. Greenaway amplifies this ontologically subversive gesture in Shakespeare's play by arranging to have the filmic image of Gielgud speaking Prospero's final soliloquy recede into a black backdrop. As Prospero exposes himself as an actor, the director exposes the actor himself as a cinematic illusion, invisibly manipulated by the whimsy of a more distant magus. Greenaway, however, has not given up his power, and therefore has not heeded the 'moral' of *The Tempest* that Western technocratic bibliotopia needs to be disavowed and dismantled.

Greenaway even rewrites the ending of the story so that, although twenty-three of Prospero's books are destroyed, the twenty-fourth and twenty-fifth books, *The Complete Works of William Shakespeare* and Prospero's own manuscript of *The Tempest*, are rescued from the water by Caliban. On the one hand, Greenaway's decision to have Caliban rescue these books is less nihilistic than Shakespeare's wholesale renunciation of the power represented by Prospero's craft. Greenaway seems to suggest that some texts should be saved – that there are some artifacts of Western literacy that have redeeming value and that the project of Western civilization itself is not irrevocably to be condemned. On the other hand, Caliban/Greenaway's rescue of these volumes suggests that Prospero's spell has not really been lifted. Whereas Shakespeare's play announces a clean break with Prospero's magic, Caliban and Greenaway smuggle a seed of this magic out of the movie and into the world. This twist in the story reflects the historical circumstances of the publication of Shakespeare's plays. Astonishingly, Shakespeare himself seems to have been content to let his own complete works drown in the sea of history, making no effort to have his plays published. He may have agreed with Prospero that personal and cultural salvation lay in the unwriting of books rather than the endless production of them. That Shakespeare's plays survive is due to the work of various Calibans and Greenaways who fished his scripts out of the water and, seven years after the playwright's death, compiled the First Folio. As a result of their labors, Shakespeare's plays have had a profound influence on the imagination of the West and of the world. Harold Bloom has even gone so far as to propose that Shakespeare's plays are responsible for 'the invention of the human', speculating that the world view that informs our social reality is itself an aftereffect of Shakespeare's representations of fictional people.[10] Greenaway's ending therefore is a truer reflection than Shakespeare's of the extent to which the magic of representation has proliferated beyond Prospero's island to usurp any notion of direct experience and to become the baseline reality for contemporary consciousness.

Notes

1 J. Baudrillard, *Simulacra and Simulation*, trans. Sheila Faria Glaser (Ann Arbor: University of Michigan Press, 1994); U. Eco, *Travels in Hyperreality*, trans. William Weaver (San Diego: Harcourt, 1986).

2 N. Frye, *Northrop Frye on Shakespeare* (New Haven: Yale University Press, 1988), 172.

3 *Ibid.*, 173.

4 Baudrillard, *Simulacra*, 1.

5 Eco, *Hyperreality*, 14.

6 'I was directing the viewers. You might say I was playing them, like an organ.' Quoted in R. P. Kolker, *Alfred Hitchcock's* Psycho: *A Casebook* (Oxford: Oxford University Press, 2004), 16.

7 'When you see Tom Sawyer immediately after Mozart or you enter the cave of *The Planet of the Apes* after having witnessed the Sermon on the Mount with Jesus and the Apostles, the logical distinction between Real World and Possible Worlds has been definitively undermined.' Eco, *Travels in Hyperreality*, 14.

8 P. Greenaway, *Prospero's Books* (New York: Four Walls Eight Windows, 1991), 12.

9 Quote from the film's description of *The Book of Universal Cosmographies*.

10 H. Bloom, *Shakespeare: The Invention of the Human* (New York: Riverhead Books, 1999).

WORKS CITED

Baudrillard, J., *Simulacra and Simulation*, trans. Sheila Faria Glaser (Ann Arbor, MI: University of Michigan Press, 1994).

Bloom, H., *Shakespeare: The Invention of the Human* (New York: Riverhead Books, 1999).

Eco, U., *Travels in Hyperreality*, trans. William Weaver (San Diego: Harcourt, 1986).

Frye, N., 'Shakespeare's Romances: *The Winter's Tale*', in R. Sandler (ed.), *Northrop Frye on Shakespeare* (New Haven and London: Yale University Press, 1986), 154–70.

Greenaway, P., *Prospero's Books* (New York: Four Walls Eight Windows, 1991).

Harrison, G. B. (ed.), *The Tempest*, in *Shakespeare: The Complete Works* (San Diego: Harcourt Brace Janovich, 1952), 1471–502.

Kolker, R. P., *Alfred Hitchcock's* Psycho*: A Casebook* (Oxford: Oxford University Press, 2004).

CHAPTER 12

The Alternating Utopic Revisions of The Tempest on Film

Delilah Bermudez Brataas

To some extent, all of Shakespeare's writings contain utopias if only as ideal moments captured in the timelessness of a sonnet, yearned for in a nostalgic soliloquy or framed by the proscenium of a stage. Among his plays, *Love's Labour's Lost* (1594), *As You Like It* (1599), *Twelfth Night* (1601) and, to an extent exceeding the others, *The Tempest* (1611), contain the clearest examples of utopian themes. Navarre's 'little academe' in *Love's Labour's Lost*, for instance, is an ideal space evoking the cloistering common to utopian literature and several scholars have reasoned as much. From one perspective, Bruce Smith names it an 'all-male utopia',[1] and from another, Irene Dash, comparing the analogous all-female space in Margaret Cavendish's *Convent of Pleasure* (1668), notes that Cavendish created the same 'possibility of utopia' in her version.[2] Even adaptations inspire similar language as John Severn describes Kenneth Branagh's filmed academe a 'study-filled utopia', evoking Prospero's book-filled cell.[3] Yet, ever since Sir Thomas More's *Utopia* (1516), perhaps no device is as indicative of utopian literature as the ideal haven discovered after a storm at sea. It appears specifically in Shakespeare's *Twelfth Night* and *The Tempest*, and more generally in *The Comedy of Errors* (1594). Shakespeare also actualized the separation of the real from the ideal through classical utopic spaces like the pastoral realm of *As You Like It*'s Arden/Eden among others. That these plays span his career demonstrates his persistence in engaging with utopia and his understanding of how utopias realize the ideal from within the real (a quality that defines utopianism in all its forms).

Among these plays, only *The Tempest* is commonly recognized for its utopian attributes.[4] This is less a problem of apposite categorization than a failure of recognizing the extent of Shakespeare's engagement with concepts that would coalesce through the early modern into the now recognizable, though troublesome, genre. However, approaching these plays as utopias reveals that a critical feature of their 'trouble' is that the ideality of the utopic spaces they posit relies on women who cannot participate in those spaces.

So fundamental is this reliance to each utopic vision that adaptations follow suit. In this chapter, I consider the revision of Shakespeare's utopia in three film adaptations of *The Tempest* focusing on Julie Taymor's *The Tempest* (2011). Using Derek Jarman's *The Tempest* (1979) and Peter Greenaway's *Prospero's Books* (1991) as context, I will demonstrate how Taymor's film captures the utopic potential of Shakespeare's play most profoundly. Though vastly different from each other, these uniquely provocative films are recognizable adaptations of Shakespeare's original yet share an ambiguity in the presence (or absence) of the play's women through an interrogation and revision of each woman's maternal potentiality. Each film evokes the materiality of the female body through the maternal conflation of birth and death (or the womb as tomb). Accordingly, their beginnings and endings, or rather, the entrances and exits into their utopic spaces, reveal these connections most clearly.

According to Lyman Tower Sargent, utopianism developed from society's essential desire for a 'return to the womb or, in a variant version of the womb, as an expression of the myth of the eternal return', although he warns against seeking 'truth' in any single explanation.[5] Consequently, there is a sense of circularity to utopia that connects with the infinite progress of birth and death that each filmmaker captures well.[6] Yet any discussion of utopia must also consider *dystopia* because it is 'a shadow of utopia' rather than its opposite, as Krishan Kumar writes, since it 'emerged in the wake of utopia and has followed it ever since. So close are the genres that it is not always clear what is a utopia and what a dystopia'.[7] Adding to the discussion, Tom Moylan defines 'critical utopias' as texts that demonstrate an 'awareness of the limitations of the utopian tradition' even as they 'reject utopia as a blueprint while preserving it as a dream'.[8] The three films I consider each demonstrate the filmmaker's awareness of the tradition's limitations in their rejection of familiar elements and simultaneous reinstatement of a dependence on women to preserve the utopic 'dream'. As such, they are critical utopias. Indeed, each film's distinct utopic vision hinges on that dependence as the means to the dream. Critical utopias also connect to the political and philosophical ideologies that contributed to the conceptualization of ideal spaces as always already failed. Marina Leslie traces utopia's 'ambiguous historical usage' and notes that even the most ahistorical utopia will vacillate 'between the antipodal positions of historical impossibility and historical imminence'.[9] Thus, in its imminence, utopia is both isolated from, and bound to, the here and now, appearing between the real and the ideal.

As one of Shakespeare's few source-less plays, *The Tempest* emerged as invention rather than adaptation in the popular imagination and so it fit our need for completion as a metatheatrical farewell with the aging Prospero paralleling a Shakespeare nearly retired from theatre, or a dramatization of England's colonial expansion. Critical readings of *The Tempest* are as varied as its adaptations, but most tend to agree on one quality: its malleability. Peter Hulme and William Sherman describe the play as a 'touchstone for critical, political and creative work throughout the modern world' which allowed the play to be 'classified as every genre, and no genre, located in every place and no place, and enlisted in the support of colonial, anti-colonial, and apolitical views'.[10] They ascribe this flexibility to 'the power and mobility of its language and its themes' which have allowed it to become 'a renewable resource like few other texts'.[11] Despite the variety of sources signalled in the play, it still seems 'unfinished' or 'full of blanks' in a way that 'tempts us to fill it in'.[12] Beyond Gonzalo's ideal commonwealth, the play's island 'tempts' us with a space that might contain utopia and the hope that *there* is a better place than *here*. Shakespeare feminizes this temptation thereby maintaining the conventions of both utopian literature and the colonial discovery accounts: the two literary forms emerged concurrently using feminized descriptions of the new land in which ideality emerges through fertility and abundance. Darby Lewes explores this connection in *Nudes from Nowhere* (2000) by identifying unexpected utopian texts. She names them 'somatopias' adapting More's denominating *Utopia* to stress the integral presence of the female body in utopian literature.[13] Emerging from the 'ancient' idea that 'women and land are somehow analogous to each other', somatopias are 'rooted in the earliest etiological myths that present the earth as a womb from which life sprang.'[14] Lewes warns that these spaces are ambiguous because they are 'composed of female bodies' and 'designed for male satisfaction' materializing as a 'body place' that must be 'either composed of a body or designed for a body (as in providing bodily pleasure)'. Thus, female bodies are analogous to a 'pseudogeographic site of male pleasure: a utopian sexual landscape.'[15] As the required substance of utopia, women embody the ideal as envisioned through masculine subjectivity and, if they provide the material of ideal spaces, they cannot participate in the ideality those spaces offer. Indeed, equating women with matter is so fundamental to literary subjectivity that Janet Adelman in her influential analysis of the maternal in Shakespeare first establishes matter as the 'diseased inheritance of the female body' that earned women the blame for human mortality. Lewes's connection is, then, less a reinstatement of a common analogy and more a recognition of how the requirement of female matter across genre allows men to imagine their ideal spaces as they do their ideal selves.[16]

The most regularly cited example of utopia in *The Tempest* is Gonzalo's commonwealth, but I would add that the same scene in which he ponders his commonwealth also offers an example of the play's reliance on the female body in capturing the ideality of the island as a utopia. When the castaways describe the island in 2.1, Adrian idealizes and feminizes it as 'a delicate wench', but also empties it by calling it a 'desert' and creates distance by declaring it 'uninhabitable, and almost inaccessible'. The 'almost' denotes potential access to a space that required a treacherous sea journey and a guide, precisely like More's *Utopia*.[17] New visions appear in their discussion but each personifies the island as female and changeable, sustaining an ambiguous image of the island that goes from 'desert' to abundance ('everything advantageous to life') and from 'temperance' to excess ('lush and lusty'). Its landscape contains both verdant 'green' grass and 'tawny' ground, smells 'sweet' but is also perfumed of 'fen' and breathes with 'rotten' lungs (2.1.34–53). Each reference contradicts the other, suggesting that each man is seeing a different island at once. Towards the end of the scene, Antonio mocks Gonzalo by noting that 'the latter end of his commonwealth forgets the beginning' (2.1.154–5), forgetting that *his* vision of the island shifted similarly. *The Tempest's* utopia appears thus in the several contradictory visions that litter this malleable play.

Curiously, *Tempest* also regularly materializes in works exploring Shakespeare's life and adaptations of other plays, such as the final scene of John Madden's *Shakespeare in Love* (1998) or the final issue of Neil Gaiman's graphic novel series *Sandman* (1989–96). One such materialization, Trevor Nunn's *Twelfth Night* (1996), offers an unexpected segue to the film adaptations of *The Tempest*. In his film, Nunn transposes the first two scenes of Shakespeare's original, thereby significantly shifting the mood from the melancholy of Orsino's courtly idyll to the tragedy of a shipwreck. Yet Nunn not only transposes the scenes, he amplifies the drama by inventing details aboard the ship, during the storm, and after the wreck, to first heighten the intimacy between the separated twins and then prolong the sense of danger on the shore. We witness Viola removing the trappings of her femininity in detail through deliberate close-ups as she casts her jewellery and corset to the ground, cuts her long blonde hair and binds her breasts. Nunn's film facilitates Viola's entry into utopia as the newly gendered Cesario. Only when s/he walks into Illyria does the film's title finally appear. Still more intriguing is the similarity of this scene to one from Taymor's *Tempest* where Prospera delivers the revels speech (4.1.146–63). The scenes echo each other through contrasting images of freedom and control, illustrating Taymor's vision for the scene of Prospera performing her decision. The 'power and freedom she has wielded on the island will now be subject to the rules of the society to which she returns'.[18] Nunn's Viola finds freedom in casting her white corset to the dark ground, but Prospera must readopt a sharp, black, patent-leather corset on her pale body. It is rigidly sculpted, accented with metal zippers and evokes a steampunk style that, on her body, contrasts against the mottled-light sky and her pale complexion. Her androgynous, earth-toned robes give way to her ducal uniform suggesting that Prospera's *leaving* of utopia is dramatized on her body just as Viola's *entrance* to utopia is dramatized on hers. Judith Buchanan argues that Taymor's regendering prevents her film from 'participating in some of the more fluid gender play already inherent in Shakespeare's *Tempest*'.[19] Yet this scene demonstrates that Prospera's transformation is more complex and multivalenced. She shifts between patriarchal master-mage, androgynous mother-mage and masculine-Duchess within her utopic realm thus reenacting the shifting gender roles of the early modern stage. Just as Viola can woo, and be wooed, across gender by entering Illyria's utopia as Cesario, Prospera's many selves relinquish utopia with a resolved 'so, so, so' (5.1.96). Considering what exactly Prospera relinquishes in this moment illustrates the fluidity of Taymor's gender play. Is Prospera reconciling the androgyny she has performed against the specific gender role she must adopt, or weighing the loss of the freedom and power utopia allowed her against the rigid social expectations of Milan? There are many unexpected parallels across adaptations, but the un-corseting and re-corseting of the fluid bodies of two women who are neither women in their original forms is a telling example of how the female body is designated as a space of utopic realization.

Taymor's film contains several examples where the play's utopia allowed for such fluid revision. For one, her film is set in the volcanic fields of the Hawaiian islands, a location that could have easily provided the paradisiacal vistas more in keeping with utopian literature. Yet her film's sweeping landscapes are nearly bereft of colour or greenery. Sublime in its unadorned scenery, it does not contain the overwhelming detail of Greenaway's film nor the Baroque styling of Jarman's climactic finale (both more in keeping with the descriptive tone of utopian literature). Instead, Taymor's setting offers a visual openness that tempts with its potential as an available space that might contain utopia. In keeping with the reliance on women, Taymor's vision for the setting also connects to Prospera's body: 'for both the landscape and the cell and her magical robe, we tapped the essence of Prospera herself as a living volcano, burning from within, primed to erupt and destroy, but ultimately to redeem and regenerate.'[20] Taymor binds her utopia to Prospera just as Shakespeare bound his to Miranda, but Taymor's vision emerges as less a conquerable/conquered island and more a Gaia-space of fluid potential. In the revelation scene (5.1.107–317), Prospera conjures a circle of fire that shifts elementally from the earth of her island clothing to the lava that hardens into the obsidian corset, exemplifying Taymor's use of the original play's transformation. All three films express the play's thematic transformation through gender, but Taymor's re-characterization of Prospero into Prospera is an exceptionally dramatic example. Taymor insists her choice was less about gender bending than about using Helen Mirren as a powerful lead, but she described the experience as 'seamless'. It was, Taymor writes, as if the play somehow 'allowed for the change', an effect I ascribe to the play's utopic elements and that Sherman and Hulme might identify as its malleability. That Nunn's transposition of *Twelfth Night*'s initial scenes was equally seamless illustrates *that* play's equally utopic text. Taymor further described the regendering as 'revelatory', claiming that it gave her new ways of thinking about how gender influences mood, tone and style. When Prospera relinquishes her power, her loss is 'much more keenly felt', just as Viola's loss emerges in the shift between comedy and tragedy in Nunn's *Twelfth Night*.[21]

Closely related to Prospera's transformation is how Sycorax materializes in Taymor's Prospera via the presence of Ovid's Medea in Shakespeare's Sycorax. Buchanan explores this connection and argues that the resulting tension leaves Prospero struggling to frame a vision of himself as always other to Sycorax's 'unruly female sorcery'. To maintain his ideal space, Prospero embodies Sycorax by wielding her words over the one remaining woman in the play – Miranda – as he does when he tempers her worry over the ship (1.2.14–16) and quiets her questions with magical sleep (1.2.185–6). This demonstrates both the need to access utopia through the female body and Buchanan's assertion that Shakespeare's Prospero gives voice 'to a dark sorcerer within'. To keep Sycorax as 'foil', Prospero acknowledges her as 'kin', and this represents 'the dramatic engine of the play'.[22] Buchanan concludes that Taymor did not need to include Sycorax in her film because Prospera becomes 'a version of Sycorax' throughout. Thus, Taymor's decision does not offer a reconciliation between the many gender roles Prospera performs, nor her loss of the utopic island, but rather a 'reconciliation with the demonized other' achieved by 'overwriting Prospera' with Sycorax. Taymor sacrifices 'the revelatory movement – the shocking shift from Sycorax as other to Sycorax as self – that characterizes Prospero's faux-obdurate but actually dynamic relationship with his off-stage nemesis'.[23]

Buchanan's reading contributes critical insight to this discussion, but I would add to her argument that a Prospera-as-Sycorax is less a reconciliation of the demonized other and more a reclamation of the excluded m/other. Indeed, Taymor reclaims *two* absent mothers at once in her film: Miranda's mother and the powerful Sycorax. A Prospera-as-Sycorax also grants her the role of disappointed mother to Caliban as demonstrated in the final scene between them. Shakespeare's Prospero reflects the 'androgynous feminine/maternal power within' and the 'patriarchal/masculine power without' that introduces the 'self-conflict and balance through the mother/father unity' contained in his masculine body that Buchanan demonstrates. However, that this conflict occurs in Prospero only emphasizes the play's dependence on women through Miranda's isolation, Sycorax's absent presence and Prospero's repeated derision of the maternal (in demonizing Sycorax and in doubting Miranda's mother). Through Prospera, Taymor's film reclaims and redeems the maternal/matter allowing the participation of *two* female bodies in the utopia their presence facilitates. This exchange accurately demonstrates Adelman's argument that 'masculine selfhood' in Shakespeare's plays (recreated in Jarman's and Greenaway's dream-states[24]) is a 'burden passed on to the women, who must pay the price for the fantasies of maternal power invested in them' regardless of how often those fantasies are actualized as men's dreams.[25]

Consequently, each film reveals a similar process in their revisions of Miranda and the play's absent women. Referring to examples from performances in which directors fill in the play's gaps by including Sycorax on stage, Buchanan notes that 'there is no gender imbalance so startlingly extreme elsewhere in Shakespeare and a stage Sycorax necessarily dilutes the visual and narrative drama of Miranda's gender isolation'.[26] It is no accident that 'tempest' aurally (in performance) and visually (as read on a page) evokes 'temptress', though the words are not etymologically connected. As the temptress at the centre of the tempest, Miranda realizes the utopic promise through her embodiment of the several women necessary to the story, but unnecessary to utopia.[27] Yet Miranda *must* be alone for the play to allow for utopia because in the presence of the other women, the play's utopias falter.[28] Thus, adaptations must confront the play's dependence on Miranda's presence to revise the play's utopia.

In Taymor's film, we see Miranda's hands and face even before the dialogue on the foundering ship that begins the play. Taymor's title shot establishes the reliance on Miranda with the first image: a close-up of a dark sandcastle against a light gray sky. The word 'THE' appears in white to the right of the sandcastle, barely discernible against the background. It then fades into 'TEMPEST' superimposed on the same space, but now stretching across the sandcastle with only the central 'M' visible against the dark sand. Through that solitary, telling 'M', Miranda (and the Mother) become(s) the single visible sign in the lingering title. The letter remains, unfading, until the tempest rains down on the sandcastle washing both away. As the camera pulls back, the forced perspective reveals that the castle is much smaller than it seemed and sits in Miranda's hand to further cement the connection. When the story begins, the scene shifts between Miranda, in white, running across the dark sand and the first scene aboard the ship. This is not a scenic transposition as we saw in Nunn's *Twelfth Night*, but a revision of the chronology that now privileges Miranda's vision. In contrast, Greenaway and Jarman minimize Miranda's presence in the same scenes. In *Prospero's Books*, Miranda first appears sleeping and remains mute because John Gielgud as Prospero voices the film's entire dialogue. Similarly, Jarman's Prospero hushes Miranda's first attempt to speak, silencing her while privileging himself. Diminishing Miranda's role in halting Prospero's tempest, Greenaway and Jarman both give the play's first scene entirely to Prospero.

They lessen Miranda's presence and introduce the absent women that the play leaves out because *The Tempest*'s utopia rests as much on the absent women as it does on Miranda's isolation. This renders Miranda irrelevant because the absent mothers Jarman and Greenaway introduce offer the required substance for their utopic revisions.

In Jarman's adaptation, Sycorax is a radically influential character played by Claire Davenport. She appears monstrous in a dark tableau in which she looms central and powerful, unsettling because she breastfeeds the adult, naked Caliban in a dungeon and tugs on a chain that holds captive the naked, crying Ariel. She is more disruptive than Shakespeare's Caliban alone because her presence grants Caliban access to her body. Voiced over by Prospero reminding Ariel of his imprisonment (1.2.258–96), the scene should be a flashback, but it does not show Caliban's infancy, and so it threatens with a warped sense of 'here' in that Caliban is as grown as he is in a dreamlike 'now' that is not. The scene also acts as foil to the film's elaborate masque that introduces another woman, though not one usually counted among the play's absent women. Instead of the metamorphic Ariel who conventionally transforms into, or conjures, the masque's goddesses, Elisabeth Welch appears dressed in gold lamé quieting the frenzied pipe music of the preceding dance sequence by singing 'Stormy Weather'[29] (a version of the play's name). Her calming song also introduces Ariel's unwilling surrender to Prospero's closing dream. Shakespeare left out the powerfully maternal Sycorax because her presence threatened his play's utopic vision, but Jarman recalls that maternal power from the fringes of the play only to corrupt it in a subversion of Michelangelo's Pietà. Kate Chedgzoy argues that the tensions surrounding Caliban's representations in this scene are 'exacerbated by the screen image of Sycorax'.[30] Alternatively, Jim Ellis argues that Elisabeth Welch's appearance is a 'salvaging of Sycorax and all her demonized sisters' allowing them an 'avenue of reconciliation and transcendence' so they share in the film's 'final triumph'.[31] Jarman does grant Welch the power of the definitive song but this does not salvage the maternal that Sycorax perverts, nor is Sycorax's presence at odds with Caliban's representation, as Chedgzoy asserts. Instead, the maternal and sexual converge into monstrosity and introduce the subversion from which he realizes a utopia that required an infantilized Caliban and an objectified Ariel leaving Welch reduced to a song that will not remain hers.

Jarman also negates the nurturing that a breastfeeding mother should evoke in the same moment that he foregrounds the threatening sexuality that motifs like the dungeon, the adult-child nursing and the presence of the bound Ariel, suggest. Combined, these images recall fetish, taboo and the unconventional sexuality and desire so often speciously linked to homoeroticism. To dismantle that connection further, Jarman elevates the affections between Ariel and Prospero. We sense this most poignantly when the camera shifts from Welch to Ariel in an extreme close-up.[32] Ariel longingly touches his lips just as Welch sings: 'I can't go on, everything I had is gone. Stormy weather, since my man and I ain't together'.[33] Ariel's freedom visually and aurally connects through his lips to the loss of 'his man' much as our vision of the island is bound to Miranda's eyes in the play. The play's androgynous Ariel becomes Prospero's lover and this strategic close-up grants him (not Welch) the telling lyrics. Ariel's love quietly fades into a melancholy loss that, for Jarman, belongs to Ariel instead of Prospero who is only ever dreaming. Ariel then walks into a darkness that shocks after the brightness of the masque and sings his song of release from 5.1 as an unaccompanied dirge. The still sadness of this moment contrasts sharply with Jarman's Prospero freeing Ariel. He does so with an offhanded 'to the elements, be free' during the masque that comes across as more thoughtless dismissal than thankful emancipation. The fluidity of Shakespeare's Ariel allows for Jarman's homoerotic Ariel, but Shakespeare's play demands that Jarman access utopia not through the fluid Ariel but through Sycorax and the Masque Goddess who, together, introduce the female bodies that allow for utopic freedom as Bakhtinian bodies.[34] Jarman's Prospero awakening would reinstate the real, but until then, the carnivalesque ideal reigns by way of the maternal bodies.

Greenaway goes further still by making grotesque mothers of *all* the play's absent women within the relentless carnival of his film. *Prospero's Books* includes crowds of women, but Greenaway treats them as spirits, or manifestations of Prospero's mind, rather than characters. Sycorax is a bald, pale demon who gives birth to a pig-snouted Caliban we witness emerging from her vagina. We carry that bestial maternity to Miranda's mother, here named Suzanne, whose entire presence in the film reflects the maternal. She bathes the young Miranda at the start of a scene that pans from that tender image to her tearing open her naked belly to expose living organs and a growing child in her womb. The camera then pans to Prospero watching a screen showing Suzanne in her casket as if it was only ever a *mise en abyme* of films within films revealing female bodies within female bodies as wombs literally becoming tombs. Greenaway sustains the connection by then introducing Claribel in a further perversion of the maternal. At first, she stands statuesque behind her reclining husband but, in a later scene, she lies high on a dais, crying and holding her bleeding groin while servants massage Tunis as he stands by, indifferent to her pain. His presence points to rape in a scene that otherwise might suggest the aftermath of violent childbirth. The maternal and sexual blur as violence on the female body because the absent women provide the matter of Jarman and Greenaway's visions of utopia. Indeed, this violence is 'much more keenly felt', to borrow Taymor's phrasing, given the artistic tenor of both films. Because they must not participate in the utopic potential their bodies allow, introducing the absent mothers required barring Miranda from utopia. Thus, for Jarman, she is a flirtatious adolescent who plays with toys and, for Greenaway, a puppet to Prospero's ventriloquism. Curiously, Caliban grows less monstrous as Miranda fades and the absent mothers appear; he is an infantilized clown for Jarman and for Greenaway a powerful dancer whose words vibrate in Gielgud's voice-over. That audible reverberation is surprisingly different from the other characters Gielgud performs, but so is the scene when Prospero calls him forth. Caliban emerges from a vaginal cave from which water flows and splashes into a pool before he begins his dance.[35] Realizing a cleaner, ideal birth requiring only a father demonstrates Prospero's role as the solitary agent of 'generative power' on the island, as Janet Adelman argues by noting that Prospero releases Ariel from the womb of the tree and brings Miranda through the ocean waters, granting Prospero an 'ideal bodiless son' and a daughter without maternal/material stain.[36] Greenaway's Prospero thus gives birth to Caliban claiming him as his son and thereby diminishing Sycorax's maternal authority over the island utopia.

By not naming Miranda's mother as other to Prospero or sentimentalizing her memory, Taymor reclaims utopia for the absent women and allows Miranda to emerge as more than an anchor to 'other' women or the substance of utopia. She participates in the island's utopia just as her mother does, because Taymor does not reinvent the absent women at the cost of Miranda. Unlike Jarman and Greenaway, Taymor's strategic introduction of the one absent woman resurrects the maternal but not through absent presence, nor through maternal violence, but through the erasure of the father. In effect, Prospera bars Prospero from *his* utopia only to then return the island to its rightful maternal successor. This grants her film an unexpected dimension that Shakespeare's play facilitates but cannot realize because only through Prospera is the maternal reclaimed and Miranda's burden lifted. Taymor does not resurrect Sycorax, nor does she grant us Claribel's reality, good or bad. She does not need to invent a name for Miranda's mother because she gives the film over to her entirely by a seamless re-gendering of the name of the father (given the gender of Italian names, the shift is also orthographically seamless).[37] Prospera does embody aspects of Sycorax in Taymor's film as Buchanan argues, but this does not lessen her erasure of the father, nor Miranda and Prospera's participation in the utopia, nor even the reintroduction and reclamation of the maternal that proves more instrumental to Taymor's revision of the play's utopia.

To realize her utopia fully, Taymor's Prospera never speaks the play's epilogue despite the rich potential of the soliloquy. Greenaway includes the epilogue as a voice-over, while Jarman prefers to close with the revels speech (also as a voice-over) to bolster the primacy of dreams that frame his film. Prospera first appears at a cliff conjuring the storm holding her staff vertically, a position she returns to when she shatters the staff on the rocks below and we see her no more. The next scene shows green-filtered dark waters with books sinking slowly as air bubbles float upwards. The closing credits appear in white, fading in and out to evoke gentle waves. Over this image, a bleak tone sounds before the voice of Beth Gibbons, of Portishead fame, sings 'Prospera's Coda'. Neither the music nor her ominous interpretation of the epilogue reflect melancholy loss or hope for what is to come. Gibbons's delivery is as sharp and unyielding as Prospera's corset in contrast with the blurry final image. The song begins hesitantly but its volume builds towards a heavier, rock tempo that reverberates with discordant feedback. Her voice enters randomly, just as the tone and tempo of the music speeds and slows with neither a connection to her singing nor a regular pattern. Straining against the accompaniment, growling and harsh, her voice generates conflict with the music. Prospera's epilogue (her return to the real) lingers beyond the film's end through an unrelenting song that is nearly eight minutes of conflict and frustration, whereas, spoken in performance, the epilogue runs only about two to three minutes or less. While Prospero's epilogue suggests resignation, Prospera in this disembodied epilogue will not go so gently. Compared to the ethereal, operatic 'Prospero's Speech' as sung by Loreena McKennitt in *The Mask and The Mirror* (Warner Brother's Records, 1994), to offer one example, it sounds like a different text altogether. While McKennitt accents Prospero's hope by resting and repeating the 'please' of 'which was to please' (Epilogue 13), Gibbons accents and rests on 'despair' in 'my ending is despair' returning to it several times during the song (Epilogue 15). Yet Shakespeare's malleable text allows for such adaptation and duality.

It is at the entrance and exit of utopia where we sense utopia best; on stage this is from prologue to epilogue and on screen from title to closing credits, when the boundaries blur between the real and the ideal. In Mirren's hands, the epilogue would have been powerful but it would have unbalanced the film's utopia by granting a resigned finality to Prospera leaving the island. Taymor diminishes this resignation by separating words from body and then further detaches it through the extended song that sustains the separation in the conflict between music and voice, and image and song. She may have cast away her staff, but Prospera herself never declares her charms overthrown, nor admits her waning strength, nor does she ask for release from the utopia she enjoys because we never see her speak the words or leave the island. It is at the film's threshold where we glimpse the utopia that was, and still is, in Prospera's hands. By never hearing her relinquish it, it remains always already lost, but never quite.

The profound intricacy of Taymor's revision of Shakespeare's utopia is felt at many levels in her film, but perhaps most poignantly where we least expect it. In Caliban's yearning for a familial utopia, Taymor's revision transforms Prospera's confrontation of Caliban into a moment of familial loss rather than chastisement. Caliban (played by Djimon Hounsou) walks up a triangular, two-sided staircase as he leaves Prospera's cell already more beautiful and proportioned than the 'thing of darkness' (5.1.274) of Shakespeare's play. Moreover, Taymor's Caliban is angry and resolute, not fearful of being 'pinched to death' (5.1.275), nor a regretful 'thrice-double ass', nor a penitent slave promising that he should 'be wise hereafter' (5.1.292–3). With head held high and piercing eyes fixed, he looks at Prospera while standing on a lava flow before climbing the stairs and opening the door to leave. A clear blue sky then frames his dark body at the summit of the staircase when he stands at the open door high above Prospera who remains below, pale and mute/d. Caliban and Prospera share a poignant exchange of mutual loss in that moment: one from anger, the other from regret. This intensifies Prospera's loss of utopia because she emerges as more of a disappointed mother than a resigned master reluctantly acknowledging Caliban. Consequently, just as Taymor frees Miranda, in this scene she grants Caliban freedom as well, a point that remains uncertain in Shakespeare's play. Caliban's demeanour and body language suggest he is *choosing* freedom in that moment as if he always could. Taymor thus shrewdly grants him an ambiguous freedom through which she reclaims Sycorax's legacy and reveals Caliban's blame at once. Unlike Shakespeare, Taymor acknowledges Caliban's loss and accedes to his demand to restore the island that is his maternal legacy: 'This island's mine by Sycorax my mother,/Which thou tak'st from me' (1.2.332–4). Yet this scene delivers a more telling message. Shakespeare's vision for *The Tempest*'s utopia depends on Prospero claiming and possessing the island and expelling the powerful women, but for Caliban, Miranda's presence was more important than the island itself. By granting him the island he demands, Taymor demonstrates that Caliban's actions against the women, and *not* Prospera's enslavement of him, was the operative factor that, at once, hindered the women's participation in the island's ideal space and thereby barred him from realizing his familial utopia. The conventional somatopia of Shakespeare's play reappears in Jarman and Greenaway critical utopic visions, but Taymor revises that convention as a newly gendered, fluid somatopia by allowing the women *and* Caliban to participate in the ideal world their bodies helped build.

Notes

1 B. R. Smith, *Homosexual Desire in Shakespeare's England* (Chicago: Chicago University Press, 1991), 66.

2 I. G. Dash, 'Single-Sex Retreats in Two Early Modern Dramas: *Love's Labor's Lost* and *the Convent of Pleasure*', *Shakespeare Quarterly* 47:4 (1996), 394.

3 J. R. Severn, 'Interrogating Escapism: Rethinking Kenneth Branagh's *Love's Labour's Lost*', *Shakespeare Bulletin* 31:3 (2013), 467.

4 Several scholars establish *The Tempest*'s thematic and structural connections to utopia, its expression of utopian themes and its engagement with critical utopia including M. Seiden's 'Utopianism in *The Tempest*', *Modern Language Quarterly* 31:1(1970), 3–21 and J. X. Evan's exploration of More's text in the play '*Utopia* on Prospero's Island', *Moreana XVIII: Bulletin Thomas More* 69 (1981), 81–3. While J. Knapp's *An Empire Nowhere* (Berkeley: University of California Press, 1992) explores the discovery of the New World and the development of the English Renaissance between the two utopian texts.

5 In his influential definition, Sargent identifies the three forms of utopianism: utopian literature, utopian thought (i.e., in theory, philosophy or politics) and communitarianism (i.e., planned communities). L. T. Sargent, 'The Three Faces of Utopianism Revisited', *Utopian Studies* 5:1 (1994), 3.

6 Jarman returns to Prospero's dreaming at the end of his film, Greenaway's mindscape is unrelenting in its circular repetition and Taymor conjures a similar circularity with Prospera standing at the cliff, as I will discuss later.

7 K. Kumar, 'Utopia's Shadow', in F. Vieira (ed.), *Dystopia(n) Matters* (Newcastle: Cambridge Scholars Press, 2013), 19.

8 T. Moylan, *Demand the Impossible* (London: Methuen, 1986), 10.

9 M. Leslie, *Renaissance Utopias and the Problem of History* (Ithaca: Cornell University Press, 1998), 4.

10 P. Hulme and W. Sherman, Preface to *The Tempest and Its Travels* (Philadelphia: University of Pennsylvania Press, 2000), xi.

11 *Ibid.*, xi.

12 *Ibid.*, xiii.

13 D. Lewes, *Nudes from Nowhere* (Maryland: Rowman and Littlefield, 2000).

14 *Ibid.*, 3.

15 *Ibid.*, 2–3.

16 J. Adelman, *Suffocating Mothers* (New York: Routledge, 1992), 8–10.

17 *Utopia* was written as an 'accessible' space accompanied by a map and vague directions, not as the Platonic dialogue that More was emulating. The possibility that Utopia *could* be found is what mattered. Louis Marin offers an insightful argument on More's description of the rocky inlet into Utopia: 'More explains that it is very dangerous to enter into the gulf. A Utopian pilot must accompany all who attempt it. And even he must follow the signals from a number of landmarks erected on shore', L. Marin, *Utopics* (New Jersey: Humanities Press International, 1990), 102–3. Access depends on knowing the way with the help of one who has 'known' her, or has lost her and hopes to regain her perfection. Following the pointed church spires on *Utopia*'s map directs us to the hazardous opening into the womb-like island that only man's divine 'erections' can access.

18 J. Taymor, 'Rough Magic', in S. Carson and H. Bloom (eds.), *Living with Shakespeare* (New York: Vintage, 2013), 467–8.

19 J. Buchanan, 'Not Sycorax', in G. McMullan, L. Cowen Orlin, and V. M. Vaughan (eds.), *Women Making Shakespeare* (London: Bloomsbury, 2014), 343.

20 Taymor, 'Rough Magic', 477.

21 *Ibid.*, 482.

22 J. Buchanan, 'Not Sycorax', 339.

23 *Ibid.*, 340–4.

24 Harris and MacDonald offer the same argument from a different position regarding Jarman's use of the dreams as reflecting a 'Jungian search for selfhood'. D. Harris and J. MacDonald, 'Stormy Weather: Derek Jarman's *The Tempest*', *Literature/Film Quarterly* 25:2 (1997), 90.

25 J. Adelman, *Suffocating Mothers*, 10.

26 J. Buchanan, 'Not Sycorax', 338.

27 Several critics have discussed the 'presence' of the absent women of *Tempest*, notably Stephen Orgel's 'Prospero's Wife' in *Representations* 8 (Fall 1984), 1–15.

Orgel describes Miranda's mother as 'absent' and 'unspoken' and yet still 'the most powerful and problematic presence' in the play.

28 From Caliban's familial utopia that requires Miranda to people the island with not Mirandas but Calibans (1.2.351), to Prospero's nostalgic paternal utopia and maintenance of his academic space (1.2.152–158, 166–8), to Stephano and Trinculo's Bacchanalian rule with Miranda as queen (3.2.99–101), each requires Miranda's physical presence as the means to utopia.

29 Written by Harold Arlen and Ted Koehler in 1933, Welch performed and recorded 'Stormy Weather' that year and it came to be her signature song.

30 K. Chedgzoy, *Shakespeare's Queer Children* (Manchester: Manchester University Press, 1995), 202–3.

31 J. Ellis, 'Conjuring *The Tempest*: Derek Jarman and the Spectacle of Redemption', *GLQ: A Journal of Lesbian and Gay Studies*, 7:2 (2001), 279.

32 Harris and MacDonald note that Jarman desentimentalizes the lovers' romance with 'comedy and burlesque' and indeed when this close-up shifts to the lovers kissing it is more friendly than passionate, but their banality grants greater pathos to Ariel's loving moment. 'Stormy Weather', 90.

33 For a related reading of this exact moment, see Harris and MacDonald, 'Stormy Weather', 96.

34 In particular, wedding masques were a 'utopian kingdom of absolute equality and freedom' during which a 'utopian element' acquired 'a sharply defined material bodily form'. Miranda and Welch both offer the bodies for this freedom. M. M. Bahktin and Hélène Iswolsky, trans., *Rabelais and His World* (Bloomington: Indiana University Press, 1984), 264–5.

35 It is not coincidental that one of the 'books' of Greenaway's film is titled 'The Book of Utopias' and appears directly before Claribel's scene; her material/maternal downfall signals the film's realization of utopia and, furthermore, to reinvest Prospero's paternal birth with the control of matter, the 'Book of the Earth' precedes Prospero birthing Caliban.

36 Adelman, *Suffocating Mothers*, 237.

37 Discussing recent productions of female directed and performed *Tempest*s, Vaughan writes that Prospero's parental affection resonates more fully with a mother figure. 'By stereotyping the female Prospero in a maternal role' some productions fail to make the play 'into a critique of patriarchal control or question in any way the play's emphasis on female chastity and fecundity'. Taymor's film realizes this maternal dimension and questions patriarchal power. V. M. Vaughan, '"Miranda, where's your mother?": Female Prosperos and What They Tell Us', *Women Making Shakespeare* (London: Bloomsbury, 2014), 349–50.

WORKS CITED

Adelman, J., *Suffocating Mothers: Fantasies of Maternal Origin in Shakespeare's Plays, Hamlet to* The Tempest (New York: Routledge, 1992).

Bahktin, M. M. and H. Iswolsky, trans., *Rabelais and His World* (Bloomington: Indiana University Press, 1984).

Buchanan, J., 'Not Sycorax', in G. McMullan, L. Cowen Orlin, and V. M. Vaughan (eds.), *Women Making Shakespeare: Text, Reception, and Performance* (The Arden Shakespeare. London: Bloomsbury, 2014), 334–45.

Carson, S. and H. Bloom, *Living with Shakespeare: Essays by Writers, Actors, and Directors* (New York: Vintage, 2013).

Chedgzoy, K., *Shakespeare's Queer Children: Sexual Politics and Contemporary Culture* (Manchester: Manchester University Press, 1995).

Dash, I. G., 'Single-Sex Retreats in Two Early Modern Dramas: *Love's Labor's Lost* and the *Convent of Pleasure*', *Shakespeare Quarterly* 47:4 (1996), 387–95.

Ellis, J., 'Conjuring *The Tempest*: Derek Jarman and the Spectacle of Redemption', *GLQ: A Journal of Lesbian and Gay Studies* 7:2 (2001), 265–84.

Harris, D. and J. MacDonald, 'Stormy Weather: Derek Jarman's *The Tempest*', *Literature/Film Quarterly* 25:2 (1997).

Hulme, P., W. H. Sherman and R. Kirkpatrick, *'The Tempest' and its Travels* (Philadelphia: University of Pennsylvania Press, 2000).

Knapp, J., *An Empire Nowhere: England, America, and Literature from Utopia to The Tempest* (Berkeley, CA: University of California Press, 1992), 19–22.

Kumar, K., 'Utopia's Shadow', in F. Vieira (ed.), *Dystopia(n) Matters: On the Page, on Screen, on Stage* (Newcastle: Cambridge Scholars Press, 2013), 19–22.

Lewes, D., *Nudes from Nowhere: Utopian Sexual Landscape* (Maryland: Rowman and Littlefield, 2000).

Marin, L. and R. A. Vollrath, trans., *Utopics: The Semiological Play of Textual Spaces*, (Contemporary Studies in Philosophy and the Human Sciences. New Jersey: Humanities Press International, 1990).

Moylan, T., *Demand the Impossible: Science Fiction and the Utopian Imagination* (London: Methuen, 1986).

Orgel, S., 'Prospero's Wife', *Representations* 8 (1984), 1–13.

Sargent, L. T., 'The Three Faces of Utopianism Revisited', *Utopian Studies* 5:1 (1994), 1–37.

Severn, J. R., 'Interrogating Escapism: Rethinking Kenneth Branagh's *Love's Labour's Lost*', *Shakespeare Bulletin* 31:3 (2013), 453–83.

Smith, B. R., *Homosexual Desire in Shakespeare's England* (Chicago: Chicago University Press, 1991).

Vaughan, V. M., '"Miranda, where's your mother?': Female Prosperos and What They Tell Us', in G. McMullan, L. Cowen Orlin, and V. M. Vaughan (eds.), *Women Making Shakespeare: Text, Reception, and Performance* (The Arden Shakespeare. London: Bloomsbury, 2014), 347–56.

CHAPTER 13

Screen Magic in Greenaway's Prospero's Books and Taymor's The Tempest

Victoria Bladen

In *The Tempest*, the performance of magic involves utilizing language and knowledge (of the natural world and the cosmos) and exercising control, over humans, spirits and nature. It also involves the creation of illusions and theatrical display, rendering the play highly metatheatrical. The exercise of supernatural power invokes a range of implications, moral, political, gendered and post-colonial, providing rich scope for contemporary directors to explore. This chapter examines the screen magic of Peter Greenaway's *Prospero's Books* (1991)[1] and Julie Taymor's *The Tempest* (2010),[2] considering the aesthetics and ideological implications of magic and how each production harnesses early modern ideas and iconography. Both films are metafilmic and alert to the central paradox of *The Tempest* that a play intensely concerned with control is also ultimately about release and the relinquishing of power.

The Palimpsest of *Prospero's Books*

As Russell Jackson observes, Shakespearean films can be thought of as 'constituting a distinctive genre of their own, claiming kinship with various other kinds of film but always distinguished by their origins in texts that are at once theatre scripts and cultural icons'.[3] Greenaway foregrounds this intertextual relationship with script and cultural iconicity, not only Shakespeare's but also other early modern artists. *Prospero's Books* is conceived as a visual and ideological palimpsest, whereby multiple layers are concurrently present and intertexts suggestively invoked. As Peter S. Donaldson describes, 'At times, when the levels of illusion and reality, or present narration and memory, proliferate, there are three and four images on the screen at once, one nested in another, each permitting a partial view of the screen beneath'.[4] Greenaway is a visual artist as well as filmmaker, identifying himself as primarily a painter, but with a substantial body of work in collage and installation as well.[5]

For Greenaway, *The Tempest* was an opportunity to play in and around the imaginative spaces created by the play; while Shakespeare's work inspired the film, the director was not concerned with a close relationship with the play's narrative. As Sarah Hatchuel observes, 'The density of visual signs becomes more essential than the story of the film'.[6] This grants more autonomy to the audience to construct the narrative and choose their own pathways through the labyrinth of intertextual references. Greenaway's 'aesthetic discontinuity forces each member of the audience to create a highly personal movie through ceaseless construction and deconstruction of meaning'.[7] Similarly Mariacristina Cavecchi perceives that 'we move around among the sights, sounds, and accidentals which constitute the film, assembling and disassembling the meanings as they fleetingly present themselves'.[8]

Magic is foregrounded through the central focus on Prospero's (John Gielgud) books, which provide an organizing structure around which the narrative is presented. There are frames within frames, suggesting a potentially infinite number of layers that are partially veiled, transparent and overlapping. The various screen layers, with their animate borders and moving inserts, diffuse the focus for the viewer such that rather than a single focal point in any one shot, there are multiple areas of visual interest. The aesthetics also invoke multiple media. The sensory qualities of physical books, of paper and leather bindings, and the slow pleasures of writing in pen and ink are evoked. Yet the work also explores the medium of film and contemporary digital techniques of manipulation, layering and montage (using Quantel Paintbox), transforming the concept of an inanimate book into a highly animate, generative object and the two-dimensional page into a three-dimensional window onto other spaces and worlds. The film screen becomes akin to the surface of a book, while page surfaces become little screens; various media are juxtaposed, and old technology and new are interconnected. The effect for the viewer is one of sensory overload; there is an abundance of details, both static and moving, too much to absorb at a single viewing. These multi-faceted layers suggest a multiplicity of truths, viewpoints and realities, a particularly Shakespearean quality.

Taymor's Natural Magic

Taymor is also highly alert to the idea of magic in the play and uses special effects to create spectacle and convey magical power. In contrast to Greenaway's film, situated indoors with the *mise-en-scène* of a theatre set, Taymor's film, shot in Hawaii, is predominately set outdoors, utilizing the natural elements of sea, volcanic rock, natural vegetation and the natural weather patterns. The volcanic island location of the film influenced other elements of the production, such as costumes and the design of Prospera's (Helen Mirren) cave. For example, Prospera's magic cloak, comprised of plastic segments, evokes volcanic rock, lava flow and the sea.[9] The colours of the cave design were intended to suggest layers of volcanic rock, earth and shell.[10] The predominance of nature in this adaptation emphasizes a vision of magic grounded in control of the elements.

The strong sense in the film of immersion in nature, and humanity's subjection to the elements, is continued in *Raising the Tempest*, the documentary on the making of the film, which accompanies the DVD. Shooting was affected by rain on occasions, while for other shots, the weather and waves provided natural backdrops for scenes. The documentary includes shots of the crew and cast having the production blessed with a charm to ensure good weather for the shoot. As well as constituting respect for the local Hawaiian customs, the ritual resonates with *The Tempest* and reflects on continued belief in certain cultures of the power of magic to control the elements through language.

Recreating Magic

Both films use a range of effective techniques to suggest the idea of magic and to create the effect of magic on an audience, presenting a range of rich visuals designed to reference various types of knowledge, using images and iconography with a medieval or early modern aesthetic. The *otherness* of historical imagery thus serves to create the idea of esoteric knowledge, the full meaning of which remains opaque however; full knowledge implicitly resides only with the magus, not with the viewer.

Magic Books

In Greenaway's film, the magical books are presented in a frontal mode so that the audience is given visual access to them, aligning us with Prospero, and inviting us to marvel at their strange contents and experience their magic. The books often correspond thematically with events in the narrative; for example, the Book of Earth is bound up with the idea of Caliban (Michael Clark). It contains details of the colours and textures of the natural world and is the target of Caliban's frustrated rage at his captivity; he inflicts the book with harsh scoring, eggs, human excrement and urine. These wanton acts of destruction paradoxically align Caliban with Prospero, prefiguring the final destruction of the books.

As Donaldson observes, the books 'are used by Prospero to create the world we see in the film'.[11] While Prospero's ownership of the books leads us to see the sequence of themed magic books as the sole domain of Prospero, it is important to recognize that the books were chosen by Gonzalo; it is he who has picked the most important books from the library and it is his voice-over (Erland Josephson) that describes them. Thus, the vision of the world created by the books derives in some part from Gonzalo, the utopian idealist and ghostly librarian who haunts the selection and sequence of the magic books.

Taymor's *mise-en-scène* of Prospera's study emphasizes alchemical and cosmological equipment, rather than books. However, she references the idea of magical books in alternative ways. The design of the outer entrance to the cell, with its stone steps leading up, is conceived of as an open book.[12] There is also the elaborate sequence of the closing credits, with multiple volumes falling through water, the drowning of the library, which implicitly owes a debt to Greenaway.

Cosmology, Astronomy and Astrology

In Taymor's film, Prospera's study features a three-dimensional model of the cosmos, the various globes suggesting planets and stars. This structure suggests Prospera's overarching view of the cosmos and the necessity of this knowledge in order to understand and manipulate the occult forces in nature. She is able to effect an eclipse by adjusting elements of the cosmological model. The room also features a giant astrolabe marked with astrological signs. The circular shapes of her implements, evoking the cycles of nature and orbits of the heavens, are echoed in her drawing of a magic circle of fire at the climax of the play. The magic circle was a traditional aspect of magical practice and featured in depictions of Dr Faustus.[13]

Taymor replaces the betrothal celebration masque of the play-text (4.1) with a cosmic light show. Special effects create a brief, but awe-inspiring, spectacle, which suggests the magician's knowledge of the universe. Images invoke both the stars and their astrological signs. A shot of Miranda's (Felicity Jones) and Ferdinand's (Reeve Carney) heads against the backdrop of cosmological wonders emphasizes the idea in the play-text that this marriage is intended to ensure not only restoration of the political schism and Prospero and Miranda's reintegration into European society, but also universal harmony. This linking of the microcosm with the macrocosm is also

Figure 13.1. Prospera as Magus – Helen Mirren in Taymor's 2010 *The Tempest.*

implicit in the flower patterns integrated within cosmic grids and with imagery of the human figure as the fulcrum of a cosmological and astrological map, analogous to common medieval and Renaissance diagrams emphasizing astral influence over the human body, character and mortal fate, and also invoking Leonardo's Vitruvian man. The link between the minute and the immense is also invoked where the astrological figures seem to proliferate, suggesting microorganisms under the microscope and reiterating the scientific knowledge that underpins Prospera's knowledge. Mathematical numbers and geometric symbols conflate with kaleidoscopic patterns and a dove, which evokes the common iconography of the Holy Spirit. When Prospera's troubled countenance is set against the cosmographical background, which also reflects on her face (see Figure 13.1), although her primary concern, pursuant to the play-text, is the rebellion of Caliban and friends, her mood also seems reflective of the immensity of the knowledge and power she will have to relinquish.

Alchemy

The alchemical concept of *solve et coagula*, breaking up components using the liquid solvent as the medium in order to transform and recreate, resonates with the themes and imagery of *The Tempest*.[14] As most editors of the play observe, the play itself can be compared to the alchemical process; the tempest invokes the boiling of the solution in the alembic to remove impurities and transform the base metal into gold, and Prospero's language at the beginning of Act 5, 'Now does my project gather to a head' (5.1.1), suggests alchemical practice.[15] In rendering his enemies 'spell-stopped' (5.1.61), Prospero refers to their brains as 'boiled within' (5.1.60) their skulls, suggesting the boiling process of an experiment.[16]

The Arden editors comment: 'If we see Prospero's goal as the transformation of fallen human nature – Caliban, Antonio, Sebastian and Alonso – from a condition of sinfulness to a higher level of morality, the play's episodes mirror the alchemical process'.[17] Of course the issue of reformation raises a series of questions, including Prospero's hubris, his right to pursue vengeance, and his right to 'reform' Caliban, which is based on assumptions about Caliban that the play counters in many ways. Prospero's own character is likewise in need of reformation and undergoes a process of self-awareness, notably learning compassion from the non-human Ariel. Most of the characters experience a transformative process, with the exception of perhaps Sebastian and Antonio, whose violent potential is at least arguably neutralised for the present.

Taymor's depiction of Prospera's cell foregrounds alchemy, with a vertical structure of glass vials and glass vessels featuring in the flashback of her practices in Milan. The invocation of alchemy is consistent with the emphasis throughout the film on the four elements – earth, fire, air and water; alchemy constituted the search for the fifth element, quintessence, the path to immortality, as well as the transformation of base metals to gold. As Samuel Crowl observes, 'Taymor's Prospera is a scientist as well as a student of the "liberal arts"'.[18] Interestingly, there is an echo of the glass bottles in Caliban's dugout, where various empty bottles lie to his left in the first shot of him. This has the effect of linking the two figures, while also emphasizing the discrepancy between them in terms of access to scientific, book-based knowledge. While Prospera's bottles evoke specialized knowledge of alchemy, Caliban's meagre cluster of scavenged bottles conveys his restricted resources (and foreshadows how Stephano and Trinculo will gain a measure of control over him through the bottle of alcohol).

Greenaway invokes alchemy in an alternative way through his foregrounding of water, central to alchemical procedure since it was the solvent which broke down the various components in order to recreate and refine them in the search for quintessence – the philosopher's stone. Greenaway emphasizes the visual and sensual qualities of water, reiterating the evocative idea of drowning the book. An aesthetic of immersion is constant, from the opening shots of water drops to the final scenes of book destruction. The first magical book is 'The Book of Water,' introduced with a drawing of water by Leonardo da Vinci, the paper of which appears rumpled and rippled, as if the drawing itself had been soaked and dried, drowned and then retrieved, as Caliban does with the Folio and the play manuscript. The saturation of naked figures in the majority of scenes can also be read as an immersive medium, the protagonist swimming amidst the allegories of Prospero's masque-like imagination.

Elemental Magic

Ariel and Caliban can be read to some degree as personifications of the elements of air and earth, thus Prospero's control over both is at the thematic level a manifestation of his magical practice. Taymor emphasizes Ariel's (Ben Wishaw) association with the element of air through a range of special effects. He is often depicted against the sky and his speed conveyed by multiple images of the figure. The spirit's magical nature is also emphasized through variations of scale. When creating the tempest, Ariel is a giant in comparison with the beleaguered ship and yet in other shots he appears as miniscule in scale compared with humans. Taymor drew on the skills of photographer Brian Oglesbee, who worked with glass and water to create effects of immersion.[19]

Taymor's Caliban is strongly identified with nature and natural elements. Taymor observes that he 'has nature in him'; Djimon Hounsou, who played the role of Caliban, observes that 'he is the land'.[20] The costume figures Caliban's skin as like the surface of a map. Intriguingly, the patchwork pattern may have been subliminally suggested by Greenaway's earlier film.[21] The encrustations on the skin of Taymor's Caliban, designed to evoke pieces of volcanic rock and shell, suggest the natural surfaces of the island. It emphasizes Caliban's connection with the earth, while also evoking the confrontation of white and black, between colonialism and indigenous resistance that Caliban has come to embody in the critical reception of the play.[22]

Taymor sought to make the figure of Caliban 'slightly surreal,' drawing on the idea of the 'moon-calf' (2.2.94; 113), the splotches of white on black intended to evoke the patterning of a cow.[23] Caliban's unusual skin constructs him as a type of marvellous or 'monstrous' race, associated in the early modern imagination with lands beyond the known regions of the world.[24] Caliban is also marked, literally, with the language of cursing; Elizabethan swear words were formed in raised patterns on his skin as part of his costume. The suggestion is that his body, and implicitly the land with which he is connected, is marked with the conflict over power, agency and language.

Both Ariel and Caliban are also closely associated with water in both productions. Taymor's Ariel is often aquatic and first appears below the surface of Prospera's magic pond, which represents the boundary between the mortal and spiritual dimensions. Caliban is given webbed hands, linking him with the sea and picking up on Trinculo's question: 'a man, or a fish?' (2.2.23). In Greenaway's film, Ariel is introduced as a source of endless urine, part of the systems of water that surround Prospero.[25] Caliban is also given a strong association with water. We first see him perched on a miniature island, which emblematizes his prior occupancy of and belonging to the larger island. At the end of the encounter, he slinks beneath the water's surface, suggesting an amphibious nature equally at home on earthy terrain and water. His dancing movements are also fluid and aquiline, in tune with the liquid flow of the film's aesthetic.

Control and Knowledge

Magic, as a practice of control, resonates with other forms of control over others in the play. As David Lindley observes, many interpretations of Prospero's magic 'see it simply as a metaphor for any kind of authority or power'.[26] As well as evoking natural elements, Ariel and Caliban are alternative children of Prospero, who has quasi-parental relationships with both, in addition to relationships of master and servant/slave. Consequently, both Ariel and Caliban are voices of protest against control and slavery. In juxtaposition to Prospero's magical knowledge, Caliban and Ariel teach Prospero different kinds of knowledge that save his body and soul. Caliban's natural knowledge of the island is undoubtedly the reason for Prospero's and Miranda's survival. Ariel is also crucial in teaching Prospero forgiveness and in restraining him from giving way to the desire for full revenge. Within a paradigm of Christian ideology, the Old Testament ethos of punishment has to give way to the New Testament ethos of mercy; the tempest, recalling the Biblical Flood narrative, subsides to Baptism and renewal.

Ariel and Caliban also reflect aspects of Prospero and are manifestations of humanity in its divine aspiration and bounded earthiness.[27] They are thus mirrors facilitating self-knowledge. To become a reformed human, Prospero must learn to find the *via media*, curb his ambitious magical arts, which constitute a dangerous usurpation of divine knowledge, as well as curb his human impulses towards rage and vengeance, akin to Caliban's uncontrolled appetite in attempting to rape Miranda (1.2.348–51). Prospero also has to learn to relinquish power and release those under his control.[28] Just as Prospero relinquishes his magic at the end of the play, an act bound up with his decision to exercise mercy towards his enemies, he also releases Ariel. Whether he releases Caliban is not specified in the play, leaving it as a decision for directors. Logically Caliban belongs on the island and both Greenaway and Taymor assume the release of Caliban. Taymor's Prospera and Caliban engage in a silent moment of at least partial understanding of each other before, in a low-angle shot, Caliban transcends the 'book' of the cell, with its implications of knowledge and power over others, before leaving. Greenaway's Caliban intriguingly is the preserver of the Folio and play manuscript, making him an aquatic librarian and linking him with Gonzalo.

Magic and Gender

Prospero's magic is ambiguous; is he a practitioner of 'white magic' (also termed 'theurgy' and 'natural magic'), or 'black magic' (also termed 'necromancy', 'nigromancy' or 'goety')?[29] As Richard Kieckhefer outlines:

> Broadly speaking, intellectuals in medieval Europe recognized two forms of magic: natural and demonic. Natural magic was not distinct from science, but rather a branch of science. It was the science that dealt with 'occult virtues' (or hidden powers) within nature. Demonic magic was not distinct from religion, but rather a perversion of religion. It was religion that turned away from God and toward demons for their help in human affairs.[30]

The word 'magic' in classical antiquity referred to the arts of the magi, Zoroastrian priests of Persia who were known to practise astrology, claim the power to cure people and pursue occult knowledge.[31] As the practice of suspect foreigners to the eyes of the Greeks and Romans, magic from the outset was something potentially threatening and likely to arouse apprehension.[32]

Perceptions of the status of magic in the medieval and early modern period differed widely. According to the Christian Church, even ostensibly white magic was suspect and to be condemned; anxiety over this issue was exacerbated by the often-blurred lines between the rituals and ideology of the Church, often close in character to magic, and what the Church condemned as demonic magic. Where precisely was the line to be drawn between prayers and charms?[33] The political state also generally took a dim view, evidenced by the introduction of witchcraft legislation into England in the sixteenth century.[34]

Traditionally, the practice of magic was highly gendered and subject to class distinctions. Higher magic, ostensibly white magic, was based on learned, scholarly knowledge and seen as the preserve of male magicians, the respected and revered (at least by some) magus figure. In this context, magic was an extension of book-based knowledge, generally inaccessible to women because of gendered access to education. In comparison, lower magic was based on local, experiential and folkloric knowledge, not derived from bookish learning. This was the preserve of 'cunning' women and men. Although this too was generally claimed and often believed to be based on natural magic, that is understanding of occult forces in nature, this was perceived as more easily sliding into dubious black magic, requiring demonic assistance, and was more often associated with the female witch, feared for her ability to cause harm to people and animals, *maleficium*.[35] As Kieckhefer states, 'It was men who were more likely to arouse anxiety by actually standing in magic circles and conjuring demons; it was women who were far more likely to be burned in the ensuing bonfires'.[36]

In the play, this traditional, gendered polarity is represented by the juxtaposition of Prospero, presented as an ennobled, scholarly sorcerer, and Sycorax, described as a 'foul witch' (1.2.258) (although, since she never appears onstage, the audience only has Prospero's word for this). According to Prospero she was exiled from Algiers for 'mischiefs manifold, and sorceries terrible/To enter human hearing' (1.2.264–5). Greenaway's version encapsulates this gendered distinction. While Prospero is ennobled and encased in books, presented in a dignified manner even when naked in his bath, Sycorax is presented as a wild thing, her privacy violated when the camera insists on giving us full access to her in the process of giving birth. A pig's snout emerges from her vagina, the monstrous birth suggesting that she had sex with the Devil, a common allegation in early modern witchcraft trials, and echoing Prospero's allegation that Caliban was 'got by the devil himself' (1.2.320). That this vision is Prospero's distorted perception of his magical rival, rather than an 'actual' event, is confirmed by the appearance of Caliban, who has nothing piggish about him and in fact is a highly graceful and lithe figure.

In the play-text, Shakespeare invites questions over Prospero's distinction between his magic and Sycorax's by drawing heavily for Prospero's 'Ye elves of hills' speech (5.1.33) from the incantations of Medea in Ovid's *Metamorphoses*, as translated by Arthur Golding.[37] As Lindley observes of this invocation 'of the archetypal witch', 'the potential blasphemy of [Prospero's] magic power becomes frighteningly apparent' and 'the issue of the legitimacy of Prospero's magic is brought sharply into view'.[38] Furthermore, Prospero's power is generally performed through the agency of Ariel, who fulfils the traditional role of the familiar, a sign of demonic magic. The creation of tempests was also generally associated with witchcraft.[39]

In casting Mirren, Taymor further strengthens the symbolic fusion between Prospero and Sycorax, as does the exile of Prospera for witchcraft. While in theory Prospera practises white magic, aspects of her magical display, such as Ariel's appearance as the Harpy and the flaming dogs emerging from the mouth of hell, suggest the potential for diabolical powers to be drawn on in the pursuit of revenge. Taymor's choice of fire for the magic circle also invokes a potentially demonic element, cautioning that white magic may slide towards necromancy.

By casting a woman as the lead, Taymor implicitly intervenes in the play's patriarchal power struggles. The usurpation of Prospera by Antonio (Chris Cooper) introduces gender as a contributing factor in her deposition. This has further implications for Prospera's return from exile. As Crowl observes, 'To return to Milan is to become re-embedded in a masculine world'.[40] Thus magic has provided a world of comparative intellectual freedom, which she must give up in returning from exile.

Metatheatrical and Metafilmic Magic

In *The Tempest*, Prospero performs magic in order to assert power over his enemies and servants/slaves but also to entertain, evident in the masque of 4.1 and echoed in the metatheatrical epilogue, where he asserts that his 'project' was 'to please' (Epilogue 12–13). With both films, the magic of Prospera/o is bound up with the magical capabilities of the director to create an intricate illusion on a flat screen (in conjunction of course with the many other skilled individuals involved in diverse capacities). Both productions create lavish visuals that generate awe and spectacle; implicitly directors are magi. In Greenaway's film, writing, language and utterance are presented as having the ability to create realities. Digital technologies become analogues of Prospero's generative magic and many of the books generate live creatures or throb with human body parts, blurring lines between animate and inanimate objects, and between bodies and books.[41] This has moments of disquieting implications. Elsewhere in Greenaway's work, in art predating but linked with the vision of the film, he makes specific connections between women's bodies and the open book. This link has misogynist implications for representations of the destruction of books and echoes the film's most disturbing fantasy of the violent abuse of Claribel.[42]

Greenaway's work is particularly metafilmic.[43] Prospero's library appears as a stage set and he is both inside and outside of the play, emphasized with scenes where Prospero is literally doubled and both intradiegetic and extradiegetic figures appear. Prospero with a blue magic cloak is the writer in the process of creating, while Prospero with the red cloak is the protagonist inside the narrative and his mindscape. In shifting Prospero to the extradiegetic space, 'outside' of the frame of the play as it is being written, he becomes blurred with Shakespeare and implicitly Greenaway. Further references to genius/magus figures invite the audience to make links between various magical, genius figures: Leonardo da Vinci, Michelangelo, Shakespeare, Prospero, Gielgud, Greenaway. Taymor's casting of Mirren specifically counters such discourses of masculine genius since the shift to a female sorcerer and prominent female actor in Mirren inevitably reflects on Taymor as a female director asserting her claim and power to interpret and adapt Shakespeare in a field of mostly male directors. There are implicit links between the concepts of magus and film director as creators of powerful illusions, thus the female magician has the effect of constantly evoking the female director, drawing attention to the way that both magic and film direction have traditionally been gendered.

Both adaptations explored here draw on the aesthetics of occult knowledge, the idea of mysterious knowledge beyond our grasp but sufficiently powerful to create awe and wonder in the audience. While both productions utilize the wonders of contemporary digital technology, the directors also rely on the powerful magic of history, the *otherness* of historical conceptions of the cosmos and its forces.

The concept of the four elements, of water, earth, air and fire, are important to the aesthetics of both productions. By emphasizing physical environment, Taymor's adaptation could also be read as invoking ecocritical readings, raising questions about humanity's attempts to control natural forces. In a new world that will need to be brave in the face of climate change, likely to bring tempests and fire, as well as the loss of low-lying islands due to rising sea levels, human intervention in nature is increasingly understood as having wrought destruction through technological knowledge. Nature will wreak her own tempestuous revenge. The splintering of Prospera's magic staff against the volcanic rock of the cliff speaks eloquently of the failures of human dominion and stewardship.

In *The Tempest* magical knowledge is finally cast away. The extreme control it facilitates is recognized as dangerous, not so much because natural magic can veer into necromancy but because revenge becomes too tempting, thus endangering the soul. Prospero recognizes that in the search for vengeance he risks becoming dehumanised, a lesson he learns ironically from the non-human spirit Ariel. Just as magical power needs to be relinquished, so do other relationships of control.

In Taymor's adaptation, Prospera must leave the world of nature and reenter the world of culture to facilitate her daughter's need to be reintroduced into European society, crucial to Miranda's happiness with Ferdinand. Because Prospera is female, this reentry involves donning once again gendered roles of confinement and restriction, contrary to the other thematic impulses of the play's ending. Ironically Ariel, in one of his last duties before he is released, must bind up his master into the gendered confinements central to European society. As a master releases a slave, the master also reenters a different type of gendered slavery.

Paradoxically, while *The Tempest* appears initially to be about control and domination, it is ultimately concerned with letting go, in light of the recognition of the ultimately ephemeral, temporal and insubstantial nature of both culture and nature in the cosmos, encapsulated in Taymor's opening shot of the dissolving sandcastle in Miranda's hand. The mirage of the island space, the alchemical vessel of transformation, separates the constituents and unlocks the hostile bonds between Prospero and his three children, Ariel, Caliban and Miranda. Ultimately the elements under Prospero's control are released to their spaces of belonging: Ariel to the air, Caliban to the terrain of the island, and Miranda to European culture. In alchemical discourse, 'the solve is the softening of hard things'.[44] The magus exchanges occult knowledge for self-knowledge, learning compassion from Ariel and responsibility from Caliban.

Magic is also about performance, in Shakespeare's play-text, and emphatically in both Taymor's and Greenaway's productions. Thus filmic performance of digital wonders casts directors as magi, reflecting on the process of filmic spectacle making and film as an ephemeral, yet powerful medium to reflect on the stuff of dreams that we are made of. In the epilogue to Shakespeare's play, the role of the playwright is constructed as a different type of servitude, in which the audience holds the power to release the creative, magical artist from suffering through audience appreciation of a play's artistry. Both Greenaway's and Taymor's visions likewise invite their audiences to actively engage with their powerful screen magic.

Notes

1 An Allarts-Cinéa/Camera One-Penta co-production. Music by Michael Nyman.
2 Produced by Julie Taymor, Robert Chartoff, Lynn Hendee, Julia Taylor-Stanley and Jason K. Lau. Music by Elliot Goldenthal.
3 R. Jackson, 'Shakespeare's Comedies on Film', in A. Davies and S. Wells (eds.), *Shakespeare and the Moving Image: The Plays on Film and Television* (Cambridge: Cambridge University Press, 1994), 100–1.
4 P. S. Donaldson, 'Shakespeare in the Age of Post-Mechanical Reproduction: Sexual and Electronic Magic in *Prospero's Books*', in R. Burt and L. E. Boose

(eds.), *Shakespeare, the Movie, II: Popularizing the Plays on Film, TV, Video, and DVD* (London: Routledge, 2003), 106.

5 B. Elliott and A. Purdy, *Peter Greenaway: Architecture and Allegory* (Chichester: Academy Editions, 1997); D. Pascoe, *Peter Greenaway: Museums and Moving Images* (London: Reaktion Books, 1997).

6 S. Hatchuel, *Shakespeare from Stage to Screen* (Cambridge: Cambridge University Press, 2004), 29.

7 *Ibid.*, 99.

8 M. Cavecchi, 'Peter Greenaway's *Prospero's Books*: A Tempest between Word and Image', *Literature/Film Quarterly* 25:2 (1997), 87.

9 The shape of the cloak was also intended to evoke the shape of a volcano. See *Raising the Tempest*, included as an extra feature of the DVD. Sandy Powell was costume designer.

10 See *Raising the Tempest*.

11 Donaldson, 'Post-Mechanical', 106.

12 Director's comment in *Raising The Tempest*, DVD extra.

13 For example, see the frontispiece to Christopher Marlowe's *The Tragicall Historie of the Life and Death of Doctor Faustus* (1631), which depicts the traditional magic circle. Available via *Early English Books Online* (EEBO) and reproduced in the Arden edition of *The Tempest* at 65.

14 For the process of *solve et coagula*, dissolution and coagulation, as essential to the alchemical process of refining the philosopher's stone, see L. Abraham, *A Dictionary of Alchemical Imagery* (Cambridge: Cambridge University Press, 1998), 187.

15 William Shakespeare, *The Tempest*, The New Cambridge Shakespeare, D. Lindley (ed.), 2nd ed. (Cambridge: Cambridge University Press, 2013), 216. Also see: V. M. Vaughan and A. T. Vaughan, 'Introduction' in V. M. Vaughan and A. T. Vaughan (eds.), *William Shakespeare's The Tempest*, The Arden Shakespeare. Third Series (London: Arden Shakespeare, 1999) 63–4; S. Greenblatt, W. Cohen, J. E. Howard, K. Eisaman Maus (eds.), *The Norton Shakespeare: Based on the Oxford Edition*. 2nd ed. vol. 2 (New York: Norton, 2008), 1373, note to 5.1.1.; J. S. Mebane, *Renaissance Magic and the Return of the Golden Age* (Lincoln, NE: University of Nebraska Press, 1989), 181; P. Munoz Simmonds, '"My Charms Crack Not": The Alchemical Structure of *The Tempest*', *Comparative Drama* 32 (1998), 538–70.

16 Vaughan and Vaughan, 'Introduction' 64; Munoz Simmonds, 'Charms'.

17 Vaughan and Vaughan, 'Introduction' 63–4.

18 S. Crowl, '*The Tempest* (Review)', *Shakespeare Bulletin* 29:2 (2011), 177–8.

19 Kyle Cooper was responsible for the visual effects on the film.

20 *Raising the Tempest*.

21 In Greenaway's film, there is a brief passing shot of a boy on a horse, both with black and white patched skin.

22 Michael D. Friedman has argued that although Hounsou's casting invokes the history of trans-Atlantic slavery, an opportunity to reference local Hawaiian history was missed. M. D. Friedman, 'Where Was He Born? Speak! Tell Me!:

Julie Taymor's *Tempest*, Hawaiian Slavery and the Birther Controversy', *Shakespeare Bulletin* 31:3 (2013), 431–52.

23 *Raising the Tempest.*

24 On the monstrous races generally, see J. B. Friedman, *The Monstrous Races in Medieval Art and Thought* (Syracuse, NY: Syracuse University Press, 2000).

25 Greenaway's Ariel is played by four actors: Orpheo, Paul Russell, James Thierrée and Emil Wolk.

26 D. Lindley, 'Introduction' in D. Lindley (ed.), William Shakespeare, *The Tempest*, The New Cambridge Shakespeare. 2nd ed. (Cambridge: Cambridge University Press, 2013), 41.

27 On the idea of Ariel and Caliban as aspects of Prospero's psyche, see L. Hopkins, *Screen Adaptations: Shakespeare's* The Tempest*: The Relationship between Text and Film* (London: Methuen Drama, 2008), 19–20.

28 On how the play's dramatic design emphasizes the themes of 'service, subjection and freedom', see Lindley, 'Introduction', 15.

29 Richard Kieckhefer, *Magic in the Middle Ages* (Cambridge: Cambridge University Press, 2000), xi; Vaughan and Vaughan, *Tempest*, 62; B. Howard Traister, *Heavenly Necromancers: The Magician in English Renaissance Drama* (Columbia, MO: University of Missouri Press, 1984).

30 Kieckhefer, *Magic*, 9. Also see Lindley, 'Introduction', 40.

31 Kieckhefer, *Magic*, 10.

32 *Ibid.*

33 See generally Kieckhefer, *Magic*, on this issue.

34 In 1542, Henry VIII passed the first Witchcraft Act (subsequently repealed in 1547 by Edward VI). In 1563, Elizabeth I passed a new Witchcraft Act, which penalised those convicted of damage to property or persons by witchcraft with one year's imprisonment, and those convicted of murder by witchcraft with the death penalty. P. C. Almond, *England's First Demonologist: Reginald Scot & 'The Discoverie of Witchcraft'* (London, New York: I. B. Tauris, 2011), 14–16. This legislation was subsequently broadened in scope by James I in 1604. Originally practitioners could only be prosecuted if their magic resulted in harm, however the legislation became more draconian under James I and the mere practice of magic, regardless of its consequences, could attract prosecution.

35 It is estimated by Brian Levack that there were approximately 90,000 prosecutions for witchcraft across Europe, of which around half resulted in executions. In Britain, it is estimated there may have been up to 5,000 trials and 1,500–2,000 executions. The most common profile for those convicted and executed was elderly women. See generally B. P. Levack, *The Witch-Hunt in Early Modern Europe*, 3rd ed. (Harlow: Pearson, 2006). For alternative estimates from various authors, see A. P. Coudert, 'The Myth of the Improved Status of Protestant Women: The Case of the Witchcraze', in J. R. Brink, A. P. Coudert and M. C. Horowitz (eds.), *The Politics of Gender in Early Modern Europe* (Kirksville, MO: Sixteenth Century Journal Pubs., 1989), 61–89, n2.

36 Kieckhefer, *Magic*, xi.

37 The New Cambridge Shakespeare edition reproduces Arthur Golding's translation of the Latin at Appendix 2 (273–4). Also see Lindley, 'Introduction', 8. For a modern translation, also see Ovid, *Metamorphoses*, trans. S. Lombardo (Indianapolis: Hackett Publishing, 2010), 7.233–51.

38 Lindley, 'Introduction', 8.

39 M.-F. Wilson, 'English Epicures and Scottish Witches', *Shakespeare Quarterly* 57:2 (2006), 143; C. Zika, *The Appearance of Witchcraft: Print and Visual Culture in Sixteenth-Century Europe* (London, New York: Routledge, 2007), fig. 1.4. However, Lindley argues that the ability to generate storms could also be classified as natural, not demonic, magic, so the issue was far from clear. Lindley, 'Introduction', 41.

40 Crowl, '*Tempest*', 178.

41 See Donaldson's argument on Prospero's appropriation of maternal reproduction.

42 Pascoe, *Greenaway*, 161, fig. 67, 236, n4. For an analysis of this scene, in the context of an argument that Greenaway's film rewrites the play's absent women, see also Simon Ryle's chapter 4, 'Re-nascences: *The Tempest* and New Media', in *Shakespeare, Cinema and Desire: Adaptation and Other Futures of Shakespeare's Language* (Houndsmills, Basingstoke, Hampshire, New York: Palgrave Macmillan, 2014).

43 Hatchuel, *Shakespeare*, 29; Cavecchi, 'Greenaway', 83.

44 Abraham, *Dictionary*, 187.

WORKS CITED

Abraham, L., *A Dictionary of Alchemical Imagery* (Cambridge: Cambridge University Press, 1998).

Almond, P. C., *England's First Demonologist: Reginald Scot & 'The Discoverie of Witchcraft'* (London, New York: I. B. Tauris, 2011).

Cavecchi, M., 'Peter Greenaway's *Prospero's Books*: A Tempest between Word and Image', *Literature/Film Quarterly* 25:2 (1997), 83–9.

Coudert, A. P., 'The Myth of the Improved Status of Protestant Women: The Case of the Witchcraze', in J. R. Brink, A. P. Coudert and M. C. Horowitz (eds.), *The Politics of Gender in Early Modern Europe* (Kirksville, MO: Sixteenth Century Journal Pubs., 1989), 61–89.

Crowl, S., '*The Tempest* (Review)', *Shakespeare Bulletin* 29:2 (2011), 177–81.

Donaldson, P. S, 'Shakespeare in the Age of Post-Mechanical Reproduction: Sexual and Electronic Magic in *Prospero's Books*', in R. Burt and L. E. Boose (eds.), *Shakespeare, the Movie, II: Popularizing the Plays on Film, TV, Video, and DVD* (London: Routledge, 2003), 105–19.

Elliott, B. and A. Purdy, *Peter Greenaway: Architecture and Allegory* (Chichester: Academy Editions, 1997).

Friedman, J. B., *The Monstrous Races in Medieval Art and Thought* (Syracuse, NY: Syracuse University Press, 2000).

Friedman, M. D., 'Where Was He Born? Speak! Tell Me!: Julie Taymor's *Tempest*, Hawaiian Slavery and the Birther Controversy', *Shakespeare Bulletin* 31:3 (2013), 431–52.

Greenblatt, S., W. Cohen, J. E. Howard, K. Eisaman Maus (eds.), *The Norton Shakespeare: Based on the Oxford Edition*, 2nd ed. (New York: Norton, 2008).

Hatchuel, S., *Shakespeare from Stage to Screen* (Cambridge: Cambridge University Press, 2004).

Hopkins, L., *Screen Adaptations: Shakespeare's* The Tempest*: The Relationship between Text and Film* (London: Methuen Drama, 2008).

Howard Traister, B., *Heavenly Necromancers: The Magician in English Renaissance Drama* (Columbia, MO: University of Missouri Press, 1984).

Jackson, R., 'Shakespeare's Comedies on Film', in A. Davies and S. Wells (eds.), *Shakespeare and the Moving Image: The Plays on Film and Television* (Cambridge: Cambridge University Press, 1994), 99–120.

Kieckhefer, R., *Magic in the Middle Ages* (Cambridge: Cambridge University Press, 2000).

Levack, B. P., *The Witch-Hunt in Early Modern Europe*, 3rd ed. (Harlow: Pearson, 2006).

Lindley, D., 'Introduction', in D. Lindley (ed.), *The Tempest*, The New Cambridge Shakespeare. 2nd ed. (Cambridge: Cambridge University Press, 2013), 1–101.

Mebane, J. S., *Renaissance Magic and the Return of the Golden Age* (Lincoln, NE: University of Nebraska Press, 1989).

Munoz Simmonds, P., '"My Charms Crack Not": The Alchemical Structure of *The Tempest*', *Comparative Drama* 32 (1998), 538–70.

Ovid, *Metamorphoses*, trans. S. Lombardo (Indianapolis: Hackett Publishing, 2010).

Pascoe, D., *Peter Greenaway: Museums and Moving Images* (London: Reaktion Books, 1997).

Ryle, S., *Shakespeare, Cinema and Desire: Adaptation and Other Futures of Shakespeare's Language* (Houndsmills, Basingstoke, Hampshire, New York: Palgrave Macmillan, 2014).

Vaughan, V. M. and A. T. Vaughan, 'Introduction', in V. M. Vaughan and A. T. Vaughan (eds.), William Shakespeare, *The Tempest*, The Arden Shakespeare. Third Series (London: Arden Shakespeare, 1999), 1–138.

Wilson, M.-F., 'English Epicures and Scottish Witches', *Shakespeare Quarterly* 57:2 (2006), 131–61.

Zika, C., *The Appearance of Witchcraft: Print and Visual Culture in Sixteenth-Century Europe* (London, New York: Routledge, 2007).

CHAPTER 14

Almereyda's Cymbeline
The End of Teen Shakespeare

Douglas M. Lanier

What happened to the teen Shakespeare film? Arguably the dominant screen Shakespeare genre at the turn of the twenty-first century, the teen Shakespeare film can trace its origins to the unexpected success of *Clueless* (dir. Amy Heckerling, 1995), which hit upon the market-savvy strategy of melding the plot of an English classic (in this case, Jane Austen) with the dynamics of contemporary American high school culture. Baz Luhrmann's *Romeo + Juliet* (1996) broadened out the social scope of this formula, extending it to a post-modern Los Angeles gripped by corporate rivalries and gang violence and becoming in the process the iconic Shakespeare film for its generation. In the years that followed, the 'Shakespeare-plus-teen social dynamics' formula largely retreated back to the American high school milieu and was repeated with variations in the following decade: *10 Things I Hate About You* (dir. Gil Junger, 1999), *Never Been Kissed* (dir. Raja Gosnell, 1999), *Get Over It* (dir. Tommy O'Haver, 2001), '*O*' (dir. Tim Blake Nelson, 2001), *She's the Man* (dir. Andy Fickman, 2006) and *Romeo and Juliet in Yiddish* (dir. Eve Annenberg, 2010), to mention the most prominent examples, along with myriad high school films with classroom scenes involving Shakespeare.[1] The production trend even became internationalized, though most of the non-Anglo versions eschew the high school setting – see, for instance, *The Chicken Rice War* (dir. Chee Kong Cheah, 2000, from Singapore), *Amar te Duele* (dir. Fernando Sariñana, 2002, from Mexico), *Gedebe* (dir. Namron, 2003, from Malaysia), and *Iago* (dir. Volfango De Biasi, 2009, from Italy). By the middle of the 2000s, however, this film cycle seemed to have run its course. Carlo Carlei's *Romeo & Juliet* (2013), the most recent entry, featured contemporary language and attractive teenage leads and remained faithful to Shakespeare's plot. However, it opted for a period rather than contemporary *mise-en-scène*, even though posters for the film, apparently mindful of the teen market, rather cleverly sought to obscure that fact. Despite (or because of) its contemporizing half-measures, critics widely panned the film (most fastened on Julian Fellowes's anachronistic dialogue) and, more to the point, *Romeo & Juliet* failed miserably at the box office. Many major studio teen Shakespeare projects once rumoured to be in development have apparently come to naught and even independent filmmakers seem uninterested in the genre. The association of Shakespeare with cool youth culture seems to have faded from the cinematic mainstream (or migrated elsewhere[2]) and, with it, much of the energy that fueled the Shakespeare film boom at the turn of the millennium.

I have omitted one crucial film from the previous list – Michael Almereyda's *Hamlet* (2000). Almereyda approached the youth-market Shakespeare film by focusing on the next frame out of teen life, the plight of Generation X post-high-school, attending especially to that generation's disaffection from the Reagan-era culture of their parents and from the corporate-media complex within which they came of age. Hamlet's dilemma within the film is that he resists his parents and mainstream media culture (they become one and the same) by using their own materials and techniques, both of which are in his hands inadequate to so formidable a task.[3] Played by indie film icon Ethan Hawke, Hamlet is an amateur filmmaker and an adept at media bricolage, like Claudius a manipulator of screen culture. Yet when he tries to use images to craft tactics of resistance and independence, to 'take arms against a sea of troubles' (*Hamlet*, 3.1.59), he discovers that his oppositional gestures have been co-opted by the very media culture he seeks to resist. As he walks, anguished, down the action film aisle of Blockbuster Video, confronted by box after box of commercialized rebel or revenge narratives, he bemoans how his 'enterprises of great pitch and moment/With this regard their currents turn awry/And lose the name of action' (*Hamlet*, 3.1.86–8), in the process aptly illustrating the defining dilemma of the disaffected, media-savvy millennial. Hamlet's valiant but finally futile rage against the corporate machine, a phantom empire that extends far beyond Claudius's shadowy Denmark Corporation, is cast by Almereyda as the stuff of indie tragedy, his Hamlet a Gen-X melancholic of a poetic bent, an ideal-minded wannabe bohemian crushed by the enormous burden of carving out a media space of his own. Heir to Romantic Hamlets of the past, Hamlet is the alienated loser as tragic hero. Almereyda was perhaps the most self-conscious of the filmmakers of this period about the cultural politics of hybridizing Shakespeare and contemporary teen culture. Whereas others were by and large content to assert an easy congruence between Shakespeare and the youth culture mainstream, Almereyda was interested – albeit warily – in Shakespeare's potential as an icon for alternative culture, a means through which he might meditate upon the quandary of the contemporary hipster, confronted by a ubiquitous media mainstream voraciously appropriating gestures of alienation. It is hard not to see in Almereyda's *Hamlet* an allegory of his own vexed position as an indie Shakespeare filmmaker, for at the time the film was made he was swimming against a very strong ideological current in screen Shakespeare, one promulgated in part for market reasons by major studios. Like Hamlet within the film, whose disgust for Claudius is valorized by his ghostly father, played by Sam Shepard, dissident American playwright, Almereyda finds in Shakespeare legitimation for indie cinema and the alternative pop culture it presents. What complicates this reclaiming of Shakespeare's oppositional status is that it is not clear that Hamlet's hipsterism is in fact oppositional rather than just another species of mainstream 'cool' and, even if it is, it is politically inert, ineffective, implosive.

It is surprising, then, that Almereyda would return to Shakespeare in 2014, at a moment when the teen Shakespeare subgenre seems to have played itself out. Surprising too is that he would choose *Cymbeline* for screen adaptation, a play so obscure that it would not be immediately recognizable to most viewers as Shakespeare (and perhaps this was part of a commercial strategy). Given the status of the subgenre and the obscurity of the play, *Cymbeline* came and went from screens almost immediately, premiering to mostly hostile or uncomprehending reviews[4] and appearing on pay-per-view video on the day of its theatrical release, a sign of its producers' lack of faith in its market viability. However, I want to make the case for Almereyda's *Cymbeline* as a thematic sequel, a return, a generation later, to issues which animated his *Hamlet*: the fate of the hipster in contemporary American culture, the effects of media on youth culture (in this case, social media) and the possibilities for cultural dissidence from the American mainstream. As is Almereyda's wont, the film also reflects upon the very genres within which he is working – the youth market Shakespeare adaptation and indie film – both of which have fallen out of fashion. Instead of Hamlet, Imogen serves as Almereyda's primary surrogate within the film. Her journey from preppy high-school sweetheart meeting her lover under the bleachers to butch biker chick striking out on her own marks Shakespeare's passage from mainstream teen culture to a dissident alternative; it also charts the affective journey of a generation from adolescent millennial to alienated adulthood. In the process, Almereyda rearticulates his case for Shakespeare's oppositional orientation, an orientation which lines up well with the concerns of indie cinema. In Almereyda's hands, *Cymbeline*, like his *Hamlet*, becomes a meditation on the conditions, contradictions and possibilities for alternative culture in America.

Almereyda conducts his discussion of the state of American counterculture through the tale of Imogen and Posthumus's romantic rebellion. Most scholars agree that *Cymbeline* provides, through the plotline of conflict between Cymbeline and the Romans, a foundation myth for the British nation and with it, a conception of British identity rooted in principles of liberty and empire.[5] Understandably, Almereyda downplays this narrative thread as inappropriate for an adaptation so firmly situated in American culture,[6] transforming Cymbeline's Britons into a biker gang and Caius Lucius's Romans into the local police force. In place of this British nationalistic strain, Almereyda emphasizes the play's other plotline, the blocked romance between the young lovers. In interviews, Almereyda has characterized Imogen and Posthumus's tale as 'timeless' and resonant for modern audiences. His adaptation stresses, so he claims, 'the way the men were underestimating the women in their lives, and misjudging them, mistrusting them, and trying to manipulate them.'[7] Certainly focusing the film on the blocked romance makes Almereyda's version of the play more recognizable to audiences familiar with Shakespearean stalwarts like *Romeo and Juliet* and *A Midsummer Night's Dream*. But the specific forces that pull this couple apart, the particular arc each travels from romantic innocence and adolescent rebellion to painful, redemptive knowledge and reconciliation, as well as the choices they make upon gaining that knowledge, allow Almereyda to consider the possibilities for an authentic counterculture sensibility in contemporary America. Almereyda has commented that, as he wrote the film in 2009, he was contemplating 'the American empire, fatigued and confused.'[8] That thinking, I argue, surfaces rather surprisingly in his handling of the rebellious lovers' tale of love lost and regained, in which questions of national identity in Shakespeare's original are addressed in updated and culturally transposed form. In Almereyda's hands, the lovers' plot becomes an allegorical tale about countercultural integrity in contemporary America. Imogen and Posthumus take very different journeys to knowledge in the film and, as is typical of Shakespearean romance, those journeys involve symbolic death and rebirth.

Almereyda's *Cymbeline* evokes myths of American alternative culture in a number of ways.[9] The film is chock-a-block with American alt-cult archetypes, the most potent of which is the image of the leather-jacketed biker, reminiscent of rebel icons like Marlon Brando and James Dean, the uniform of Cymbeline's 'Britons'.[10] More contemporary are the portrayals of Posthumus as an emo skateboarder – his red tee festooned with a skull, modern sign of the cultural dissident – and of Iachimo (played by Ethan Hawke) as a sneering, casually superior hipster, living in a fashionably shabby flat, clad in American Apparel outfits, driving a vintage lemon-yellow Mustang convertible. Belarius's cave becomes a location meant to suggest what remains of the American frontier ideal, an off-the-grid cabin decorated with, among other telling items, an American flag pillow, home to a decidedly unconventional, interracial, working-class family.

The film's locations – pointedly mundane and non-descript, except for Cymbeline's grand suburban home – situate the action far from the metropolitan centres of corporate and cultural hegemony that were the focus of *Hamlet*. The gritty settings of *Cymbeline*, many of which are in Brooklyn, ground zero for American hipsterism in the nineties and naughts, would seem to offer fertile ground for American indie sensibilities to take root. Notable too are elements of production design that evoke all manner of indie culture – the Queen smokes an e-cigarette; John Cage, Bob Dylan, Patti Smith, reggae and brooding electronica are featured on the soundtrack; we first meet Iachimo as he gets a homemade hipster hair-cut; all the ubiquitous computer products are Apple-branded; Iachimo's box is disguised as rock band equipment; Posthumus buys a gun from a bald, ambiguously gendered saleswoman; as Imogen wanders the countryside, she encounters a scarecrow in a Guy Fawkes mask; and Arvigarus plays LPs on a turntable in Belarius's cabin. The concatenation of signifiers of oppositional or alternative culture affiliates Shakespeare – and *Cymbeline* specifically – with an indie sensibility,[11] but more importantly, it keeps before the viewer the question of contemporary American alt-culture.

And yet despite the film's impressive catalogue of American alt-culture motifs and allusions, the social groups we see on the screen hardly seem alternative at all. For all its rebel regalia, the Briton biker gang has degenerated into a drug-dealing operation, affording Cymbeline and his family life in a sprawling home in the suburbs (with servants and antique furnishings to boot). One is reminded of Thomas Frank's trenchant critique of what has become of American dissident culture, now merely a matter of the consumption of signs of rebellion rather than a dissident perspective on mainstream American culture.[12] An avatar of America's youth culture past, Cymbeline is portrayed as aged, wolfing down a handful of vitamins and heart pills with his breakfast, crippled by news of Imogen's absence from his Pleasant Valley court. This incongruous mix of bikers and bourgeois complacency suggests the degraded state of earlier ideals of American alternative culture. Those ideals have corroded into tyranny and violence, the first manifestation of which is Cymbeline's opposition to Posthumus's romance with Imogen, an edict he enforces by threatening to blow off Posthumus's head. A montage of the simmering war between the Britons and the Roman police makes clear that Cymbeline's brutality is indistinguishable from that of his oppressive foes. Unprovoked, Cymbeline and his men open fire on the cops, as the cops mercilessly beat a suspect and Caius Lucius counts money and smirks at his fortune from a fortune cookie. The two form a symbiotic circle of corruption that is broken so that Cloten, like the Dauphin in *Henry V*, with an insulting tribute (of candy kisses) can make a callow display of princely bravado. The Queen exemplifies this degraded version of rebellion. She may vape like a hipster but, like a Lady Macbeth crossed with a footballer's wife, she seems far better suited to the comforts of suburban life – coifed hair, stylish clothes, patrician manner – than to Cymbeline's bikers. Dylan's 'Dark Eyes,' the song she sings for a biker party, concerns the possibility of redemption of a world of loss, conflict and exploitation. That redemption takes the form of the narrator's fleeting vision of beauty, a dark-eyed woman. Yet in the Queen's mouth, the song becomes a narcissistic self-advertisement, an anthem to the erotic power she, as bourgeois bitch-goddess, holds over the aging Cymbeline. That is, her performance of Dylan's song – turning a dissident work on its head – epitomizes the effect she has more generally on the countercultural sensibility for which Cymbeline might stand.

This disconcerting amalgam of rebel subculture with middle-class mainstream is the debased milieu from which Imogen must divide herself in the course of the film. As the film begins, she is a preppy naïf. The only indication of the violence that underlies her comfortable existence is the Old Master painting of dogs attacking a stag that hangs in her spacious bedroom. Like a lovesick schoolgirl, she surreptitiously meets her lover Posthumus under the bleachers at night, exchanging tokens with him amidst bars that subtly hint of prison. Almereyda slyly indicates Imogen's initial innocence by repeatedly filming her head in medium shot while blocking view of her body, one of the film's witty riffs on the motif of headlessness. We see this shot when she is first introduced in the film's expositional prologue, seated at the foot of her bed and, again, when she peruses Iachimo's box before retiring to sleep, both indications of her divorce from the ugly realities of her situation. Cymbeline's opposition to Imogen's liaison with Posthumus is somewhat surprising, given that he seems Cymbeline's natural cultural heir, with James Dean looks and a rebellious streak (at first, he stands up to Cymbeline), unlike the wannabe biker Cloten, a spoiled brat whose perverse desire for Imogen smacks of incest and jealousy. For Imogen to separate from her father's tyranny and more generally from the compromised oppositional ideals of her home, Imogen must first give up her identity, not just her femininity (she bobs her hair) but also more crucially her class status (she bloodies her beloved white cardigan and dresses in thrift-store clothes like a homeless person).

Imogen's passage to understanding entails not just shedding her former identity but making contact with working-class values, those at the margins of dominant society, exemplified by Belarius and his wholesome, milk-drinking sons. In this context, Belarius's blackness serves to intensify the authenticity of his underclass status, his difference from the corrupted and almost exclusively white suburban regime of Cymbeline. His realm is an off-the-grid cabin in the woods, a locale which evokes not only working-class subsistence and pre-digital American life, but also Thoreau's home on Walden Pond and the frontier cabin, mythic American sites of independence and self-reliance. The cabin is filled with signs that identify this space with various strains of political liberation and hope. In one establishing shot, we see President Obama delivering an address on an outdated TV, a reminder that his election was a triumph for progressive culture against conservative hegemony; indeed, Belarius's quietly authoritative manner seems distantly reminiscent of Obama's no-drama. On the wall is a banner reading 'Work Rest Play,' an allusion to the Subhumans' song 'Work Rest Play Die'[13] (Imogen's 'death' supplies the 'die'), a punk anthem decrying the impoverished state of dissident culture. In the context of Belarius's cabin, the banner reads like a wholesome American credo evoking the uncomplicated life of the frontier. In a gesture which reads like a gesture of reflexive class privilege, Imogen, having broken into Belarius's home, tries to pay for the food she has stolen, but like proper anti-capitalists the sons scorn talk of money: 'All gold and silver rather turn to dirt,' responds Guiderius, for money is fit only for 'those/Who worship dirty gods' (3.6.52, 54).[14] Arvigarus wears a Che tee-shirt, a global image of counterculture affiliation that prompts Imogen, when cornered about her identity, to take the name 'Fidel,' in the process transposing Imogen's pseudonym in Shakespeare's text – 'Fidele,' the faithful one – into a political revolutionary key. When Belarius and his sons sit down to dinner with Imogen, Guiderius plays Toots and the Maytals's 'Pressure Drop' (on a turntable, of course). This classic reggae indictment of mainstream society, predicting rough justice on those who 'know that you were doing wrong,' speaks with some irony to Imogen, who has broken into Belarius's home, but it also resonates more generally and more forcefully with Almereyda's positioning of Belarius's space in opposition to the American mainstream.[15] Tellingly, it is at this dinner table, with 'Pressure Drop' playing, that Imogen experiences unexpected kinship with this alternative family, this in sharp contrast to the rather tense breakfast table over which Cymbeline presides in his suburban 'court,' a setting where Imogen never appears. Imogen's meal in Belarius's cabin becomes her initiation to an alternative American culture and to a new identity she will come to embrace. Even so, the death of her old identity as mainstream naïf is not completed until she fully 'dies,' drinking the Queen's potion and ending up next to what she thinks is Posthumus's body, making her way fully to the American margins by ending up buried with the slag in a strip mine. It is her discovery of the body of 'Posthumus', identified by the red skull tee that Cloten stole, that brings Imogen to tears and, with his 'death,' reconfirms her love for him. The Imogen who emerges from this process is the Imogen we see in the back of a squad car in an extended and affecting close-up in the film's exposition. Her hair cut androgynously short, her clothes shabby, she is no longer affiliated with her rebel father or bourgeois mother, but is reborn as a disaffected alt-cult youth. Her burnt-out affect signifies a newfound, world-weary wisdom about what she surmises are the violent lengths her family will go to control her romantic life and class affiliations.

Posthumus takes a different path of symbolic death and rebirth in his journey from innocence to wised-up disaffection. Like Imogen, Posthumus enters the film as a naïf. Unlike Imogen, however, he is affiliated at the start with a particularly American form of adolescent 'rebellion lite' signified by his skateboarding and skull-emblazoned tee. Almereyda leaves unclear why Posthumus's arm is in a cast. Has he fallen from his skateboard, an indication of loser status? Has Cymbeline previously broken his arm to warn him away from Imogen? Whatever the reason, the broken arm symbolically suggests, like Oedipus's lame foot, that Posthumus is operating with insufficient wisdom and will suffer a fall for it. Exiled by Cymbeline and homeless, he crashes at Iachimo's shabby chic flat. Iachimo is yet another incarnation of American alt-culture tradition, the contemporary hipster. His stock in trade is sneering irony and, in this case, confronted with Posthumus's romantic idealization of Imogen, it takes the form of misogynistic demythologization of women – 'I have not seen the most precious diamond that is,' says Iachimo provocatively, 'nor you the lady' (1.4.60–1). When Iachimo declares 'I make my wager rather against your confidence than her reputation' (1.4.89–90), he identifies the true stakes of the bet –what is at issue is a contest between idealism and cynicism. What provokes Posthumus as much as the insult to Imogen is Iachimo's casual hipper-than-thou attitude and superior smirk; he too quickly takes up the wager and falls into Iachimo's trap. The photo of Imogen that Posthumus shares with Iachimo is rather surprisingly of her as a child, the very image of pre-sexual innocence. The image too presents Imogen as something of a be-garlanded flower child, wearing a peasant dress in a pastoral setting. That is, this image conveys the nature of Posthumus's symbolic investments in her – for him, Imogen exudes not just erotic innocence and purity but a countercultural quality which the real Imogen does not seem to have.

Iachimo's means for undermining the couple's idealization of each other and spreading rumor is one of Almereyda's targets for critique, social media – a lifeblood of contemporary youth culture, much lauded for its progressive political potential. In Iachimo's hands, however, digital technology is a tool only to spread his own brand of romantic cynicism. He takes surreptitious selfies to provide evidence of Imogen's infidelity, a strategy that changes significantly the dynamic of Shakespeare's text. In Shakespeare's version, Iachimo's power depends upon his storytelling skills, his ability to weave a believable tale of betrayal around the tokens he has collected. In Almereyda's, the scene turns far more on the power of the photographic image to generate scandal in itself, underlined when Iachimo snaps away, 'Here's a voucher,/Stronger than ever law could make' (2.2.39–40).[16] To add insult to injury, Iachimo, sitting in front of his box, even rolls his photo across the table to Posthumus atop Posthumus's skateboard. When he visits Imogen, he ups the ante by photoshopping pictures on his iPad to convince Imogen that Posthumus has betrayed her. The association of screen technologies with troubling elements of manipulation and surveillance extends well beyond Iachimo. As the sinister queen waits for Cymbeline in the first scene, she checks her iPhone and texts; Cymbeline himself uses surveillance cameras around his biker headquarters; Cloten checks Imogen's browser history to trace her whereabouts; even Posthumus directs Pisanio to kill Imogen by phone message, a message Pisanio shares with Imogen. The ambivalent view of contemporary tech that Almereyda explored in *Hamlet*, the potential of the camera and laptop as means for individual resistance but also as conduits for hegemonic power, becomes in *Cymbeline* rather more pessimistic about screen technology as a vehicle for alternative culture. What the film seems to process subtextually, especially through Iachimo's actions, is an anxiety about the general effect of social media, its capacity to poison the social fabric, to breed and propagate mistrust. Iachimo's powerful line, 'hell is here' (2.2.50), refers not just to his pang of conscience as he creeps about Imogen's bedchamber but also to the very means he uses to destroy her and Posthumus's relationship. This may explain why the media technology in Belarius's home, Almereyda's alt-cult 'green world,' is pre-digital. His is a realm in which human relationships are comparatively *un*mediated, direct, less susceptible to digital manipulation and interpretive reframing, a realm where positive cultural alternatives might take root and thrive.

Though Posthumus's romantic disillusionment certainly springs from his wounded male pride, I suggest that it also has a cultural-political dimension: he is victim to the postmodern regime of the social image over which Iachimo is cynical master. Before he is infected with Iachimo's lies about Imogen, Posthumus's aesthetic is resolutely lo-fi and handmade – he records his thoughts in a composition notebook with a pen (he doesn't seem to own a laptop), and the love token he sends Imogen is a woodcut he crafts himself.[17] However, once Posthumus accepts the 'truthiness' of the screen images Iachimo purveys, he loses faith and becomes, like Imogen, a homeless exile. It's noteworthy that as he forsakes Iachimo's hipster pad, he passes in front of a graffitoed wall on which the camera lingers. The graffito is of a childlike blonde girl, vaguely angelic, duplicated freely in the public space, a manifestation of the dissemination and degradation of Imogen's image in Iachimo's realm.

After this sequence, Posthumus is a man without a culture. Though he finds momentary focus for his rage by buying a gun, he does not use it nor does he go to court to take revenge as promised. Instead, he wanders the streets on his skateboard, eventually getting picked up by Caius Lucius and the Roman cops. By rearranging portions of the play's opening expositional scene and placing them in Caius Lucius's mouth, Almereyda suggests that the Roman police have framed Posthumus for Cloten's murder, only to release him so that he can be dealt with by Cymbeline and his men. Ironically, upon his release, Posthumus is welcomed back into the hipster fold by Iachimo but, when he is handed Imogen's bloody sweater (evidence that Pisanio has carried out his order to kill her), the concatenation of betrayals is too much for him to bear. Like Imogen, he comes to recognize the depth of his love for his beloved only when he thinks she is dead. With that recognition, he lashes out mindlessly, shooting at Cymbeline's men in hopes of provoking his biker-assisted suicide. It is as if Posthumus, forced to occupy the darkly cynical, 'un-green world' of Iachimo, brings Iachimo's cynical hipster perspective to its logical conclusion – nihilism.

Posthumus's redemption, like Imogen's, involves a symbolic death and rebirth and contact with a positive model of alternative culture. That final passage occurs when Posthumus, bound and readied for execution, is laid out on a metal prep table, as if already a corpse at a morgue. Almereyda rewrites significantly the *deus ex machina* in Shakespeare's text, jettisoning the vision of Jupiter and Posthumus's extended family. Instead, the mechanism for Posthumus's redemption is a *pater ex machina*, the ghostly appearance of his father Sicilius. Over Posthumus's body he reads what is Almereyda's substitute for Jupiter's riddling prophecy in Shakespeare's version: 'Of God we ask one favor' by Emily Dickinson, yet another American

maverick. Dickinson's oracular poem points in several directions: it continues Almereyda's Americanization of Shakespeare's play – if Sicilius is
Posthumus's Briton father, Dickinson serves here as the American 'mother'
of his rebirth; it announces the theme of forgiveness that will run throughout the final reconciliation scene; and, most important, it informs Posthumus that he still lacks full knowledge of the sin he has committed, locked
as he is within an ideological 'magic prison'. Potent and resonant as the
Dickinson text is, the film's renewal of faith in an alt-cult ideal takes place
just as much in terms of the figure of Sicilius himself, yet another avatar
of biker culture, but this time in a heroic, benevolently paternal key, the
'un-Cymbeline'. Sicilius establishes Posthumus as heir to the proper legacy
of American alternative culture for which he stands, just as Belarius adopts
Imogen into his alternative family. Upon waking up, Posthumus at first
shakes off – literally – Sicilius's legacy in the form of the 'tablet' he leaves
on his son's chest. Consumed by guilt over what he thinks is Imogen's
murder, he longs for death, a state he claims he alone now finally understands: 'There are none want eyes to direct them the way I am going,' he
tells his executioner, 'but such as wink and will not use them' (5.3.243–4).
Nonetheless, his fixation on guilt, expressed as a world-weary angst, seems
somewhat overwrought and self-regarding. The executioner remarks presciently, 'What an infinite mock is this, that a man should have the best
use of eyes to see the way of blindness!' (5.3.245–6); and when Imogen puts
her arm around Posthumus as he begs death from the king, he butts her
with his elbow, the one sardonically comic moment in the final scene. Only
after the two lovers reconcile does Posthumus take up his father's legacy by
forsaking his skateboard for a motorcycle at the film's end. Notably, he is
not a means, as he is in Shakespeare's version, for fortifying Cymbeline's
empire.

Throughout the film, Pisanio, like the king clad in motorcycle regalia,
offers a telling contrast to the corrupted alt-cult ideal embodied by Cymbeline and his household.[18] Seemingly a loyal henchman – he participates
in the king's ambush of the police and ferries drugs for the Queen – he
nonetheless has qualms about their activities, as his sidelong glance at Cymbeline during the ambush and growing distance from the royal family indicates. Almereyda often positions him as a witness of events, exuding a
blank-faced, knowing melancholy as he watches Imogen become caught
up in Cloten's lovelorn scheming. More than any other character in the
film, he exemplifies the problem of maintaining his rebel integrity while
navigating the oppressive demands of Cymbeline's household. It is Pisanio
who tosses Imogen a motorcycle helmet as she speaks of going to Milford

Haven, the first harbinger of her trajectory at the end of the film; and it is he who sets her on a path to genuine independence by supplying her with a new male identity, the catalyst for her symbolic death and rebirth in exile. He also refuses to give her up when Cymbeline, in a moment of particular cruelty, tortures him regarding Imogen's whereabouts. Almereyda's approach to this scene – Pisanio is stripped naked, placed in a dog cage, and nearly strangled to death with a plastic bag – emphasizes his vulnerability at the king's hands and his embrace of martyrdom for Imogen's cause. Indeed, he too undergoes something of a symbolic death and rebirth by committing himself to a truer ideal of rebel culture. Pisanio is also instrumental in Posthumus's release from his death sentence, for it is he who removes Posthumus's noose at the last moment and orders him taken to the king. Unlike Shakespeare's version, it is not at all clear that this reprieve came from Cymbeline. When Posthumus marches in slo-mo to see the aftermath of the battle between the Britons and Romans (in Almereyda's version he is not a participant), he passes Pisanio who, centre-frame, is brooding, his worried face turned toward the battle and the king outside. In a voice-over, Posthumus offers this commentary as he passes, 'Every good servant does not all commands;/No bond, but to do just ones' (5.1.6–7). This juxtaposition reinforces the dramatic irony of the original (Posthumus does not yet know that Pisanio did not kill Imogen as he commanded) but, more importantly, it summarizes Pisanio's growing moral integrity throughout the film, as the one servant who keeps most genuine faith with the ideal of countercultural independence his motorcycle jacket signifies.

The final scene of Shakespeare's *Cymbeline* is notoriously difficult to stage convincingly. The preposterous cascade of revelations is particularly ill-suited to cinematic adaptation, given the medium's basic orientation toward realism. Interestingly, in this scene, Almereyda emphasizes rather than covers over the gap between his film's low-budget naturalism and Shakespeare's patently fantastical approach. It is tempting to think that the mismatch is intentional, a way of introducing a Brechtian quality (or just plain doubt) regarding the comic social order established by Cymbeline's victory and 'pardon' for all. In any case, Almereyda recasts the final scene so that considerable attention falls to Iachimo's and Cymbeline's takedowns. Captured after Posthumus's gunfight with Cymbeline's men, bound and roughed up, Iachimo is forced to suffer the consequences of Posthumus's disillusionment that he himself set in motion. His smirking bravado stripped away, he is exposed as a cringing coward, confessing his villainy to the king and Posthumus (but not to Imogen, as in Shakespeare's version) and afterward slinking ignobly away, his hipster attitude revealed as empty lies.[19] When Cymbeline learns of the Queen's death and abhorrence for him, rather absurdly her body is brought to the parking-lot 'battlefield' so that he can have one last encounter in which he confesses his own weakness for her charms. Afterward, he pushes the body away and orders that it be burnt, as if he were purging all that she stood for in his life, particularly her raw bourgeois aspiration. Indeed, throughout this scene, Almereyda projects the failings of Cymbeline's regime onto the Queen so that they can be symbolically excised. By contrast, the restoration of the lovers and the royal family is hurried along, signified by a sequence of silent embraces over which the camera does not linger; Imogen's cross-dressing as Fidel is not remarked upon at all. The reconciliation between the Britons and the Romans – with Cymbeline's summary line, 'Pardon's the word to all' (5.4.422) – seems strangely unmotivated. Within the politics of the film, it plays as an unforeseen restoration of the corrupt arrangement between bikers and cops that inexplicably jeopardizes the Britons' hard-won independence, as if Cymbeline had simply traded affiliation with 'our wicked Queen' for alliance with the police.

Little wonder, then, that Imogen and Posthumus do not integrate themselves into the 'comic' community that emerges at the end. They back away unseen, and then ride off on a motorcycle, with Imogen at the handlebar, giving a brief backward glance before roaring to destinations unknown. The two constitute a new alt-cult community of their own, wised-up about the failings of the cultural alternatives.

Throughout their journey to this moment of liberation, they have been shadowed by Posthumus's woodcut, a picture of a wide-eyed girl side-by-side with a skeleton, with the logo 'Fear No More' in reference to 'Fear no more the heat o'th'sun' (4.2.257) in Shakespeare's text. This image is Posthumus's love token for Imogen and, at first, it signifies the lovers, with Imogen as the girl and Posthumus with his skull-adorned tee as the skeleton. 'Fear no more' is his exhortation to her that she should not fear her father's wrath and that he will remain faithful to her.[20] Imogen looks it over as she journeys into the wilderness in exile, encountering a scarecrow with a Guy Fawkes mask that reminds her of Posthumus, another hollow seeming-revolutionary, at which she lets the image go. But as the film moves along and we encounter the woodcut in other contexts, it gains resonance. Cloten finds it at the quarry near Belarius's home and it presages his death and Imogen's 'poisoning' soon after. Here the image becomes associated with the actual experience of death but also with its transformative potential in the form of symbolic 'rebirth,' a passage through which Imogen (and Posthumus) must pass to experience loss, achieve knowledge and mature. Almereyda suggests that this potential is lost on mainstream American society, for he includes myriad references to Halloween paraphernalia, all of which masks the truth of death and trivializes its pain and power. As Imogen and Posthumus roar away on the motorcycle, the woodcut appears again in an extended close-up. Here the two connotations of the woodcut become interwoven: the image signifies the reconciliation of the couple but it also reminds us of their transformative encounters with death and their passage to an alternative cultural space where they can 'fear no more'.

Writing in the sixties, Norman Mailer characterized the quest for an alternative to mainstream American culture in this way:

> It is on this bleak scene that a phenomenon has appeared: the American existentialist – the hipster, the man who knows that if our collective condition is to live with instant death by atomic war, relatively quick death by the State as *l'univers concentrationnaire*, or with a slow death by conformity with every creative and rebellious instinct stifled [. . .], if the fate of twentieth-century man is to live with death from adolescence to premature senescence, why then the only life-giving answer is to accept the terms of death, to live with death as immediate danger, to divorce oneself from society, to exist without roots, to set out on that uncharted journey with the rebellious imperatives of the self.[21]

The ending of *Cymbeline* – Imogen and Posthumus's refusal of the 'comic' resolution, their exit to parts unknown, the camera's return to the woodcut, an image of an embrace with death – suggests Almereyda's desire for a return to a heroic conception of youthful rebellion of the sort Mailer articulates here, for a recovery of existential angst – and not merely gangsta posturing or caustic cynicism – as a basis for an American counterculture. The rising roar of cycle engines on the soundtrack as the woodcut image fades to black, then, reads two ways. The engine sounds remind us of the roar we hear as Imogen and Posthumus first kiss under the bleachers, a roar signaling the arrival of Cymbeline and his retinue, the corrupt rebel regime that blocks the lovers' happiness. That regime, the social dominant of the film's fictional world, remains firmly in place at the end, ostensibly all the stronger since Cymbeline has renewed his arrangement with the police and received his once-lost sons. The sense that the forces against which the protagonists are pitted are vast and powerful is consistent with the ending of *Hamlet*, in which the last shot (of a teleprompter) reminds us of the media-industrial complex, Hamlet's ultimate foe. But the roar of motorcycle engines at the end of *Cymbeline* also introduces a tentatively hopeful note, since it reminds us of an alternative possibility, the 'heroic' biker ideal

incarnated by Sicilius, the road taken by Imogen and Posthumus as they
ride away.

In very surprising, even unlikely, ways, Almereyda's *Cymbeline* uses
Shakespeare's late romance to reflect upon the ideological conditions of,
and potential for, indie culture in contemporary America. In Imogen's case,
he remakes her encounter with the 'green world' of aboriginal Britain into
a rejuvenating experience of working-class America; in Posthumus's case,
he remakes his visionary encounter with Jupiter into a Hamlet-like con-
fronting of his father and the lost cultural ideal he represents. The symbolic deaths and rebirths they undergo have as much to do with their
visions of American culture as they do with their understandings of love
for one another. Part of Almereyda's concern here too is the relationship
between Shakespeare and indie film and more generally how Shakespeare
might remain relevant to movies addressed to a youth market. Certainly,
the style of his *Cymbeline* – laconically understated, committed to the grit-
tiness of the street, saturated with hip references, often brooding in tone –
seems a very poor match with Shakespeare's play, filled as it is with fantastical events, coincidence and supernatural intervention, ancient history, and
extravagant emotion and rhetoric. Nonetheless, Almereyda makes the quite
unexpected case that the two have shared ideological ground, a concern
for what constitutes genuine liberty. In Almereyda's hands, Shakespeare
emerges, at least deep-structurally, as an indie artist, one to which he and
the indie film genre can claim to be distant heirs. The ending of his *Cymbeline*, with the leave-taking of its youthful protagonists, also seems intent to
signify definitively the end of a production trend, a growing up and moving
on of all those adolescent Shakespearean lovers to parts unknown, a book-
end – and riposte – to Luhrmann's elaborate, relentlessly hip *Romeo +
Juliet*. By saying goodbye to all that teen Shakespeare while himself producing a form of just such a film, Almereyda seeks to propel Shakespeare
on film into a new, as yet uncharted, phase – an act of adaptational independence whose ultimate fruits remain to be seen.

Notes

1 Arguably, *Scotland PA* (2001) also falls in the teen Shakespeare category because
  even though its protagonists are decidedly post-adolescent, they still act like
  immature teenagers.
2 As to that migration, one might point to the proliferation of Shakespeare-
  themed web series since 2014.
3 For discussions of this film, see D. M. Lanier, 'Shakescorp Noir', *Shakespeare
  Quarterly* 53:2 (2002), 157–80; M. T. Burnett, '"To Hear and See the Matter":

Communicating Technology in Michael Almereyda's *Hamlet*', *Cinema Journal* 42:3 (Spring 2003), 48–69; K. Rowe, '"Remember Me": Technologies of Memory in Michael Almereyda's *Hamlet*', in R. Burt and L. Boose (eds.), *Shakespeare, the Movie, II: Popularizing the Plays on Film, Television, Video, and DVD* (New York: Routledge, 2003), 37–55; P. Donaldson, 'Hamlet among the Pixelvisionaries: Video Art, Authenticity and Wisdom in Michael Almereyda's *Hamlet*', in D. Henderson (ed.), *A Concise Companion to Shakespeare on Screen* (Oxford: Blackwell, 2006), 216–37; Y. J. Ko, '"The Mousetrap" and Remembrance in Michael Almereyda's *Hamlet*', *Shakespeare Bulletin* 23:4 (2005), 19–32; and P. Cook, 'Michael Almereyda's *Hamlet*: Uncanny Imagination', *Cinematic Hamlet: The Films of Olivier, Zeffirelli, Branagh, and Almereyda* (Athens, OH: Ohio University Press, 2011), 161–216.

4 The critical reception after its premiere at the 2014 Venice Film Festival was especially harsh. For a sampling of reviews, see J. Kiang, 'Review: Shakespeare's "Cymbeline" Gets Teleported from the Past, but the Problems Remain the Same', *The Playlist*, 2 September 2014; E. Walkuski, 'Review: Cymbeline', *JoBlo .com*, 11 March 2015; T. Derakhshani, 'Somnolent, updated take on Bard's "Cymbeline"', *The Philadelphia Inquirer*, 13 March 2015, W11; M. Halperin, '"Cymbeline", Baz Luhrmann's "Romeo + Juliet", and Why Shakespeare is so Hard to Adapt for the Screen', *Flavorwire.com*, 13 March 2015; B. Sharkey, '"Cymbeline" in the Instagram age. Bring Shakespeare's drama of deception into today's social media world: a good idea gone awry', *Los Angeles Times*, 13 March 2015; R. Samuelson, 'Cymbeline Review: The Limits of Modernity', *Haystack Magazine Online*, 20 March 2015; and P. Sobczynski, 'Cymbeline', *RogerEbert.com*, 13 March 2015. M. Dargis's review for the *New York Times* ('Review: In "Cymbeline", a Drug Kingpin Cymbeline', 12 March 2015) was one of the few sympathetic assessments of the film.

5 For versions of this argument, see C. Jordan, '*Cymbeline*', *Shakespeare's Monarchies: Ruler and Subject in the Romances* (Ithaca: Cornell University Press, 1997), 69–106; W. Maley, 'Postcolonial Shakespeare: British Identity Formation and *Cymbeline*', in J. Richards and J. Knowles (eds.), *Shakespeare's Late Plays: New Readings* (Edinburgh: Edinburgh University Press, 1999), 145–57; B. Lockey, 'Roman Conquest and English Legal Identity in *Cymbeline*', *Journal for Early Modern Cultural Studies* 3:1 (2003), 113–46; and R. King, '*Great Britain*', Cymbeline: *Constructions of Britain* (Aldershot: Ashgate, 2005), 47–92.

6 S. Mears, 'Interview: Michael Almereyda', *FilmComment*, 13 March 2015.

7 Mears, 'Interview'. In his interview on the DVD extras, Ethan Hawke, a close collaborator with Almereyda on the film, also highlights this theme, noting that 'the men in the play are interested more in competing for the women than in the women themselves.'

8 This citation is taken from the commentary of the DVD edition of *Cymbeline*, dir. Michael Almereyda, Lionsgate, 2015, starring Ethan Hawke, Dakota Johnson and Ed Harris, color. See also Almereyda's comments in his interviews with Emily Rome for *Hitfix.com* ('Interview: "Cymbeline" director Michael Almereyda on reuniting with Shakespeare and Ethan Hawke',

13 March 2015, available at www.hitfix.com/news/interview-cymbeline-director-michael-almereyda-on-reuniting-with-shakespeare-and-ethan-hawke) and with Dave Odegard for *Word&Film* ('On Shakespeare & Street Life: Q&A with Michael Almereyda', *Word&Film*, 11 March 2015, available at www .wordandfilm.com/2015/03/on-shakespeare-street-life-qa-michael-almereyda).

9 Much of the recent analysis of American alternative culture has focused on contemporary hipster culture, which is dated from its emergence in 2007 in Williamsburg, Brooklyn, and spread throughout the States during the 2010s. In my discussion of *Cymbeline*, I have profited especially from these works: J. Kinzey, *The Sacred and the Profane: An Investigation of Hipsters* (Alresford, Hants, UK: Zero Books, 2010); M. Greif, K. Ross, and D. Tortorici (eds.), *What was the Hipster? A Sociological Investigation* (New York: n+1 Foundation, 2010); K. Henke, 'Postmodern Authenticity and the Hipster Identity', *Forbes & Fifth* (2013), 117–28; and B. Schiermer, 'Late-modern hipsters: New tendencies in popular culture', *Acta Sociologica* 57:2 (May 2014), 167–81.

10 For contemporary viewers, *Cymbeline*'s biker dynasty resembles the Sons of Anarchy bike club in the American television series *Sons of Anarchy* (2007–14), which several fans and scholars have seen as a free adaptation of *Hamlet*. Over the objections of Almereyda (who claims he never heard of *Sons of Anarchy* before writing the film), the distributor of *Cymbeline*, Lion's Gate, briefly renamed the film *Anarchy* in an attempt to create a wider market. The title was changed back to *Cymbeline* before its Anglo-American release, but not before some posters were created with the *Anarchy* title. The film was released under the title *Sons of Anarchy* in several European and Latin American markets; the poster for the English language market misleadingly characterizes the film as a 'mash-up of *Sons of Anarchy* with *Game of Thrones*'.

11 If part of the hipster aesthetic is to find value in obscure cultural products that have been discarded or denigrated by the mainstream as irredeemably kitschy, making an indie film from *Cymbeline*, one of Shakespeare's least critically regarded plays, would seem to fit the designation of hipster Shakespeare.

12 T. C. Frank, *The Conquest of Cool: Business Culture, Counterculture, and the Rise of Hip Consumerism* (Chicago: University of Chicago Press, 1997).

13 The song's title is also a sardonic reference to a long-lived slogan for Mars candy bars.

14 All citations of *Cymbeline* have been checked against the soundtrack of the film.

15 This sequence – with 'Pressure Drop' lapped on the soundtrack – is intercut with Cymbeline's brutal imprisonment of Imogen's faithful servant Pisanio in what seems to be a room in Cymbeline's home, a reminder yet again of the strange mix of brutality and bourgeois status his regime stands for.

16 On the DVD commentary track, Hawke tells an anecdote that underlines the selfie's power to generate scandal. The iPhone he used in Iachimo's bedroom scene with Imogen was his own. Hawke's wife found the pictures on his phone and demanded an explanation; the issue was finally resolved only when she saw the film at its premiere. It's notable that the image Iachimo/Hawke takes

of Imogen/Johnson's breast beneath the sheets is never shown to the viewer or to Posthumus.

17 The love token Imogen sends him in reply, a token hand-delivered by Iachimo, is a sheet of paper out of which stars have been cut. It wittily alludes to Juliet's ominous praise of Romeo, spoken as the storm clouds of tragedy gather over their relationship after Tybalt's death:

> Give me my Romeo, and when I shall die,
> Take him and cut him out in little stars,
> And he will make the face of heaven so fine
> That all the world will be in love with night,
> And pay no worship to the garish sun. (3.2.21–5)

18 Ethnicity may be relevant here. One line of critique of modern hipsterism is that it is inauthentic poaching of ethnic and working-class culture by privileged white youth, in effect a mode of strategically displaying rebellion against the cultural mainstream without giving up any real cultural power (and in the process destroying the organic connection between alternative cultural styles and marginal identities). Pisanio is played by John Leguiziamo, and his Latino ethnicity provides him with a measure of alt-cult authenticity that his white counterparts in the Briton royal family lack, just as Delroy Lindo's African-American Belarius is by virtue of his race situated more organically outside the hegemonic mainstream of the film's social matrix. That said, it must be added that this ethnic schematization is not entirely consistent – Lucius is African-American, and Belarius's 'sons' are white.

19 In earlier scenes, Posthumus's lack of knowledge was indicated by his arm splint. Interestingly in the final scene, it is Iachimo's arm that is in a sling; Posthumus, who now recognizes his error in believing Iachimo, no longer wears his splint.

20 We see this image even before Posthumus makes his woodcut, when early in the film Cloten in a Halloween costume passes two trick-or-treaters, one a young girl dressed as a bride (with a cap for a veil and cotton candy for a bouquet) and a boy in a headless skeleton costume. In one of the film's many head jokes, Cloten is wearing a skull mask, foreshadowing his eventual beheading.

21 N. Mailer, 'The White Negro', in G. O'Brien (ed.), *The Cool School: Writing from America's Hip Underground* (New York: Library Classics of the United States, 2013), 159.

WORKS CITED

Burnett, M. T., '"To Hear and See the Matter": Communicating Technology in Michael Almereyda's *Hamlet*', *Cinema Journal* 42:3 (Spring 2003), 48–69.

Cook, P. 'Michael Almereyda's *Hamlet*: Uncanny Imagination', *Cinematic Hamlet: The Films of Olivier, Zeffirelli, Branagh, and Almereyda* (Athens, OH: Ohio University Press, 2011), 161–216.

Donaldson, P., 'Hamlet among the Pixelvisionaries: Video Art, Authenticity and Wisdom in Michael Almereyda's *Hamlet*', in D. Henderson (ed.), *A Concise Companion to Shakespeare on Screen* (Oxford: Blackwell, 2006), 216–37.

Frank, T. C., *The Conquest of Cool: Business Culture, Counterculture, and the Rise of Hip Consumerism* (Chicago: University of Chicago Press, 1997).

Greif, M., K. Ross, and D. Tortorici (eds.), *What was the Hipster? A Sociological Investigation* (New York: n+1 Foundation, 2010).

Henke, K., 'Postmodern Authenticity and the Hipster Identity', *Forbes & Fifth* (2013), 117–28.

Jordan, C., *Shakespeare's Monarchies: Ruler and Subject in the Romances* (Ithaca: Cornell University Press, 1997).

King, R., Cymbeline: *Constructions of Britain* (Aldershot: Ashgate, 2005).

Kinzey, J., *The Sacred and the Profane: An Investigation of Hipsters* (Alresford, Hants, UK: Zero Books, 2010).

Ko, Y. J., '"The Mousetrap" and Remembrance in Michael Almereyda's *Hamlet*', *Shakespeare Bulletin* 23:4 (2005), 19–32.

Lanier, D. M., 'Shakescorp Noir', *Shakespeare Quarterly* 53:2 (2002), 157–80.

Lockey, B., 'Roman Conquest and English Legal Identity in *Cymbeline*', *Journal for Early Modern Cultural Studies* 3:1 (2003), 113–46.

Maley, W., 'Postcolonial Shakespeare: British Identity Formation and *Cymbeline*', in J. Richards and J. Knowles (eds.), *Shakespeare's Late Plays: New Readings* (Edinburgh: Edinburgh University Press, 1999), 145–57.

Rowe, K., '"Remember Me": Technologies of Memory in Michael Almereyda's *Hamlet*', in R. Burt and L. Boose (eds.), *Shakespeare, the Movie, II: Popularizing the Plays on Film, Television, Video, and DVD* (New York: Routledge, 2003), 37–55.

Schiermer, B., 'Late-modern hipsters: New tendencies in popular culture', *Acta Sociologica* 57:2 (May 2014), 167–81.

CHAPTER 15

Ghost Towns and Alien Planets
Variations on Prospero's Island

Kinga Földváry

Film versions of *The Tempest* cannot avoid at least some sketchy visualisation of the location in which this story of love, magic, revenge and reconciliation is set – and, when looking at cinematic islands of Prospero's, we can easily recognize them as clues to the understanding of the films as a whole. In this chapter, I argue that the various screen depictions of the island are intricately linked to the films' cinematic genres, which in turn are tell-tale signs of the sociocultural issues the films and their creators were trying to address. The films I use to illustrate my point can all be classified as derivatives or free adaptations of the drama, including a western, *Yellow Sky* (dir. William A. Wellmann, 1948); a science fiction film, *Forbidden Planet* (dir. Fred M. Wilcox, 1956); two films that do not lend themselves easily to genre categories but can be classified as *auteur* films, *Age of Consent* (dir. Michael Powell, 1969), and *Tempest* (dir. Paul Mazursky, 1982), and a television production, *The Tempest* (dir. Jack Bender, 1998). However distant some of these films' connections to the Shakespearean text are (apart from Mazursky's and Bender's *Tempest*s, they do not even mention Shakespeare in their credits), I believe the presence of a variety of motifs makes them worthy of examination as Shakespearean adaptations. Even if a few better-known adaptations, notably Peter Greenaway's *Prospero's Books* (1991) and more recently Julie Taymor's *The Tempest* (2010), make more conscious use of the Shakespearean text, we need to investigate in what way the 'illegitimate variations' approach the play (to paraphrase Douglas Brode, who complains that there is 'no legitimate film of *The Tempest*').[1] I believe that an examination based on the films' cinematic qualities, particularly their associations with film genres may prove more fruitful than ill-advised considerations of legitimacy or the use of fidelity-based taxonomies, which are random at most, and often useless when it comes to understanding a film's relationship to audiences, or their production teams' creative decisions.

At the same time, I am convinced that the better known or more recent adaptations could fit this investigation equally well – Derek Jarman's 1979 avant-garde version of *The Tempest*, representative of his own vision of an 'island of the mind',[2] in which the haunted, cavernous setting of Stoneleigh Abbey 'becomes virtually a character in its own right';[3] Peter Greenaway's dreamlike spaces of the creative subconscious in *Prospero's Books* (1991), and even Julie Taymor's fantastic, uncannily artificial microcosm (2010), which not only builds on twenty-first-century viewers' acquaintance with the fantasy genre, but also speaks volumes of contemporary fears of the demise of the natural universe. In each and every case, the particular version of the isolated location that the filmmakers chose to represent Prospero's island serves as the key to interpreting the films by associating them with either the cinematic genre or the *auteurial oeuvre* into which the Shakespearean text is adapted.

'An un-inhabited Island'

As Frank Kermode remarks in his Introduction to *The Tempest*, the play 'has the unusual distinction of bearing an indication of locality ("An un-inhabited Island"),' a rarity in the Shakespearean *oeuvre*.[4] In the First Folio this reference to the setting is typographically emphasized by being printed at the very end, after the last scene of the play, in surprisingly large Roman letters, considerably larger than stage directions in the text, and nearly the same size as titles in the volume, which gives this specification unusual visual emphasis.

It is another critical commonplace that the island as a concept boasts of a rich history of symbolism in mythological and religious traditions, allowing cinematic representations to emphasize slightly different elements from a diversity of symbolic associations. Whereas islands can be seen as places of shelter and safety, they are also symbols of isolation and solitude; moreover, they may represent a utopian ideal, an unreachable location where Atlantis, Paradise, the remnants of a Golden Age can be found. In Celtic mythology, islands also stand for a spiritual centre, a place of otherworldly peace and knowledge, associated with magic and enchantment.[5] In Shakespeare's play, the 'un-inhabited island' in the Mediterranean – if we rely on the geographical names mentioned in the play (Tunis, Milan and Naples) – may be interpreted in a variety of ways, depending on each and every character's individual disposition. It is just as much a place of forced isolation as one of shelter, nurture and magic for Prospero and Miranda; one of imprisonment for Caliban and Ariel; but Gonzalo envisions a utopian republic here; Ferdinand and Miranda find their future and happiness; and sinners meet divine retribution but also forgiveness for their past and present crimes.

Out of this variety of abstract interpretations, there are many types of evidence to suggest that early modern audiences could perceive the uninhabited island not only as a symbolic, unreachable, imaginary location, but also as a local or otherwise recognisable place. On the one hand, Todd Andrew Borlik argues that the play is at least partly based on legends of Lincolnshire fen spirits and a lost play on the life of St Guthlac, an Anglo-Saxon hermit, and therefore contemporary viewers may have noticed its local references.[6] Another type of contemporary relevance is observed by Alden T. Vaughan and Virginia Mason Vaughan, editors of the third Arden Shakespeare edition:

> The topicality of a south Mediterranean setting and characters of African origin would not have been lost on *The Tempest*'s early audiences. Information was abundant about western Europe's ongoing exploration of Africa and its brazen enslavement of African people.[7]

It is not surprising therefore that the uninhabited island as a motif and setting has continued to invite diverse interpretations, particularly by virtue of its extraordinary adaptability, as the Vaughans observe: 'Prospero's enchanted island could be almost anywhere – and, indeed, in modern productions and appropriations has been set in several continents and even in outer space'.[8] In what follows, this adaptability will be exemplified by five different visualisations of the uninhabited island, each case providing clues to identifying the cinematic genre or *auteurial* background of the films. While all localisations can be seen as appropriately specific for the film genre selected for the individual productions, I believe that the more successful attempts are the ones which at least retain the possibility of interpreting the islands as being 'nowhere' or 'anywhere' – somewhere in the West, in space, or any odd island, either in the Mediterranean, or in one of the oceans – rather than sacrificing this opportunity for a clearly defined place at a very specific moment in historical time.

The Endless Spaces of Classical Hollywood Cinema: Western and Science Fiction

Searching for diverse cinematic representations of Prospero's island, two examples of classical Hollywood cinema lend themselves to examination: a western from the late 1940s, and a science fiction film from the 1950s. Although at first sight there is not much to connect the two genres, Ruth Morse convincingly argues in her article on science fiction adaptations of *The Tempest* that 'in the films science fiction has never been altogether

remote from the genre of the western, with its own problems of first contact, law and the frontier, asymmetries of power, knowledge, and what used
to pass for civilization'.⁹ The two genres' visualisations of space, however,
are clearly different. The western is primarily defined by its setting: the
Wild West, a place always imbued with nostalgia on the screen, since it
survives only in cultural memory by the middle of the twentieth century.
The favoured locations of science fiction, on the other hand, are not remnants of the past but projections of an imagined – desired or feared – future:
distant planets and galaxies, far beyond the known universe of mankind.
Their attitudes to Prospero's island, however, are similar: both films examined here represent radically altered spaces, which recall the island only in
indirect, metaphorical ways, as isolated spaces where knowledge is power,
not to be renounced lightly.

Yellow Sky (1948)

The Wild West of the North American continent, the endless open space
of the frontier is a setting that embodies the lure of adventure, the menace of the unknown and, as Kathleen Stewart summarizes, its complex
'strangeness': 'it is too local, too out of the way, too much a separate place
with laws of its own'¹⁰ not to appear as a threat to the outsider. It is therefore
fitting that the first film to be examined when searching for a cinematic representation of a spatial metaphor is the 1948 western Yellow Sky, directed by
William A. Wellman, and starring Gregory Peck, Anne Baxter and Richard
Widmark. While a quest for an island proper may prove fruitless in this
film, the symbolic significance of the Shakespearean island remains – that
of the distant, isolated place, accessible only by accident or disaster, a cruel
joke of the gods. The island here becomes an abandoned mining town (see
Figure 15.1), surrounded by a salt plain through which only the desperate
and outcast, the group of outlaws, venture, who no longer have anything
to lose. (The salt plain, as a remnant of a dried-out, dead sea, needs hardly
to be spelled out here.)

Yellow Sky was made in the middle of the period described as the Golden
Age of the western, spanning roughly from Stagecoach (1939) to the end of
the 1950s, possibly even to the 1960s.¹¹ The setting is therefore meaningful
to its audiences in more ways than one: it is one that evokes nostalgia for an
age of heroic greatness in American history but the untamed countryside
of the West also identifies the genre as enjoying considerable popularity in
the present of its creation. In the film, the dilapidated, dead town, bearing
the uncanny name of Yellow Sky, bodes no good for the protagonists who

Figure 15.1.   Ghost town in the middle of the salt plain in Wellman's 1948 *Yellow Sky*.

are in various kinds of trouble anyway. After a successful bank robbery, a group of gangsters in need of a hideout and a place to rest escape their pursuers by crossing the salt plains, a journey that nearly kills them, making their arrival at Yellow Sky not simply unexpected but indeed miraculous. Similarly to the uninhabited island of *The Tempest*, which turns out to be rather crowded by the time the plot begins – with at least four creatures of various degrees of (non)humanity dwelling permanently on it – Yellow Sky is equally deceptive as a ghost town, since there are two residents living on the outskirts of the locality, both of whom provide diverse attractions to the newcomers. The young tomboy of a girl, Constance Mae, or 'Mike' for short (a Miranda character with a similar naïve innocence concerning her own feminine attractions) wreaks havoc with her widely swinging hips among the exhausted bank robbers who are hungry and thirsty for food and female company alike. Her grandfather, however, possesses knowledge that is even more attractive: as the deceptive robber, Dude, sniffs out, the old man has put aside a considerable amount of gold from the seemingly deserted mines.

However comic some of the *Tempest*-allusions may be, from the pot-bellied drunkard through the lovelorn young kid, and the blossoming romance between not-such-a-bad-guy-after-all James 'Stretch' Dawson (played by Gregory Peck) and Mike (played by Anne Baxter), the desolation of the place still tells us another story that seems to haunt post-war American society. The first frames of the film specify the date as 1867 – only two years after the end of the Civil War – and the place as 'The West,' the latter being not much more specific than the Shakespearean location of the 'uninhabited island,' and equally and noticeably allegorical. The film itself was made in 1948, just after another upheaval that shook the world in its foundations; thus it is easy to look for connections between the socio-historical context of the film's creation and the time and place specified in the narrative itself. Similar to the way the gunmen involved in the American Civil War needed to be disbanded and persuaded to go back to a civilian lifestyle, late 1940s America was haunted by anxieties of poverty and unemployment, but also a need to return to a peaceful and civilized existence within a human community. It is no accident that in the film's narrative we learn about each and every character in turn that they come from good families and that it was only fate that had driven them out of society where they long to return now that the war is over.

The ghost town, still bearing the sign of 'Yellow Sky – Fastest Growing Town in the Territory' is no more than a couple of dilapidated ruins, where the only source of life – water – can be found outside the settlement, suggesting that this is no earthly paradise, no utopian island, but rather a place at the end of the universe, at the far edge of human civilisation. The inclination to stay on and brood over the greatness of the past, however, turns out to be self-destructive, and the conclusion makes it clear that both domestic happiness and socially acceptable citizenship are available for the ones who turn to the future. Mike, whom we have long suspected of cherishing feminine traits under her tomboyish appearance (the camera has repeatedly observed her curvaceous body in moonlit scenes), is offered a way to find her real feminine self, symbolically represented by the hat that Stretch buys her when he returns the money to the bank they robbed in the opening scene. While we may feel slightly anxious for Mike, doubting her ability to adapt to the kind of small town social life that her new hat appears to be representative of (just like Miranda may find it hard to adapt to Milanese society), the film ends on a positively cheerful note – the company of Mike, her Grandpa, Stretch and his two surviving companions leave the place for good and begin a new life. The message to the 1948 audience could not be clearer: the war is over and what it represented should be a thing of the past too, just like the dead town beyond the salt plains in the Wild West – there is law and order, peace and prosperity ahead, and an opportunity to start with a clean slate, for anyone willing to work for it. The changing landscape of the final scenes reinforces this message; but just as Prospero's epilogue is necessarily tainted by a bitter resignation from his position of control and his farewell to the island, the ending of *Yellow Sky* also suggests that Grandpa and the old generation may find it hard to make the transition to a post-war brave new world.

Forbidden Planet (1956)

Made nearly a decade after *Yellow Sky*, *Forbidden Planet* may have the dubious distinction of being the most commonly discussed one among the five films examined here, both in critical and popular literature. The reasons for this are partly obvious – it was the first of its kind in several ways: 'MGM's first big foray into A-level science-fiction, [featuring] state-of-the-art special effects,'[12] and the genre to which it belongs has enjoyed almost continuous popularity ever since its first appearance.

The suitability of *The Tempest* for being adapted to the genre of science fiction has been noted many times. As the editors of the third Arden edition of *The Tempest* observe: '[t]he play's imprecise location attracts writers and artists to *The Tempest* for what science-fiction writers call a "second world" structure, in which faraway islands, imaginary and often "enchanted", are ideal'.[13] Thus the question that Ruth Morse asks in her discussion of science fiction adaptations of *The Tempest* – what it is precisely that draws creative adaptors to this play rather than any other – may be answered by direct reference to the play's setting: if *The Tempest* is characterized by such an open and unspecific, therefore adaptable, space, then it is inherently connected to the central theme (space travel) of 1950s science fiction, which makes the two such a perfect match. It is no accident that the golden age of science fiction coincides with the Cold War and the space race,[14] and this constant threat resulted in literature and cinema, *Forbidden Planet* among the first of its kind, presenting 'science and technology as a source of danger rather than progress. Its theme was [. . .] appropriate to the Cold War, a period ambiguously split between the celebration of one's own (American) technology and the intense mistrust of the Other's (Soviet) science'.[15] Thus in the age when both the advances of technology and the Communist threat were ever present in the media and in the popular imagination, the island of *The Tempest* is unsurprisingly reborn in the favoured location of science fiction, that is, the distant planet.

What is, however, also interesting in this choice is that the revision of the Shakespearean theme includes a transformation of the characters' attitudes to the island, which may be even more significant than the re-imagining of the external qualities of the place. While the planet Altair IV appears to be a safe haven for Dr Morbius (the Prospero figure), where he can experiment safely and where he stumbles upon resources he would be unable to access on Earth, it is also significant that his connection to the island has turned into an unnatural attachment, and his access to the knowledge of earlier civilizations brings forth a monster from his own id with the destructive power of hundreds of Calibans combined. Therefore, he is not the one planning his escape and the retribution-cum-reconciliation event by misdirecting the visitors' vehicle to accidentally land on his doorstep. The visitors are there of their own accord, neither lost nor disconnected from their homes, and eventually they are not even overpowered by Prospero-Morbius, the former ally whose advances in science and technology have turned him into a threat and an enemy.

This attitude, however, appears to fit the controversial post-war definition of the threat of the monstrous Other: the Soviet Union was not that long ago the ally of the United States in the war against Nazism, but it suddenly became redefined as an opponent, a rival, a menacing monster whose claws may reach and sabotage American development both inside and out of the country. The alien planet which could have been a common destination without the Space Race, has thus become contested territory, with all potentially dangerous weaponry to be destroyed, rather than allowed to fall into enemy hands – particularly if that enemy was a former ally, a snake one has warmed in one's bosom. That is why the 1956 science fiction Prospero is not allowed to return to his former world, but has to be destroyed with his island-planet, this sacrifice being the only way to protect the new generation from total destruction.

Every Man Has an Island – The *Auteur* Visions of Michael Powell and Paul Mazursky

Moving on from classical Hollywood genre cinema towards *auteur* films of the 1960s and 1980s, we can witness a surprising transformation in the cinematic manifestations of the uninhabited island. The two *auteur* films' settings are deceptively close to the Shakespearean instructions: both of them are indeed set on (nearly uninhabited) islands, one even in the Mediterranean. Nonetheless, these locations have just as much a particular, individual meaning in their *auteurs*' own self-representation as the ghost town and the alien planet of the earlier genre films. *Age of Consent*, directed by Michael Powell, and *Tempest* by Paul Mazursky share several significant features concerning their settings: among other things, we are also presented with the worlds the protagonists choose to leave behind. In both cases, this world is set in the city of New York and both protagonists are artists who find their talents on the wane amongst high society, so antagonistic to the magic of inspiration and creation; therefore, they decide to leave the bustle of the city behind and go to an island where they can live the life of their dreams. The dissatisfaction and *ennui* that these artists manifest is easily associated with social issues that defined late 1960s Britain and early 1980s America, respectively. We are also introduced to other steps along their journeys, the places of transition which prove to be inadequate as places of refuge and reinvigoration, suggesting that transformation – whether social or personal – requires one to travel all the way.

Age of Consent (1969)

On the British front, Dominic Sandbrook refers to the sociocultural context of the 1960s as fraught with contradictions below the surface:

> beneath the glamorous veneer of swinging London, Britain under Harold Macmillan, Sir Alec Douglas-Home and Harold Wilson remained a remarkably conservative, even anxious society. [. . .] Meanwhile, despite the much-discussed stereotype of the 'permissive society', popular attitudes to moral and sexual issues remained strikingly slow to change.[16]

This slow change in attitudes may explain why Michael Powell felt he was forced to leave his native Britain after his 1960 film *Peeping Tom* (today regarded as one of his most significant, though unsettling, directions) received disastrous reviews, nearly ending his career. He continued filming in Australia, making *Age of Consent* in 1969, another film that was unfavourably received in Britain for 'too much nudity,' as Powell said in an interview in 1986[17] – a clear indication of the slow change in sexual attitudes that felt oppressive for the artist.

Age of Consent, a little known late film by Powell (one of the few he made without scriptwriter Emeric Pressburger), is hard to categorize in any of the commonly used Hollywood genres but it clearly fits the bill of a Powell film. Andrew Moor goes as far as saying that the painter Bradley Morahan, protagonist of *Age of Consent* (played by James Mason) is an 'expression of Powell's persona,'[18] similarly to other 'charismatic, powerful men' in Powell's films who are in fact alter egos on-screen, being 'another sign of Powell and Pressburger as "auteurs"'.[19]

The film is in fact an adaptation of a novel by Australian artist Norman Lindsay and thus only indirectly based on *The Tempest*, which may explain why the Shakespearean island is given a very specific and recognisable manifestation here: it becomes Dunk Island in Australia's Great Barrier Reef and the natural beauty of the landscape, complete with corals, fish, jungle and sandy beaches, is made great use of in the film. This centrality of the landscape may be what Powell's earlier films manifested, although characteristically it was the British countryside that played such a significant role in his films, his being 'intrinsically British,' as Robert Shail suggests, and 'his love of landscape, literature and tradition' is partly what has made him 'emblematic for a national cinema'.[20] But even if it is not his native British countryside but the Australian landscape, the landscape is in a sense the film's real protagonist or at least an equal partner to the artistic Prospero-figure and young Cora, played by an almost ethereally beautiful Helen Mirren, whose character combines traits of Miranda with some of Ariel's. The beginning of the narrative spells it out in a mediated text (the protagonist speaking on television in the background) that our hero is 'local boy made good,' and his journey is not only an escape but also a homecoming to a utopian place imbued with nostalgia. What binds thus the film and its nostalgic vision of the island setting to the Powell *oeuvre* is the sense of identity being defined by place and by belonging – in short, the recognition that there is no Prospero without his island.

The island where Powell sets his enchanting narrative of art, coming of age and romance is thus perfectly illustrative of a combination of Shakespearean and Powellian vision. In fact, I am convinced that *Age of Consent* may be just another example of the relationship between an adaptation and its adapted source that Judith Buchanan describes as strong but not 'necessarily [. . .] *strategic* on the part of its producers. Stories as fundamental and familiar as the one we know most commonly as *The Tempest* find representation constantly in various transmuted forms'.[21] This island, a place of imprisonment for the Miranda-Ariel character (by a Sycorax-like witch of a drunken grandmother) is so much alive with dreamlike natural beauties that 'give delight and hurt not' (3.2.128) that the viewer immediately sympathizes with the desire of a liberal-minded artist to escape here and create a world of his own, even if we fear with him that 'the baseless fabric of this vision' (4.1.151) shall eventually dissolve into thin air. Still, this somewhat escapist, late 1960s dream of *The Tempest* allows its Prospero to remain on the island and even to break out of the confines of his dramatic role and enter into a relationship with the Miranda-Ariel figure, who promises him artistic inspiration and earthly delights alike (see Figure 15.2).

Figure 15.2.   The artist and his Miranda-Ariel in Powell's 1969 *Age of Consent.*

Tempest (1982)

While all the previously mentioned film adaptations or variations on the *Tempest*-theme have chosen to locate their uninhabited islands in markedly non-Shakespearean, more or less unknown, or little visited parts of the universe, Paul Mazursky's 1982 *Tempest* offers an idyllic place of escape located on an island in the Mediterranean, following the scarce Shakespearean references as precisely as possible. Still, we would be very much mistaken to consider this a less imaginative choice or one that is less integral to the *auteur*–filmmaker's concept as a whole.

The first clear sign of this is the fact that the Mediterranean island is contrasted not with Milan and Naples, but again with New York City, with its protagonist not a political ruler but a jaded architect, similarly to Powell's vision – both of these films tell us a surprisingly artistic story of magic and power in the late twentieth century. It is also significant that while the two earlier genre films suggest that the Prospero characters had the means to vacate their places of exile but chose to remain there for reasons of their

Figure 15.3.   Mediterranean idyll, complete with artist and goat, in Mazursky's 1982
Tempest.

own, for the protagonists in the two *auteur* films exile is fully voluntary, in fact, a desired escape from societies whose oppressively commercial appreciation has a detrimental effect on their creative powers. However, while Powell's Prospero figure may have been fleeing from a morally conservative society, Mazursky's 1982 context is the Reagan Revolution, a reinforcement of traditional values that appeared to be endangered by the liberalism of the 1970s. According to Paul Haspel, this 'transitional period of history'[22] may be reflected in the way Mazursky's film shows 'an interest in seeing what happens when American culture and some other major culture of the world meet,'[23] the perfect place for the encounter being an isolated Greek island (see Figure 15.3), where American commercialism has already made its impact felt. Although the film is not overly political, it is hard to ignore its depiction of the American ruling class as rotten to the core and to interpret its conclusion as a return to the long-term foundations of society: work, love and the family. At the same time, this belief in a possibility of return may equally be characteristic of 'Mazursky's fundamentally comic and optimistic world view'.[24]

In a similar manner, Douglas Bruster in his overview of Mazursky's *oeuvre* as director convincingly argues for the shared thematic interests that make *Tempest* a film of Mazursky's own: 'not only an aesthetically satisfying work, but one which meaningfully charts the status of the aesthetic in the globalized culture of the late twentieth century'.[25] This combination of personal artistic concerns and topical anxieties of his time and life proves once again that *Tempest*, similarly to the previously discussed variations on the Shakespearean theme, is to be approached from its own creative context. To do it justice, an appreciation of what it successfully achieved – contemplating 'personal crisis, [...] illustrating cultural change; paying reverence to the idea of the theatre'[26] – is more relevant than searching for what it never set out to do: to create a textually faithful rendition of Shakespeare's drama for its own sake.

A Tempestuous Civil War in the Deep South

Even though the four films discussed so far exemplify the influence of the American movie industry and several cinematic genres or *auteurs* directly related to the United States of America, *The Tempest* that all reviewers label as 'American' is Jack Bender's television production from 1998, with Peter Fonda in the lead role. The Southern setting of the film – beginning in Mississippi, 1851, and ending right after the Battle of Vicksburg on 4 July 1853 – in itself is immediately associated with American history. Between the historical frame, however, the central parts of the plot are set in the Mississippi bayous, well known for the role they played in the American Civil War, thus the location standing in for the island scenes also invokes the spirit of the period. It is in the bayous where the protagonist, former plantation owner Gideon Prosper, escapes from his cruel and treacherous brother, who stops short of nothing to get rid of his liberal brother who prefers slaves and magic to proper Southern society. It is no wonder that when several reviewers invoke *Gone With the Wind* (dir. Victor Fleming, 1939) when reflecting on this choice of setting, more than a hint at criticism is included in these references, suggesting that the combination of a historical period with the romance characters produced a rather conservative, even outdated, visual work of art.

More than that, it is again the film's generic associations that may point out the reason for its failure to captivate its audiences. Recreating the most stereotypically American time period, that of the Civil War, and the most fitting location for the depiction of the War Between the States, the Mississippi bayous, the film's narrative cannot resist the temptation of engaging in broader battles than those for forgiveness and reconciliation within families. However, when the cinematic world suggests that it is not only a personal farewell to magic that is at stake, but far-reaching national concerns of life, liberty and the pursuit of happiness, then the genre label invoked is that of historical melodrama, which is markedly at odds with the romance narrative the film also wishes to retain from its Shakespearean source. Besides, the visual spectacle of magic tricks also engages in a style more at home in the fantasy genre than in melodrama, where at least a semblance of verisimilitude is typically maintained to preserve the illusion of a historically plausible context. This clash between the implications of setting, narration, visual style and cinematography may explain why the film has not been received too favourably by viewers or critics.

The decision to foreground slavery as a central issue may also be seen as a fitting choice for the location and time period but it problematizes the central character's position. From dialogues and voice-over narration, we learn that Gideon Prosper 'prefers the company of slaves' and considers it his 'great fortune to learn from a slave named Azaleigh,' replacing book-based learning with voodoo instructions. While Azaleigh clearly sides with Gideon Prosper both in his personal and the national battles, the fact that this Prospero-character displays no more extraordinary abilities than a keenness to dabble in dark magic makes us question his control over his family, plantation, slaves and associates alike. At the same time, as Lisa Hopkins summarizes one of the ways in which the melodramatic associations seem to be restrictive for the narrative as a whole, 'The workings of the mind are downplayed in Bender's film because what really matters here are the workings of God.'[27] As a result, the Christian allusions indeed problematize the spiritual backdrop that the narrative is placed against. This confusion of genres is equally apparent in the characters' frequent departures from and return to the bayous that have replaced Prospero's island here. Most of the narrative follows the requirements of historical melodrama, in which the bayous can be seen as a geographically realistic location. The significance of this setting is that it functions as a place of transition where local knowledge can be turned to the advantage of the morally superior Northern Army in 'a righteous war, a holy war!', as Captain Frederick Allen, the Ferdinand figure of the play claims when he wishes to open the eyes of Miranda to the value system of the real world. Nonetheless, the creators of the film do not seem to have been satisfied with historical realism or willing to give up Prospero's magic either. As a result, this bayou-based magic turns out to be no more than a lot of mumbo jumbo, clearly counterproductive in a film which wishes to convince its viewers that its Southern protagonist is able to see his own slaves as his equals, rather than typecasting them as the embodiments of the worst stereotypes created by slave-owner anxieties.

These clichés are topped by an equally banal cinematic narrative turn in the finale; as Ton Hoenselaars points out, 'Prosper is overcome by the traditional horror that still feeds all popular screen versions of the North-South genre, namely that a brother should be about to kill his brother'.[28] The resulting offer of forgiveness is melodramatic and futile, and again somewhat at odds with the mock-Shakespearean finale in which Gideon Prosper is given (a few of) the words of Prospero's epilogue. Having witnessed his failure to control either his daughter's emotions or his brother's murderous attempts, and seeing how his slaves, both Ariel and especially his mother, the mambo priestess Azaleigh, were the ones in actual control, there is neither catharsis nor melodramatic tear jerking when we see Prosper empty his satchel of magic dust – and thus the film disappoints all expectations raised by the variety of genres it mixed into its voodoo magic. The Mississippi bayous remain no more than a swamp, a tangle of waterways in which not only the Confederate army but also the film's narrative get hopelessly lost.

As the previous discussion pointed out, the ancient and richly symbolic setting of the uninhabited island in Shakespeare's *The Tempest* allows a variety of interpretations that the cinematic or televisual productions inevitably rely on when creating their specific visual versions of the location. At the same time, as Russell Jackson also remarked, the actualisation of a general, even abstract, concept always comes at a price: 'It's interesting how there is at once more and less at stake in these very specific islands, unlike the less identifiable locale of the play.'[29] This balance of loss and gain, however, I believe, is symptomatic of the way the adaptation process as a whole works; at the same time, it exemplifies the uses of genres as the angle from which these cinematic and televisual reimaginings should best be approached. Placing genre films in their generic contexts, *auteur* films in their director's own *oeuvre* and disregarding the impossible – to quantify or even qualify the measure of textual fidelity binding the new creation to its source work – appears to be instrumental in making meaning of film adaptations. As the variations on Prospero's islands have shown, it is the cinematic context that best explains attitudes to a directly or indirectly acknowledged source, a viewpoint that may open up new vistas of interpretation for Shakespearean scholarship as well.

Notes

1 D. Brode, *Shakespeare in the Movies: From the Silent Era to* Shakespeare in Love (Oxford: Oxford University Press, 2000), 223.

2 S. Martin, 'Classic Shakespeare for All: *Forbidden Planet* and *Prospero's Books*: Two Screen Adaptations of *The Tempest*', in D. Cartmell, I. Q. Hunter,

H. Kaye and I. Whelehan (eds.), *Classics in Film and Fiction* (London & Sterling, VA: Pluto Press, 2000), 37.

3 L. Hopkins, *Screen Adaptations: Shakespeare's* The Tempest: *The Relationship between Text and Film* (London: Methuen, 2008), 88.

4 F. Kermode, 'Introduction', in F. Kermode (ed.), *The Tempest*. The Arden Shakespeare second series (London: Methuen, 1994 [1954]), xii.

5 See J. E. Cirlot, *Dictionary of Symbols*, trans. J. Sage (London: Routledge, 2001); M. Ferber, *A Dictionary of Literary Symbols* (Cambridge: Cambridge University Press, 2007).

6 T. A. Borlik, 'Caliban and the Fen Demons of Lincolnshire: the Englishness of Shakespeare's *Tempest*.' *Shakespeare* 9:1 (2012), 21.

7 A. T. Vaughan and V. M. Vaughan. 'Introduction', in A. T. Vaughan and V. M. Vaughan (eds.), *The Tempest*, The Arden Shakespeare, third series (London: Thomas Nelson, 1999), 49.

8 *Ibid.*, 74.

9 R. Morse, 'Monsters, Magicians, Movies: *The Tempest* and the Final Frontier', *Shakespeare Survey* 53 (2000), 168.

10 K. Stewart, 'Real American Dreams (Can Be Nightmares)', in J. Dean (ed.), *Cultural Studies and Political Theory* (Ithaca: Cornell University Press, 2000), 249.

11 H. Fagen, *The Encyclopedia of Westerns* (New York: Facts on File, 2003), xviii.

12 D. Schneider, '*Forbidden Planet* Review – Anne Francis, Leslie Nielsen, Fred M. Wilcox', *Alt Film Guide*, n.d., www.altfg.com/blog/classics/forbidden-planet-anne-francis-leslie-nielsen.

13 A. T. Vaughan and V. M. Vaughan, 'Introduction', 74.

14 See, for instance, M. Hardin, 'Mapping Post-War Anxieties onto Space: *Invasion of the Body Snatchers* and *Invaders from Mars*', *Enculturation* 1:1 (1997); and S. Martin, 'Classic Shakespeare for All'.

15 Martin, 'Classic Shakespeare for All', 40.

16 D. Sandbrook, 'Introduction', *Sixties Britain: A Social and Cultural Revolution?* The National Archives. n.d. www.nationalarchives.gov.uk/education/resources/sixties-britain/#introduction.

17 T. Johnston, 'Exclusive: An Unpublished Interview with Michael Powell', *TimeOut London*. n.d. www.timeout.com/london/film/exclusive-an-unpublished-interview-with-michael-powell-1. In the same interview, Powell refers to his plans to 'do a version of *The Tempest*' with a cast similar to that of *Age of Consent*, implying that he did not consider his 1969 film a Shakespearean adaptation, and it is indeed 'only tangentially related to *The Tempest*,' although it 'does rework various motifs from Shakespeare's play'. See D. M. Lanier, 'Film Spin-offs and Citations', in R. Burt (ed.), *Shakespeares after Shakespeare: An Encyclopedia of the Bard in Mass Media and Popular Culture* (Westport, CT & London: Greenwood Press, 2007), vol. 1, 318. For more on the planned film, see J. Buchanan, *Shakespeare on Film* (Harlow: Pearson Longman, 2005), 157–9.

18 A. Moor, *Powell and Pressburger: A Cinema of Magic Spaces* (London: I. B. Tauris, 2005), 14.

19 Moor, *Powell and Pressburger*, 14.
20 R. Shail, *British Film Directors: A Critical Guide* (Edinburgh: Edinburgh University Press, 2007), 171.
21 J. Buchanan, '*Forbidden Planet* and the Retrospective Attribution of Intentions', in D. Cartmell, I. Q. Hunter, and I. Whelehan (eds.), *Retrovisions: Reinventing the Past in Film and Fiction* (London & Sterling, VA: Pluto Press, 2001), 158. Italics original.
22 P. Haspel, 'Ariel and Prospero's Modern English Adventure: Language, Social Criticism, and Adaptation in Paul Mazursky's *Tempest*', *Literature/Film Quarterly* 34:2 (2006), 136.
23 P. Haspel, 'Ariel and Prospero's Modern English Adventure', 138.
24 *Ibid.*, 130.
25 D. Bruster, 'The Postmodern Theatre of Paul Mazursky's *Tempest*', in M. T. Burnett and R. Wray (eds.), *Shakespeare, Film, Fin de Siècle* (Basingstoke: Macmillan, 2000), 26.
26 *Ibid.*
27 L. Hopkins, *Screen Adaptations*, 58.
28 T. Hoenselaars, 'Gone with *The Tempest*', *Shakespeare Society of the Low Countries* 8:1 (2001), 46–8, http://shakespeare.let.uu.nl/bayou.htm.
29 R. Jackson, 'Responses' (unpublished comments on the first version of this essay circulated in the context of the seminar 'Shakespeare on Screen: The Romances' at the Shakespeare 450 congress, Paris, April 2014), n.p.

WORKS CITED

Borlik, T. A., 'Caliban and the Fen Demons of Lincolnshire: the Englishness of Shakespeare's *Tempest*', *Shakespeare* 9:1 (2012), 21–51.
Brode, D., *Shakespeare in the Movies: From the Silent Era to* Shakespeare in Love (Oxford: Oxford University Press, 2000).
Bruster, D., 'The Postmodern Theatre of Paul Mazursky's *Tempest*', in M. T. Burnett and R. Wray (eds.), *Shakespeare, Film, Fin de Siècle* (Basingstoke: Macmillan, 2000), 26–39.
Buchanan, J., 'Forbidden Planet and the Retrospective Attribution of Intentions', in D. Cartmell, I. Q. Hunter and I. Whelehan (eds.), *Retrovisions: Reinventing the Past in Film and Fiction* (London & Sterling, VA: Pluto Press, 2001), 148–62.
Shakespeare on Film (Harlow: Pearson Longman, 2005).
Cirlot, J. E., *Dictionary of Symbols*, trans. Jack Sage (London: Routledge, 2001).
Fagen, H., *The Encyclopedia of Westerns* (New York: Facts on File, 2003).
Ferber, M., *A Dictionary of Literary Symbols* (Cambridge: Cambridge University Press, 2007).
Hardin, M., 'Mapping Post-War Anxieties onto Space: *Invasion of the Body Snatchers* and *Invaders from Mars*', *Enculturation* 1:1 (1997).
Hoenselaars, T., 'Gone with *The Tempest*', *Shakespeare Society of the Low Countries* 8:1 (2001), 46–8, http://shakespeare.let.uu.nl/bayou.htm.

Haspel, P., 'Ariel and Prospero's Modern English Adventure: Language, Social Criticism, and Adaptation in Paul Mazursky's *Tempest*', *Literature/Film Quarterly* 34:2 (2006), 130–40.

Hopkins, L., *Screen Adaptations: Shakespeare's* The Tempest: *The Relationship between Text and Film* (London: Methuen, 2008).

Johnston, T., 'Exclusive: An Unpublished Interview with Michael Powell', *Time-Out London*. n.d. www.timeout.com/london/film/exclusive-an-unpublished-interview-with-michael-powell-1.

Kermode, F., 'Introduction', in F. Kermode (ed.), *The Tempest*, The Arden Shakespeare second series (London: Methuen, 1994 [1954]), xi–xcii.

Lanier, D. M., 'Film Spin-offs and Citations', in R. Burt (ed.), *Shakespeares after Shakespeare: An Encyclopedia of the Bard in Mass Media and Popular Culture*. (Westport, CT & London: Greenwood Press, 2007), vol. 1, 132–365.

Martin, S., 'Classic Shakespeare for All: *Forbidden Planet* and *Prospero's Books*, Two Screen Adaptations of *The Tempest*', in D. Cartmell, I. Q. Hunter, H. Kaye and I. Whelehan (eds.), *Classics in Film and Fiction* (London & Sterling, VA: Pluto Press, 2000), 34–53.

Moor, A., *Powell and Pressburger: A Cinema of Magic Spaces* (London: I. B. Tauris, 2005).

Morse, R., 'Monsters, Magicians, Movies: *The Tempest* and the Final Frontier'. *Shakespeare Survey* 53 (2000), 164–74.

Sandbrook, D., 'Introduction', Sixties Britain. A Social and Cultural Revolution? *The National Archives*. n.d. www.nationalarchives.gov.uk/education/resources/sixties-britain/#introduction.

Schneider, D., 'Forbidden Planet Review – Anne Francis, Leslie Nielsen, Fred M. Wilcox', *Alt Film Guide*, n.d. www.altfg.com/blog/classics/forbidden-planet-anne-francis-leslie-nielsen/.

Shail, R., *British Film Directors: A Critical Guide* (Edinburgh: Edinburgh University Press, 2007).

Stewart, K., 'Real American Dreams (Can Be Nightmares)', in J. Dean (ed.), *Cultural Studies and Political Theory* (Ithaca: Cornell University Press, 2000), 243–57.

Vaughan, A. T. and V. M. Vaughan, 'Introduction', in A. T. Vaughan and V. M. Vaughan (eds.), *The Tempest*. The Arden Shakespeare third series (London: Thomas Nelson, 1999), 1–138.

CHAPTER 16

Grafting The Tempest *onto Allégret's* Le Bal du Comte d'Orgel

Gaëlle Ginestet

This chapter analyses the presence of *The Tempest* in Marc Allégret's adaptation of Raymond Radiguet's *Le Bal du Comte d'Orgel* that was released in 1970.[1] *Le Bal* is also the director's last work in a career spanning forty-three years, which includes several films set against a backdrop of performing arts, such as *Futures vedettes* (1955), *Félicie Nanteuil* (1944), or the classic *Entrée des artistes* (1938) where would-be actors play a scene from *The Taming of the Shrew*. Raymond Radiguet (1903–1923) was a comet in French literature. The son of a Parisian caricaturist, the young prodigy turned to journalism and writing and was befriended by artists like Picasso, Max Jacob and especially Jean Cocteau, who became his Pygmalion. Radiguet died of a typhoid fever at the age of 20 prior to the publication of *Le Bal du Comte d'Orgel* (*Count d'Orgel's Ball*,[2] 1924), his second and last novel, following *Le Diable au corps* (*The Devil in the Flesh*, 1923). *Le Bal* is the story of a love triangle taking place after the First World War, between an aristocrat, Count Anne d'Orgel, his young wife, Mahaut, and François de Séryeuse, the new friend Orgel likes so much. François soon falls in love with Mahaut, but intends to admire her in silence. The count plans to give a lavish fancy dress ball which has no specific theme. Before the ball is given, Mahaut realizes that she is in love with François. She tells her secret to Madame de Séryeuse, François's mother, hoping she will find a way to keep her son away from her. On the contrary, Madame de Séryeuse maladroitly reveals to Mahaut and François that they love each other. During an 'evening party dedicated to the final preparations for the ball',[3] Mahaut faints, out of guilt and emotion intermingled. She then tells her husband of her feelings for François. The count's response is only that a scandal must be avoided.

Radiguet's *Le Bal du Comte d'Orgel* does not comprise any mention of Shakespeare. Yet, in Marc Allégret's adaptation, the ball becomes thematic and its guiding line is 'Shakespeare's characters'. The three main protagonists rehearse a scene from *The Tempest* which is supposed to be the high

269

point of the evening. Therefore, the film is the adaptation of a literary work – a novel – into which a passage from another literary work – a play – is inserted. Why was this second literary text grafted onto the first one in its cinematic adaptation? The trigger for the graft was probably the characterisation of Count Anne d'Orgel, in the novel, as a magician. In the film, Orgel is both a theatre director and a magician (an avatar of Prospero), who will, more or less willingly, throw his wife Mahé[4] (a Miranda figure) into the arms of their friend François (a Ferdinand figure). Allégret intended *The Tempest* as a *mise en abyme* of the novel's plot. The *Tempest* scenes happen at crucial moments and prompt revelations for the characters as much as for the viewers, for they help open 'the fringèd curtains of th[eir] eye[s]' (1.2.407). The characterisation of the count as an avatar of Prospero especially reveals his latent homosexuality.

Why Shakespeare, and why *The Tempest*? Firstly, Marc Allégret (1900– 1973), in his teenage years, famously became André Gide's *protégé* and lover. He and Gide shared many intellectual interests and often discussed art and literature. Gide considered that 'no author [was] more deserving of translation than Shakespeare'.[5] Indeed, he translated *Antony and Cleopatra* and *Hamlet* into French and contemplated doing the same with *As You Like It*.[6] As a consequence of Gide's guidance, Allégret became an extremely well-read man who probably knew Shakespeare's greatest plays inside out. He signed the adaptation of *Le Bal du Comte d'Orgel* himself, assisted by his producer Philippe Grumbach and by Françoise Sagan[7] who wrote the dialogue.

Secondly, how did Allégret come to associate Radiguet's twentieth-century novel with Shakespeare's seventeenth-century play? The most obvious contact point between the two is the figure of the magician. Allégret interpreted the character of Anne d'Orgel as a Prospero figure, with Mahaut/Mahé as Miranda and François as Ferdinand (coincidentally, the count's wife and her admirer have the same initials as Shakespeare's characters). In *The Tempest*, thanks to his magical powers, Prospero is the master of the island as well as the master of his daughter Miranda's destiny, since his art allows him to match her with the young man he chose. Radiguet's short novel contains a form of manipulation too, since the author subtly makes the reader understand that in reality, Orgel, willingly or not, is the one who pushes his wife into François's arms. Allégret emphasizes this idea in the film by having Orgel play the part of Prospero in his own staging of *The Tempest*.

The link between the count and a magus appears in chapter 1 when the Orgels attend a party with their new friend François and a group of aristocrats and socialites: Hortense d'Austerlitz, Hester Wayne, Mirza, a Persian prince, and Amina, his niece. Orgel, like a magician, can concoct potions: 'The Count did not sit down. To rest from dancing, he prepared a mixture which was nearer to sorcery than to the barman's art'.[8] During the evening, François has caught the eye of Hester Wayne, an American socialite who tries to seduce him in any way she can: 'Returning to the word "sorcery" that someone had used after Anne d'Orgel's mixture, she spoke of filtres and imagined in a delicate way that he appealed to her; she whispered a recipe for the famous love potion that bound Tristan and Isolde together forever'. François, already attracted by Mahaut, 'imagined he had drunk alone with Countess d'Orgel a drink she ought to have taken with Anne, and that he who had mixed it had not drunk'.[9] At the end of the party, he realizes that he has indeed drunk the potion: he is in love with the countess.

In Allégret's film, emphasis is put on the idea of witchcraft. Orgel is the one who mixes a near-magic cocktail called Alaska. Hortense d'Austerlitz jokingly refuses to drink, warns Mahé against it and throws the contents of a glass in the fireplace: the liquid stirs up the fire.[10] Hortense comments that it is a drink from Hell and accuses Orgel of witchcraft. Amused, Orgel exclaims: 'Alright, yes, I'm a sorcerer, I prepare elixirs, philtres.'[11] Allégret's camera places him in the background of a medium shot, between his wife and François. The jocund-faced count seems to be delighted to serve them this dangerous drink. Then, François and Mahé drink the potion with Anne's blessing, looking straight into each other's eyes.

Orgel reappears as a magus at the very end of *Le Bal*. The last sentence in the novel is the traditional phrase pronounced by hypnotists – who are magicians of sorts – when they perform their art: 'And now, Mahaut, sleep! I insist.'[12] Those words are also the last ones to be uttered in the film, although Allégret added a – very clichéd – happy ending in the shape of a dream, where Mahé and François run towards each other at dawn. These words obviously echo Prospero's words to Miranda, when he charms her to sleep: 'Here cease more questions./Thou art inclined to sleep; 'tis a good dullness,/And give it way; I know thou canst not choose' (1.2.184–6).

A magician, in a certain way, is also a director: he is the one who decides what is going to happen and how. Prospero's masque in 4.1 gives him the role of a theatre director. Orgel acts and directs his life more than he lives it: he spends his time playing practical jokes, giving parties, designing dresses for his wife or costumes for the guests of his fancy dress ball. In the novel, a simile shows us that he has the manners of an actor: 'Anne d'Orgel made a stupid face, like a comedian who expresses astonishment. This astonishment was sincere, but exaggerated'.[13] Casting Jean-Claude Brialy as the count was a perfect choice, since he could put on airs effortlessly. The film starts with Orgel dressing up as a clown, complete with red nose and heavy makeup. Later on, the count expresses his distaste for anything 'natural,' which implies that his life is a work of art, hence, a show devoid of any spontaneity or genuine feeling:

> ANNE D'ORGEL: Nature has something natural which irritates me. In the end each tree should be signed by a painter.
> MAHÉ D'ORGEL: And each feeling by a writer.[14]

For him, life is a stage of which he is the undisputed director: 'He "adopted" people more than he made friends with them. In return he expected a great deal. He intended more or less to direct. He exercised control'.[15] It is no wonder, then, that he took the role of director of *The Tempest*.

As already mentioned, Radiguet's novel contains no reference to Shakespeare, nor does it seem to be remotely inspired by any of his works. The ball has no dress code: 'Everyone agreed on one point, that a fancy dress ball degenerates into a carnival unless discipline is insisted upon. There must be a general theme'.[16] And yet, no guiding line is ever found by the characters of the novel. Nevertheless, Marc Allégret chose that general theme for his film by grafting *The Tempest* onto *Le Bal*. The term 'graft' is sometimes used with a derogatory connotation: it refers to an artificial or inappropriate association. As regards the film, the insertion of *The Tempest* is a graft in the sense that it is an unexpected import from a literary work pertaining to a remote period and a different genre. With a graft, there is always a danger of rejection: will it adhere or not? It is also a *mise en abyme*, corresponding with Lucien Dällenbach's definition: 'any part embedded in a work which entertains a relation of similarity with the larger work that contains it'.[17] The passage from Act I scene 2 where Prospero orchestrates Miranda and Ferdinand's encounter mirrors the fact that, in the film, Orgel decides to cast his wife and their best friend in a love scene, at the risk of setting their hearts ablaze. In this respect, *Le Bal du Comte d'Orgel* corresponds to the second kind of Shakespeare derivatives in Kenneth Rothwell's classification, the 'mirror movie'.[18] The ball for Count d'Orgel is like the tempest for Prospero: both a display of power (be it financial, creative or magical) and the agent of a potential new relationship for two young people.

In the film, this is how Orgel introduces their roles to François and Mahé:

> Marvellous, I just wanted to talk to you about our ball! I must tell you! I've already mentioned the theme, Shakespeare's characters. The three of us will

make the last entrance, the most beautiful, of course. [*To his servant who has placed the costumes of the three characters on a sofa*] Thank you, Robert. I will be Prospero, the magician in *The Tempest*. You, François, you will be Prince Ferdinand. And you, Mahé, you will be . . . my daughter [*He arranges her hair and drapes her in a golden netted cape*], Miranda. It will be superb. Hide! I enter alone, I calm the storm, I make the monster disappear. Then Mahé enters and joins me. I wave my wand and conjure up Ferdinand. [*He puts his hands on their shoulders*] She watches him as if he were the only creature on earth. He's the first man she's ever seen. She's dazzled, she's in love; Ferdinand steps forward slowly.[19]

As was the case in the love potion scene, Orgel is positioned between the two younger characters; however, he does not mean to separate but to unite them, as is clear from his way of putting his hands on their shoulders. He looks more like a father giving his consent for his daughter's marriage than like a jealous husband.

The pause between 'And you, Mahé, you will be . . . ' and 'my daughter' creates suspense. For the spectator unfamiliar with the plot and characters of *The Tempest*, 'my daughter' comes as a surprise: why would Orgel cast his wife as his daughter? Why didn't he choose, say, *Antony and Cleopatra* or even *Macbeth* or *Othello*, in which he could have played a united couple with Mahé? Furthermore, the age gap between the count and the countess (twelve years in the book) is obvious in the film: Jean-Claude Brialy was thirty-six during the shooting, Sylvie Fennec was twenty-three but she looked even younger, while Bruno Garcin was twenty-one. During the whole film, Orgel incites Mahé and François to kiss on the cheeks, and when Mahé tells her husband that François has put his arm under hers in the carriage, he dismisses the matter as a childish trifle. Add to that Orgel's strange casting of his wife and his friend as lovers, and the seeds of doubts are sown in the spectators' minds: isn't the count putting his marriage at risk there?

What the characters will perform under Orgel's direction is not the play, but rather a silent rendering of it, which the viewers will see twice: after the first private rehearsal comes a dress rehearsal. Most of the performers wear rich Renaissance costumes, which cannot be ascribed to any Shakespearean character in particular, while others don more original outfits or props. For instance, François's friend Paul Robin (Gérard Lartigau) is carrying a donkey head mask, indicating that perhaps, a scene from *A Midsummer Night's Dream* is also on the bill, although we never get to see it. In total, all the rehearsal scenes last around fourteen minutes, interspersed with dialogue from the main plot. The second time, once again, Mahé and François just rehearse the moment when Miranda and Ferdinand first cast eyes on each other, but they do not pronounce a single word from Shakespeare's play. Anne d'Orgel stands in the pit with Mirza and the pianist and gives Mahé and François directions: 'Alright, so I've calmed the storm, I've made the monster disappear, Miranda has joined me, and with my wand I conjure up Ferdinand. There.'[20] The count is using the same trick as in the first rehearsal: he sums up the beginning of the play (the ship lost in the storm and the monster) so as to avoid performing it. Act I scene 1 might be too challenging to stage for an amateur play but above all, here, Marc Allégret's intentions become apparent: the adaptor/director is not interested in the whole play of *The Tempest*, but just in this passage from Act I scene 2 where Miranda and Ferdinand fall in love at first sight. As in the previous rehearsal, the scene is 'de-verbalized,' and long gazes are exchanged between the two would-be lovers under the count's direction. Reality merges with fiction when Mahé is so absorbed in the sight of Ferdinand that she does not even hear Anne call her name: 'Mahé! Mahé! [*Mahé jumps and looks at Orgel*] Miranda gazes at Ferdinand, she's mesmerized, she's lost, same acting for Ferdinand, you come closer slowly, very slowly, and now, you take her in your arms'.[21] Mahé no longer needs to act.

The director of the play within the film, Orgel, insists on the intense gazes between his actors, which actually replace the dialogue in Act I scene 2 where sight is an essential theme, for example when Ferdinand says that he would be happy if only he could 'once a day/Behold this maid' (1.2.489–90) or when Prospero asks his daughter to look at Ferdinand:

> The fringèd curtains of thine eye advance,
> And say what thou seest yond. (1.2.407–8)

Orgel's words 'Miranda gazes at Ferdinand, she's mesmerized, she's lost' are the equivalent of Miranda's answer:

> What is't? A spirit?
> Lord, how it looks about! Believe me, sir,
> It carries a brave form. (1.2.408–10)

What Orgel brings into relief in his staging of the passage is that it is 'love at first sight', as the English-language saying goes:

> Prospero: [. . .] At the first sight
> They have changed eyes. (1.2.439–40)

The director of the film, Marc Allégret, resorts to the visualisation of the dialogue in both rehearsal scenes: he translates the play's insistence on sight with long shots and reverse shots of Mahé and François gazing at each other. The close-ups of the first rehearsal convey the intensity of their feelings particularly well.

In lines 1.2.439–40 of *The Tempest*, Prospero rejoices at the success of his plan: making two young people meet and fall in love at first sight. We cannot assert that it is the same in Allégret's film but, still, it seems that the enigmatic count is giving his wife away to the young man he is himself so fond of. 'How fond?' is the entire question. In fact, it is now quite easy to understand why Allégret chose *The Tempest*: the rehearsal scenes, as they are a *mise en abyme* of *Le Bal's* story, function as eye-openers.

Those scenes are indeed a way for the audience – and for the characters themselves – to understand what is happening inside the characters' heads and hearts by translating it visually. Hence, *Tempest* scenes help fast-forward the action. When the first rehearsal scene comes, the spectators have long guessed that François is in love with his friend's wife, but they are still in doubt as to what she feels. Orgel's words ('She's dazzled, she's in love') probably help Mahé put a name on her feelings for François, though she believes that her love is not reciprocated. After the first rehearsal scene and the long exchange of gazes, Allégret cuts to Mahé crying and writing a letter to Madame de Séryeuse (Micheline Presle), confessing her love for her son, her shame, and urging her to find a means to keep him at a distance. The result of Madame de Séryeuse's intervention is that François and Mahé both become certain that their feelings are requited, which, of course, only strengthens those feelings.

A somewhat similar process happens in Éric Rohmer's *Conte d'Hiver* (*A Winter's Tale*, 1992) when Félicie has a revelation that she attributes to a prayer she made in a cathedral. On the same day, she watches a performance of *The Winter's Tale*. The statue scene makes a profound impression on her, leaving her in tears. Just after the play, she says she 'sees clearly' and understands that she has to look for her lost lover Charles. Barthélémy Py labels the performance a 'transition' in the film: "[i]t guides Félicie's destiny who then decides to bet on a potential reunion with Charles and to believe in it. After the grace received in the Nevers church, it is Shakespeare's play which brings her a second revelation'.[22] However, in Allégret's film, the performers of the play, not the spectators, are the ones who have the revelations; furthermore, the characters do not analyse those revelations afterwards as Félicie does in *Conte d'hiver*.

In *Le Bal du Comte d'Orgel*, the second rehearsal scene, a dress rehearsal, fast-forwards the action by allowing François and Mahé to voice their love

Figure 16.1.   The dress rehearsal – Anne d'Orgel (Jean-Claude Brialy) as Prospero in
Allégret's 1970 *Le Bal du Comte d'Orgel*. All rights reserved.

for each other. When the scene starts, the two haven't met since the revelation. The amateur actors are wearing luxurious Renaissance costumes.
Mahé/Miranda, her black hair dotted with pearls, is sporting a long white
dress and a golden netted cape. François/Ferdinand is in red and white with
a big golden necklace, while the count is even more richly attired with a
large hat, a black sparkling doublet, a red cape and, to top it all, the chain
of the Order of the Golden Fleece around his neck (see Figure 16.1). Before
the dress rehearsal, Mahé looks extremely anxious and she asks Anne if the
rehearsal is really necessary. Her husband's stage directions command her
to gaze at François lovingly and to go into his arms.

While they are hugging each other, the young man whispers in her ear:
'Mahé, I've seen my mother. I'm happy'.[23] Mahé just answers 'yes' and she
faints. Later on, while she is having a rest with her husband at her bedside,
she confesses her love for their young friend. Hence, the second *Tempest*
scene hurries the revelation of Mahé and François's chaste passion.

The scene is also an eye-opener for the audience as to the count's strange
behaviour. Mahé accuses him of being responsible for her infatuation: '*You*
are the one who introduced him in this house! *You* are the one inviting
François constantly!'[24] she shouts. This confirms the impression that he
was trying to alienate his wife at the same time as he was growing closer
to François. After Mahé's confession, Orgel shows no emotion. All he can

think of are appearances that must be kept up, as well as the ball: 'If I must, I will suffer later, and alone. For the moment, there's our ball. It must take place . . . François will attend the ball, you will be perfect. And now, Mahé, sleep, I insist.'[25] In the novel, Radiguet specified that Orgel did not really love Mahaut: 'She fell madly in love with her husband, and in return he showed her much gratitude and the warmest friendship which he himself took for love'.[26] If Anne does not love Mahaut, then isn't François the object of his affections?

Scholars of Radiguet's novel certainly have underlined its homoerotic undercurrents.[27] Radiguet's work on onomastics aims at blurring the boundaries between the sexes. The two male protagonists are given feminine-sounding names. The first name 'Anne' is no longer epicene. A few noblemen in times past have borne this name[28] but when the novel was written (and today too), it would have been more than unusual for a Frenchman to be called Anne. François de Séryeuse's last name is very close to '*sérieuse*,' the feminine form of the adjective '*sérieux*' (serious). As for the female protagonist, Mahaut/Mahé, her first name is extremely rare and the end sounds /o/ and /e/ usually belong to male names.[29] In the book as in the film, these confusing names demonstrate that there is something wrong inside the trio. Radiguet gives us a discreet clue at the beginning of the novel: '[Mahaut's] voice had an austere grace which seemed hoarse and masculine to the naïve . . . The same naïveté would have mistaken Count d'Orgel's voice for an effeminate one. He had a family voice, a falsetto, still used at the theatre'.[30] All in all, Radiguet clearly attributed a sexual ambiguity to the main characters.

As far as *The Tempest* is concerned, recent criticism, stagings and screen adaptations have engaged with its sexuality, including potential homoeroticism, as Virginia Mason Vaughan and Alden T. Vaughan point out: 'Many twentieth-century productions also highlighted *The Tempest's* underlying sexual tensions, in various combinations: Prospero and Miranda, Prospero and Ariel, Miranda and Caliban, even Caliban and Trinculo, and, newly eroticized, Miranda and Ferdinand'.[31] The sexual tension between Prospero and Ariel is what appealed to André Gide, Allégret's mentor, who had a special liking for *The Tempest*. Patrick Pollard relates that in 1891, Gide 'copied out, in French, into his notebook:

The finest passage in *The Tempest*:
ARIEL: Do you love me, master? No?
PROSPERO: Dearly, my delicate Ariel. [. . .]
It is, I think, obvious that the lines caught his attention because of the way in which they lend themselves to a homosexual interpretation.[32]

Such an interpretation could not have escaped Marc Allégret. The casting of Jean-Claude Brialy is also telling. At the end of the actor's life (he died in 2007), the French public knew that he was bisexual, although at the period when the film was shot and released (1969–70), he had not come out yet. Once more, Allégret could not have chosen a better actor for the count, because Brialy's latent homosexuality echoes that of the character. Lastly, during the dress rehearsal of the ball, just before the scene between Miranda and Ferdinand, the Persian prince Mirza and his niece Amina are the main attractions of a kind of short danced interlude. Orgel calls it a ballet and explains that Mirza is the Sun, Amina the Moon, both surrounded by four stars. It is easy for the viewers to recognize the union of the Sun, a symbol of masculinity, and the Moon, a symbol of femininity. Orgel does not indicate that it is part of his staging of *The Tempest* but, as the theme of the ball is 'Shakespeare's characters,' we can assume that it has a connection with it. Hence, the short ballet could be seen as Allégret's reconstruction of the masque of Juno and Ceres in *The Tempest*, making it the third Shakespearean scene of the film. Prospero's masque celebrates Miranda and Ferdinand's betrothal and, in the film, the interlude, placed just before Mahé and François's love scene, could be another way of showing that Orgel/Prospero is the thaumaturge who has unconsciously planned everything to estrange his wife from himself.

Has the graft of *The Tempest* taken in Marc Allégret's adaptation of *Le Bal du Comte d'Orgel*? I would answer yes. *Le Bal du Comte d'Orgel* is a costume drama with superb production (the film was partly shot in a real castle). The theatre scenes, with their luxurious costumes, perfectly fit in with the opulence of the diverse settings. Allégret's biographer tells how eagerly the film was anticipated and how the director was thought to be the best for this adaptation,[33] because he had met Radiguet before his untimely death at the age of twenty and probably also because of the literary prestige due to his intimacy with Gide. The name of Shakespeare could only add to the highbrow quality of the adaptation. More importantly, the *mise en abyme* is well thought out as regards the relationships between Shakespeare's and Radiguet's characters and gives the spectators clues as to the interpretation of their changing feelings and behaviours.

Nevertheless, all this did not save the film from being a flop. Allégret, ageing and ill, knew this was his swan song, just as *The Tempest* has sometimes been seen as Shakespeare's 'valediction to the stage'.[34] Unfortunately, *Le Bal du Comte d'Orgel* was a critical and public failure.[35] It is true that this film about repressed aristocrats was perhaps made at the wrong time, one year after the upheavals of May 1968 which heralded a social and sexual revolution and at the end of a decade in which French cinema was rejuvenated by the young Turks of the New Wave. Jean-Claude Brialy accepted the role of the count but found the script too bland.[36] As François Bott writes, Radiguet's novel is a book in which nothing happens, except arms touching.[37] It was a laudable idea to flesh out a weak script with theatre scenes visually conveying the inner feelings of the characters and the reviewers did not criticize the Shakespearean graft, perhaps because Shakespeare's presence in the film is evanescent. It is not only an ensemble of hardly contextualised fragments from *The Tempest*, to paraphrase Maurizio Calbi,[38] but it is also mute. And is Shakespeare without words still Shakespeare?

Notes

1 Within the 'Shakespeare on Screen in Francophonia' programme, a team of researchers based at Université Paul-Valéry, Montpellier 3, aims at finding, referencing and studying allusions and references to Shakespeare, or adaptations of his works, in French-speaking cinema.

2 Two English-language translations exist: the most recent one is entitled *Count d'Orgel's Ball* by Annapaola Cancogni (1989), published by New York Review Books; the other one, *Count d'Orgel*, is by Violet Schiff (first published in 1952 by Harvill Press under the title *Count d'Orgel Opens the Ball*, reissued by Pushkin Press in 1998 as *Count d'Orgel's Ball*). The latter will be used for this article.

3 R. Radiguet, *Count d'Orgel*, trans. Violet Schiff (London: Pushkin Press, 1998), 134.

4 In the film, Mahaut d'Orgel is renamed Mahé. One can only surmise that it might be to avoid confusion in the spectators' minds, because the rarely encountered medieval female name 'Mahaut' sounds exactly the same in French as 'Mao,' and Mao Zedong was still alive when the film was released.

5 '[I]l n'est pas d'auteur qui mérite plus d'être traduit que Shakespeare', A. Gide, 'Avant-propos', W. Shakespeare, *Œuvres complètes* (Paris: Gallimard, 1959), ix. Translations mine.

6 P. Pollard, *André Gide: Homosexual Moralist* (New Haven and London: Yale University Press, 1991), 262.

7 Sagan was, like Allégret, very knowledgeable about Shakespeare. Her novels are peppered with quotes from the plays. See C. Hromadova, 'Shakespeare comme ailleurs intertextuel: les épigraphes anglaises de Françoise Sagan', *Shakespeare en devenir* 4 (2010), http://shakespeare.edel.univ-poitiers.fr/index.php?id=404 (accessed 12 November 2015).

8 Radiguet, *Count d'Orgel*, 33.

9 *Ibid.*, 34.

10 This scene, which is absent from the book, is a cinematic illustration of the character's name. In French, Orgel is '*or*' (gold) + '*gel*' (frost), whose equivalent on the screen is the fire stirred up by the cocktail called Alaska. The name is a hint at the ambivalent nature of the character.

11 Original dialogue: 'Eh bien oui, je suis un sorcier, je prépare des élixirs, des philtres.'

12 Radiguet, *Count d'Orgel*, 156.

13 Radiguet, *Count d'Orgel*, 53.

14 Original dialogue: Anne d'Orgel: 'La nature a quelque chose de naturel qui m'exaspère. Finalement, chaque arbre devrait être signé par un peintre'. Mahé d'Orgel: 'Et chaque sentiment par un écrivain'.

15 Radiguet, *Count d'Orgel*, 37.

16 Radiguet, *Count d'Orgel*, 142.

17 '[T]oute enclave entretenant une relation de similitude avec l'œuvre qui la contient', L. Dällenbach, *Le Récit spéculaire* (Paris: Seuil, 1977), 18. Let us also remember that the term *mise en abyme* was coined by André Gide.

18 '[T]he second kind (mirror movies) will metacinematically make the movie's backstage plot about the troubled lives of actors run parallel to the plot of the Shakespearean play that the actors are appearing in' (K. S. Rothwell, *A History of Shakespeare on Screen: A Century of Film and Television*, 2nd ed. (Cambridge: Cambridge University Press, 2004), 209.

19 Original dialogue: 'Quelle merveille, je voulais justement vous parler de notre bal! Que je vous raconte! Je vous en ai dit le thème, les personnages de Shakespeare. À nous trois, nous ferons la dernière entrée, la plus belle, bien sûr. Merci Robert. Moi, je serai Prospéro, le magicien de *La Tempête*. Vous François, vous serez le prince Ferdinand. Et vous Mahé, vous serez . . . ma fille, Miranda. Ce sera superbe. Cachez-vous! J'entre seul, je calme la tempête, je fais fuir le monstre. Mahé entre à son tour et me rejoint. Je donne un coup de baguette magique et je fais apparaître Ferdinand. Elle le regarde comme s'il n'y avait que lui sur terre. C'est le premier homme qu'elle voit. Elle est éblouie, elle est amoureuse; Ferdinand s'avance lentement.'

20 Original dialogue: 'Bon, alors moi j'ai calmé la tempête, j'ai fait fuir le monstre, Miranda m'a rejoint, je donne un coup de baguette magique et je fais apparaître Ferdinand. Voilà.'

21 Original dialogue: 'Mahé! Mahé! Miranda regarde Ferdinand, elle est fascinée, elle est perdue, même jeu pour Ferdinand, vous approchez doucement, très doucement, et là, vous la prenez dans vos bras.'

22 'Elle guide la destinée de Félicie qui ensuite décide de miser sur d'éventuelles retrouvailles avec Charles et d'y croire. Après la grâce reçue dans l'église de Nevers, c'est la pièce de Shakespeare qui lui apporte une seconde révélation,' B. Py, ''*The Winter's Tale* de Shakespeare et *Conte d'hiver* de Rohmer (1992): vers une commune destinée des sentiments humains', *Shakespeare on Screen in Francophonia* (2010–), ed. P. Dorval & N. Vienne-Guerrin, Montpellier (France), Université Montpellier 3, IRCL, 2013, www.shakscreen.org/analysis/analysis_conte_hiver_rohmer (accessed 12 November 2015).

23 Original dialogue: 'Mahé, j'ai vu ma mère, je suis heureux.'

24 Original dialogue: 'C'est vous qui l'avez introduit dans cette maison! C'est vous qui invitez François sans cesse!'

25 Original dialogue: 'S'il le faut, je souffrirai plus tard, et seul. Pour le moment il y a notre bal. Il doit avoir lieu . . . François viendra au bal, vous y serez parfaite. Et maintenant, Mahé, dormez, je le veux.'

26 Radiguet, *Count d'Orgel*, 14.

27 See for instance C. Giardina, *L'Imaginaire dans les romans de Raymond Radiguet* (Paris: Didier Érudition, 1991), 51–3.

28 The best-known male 'Anne' in French history is probably Anne de Montmorency (1493–1567), Constable and Marshal of France, one of Francis I's close friends.

29 An in-depth study of the onomastics of the characters can be found in Giardina, *L'Imaginaire*, 50–9.

30 Radiguet, *Count d'Orgel*, 20.

31 V. M. Vaughan and A. T. Vaughan, 'Introduction', W. Shakespeare, *The Tempest*, Arden 3 (London: Methuen, 2011 [1999]), 123.

32 P. Pollard, *André Gide: Homosexual Moralist*, 262. The passage from *The Tempest* is 4.1.48–9.

33 'The preparation of *Le Bal du Comte d'Orgel* caused a big stir in the press. Celebrities were constantly giving their opinions about the adaptation. Some were for, some were against. Unanimously, it was considered that only a personality like Marc Allégret had the right to touch this work' ('La préparation du *Bal du Comte d'Orgel* fit grand bruit au niveau de la presse. Des célébrités donnaient sans cesse leur avis concernant cette adaptation. Il y avait les pour et les contre. Unanimement, on considérait que seule une personnalité comme Marc Allégret avait le droit de toucher à cette œuvre', my translation, B. J. Houssiau, *Marc Allégret, découvreur de stars* [Yens-sur-Morges: Cabédita, 1994], 190).

34 Introduction by S. Orgel, ed., William Shakespeare's *The Tempest* (Oxford: Oxford University Press, 1987), i.

35 The critics at the Cannes Festival were especially ruthless with Allégret, Jean-Claude Brialy recalls in his autobiography, *Le Ruisseau des singes* (Paris: Robert Laffont, 2000), 272. Also see B. J. Houssiau, *Marc Allégret, découvreur de stars*, 191. J. de Baroncelli, *Le Monde*'s film critic, described the film as an outright failure: 'a filmed pastiche of the original work' ('un pastiche filmé de l'œuvre originale'), 'the charm [of Radiguet's novel] has unfortunately disappeared from the screen. There remains a love story which leaves us unmoved and the evocation of a long-lost society whose customs make us smile' ('Ce charme a malheureusement disparu de l'écran. Restent une histoire d'amour qui nous laisse de glace et l'évocation d'une société engloutie dont les usages nous font sourire'), J. de Baroncelli, '*Le Bal du Comte d'Orgel* de Marc Allégret, d'après Raymond Radiguet' (*Le Monde*, 3 July 1970).

36 'Marc Allégret had overestimated his strength, he lacked authority, could not enrich this script, which was too weak, with his scenes' ('Marc Allégret avait présumé de ses forces, il manquait d'autorité, n'arrivait pas à enrichir

par les scènes ce scénario trop faible', J.-C. Brialy, *Le Ruisseau des singes*,
272).

37 F. Bott, *Radiguet, l'enfant avec une canne* (Paris: Flammarion, 1995), 178.

38 M. Calbi, *Spectral Shakespeares: Media Adaptations in the Twenty-First Century*
(New York: Palgrave Macmillan, 2013), 43.

WORKS CITED

Baroncelli (de), J., 'Le Bal du Comte d'Orgel de Marc Allégret, d'après Raymond
Radiguet', *Le Monde*, 3 July 1970.

Bott, F., *Radiguet, l'enfant avec une canne* (Paris: Flammarion, 1995).

Brialy, J.-C., *Le Ruisseau des singes* (Paris: Robert Laffont, 2000).

Calbi, M., *Spectral Shakespeares: Media Adaptations in the Twenty-First Century*
(New York: Palgrave Macmillan, 2013).

Dällenbach, L., *Le Récit spéculaire* (Paris: Seuil, 1977).

Giardina, C., *L'Imaginaire dans les romans de Raymond Radiguet* (Paris: Didier
Érudition, 1991).

Gide, A., 'Avant-propos', in W. Shakespeare, *Œuvres complètes* (Paris: Gallimard,
1959).

Houssiau, B. J., *Marc Allégret, découvreur de stars* (Yens-sur-Morges: Cabédita,
1994).

Hromadova, C., 'Shakespeare comme ailleurs intertextuel: les épigraphes anglaises
de Françoise Sagan', *Shakespeare en devenir* 4 (2010), shakespeare.edel
.univ-poitiers.fr/index.php?id=404, accessed 12 November 2015.

Orgel, S., ed., *William Shakespeare's* The Tempest (Oxford: Oxford University
Press, 1987).

Pollard, P., *André Gide: Homosexual Moralist* (New Haven and London: Yale
University Press, 1991).

Py, B., 'The Winter's Tale de Shakespeare et Conte d'hiver de Rohmer (1992): vers
une commune destinée des sentiments humains', in P. Dorval & N. Vienne-
Guerrin (eds.), *Shakespeare on Screen in Francophonia (2010–)* (Montpellier,
France: Université Montpellier 3, Institut de Recherche sur la Renaissance,
l'Âge Classique et les Lumières, 2013), www.shakscreen.org/analysis/analysis_
conte_hiver_rohmer, accessed 12 November 2015.

Radiguet, R., *Count d'Orgel*, trans. Violet Schiff (London: Pushkin Press, 1998).

Rothwell, K. S., *A History of Shakespeare on Screen: A Century of Film and Television*,
2nd ed. (Cambridge: Cambridge University Press, 2004).

Vaughan, V. M. and A. T. Vaughan, eds. *William Shakespeare's* The Tempest,
Arden 3 (London: Methuen, 2011 [1999]).

CHAPTER 17

The Romances on Screen
Select Film Bibliography

José Ramón Díaz Fernández

This chapter seeks to provide a selective reference guide to the screen adaptations of Shakespeare's late plays and includes sections corresponding to *Pericles, Cymbeline, The Winter's Tale* and *The Tempest*. These four sections will be subsequently divided into three subsections listing films, television adaptations as well as derivatives and citations. In each subsection, adaptations are classified in chronological order followed by an alphabetical list of relevant critical studies; a system of cross-references has been designed for those entries making reference to two or more screen adaptations. I have included theatrical productions such as Giorgio Strehler's *La tempesta* (1981) in the television section if there are significant changes between the original stage design and the television programme; in these cases I have only selected studies making specific reference to the recorded version. As far as the derivatives and citations are concerned, I have only listed those which have been discussed by critics. For additional titles and bibliographical entries related to the romances on screen, the reader may check the comprehensive online version of the present film bibliography on the Cambridge University Press website. Most entries here have been written in English, but I have also added a few relevant references in French, German, Italian and Spanish. Where possible, place names usually appear in their English version (e.g., 'Munich' instead of 'München'). All electronic addresses were correct at the time of going to press.

A.   PERICLES

1.   Television Adaptations

1.1   Pericles. *Dir. David Jones (BBC, 1983).*

1   Fenwick, Henry, 'The Production', in *'Pericles': The BBC TV Shakespeare*, ed. Peter Alexander et al. London: British Broadcasting Corporation, 1984, 17–27.

I would like to thank the Andalusian Regional Government for funding the research that allowed me to work at the Folger Shakespeare Library and the British Film Institute and led to the writing of this chapter (research project no. P07-HUM-02507).

2 Hartwig, Joan, '*Pericles*: An Unclaimed World'. *Shakespeare on Film Newsletter* 9:2 (Apr. 1985), 1–2.

3 Nelsen, Paul, 'Shot from the Canon: The BBC Video of *Pericles*', in *'Pericles': Critical Essays*, ed. David Skeele. New York and London: Garland-Taylor and Francis, 2000, 297–324.

4 Willems, Michèle and J.-P. Maquerlot, 'Entretien avec David Jones, réalisateur de *The Merry Wives of Windsor* et de *Pericles*', in *Shakespeare à la télévision*, ed. Michèle Willems. Rouen: Publications de l'Université de Rouen, 1987, 31–9.

5 Willis, Susan, 'A Study in Diversity: The Televised Shakespeare Canon', in her *The BBC Shakespeare Plays: Making the Televised Canon*. Chapel Hill and London: University of North Carolina Press, 1991, 187–225.

1.2   Pericles. *Dir. Maciej Prus*
(Telewizja Polska, 1995).

6 Fabiszak, Jacek, 'The 1995 *Pericles*, or the Power of Words', in his *Polish Televised Shakespeares: A Study of Shakespeare Productions within the Television Theatre Format*. Poznań: Motivex, 2005, 225–32.

2.   Derivatives and Citations

2.1   Paris nous appartient/Paris Belongs to Us. *Dir. Jacques Rivette (France, 1961).*

7 Burt, Richard, 'Mobilizing Foreign Shakespeare in Media', in *Shakespeare in Hollywood, Asia, and Cyberspace*, ed. Alexa Huang and Charles S. Ross. West Lafayette: Purdue University Press, 2009, 231–9.

8 Burt, Richard, 'Jacques Rivette and Film Adaptation as "Dérive-ation": *Pericles* in *Paris Belongs to Us* and *The Revenger's Tragedy* in *Noiroit*', in *The English Renaissance in Popular Culture: An Age for All Time*, ed. Greg Colón Semenza. New York and Basingstoke: Palgrave Macmillan, 2010, 167–86.

9 Calbi, Maurizio, 'Exilic/Idyllic Shakespeare: Reiterating *Pericles* in Jacques Rivette's *Paris nous appartient*'. *SEDERI* 25 (2015), 11–30.

10 Caratini, Fabienne, 'Le fantôme du théâtre dans le cinéma de Jacques Rivette'. *CinémAction* 93 (1999), 214–19.

11 Jackson, Russell, 'Three *Auteurs* and the Theatre: Carné, Renoir and Rivette', in his *Theatres on Film: How the Cinema Imagines the Stage*. Manchester: Manchester University Press, 2013, 221–68.

12 Morrey, Douglas and Alison Smith, 'Play, Theatre and Performance', in their *Jacques Rivette*. Manchester: Manchester University Press, 2009, 147–76.

13 Wiles, Mary M., 'From Shakespeare to Sartre: *Paris nous appartient*', in her *Jacques Rivette*. Urbana and Chicago: University of Illinois Press, 2012, 8–22.

B. CYMBELINE

1. Film Adaptations

1.1 Cymbeline. *Dir. Frederick Sullivan (USA, 1913).*

14 Ball, Robert Hamilton, 'Increase the Reels: 1912 to World War I', in his *Shakespeare on Silent Film: A Strange Eventful History.* New York: Theatre Arts Books, 1968, 135–215.

15 Buchanan, Judith, '"An Excellent Dumb Discourse": British and American Shakespeare Films, 1899–1916', in her *Shakespeare on Film.* Harlow: Pearson Longman, 2005, 21–48.

1.2 Cymbeline/Anarchy/Anarchy: Ride or Die. *Dir. Michael Almereyda (USA, 2015).*

16 Infante, Gabriella, Rev. of *Anarchy: Ride or Die. Shakespeare Bulletin* 34 (2016), 144–6.

2. Television Adaptations

2.1 Cymbeline. *Dir. Elijah Moshinsky (BBC, 1982).*

17 Fenwick, Henry, 'The Production', in *'Cymbeline': The BBC TV Shakespeare*, ed. Peter Alexander et al. London: British Broadcasting Corporation, 1983, 16–26.

18 Jacobs, Henry E., 'The Shakespeare Plays on TV: *Cymbeline*'. *Shakespeare on Film Newsletter* 7:2 (Apr. 1983), 6.

19 Jones, Gordon P., 'Nahum Tate Is Alive and Well: Elijah Moshinsky's BBC Shakespeare Productions', in *Shakespeare on Television: An Anthology of Essays and Reviews*, ed. J. C. Bulman and H. R. Coursen. Hanover and London: University Press of New England, 1988, 192–200.

20 Simonds, Peggy Muñoz, 'Jupiter, His Eagle and BBC-TV'. *Shakespeare on Film Newsletter* 10:1 (Dec. 1985), 3.

21 Taylor, Neil, 'Two Types of Television Shakespeare', in *Shakespeare and the Moving Image: The Plays on Film and Television*, ed. Anthony Davies and Stanley Wells. Cambridge: Cambridge University Press, 1994, 86–98.

22 Warren, Roger, '"The Neuroticism of Tragedy": Elijah Moshinsky's BBC Television Version, 1982', in his *Cymbeline*. Manchester and New York: Manchester University Press, 1989, 62–80.

23 Willis, Susan, 'Moshinsky's Television Artistry', in her *The BBC Shakespeare Plays: Making the Televised Canon*. Chapel Hill and London: University of North Carolina Press, 1991, 135–64.

3. Derivatives and Citations

3.1   Theatre of Blood. *Dir. Douglas Hickox (Great Britain, 1973).*

24 Ardolino, Frank, 'Metadramatic Grand Guignol in *Theater of Blood*'. *Shakespeare on Film Newsletter* 15:2 (Apr. 1991), 9.

25 Cartmell, Deborah, 'Shakespeare, Film and Violence: Doing Violence to Shakespeare', in her *Interpreting Shakespeare on Screen*. Basingstoke: Macmillan, 2000, 1–20.

26 Gearhart, Stephannie S., '"Only he would have the temerity to rewrite Shakespeare": Douglas Hickox's *Theatre of Blood* as Adaptation'. *Literature/Film Quarterly* 39 (2011), 116–27.

27 Holdefer, Charles, 'Bad Shakespeare: Adapting a Tradition', in *Screening Text: Critical Perspectives on Film Adaptation*, ed. Shannon Wells-Lassagne and Ariane Hudelet. Jefferson and London: McFarland, 2013, 197–206.

28 Hutchings, Peter, 'Theatres of Blood: Shakespeare and the Horror Film', in *Gothic Shakespeares*, ed. John Drakakis and Dale Townshend. London and New York: Routledge, 2008, 153–66.

29 Loiselle, André, '*Cinéma du Grand Guignol*: Theatricality in the Horror Film', in *Stages of Reality: Theatricality in Cinema*, ed. André Loiselle and Jeremy Maron. Toronto: University of Toronto Press, 2012, 55–80.

30 Lowe, Victoria, '"Stages of Performance": Adaptation and Intermediality in *Theatre of Blood* (1973)'. *Adaptation* 3 (2010), 99–111.

31 Pendleton, Thomas A., 'What [?] Price [?] Shakespeare [?]' *Literature/Film Quarterly* 29 (2001), 135–46.

32 Tibbetts, John C., 'Backstage with the Bard: Or, Building a Better Mousetrap', in *The Encyclopedia of Stage Plays into Film*, ed. John C. Tibbetts and James M. Welsh. New York: Facts on File, 2001, 541–70.

C. THE WINTER'S TALE

1. Film Adaptations

1.1   Winter Tale/A Winter's Tale. *Dir. Barry O'Neil (USA, 1910).*

33 Ball, Robert Hamilton, 'Cranks and Offices: Others American (1908–1911)', in his *Shakespeare on Silent Film: A Strange Eventful History*. New York: Theatre Arts Books, 1968, 61–73.

34 Buchanan, Judith, 'Corporate Authorship: The Shakespeare Films of the Vitagraph Company of America', in her *Shakespeare on Silent Film: An Excellent Dumb Discourse*. Cambridge: Cambridge University Press, 2009, 105–46.

35 Coursen, Herb, 'The 1910 Thanhouser *Winter's Tale*'. *Shakespeare Newsletter* 61 (2011–12), 61, 68.

36 Guneratne, Anthony R., 'Featuring the Bard: Frederick Warde's Shakespeare and the Transformation of American Cinema', in his *Shakespeare, Film*

Studies, and the Visual Cultures of Modernity. New York and Basingstoke: Palgrave Macmillan, 2008, 95–113.
See also 15.

1.2   Una tragedia alla corte di Sicilia/The Lost Princess/The Winter's Tale.
Dir. Baldassare Negroni (Italy, 1913).
See 14.

1.3   The Winter's Tale. *Dir. Frank Dunlop (Great Britain, 1968)*.

37 Manvell, Roger, 'Theatre into Film', in his *Shakespeare and the Film*. Revised, updated edn. South Brunswick and New York: A. S. Barnes, 1979, 114–32.

2.   Television Adaptations

2.1   Zimowa opowieść/The Winter's Tale. *Dir. Zofia Mrozowska (Telewizja Polska, 1977)*.

38 Fabiszak, Jacek, 'The 1977 *The Winter's Tale*, or B(e)aring the Conventions', in his *Polish Televised Shakespeares: A Study of Shakespeare Productions within the Television Theatre Format*. Poznań: Motivex, 2005, 133–42.

2.2   The Winter's Tale. *Dir. Jane Howell (BBC, 1981)*.

39 Cook, Ann Jennalie, 'Jane Howell's Manipulation of Distance in *The Winter's Tale* (BBC-TV)'. *Shakespeare Bulletin* 11:3 (Summer 1993), 37–8.

40 Coursen, Herbert R., 'Using Film and Television to Teach *The Winter's Tale* and *The Tempest*', in *Approaches to Teaching Shakespeare's 'The Tempest' and Other Late Romances*, ed. Maurice Hunt. New York: MLA, 1992, 117–24.

41 Dunbar, Mary Judith, 'Jane Howell's Television Production for the British Broadcasting Corporation, 1980', in her *The Winter's Tale*. Manchester and New York: Manchester University Press, 2010, 134–50.

42 Fenwick, Henry, 'The Production', in *'The Winter's Tale': The BBC TV Shakespeare*, ed. Peter Alexander et al. London: British Broadcasting Corporation, 1981, 17–27.

43 Hedrick, Donald K., 'The Shakespeare Plays on TV: *The Winter's Tale*'. *Shakespeare on Film Newsletter* 6:1 (Jan. 1982), 4, 6.

44 Rothwell, Kenneth S., '"The Shakespeare Plays": *Hamlet* and the Five Plays of Season Three'. *Shakespeare Quarterly* 32 (1981), 395–401.

45 Willems, Michèle, 'Entretien avec Jane Howell, réalisatrice de la première tétralogie, de *The Winter's Tale* et de *Titus Andronicus*', in *Shakespeare à la télévision*, ed. Michèle Willems. Rouen: Publications de l'Université de Rouen, 1987, 79–90.

46 Willis, Susan, 'Jane Howell's Approach', in her *The BBC Shakespeare Plays: Making the Televised Canon*. Chapel Hill and London: University of North Carolina Press, 1991, 165–86.

3. **Derivatives and Citations**

3.1 Conte d'hiver. *Dir. Éric Rohmer (France, 1992).*

47 Cartelli, Thomas and Katherine Rowe, 'Adaptation as a Cultural Process', in their *New Wave Shakespeare on Screen*. Cambridge and Malden: Polity, 2007, 25–44.

48 Cavell, Stanley, 'Shakespeare and Rohmer: Two Tales of Winter', in his *Cities of Words: Pedagogical Letters on a Register of the Moral Life*. Cambridge, MA and London: Belknap-Harvard University Press, 2004, 421–43.

49 Costantini-Cornède, Anne-Marie, '"It is required/You do awake your faith": *Un Conte d'hiver* à la Rohmer ou le miracle de la foi dans la comédie du remariage', in *Lectures de 'The Winter's Tale' de William Shakespeare*, ed. Delphine Lemonnier-Texier and Guillaume Winter. Rennes: Presses Universitaires de Rennes, 2010, 181–98.

50 Leigh, Jacob, '*Contes des quatre saisons* – Part 1', in his *The Cinema of Eric Rohmer: Irony, Imagination, and the Social World*. New York: Continuum, 2012, 157–96.

51 Py, Barthélémy, '*The Winter's Tale* de Shakespeare et *Conte d'hiver* de Rohmer (1992): Vers une commune destinée des sentiments humains', in *Shakespeare on Screen in Francophonia*, ed. Patricia Dorval and Nathalie Vienne-Guerrin, www.shakscreen.org/analysis/analysis_conte_hiver_rohmer.

52 Rhu, Lawrence F., 'Competing for the Soul: Cavell on Shakespeare', in *Stanley Cavell and Literary Studies: Consequences of Skepticism*, ed. Richard Eldridge and Bernard Rhie. New York and London: Continuum, 2011, 136–51.

3.2 The Winter's Tale – Shakespeare: The Animated Tales. *Dir. Stanislav Sokolov (Great Britain and Russia, 1994).*

53 Boguszak, Jakub, 'The Poetics of Shakespearean Animation'. *Shakespeare Bulletin* 32 (2014), 159–83.

54 Coursen, H. R., 'Animated Shakespeare: Second Season', in his *Shakespeare in Space: Recent Shakespeare Productions on Screen*. New York: Peter Lang, 2002, 113–28.

55 Osborne, Laurie, 'Mixing Media and Animating Shakespeare Tales', in *Shakespeare, the Movie, II: Popularizing the Plays on Film, TV, Video, and DVD*, ed. Richard Burt and Lynda E. Boose. London and New York: Routledge, 2003, 140–53.

56 Rokison, Abigail, '*Shakespeare: The Animated Tales*', in her *Shakespeare for Young People: Productions, Versions and Adaptations*. London and New York: Bloomsbury, 2013, 128–44.

57 Young, Michael W., 'Editing an Aery Nothing into a Local Animation: The HBO *Shakespeare's Animated Tales* Series'. *Shakespeare and the Classroom* 6:1 (Spring 1998), 69–71.

D. THE TEMPEST

1. Film Adaptations

1.1   The Tempest. *Dir. Percy Stow (Great Britain, 1908).*

58 Ball, Robert Hamilton, 'Inexplicable Dumbshows: English Films (1908–1911)', in his *Shakespeare on Silent Film: A Strange Eventful History*. New York: Theatre Arts Books, 1968, 74–89.

59 Buchanan, Judith, 'Conflicted Allegiances in Shakespeare Films of the Transitional Era', in her *Shakespeare on Silent Film: An Excellent Dumb Discourse*. Cambridge: Cambridge University Press, 2009, 74–104.

60 Coursen, H. R., 'Silents', in his *Shakespeare in Space: Recent Shakespeare Productions on Screen*. New York: Peter Lang, 2002, 95–111.

61 Fabiszak, Jacek, 'Caliban, the Salvage and Deformed Slave: On Representations of Ugliness in Film Versions of Shakespeare's *The Tempest*', in *Faces and Masks of Ugliness in Literary Narratives*, ed. Ryszard W. Wolny and Zdzisław Wąsik. Frankfurt: Peter Lang, 2013, 65–83.

62 Forsyth, Neil, 'Shakespeare and Méliès: Magic, Dream and the Supernatural'. *Études Anglaises* 55 (2002), 167–80.

63 González Campos, Miguel Ángel, '"No Tongue! All Eyes! Be Silent!": Versiones cinematográficas de *The Tempest* en la época muda', in his *Adaptaciones a la pantalla de 'The Tempest' de William Shakespeare*. Málaga: Universidad de Málaga, 2006, 31–59.

64 Holland, Peter, 'Magical Realism: Raising Storms and Other Quaint Devices', in *Revisiting 'The Tempest': The Capacity to Signify*, ed. Silvia Bigliazzi and Lisanna Calvi. Basingstoke and New York: Palgrave Macmillan, 2014, 185–201.

65 McCombe, John P., '"Suiting the Action to the Word": The Clarendon *Tempest* and the Evolution of a Narrative Silent Shakespeare'. *Literature/Film Quarterly* 33 (2005), 142–55.

66 Vaughan, Virginia Mason, '*The Tempest* on Film and Television', in her *The Tempest*. Manchester and New York: Manchester University Press, 2011, 168–91.

67 Walker, Elsie M., 'When Past and Present Collide: Laura Rossi's Music for Silent Shakespeare (1999)'. *Literature/Film Quarterly* 33 (2005), 156–67. See also 15.

1.2   The Tempest. *Dir. Derek Jarman (Great Britain, 1979).*

68 Barber, Sian, '*The Tempest*: A Brave New World of Creative Endeavour?' in her *The British Film Industry in the 1970s: Capital, Culture and Creativity*. Basingstoke and New York: Palgrave Macmillan, 2013, 160–76.

69 Bourne, Stephen, 'Derek Jarman and *The Tempest*', in his *Elisabeth Welch: Soft Lights and Sweet Music*. Lanham: Scarecrow Press, 2005, 81–6.

70 Buchanan, Judith, 'Historically Juxtaposed Beans (II): *The Tempest* on Film', in her *Shakespeare on Film*. Harlow: Pearson Longman, 2005, 150–83.

71 Buhler, Stephen, 'Transgressive, in Theory', in his *Shakespeare in the Cinema: Ocular Proof*. Albany: State University of New York Press, 2002, 125–56.

72 Cartmell, Deborah, 'Shakespeare, Film and Race: Screening *Othello* and *The Tempest*', in her *Interpreting Shakespeare on Screen*. Basingstoke: Macmillan, 2000, 67–93.

73 Cavecchi, Mariacristina and Nicoletta Vallorani, 'Prospero's Offshoots: From the Library to the Screen'. *Shakespeare Bulletin* 15:4 (Fall 1997), 35–7.

74 Charlesworth, Michael, 'The Feature Films of the 1970s', in his *Derek Jarman*. London: Reaktion Books, 2011, 55–78.

75 Chedgzoy, Kate, '"The past is our mirror": Marlowe, Shakespeare, Jarman', in her *Shakespeare's Queer Children: Sexual Politics and Contemporary Culture*. Manchester and New York: Manchester University Press, 1995, 177–221.

76 Collick, John, 'Symbolism in Shakespeare Film', in his *Shakespeare, Cinema and Society*. Manchester and New York: Manchester University Press, 1989, 80–106.

77 Crowl, Samuel, 'Stormy Weather: A New *Tempest* on Film'. *Shakespeare on Film Newsletter* 5:1 (Dec. 1980), 1, 5–7.

78 Coursen, H. R., 'The Play in Performance: *The Tempest* on Film and Television', in *'The Tempest': A Guide to the Play*. Westport and London: Greenwood, 1999, 177–95.

79 Davis, Hugh H., '"Rounded with a sleep": Prospero's Dream in Derek Jarman's *The Tempest*'. *Literature/Film Quarterly* 41 (2013), 92–101.

80 Dillon, Steven, 'Poetry and Interpretation in Three Early Features: *Sebastiane*, *Jubilee*, and *The Tempest*', in his *Derek Jarman and Lyric Film: The Mirror and the Sea*. Austin: University of Texas Press, 2004, 62–99.

81 Ellis, Jim, 'The Elizabethan Future', in his *Derek Jarman's Angelic Conversations*. Minneapolis and London: Minnesota University Press, 2009, 49–87.

82 González Campos, Miguel Ángel, 'El sueño y el laberinto: Versiones posmodernas de *The Tempest*', in his *Adaptaciones a la pantalla de 'The Tempest' de William Shakespeare*. Málaga: Universidad de Málaga, 2006, 145–235.

83 Harris, Diana and MacDonald Jackson, 'Stormy Weather: Derek Jarman's *The Tempest*'. *Literature/Film Quarterly* 25 (1997), 90–8.

84 Hawkes, David, '"The shadow of this time": The Renaissance Cinema of Derek Jarman', in *By Angels Driven: The Films of Derek Jarman*, ed. Chris Lippard. Westport: Praeger, 1996, 103–16.

85 Holderness, Graham, 'Shakespeare Rewound'. *Shakespeare Survey* 45 (1993), 63–74.

86 Hopkins, Lisa, *Shakespeare's 'The Tempest': The Relationship between Text and Film*. London: Methuen Drama, 2008.

87 Jackson, Russell, 'Shakespeare's Comedies on Film'. *Shakespeare and the Moving Image: The Plays on Film and Television*, ed. Anthony Davies and Stanley Wells. Cambridge: Cambridge University Press, 1994, 99–120.

88 Kennedy, Harlan, 'Prospero's Flicks'. *Film Comment* 28:1 (Jan.–Feb. 1992), 45–9.

89 MacCabe, Colin, 'A Post-National European Cinema: A Consideration of Derek Jarman's *The Tempest* and *Edward II*', in his *The Eloquence of the Vulgar: Language, Cinema and the Politics of Culture*. London: British Film Institute, 1999, 107–15.

90 Oggiano, Eleonora, '"This is a most majestic vision": Performing Prospero's Masque on Screen', in *Revisiting 'The Tempest': The Capacity to Signify*, ed. Silvia Bigliazzi and Lisanna Calvi. Basingstoke and New York: Palgrave Macmillan, 2014, 202–17.

91 O'Pray, Michael, 'The First Wave – *Sebastiane, Jubilee* and *The Tempest* 1975–1979', in his *Derek Jarman: Dreams of England*. London: British Film Institute, 1996, 80–121.

92 Pencak, William, '*The Tempest*: From the Renaissance to the Present', in his *The Films of Derek Jarman*. Jefferson and London: McFarland, 2002, 100–7.

93 Piazza, Antonella, 'Media *Tempests*: Preliminary Notes to a Comparative Reading of Some Film Adaptations of the Eighties in Great Britain and the United States', in *Shakespeare in Europe: Nation(s) and Boundaries*, ed. Odette Blumenfeld and Veronica Popescu. Iaşi: Editura Universităţii 'Alexandru Ioan Cuza', 2011, 248–57.

94 Renes, Cornelis Martin, 'Whose New World? Derek Jarman's Subversive Vision of *The Tempest* (1979)'. *BELLS: Barcelona English Language and Literature Studies* 17 (2008), www.publicacions.ub.edu/revistes/bells17/documentos/582.pdf.

95 Rothwell, Kenneth S., 'Shakespeare in the Cinema of Transgression, and Beyond', in his *A History of Shakespeare on Screen: A Century of Film and Television*. 2nd edn. Cambridge: Cambridge University Press, 2004, 192–218.

96 Taylor, Maggie, 'Memory, Magic and the Musical in Derek Jarman's *The Tempest* and *Edward II*', in *Musicals: Hollywood and Beyond*, ed. Bill Marshall and Robynn Stilwell. Exeter and Portland: Intellect, 2000, 157–62.

97 Vaughan, Alden T. and Virginia Mason Vaughan, 'Screen History', in their *Shakespeare's Caliban: A Cultural History*. Cambridge: Cambridge University Press, 1991, 199–214.

98 Wheale, Nigel, 'Screen/Play: Derek Jarman's *Tempest* as Critical Interpretation'. *Ideas and Production* 8 (1988), 51–65.

99 Wymer, Rowland, '"Our revels are now ended": *The Tempest* (1979)', in his *Derek Jarman*. Manchester and New York: Manchester University Press, 2005, 70–82.

100 Zabus, Chantal, 'Flaunting *The Tempest*: From "Insubstantial Pageant" to Celluloid Fresco', in her *Tempests after Shakespeare*. New York and Basingstoke: Palgrave, 2002, 243–64.

101 Zabus, Chantal, 'The New Wretched of Europe: Shakespeare, Derek Jarman, Peter Greenaway and Flaunting *The Tempest*', in *Shakespeare: Una 'Tempesta' dopo l'altra*, ed. Laura Di Michele. Naples: Liguori, 2005, 255–69.

102 Zabus, Chantal, 'Against the *Straightgeist*: Queer Artists, "Shakespeare's England", and "Today's London"'. *Études Anglaises* 61 (2008), 279–89.

103 Zabus, Chantal and Kevin A. Dwyer, '"I'll be wise hereafter": Caliban in Post-modern British Cinema', in *Constellation Caliban: Figurations of a Character*, ed. Nadia Lie and Theo D'haen. Amsterdam and Atlanta: Rodopi, 1997, 271–89.
See also 61, 62, 64, 66.

1.3   Prospero's Books. *Dir. Peter Greenaway (Great Britain, Netherlands, France and Italy, 1991).*

104 Anderegg, Michael, 'Greenaway's Baroque Mise en scene at the Imaginative Centre of Shakespeare's *The Tempest*: A Hypertextual Recapitulation of the Rivalry between Ben Jonson and Inigo Jones?', in *Peter Greenaway's 'Prospero's Books': Critical Essays*, ed. Christel Stalpaert. Ghent: Academia Press, 2000, 101–19.

105 Anderegg, Michael, 'Post-Shakespeares', in his *Cinematic Shakespeare*. Lanham: Rowman and Littlefield, 2004, 177–206.

106 Andreas, James, '"Where's the Master?": The Technologies of the Stage, Book, and Screen in *The Tempest* and *Prospero's Books*', in *Shakespeare without Class: Misappropriations of Cultural Capital*, ed. Donald Hedrick and Bryan Reynolds. New York and Basingstoke: Palgrave, 2000, 189–208.

107 Babula, William, 'Claribel, Tunis, and Greenaway's *Prospero's Books*'. *Journal of the Wooden O Symposium* 1 (2001), 19–25.

108 Besson, Florence, '*Prospero's Books* by Peter Greenaway (1991): Reflections of/on Shakespeare's *The Tempest*', in *Rewriting/Reprising: Plural Intertextualities*, ed. Georges Letissier. Newcastle: Cambridge Scholars Publishing, 2009, 217–28.

109 Brînzeu, Pia, 'Colours, Waters, and Reflections in Marina Warner's *Indigo* and Peter Greenaway's *Prospero's Books*', in *Shakespeare in Europe: Nation(s) and Boundaries*, ed. Odette Blumenfeld and Veronica Popescu. Iaşi: Editura Universităţii 'Alexandru Ioan Cuza', 2011, 71–8.

110 Brockelman, Thomas P., 'The Place of Truth: Theatricality and Modernity in Krauss and Greenaway', in his *The Frame and the Mirror: On Collage and the Postmodern*. Evanston: Northwestern University Press, 2001, 61–89.

111 Buchanan, Judith, 'Cantankerous Scholars and the Production of a Canonical Text: The Appropriation of Hieronymite Space in *Prospero's Books*', in *Peter Greenaway's 'Prospero's Books': Critical Essays*, ed. Christel Stalpaert. Ghent: Academia Press, 2000, 43–100.

112 Buchanan, Judith, 'Leaves of Brass and Gads of Steel: Cinema as Subject in Shakespeare Films, 1991–2000', in her *Shakespeare on Film*. Harlow: Pearson Longman, 2005, 220–60.

113 Burt, Richard, 'Writing the Endings of Cinema: Saving Film Authorship in the Cinematic Paratexts of *Prospero's Books*, Taymor's *The Tempest* and *The Secret of Kells*', in *The Writer on Film: Screening Literary Authorship*, ed. Judith Buchanan. Basingstoke and New York: Palgrave Macmillan, 2013, 178–92.

114 Burt, Richard and Julian Yates, 'Drown before Reading: Prospero's Missing Book . . . s', in their *What's the Worst Thing You Can Do to Shakespeare?* New York and Basingstoke: Palgrave Macmillan, 2013, 75–110.

115 Butler, Martin, 'Prospero in Cyberspace', in *Reconstructing the Book: Literary Texts in Transmission*, ed. Maureen Bell, Shirley Chew, Simon Eliot, Lynette Hunter and James L. W. West III. Aldershot: Ashgate, [2001], 184–96.

116 Carpi, Daniela, '*Prospero's Books* by Peter Greenaway and *The Tempest* by William Shakespeare: Science, Magic, and Painting'. *Symbolism: An International Journal of Critical Aesthetics* 9 (2009), 285–93.

117 Cavecchi, Mariacristina, 'Peter Greenaway's *Prospero's Books*: A Tempest between Word and Image'. *Literature/Film Quarterly* 25 (1997), 83–9.

118 Costantini-Cornède, Anne-Marie, 'De *La Tempête* à *Prospero's Books*: Vertige des sens et fragmentation du sens', in *Shakespeare et le cinéma: Actes du Congrès de 1998*, ed. Patricia Dorval. Paris: Société Française Shakespeare, 1998, 57–76, shakespeare.revues.org/948.

119 Costantini-Cornède, Anne-Marie, 'Pictorialité et pictorialisme dans *Prospero's Books* de Peter Greenaway'. *Études Anglaises* 55 (2002), 157–66.

120 Coursen, H. R., '"Tis Nudity": Peter Greenaway's *Prospero's Books*', in his *Watching Shakespeare on Television*. Rutherford: Fairleigh Dickinson University Press, 1993, 163–76.

121 DeWeese, Dan, 'Prospero's Pharmacy: Peter Greenaway and the Critics Play Shakespeare's Mimetic Game', in *Almost Shakespeare: Reinventing His Works for Cinema and Television*, ed. James R. Keller and Leslie Stratyner. Jefferson and London: McFarland, 2004, 155–68.

122 Donaldson, Peter S., 'Digital Archives and Sibylline Fragments: *The Tempest* and the End of Books'. *Postmodern Culture* 8:2 (Jan. 1998), muse.jhu.edu/journals/pmc/v008/8.2donaldson.html.

123 Donaldson, Peter S., 'Shakespeare in the Age of Post-Mechanical Reproduction: Sexual and Electronic Magic in *Prospero's Books*', in *Shakespeare, the Movie, II: Popularizing the Plays on Film, TV, Video, and DVD*, ed. Richard Burt and Lynda E. Boose. London and New York: Routledge, 2003, 105–19.

124 Donaldson, Peter S., 'Shakespeare and Media Allegory', in *Shakespeare and Genre: From Early Modern Inheritances to Postmodern Legacies*, ed. Anthony R. Guneratne. New York and Basingstoke: Palgrave Macmillan, 2011, 223–37.

125 Dragan, Richard, 'Brave New Worlds: The Book, the Cinema, and Web 2.0 in Peter Greenaway's *Prospero's Books* and *The Tulse Luper Suitcases*'. *Literature/Film Quarterly* 39 (2011), 99–115.

126 Esposito, Lucia, 'Barocco shakespeariano', in *Tragiche risonanze shakespeariane*, ed. Laura Di Michele. Naples: Liguori, 2001, 259–83.

127 Fabiszak, Jacek, 'Elizabethan Staging and Greenawayan Filming in *Prospero's Books*', in *Peter Greenaway's 'Prospero's Books': Critical Essays*, ed. Christel Stalpaert. Ghent: Academia Press, 2000, 121–39.

128 Garcia, Wilton, 'Art and Body: Intertextual Game Subjectivity in *Prospero's Books*', in *Peter Greenaway's 'Prospero's Books': Critical Essays*, ed. Christel Stalpaert. Ghent: Academia Press, 2000, 181–95.

129 Garnier, Marie-Dominique, '*Prospero's Books*: De l'écrit à l'écran, du livre à la chair', in *La littérature anglo-américaine à l'écran*, ed. Gérard Hugues and Daniel Royot. Paris: Didier Érudition, 1993, 17–24.

130 Guneratne, Anthony R., 'Six Authors in Search of a Text: The Shakespeares of Van Sant, Branagh, Godard, Pasolini, Greenaway, and Luhrmann', in his *Shakespeare, Film Studies, and the Visual Cultures of Modernity*. New York and Basingstoke: Palgrave Macmillan, 2008, 211–49.

131 Hainge, Greg, 'Tempest in Another Time: Shakespeare, Greenaway, Céline'. *Romanic Review* 97 (2006), 15–32.

132 Hotchkiss, Lia M., 'The Incorporation of Word as Image in Peter Greenaway's *Prospero's Books*', in *The Reel Shakespeare: Alternative Cinema and Theory*, ed. Lisa S. Starks and Courtney Lehmann. Madison and Teaneck: Fairleigh Dickinson University Press, 2002, 95–117.

133 Jess-Cooke, Carolyn, 'Adaptation', in her *Shakespeare on Film: Such Things as Dreams Are Made of*. London: Wallflower, 2007, 33–54.

134 Keesey, Douglas, 'Recovering the Native Body in *Prospero's Books*', in his *The Films of Peter Greenaway: Sex, Death and Provocation*. Jefferson and London: McFarland, 2006, 99–124.

135 Köhler, Christian, '*Prosperos Bücher': Friktionen, Struktur und die Grundzüge einer Monadologie des Films*. Weimar: Max Stein Verlag, 2008.

136 Lanier, Douglas, 'Drowning the Book: *Prospero's Books* and the Textual Shakespeare', in *Shakespeare, Theory, and Performance*, ed. James C. Bulman. London and New York: Routledge, 1996, 187–209.

137 Lawrence, Amy, 'Daddy Dearest: Patriarchy and the Artist: *Prospero's Books* (1991)', in her *The Films of Peter Greenaway*. Cambridge: Cambridge University Press, 1997, 140–64.

138 Lawson, Chris, 'The Greenawayan Sensory Experience: The Interdependency of Image, Music, Text and Voice as Interconnected Networks of Knowledge and Experience', in *Peter Greenaway's 'Prospero's Books': Critical Essays*, ed. Christel Stalpaert. Ghent: Academia Press, 2000, 141–59.

139 Ljungberg, Christina, 'Unbinding the Text: Intermedial Iconicity in Peter Greenaway's *Prospero's Books*', in *Semblance and Signification*, ed. Pascal Michelucci, Olga Fischer and Christina Ljungberg. Amsterdam and Philadelphia: John Benjamins, 2011, 369–88.

140 Louguet, Patrick, 'Travelling as Strolling about and Other Modes of Introducing Movement in *Prospero's Books*'. *Cycnos* 26:1 (2010), revel.unice.fr/cycnos/index.html?id=6365.

141 Ma, Kuei-Lan Anna, '*Prospero's Books* vs. *The Tempest*: A Synthesis of Shakespeare's Ideas and Style into Film Form', in *Literary Texts & the Arts*:

Interdisciplinary Perspectives, ed. Corrado Federici and Esther Raventós-Pons. New York: Peter Lang, 2003, 209–18.

142 Mancini, Carmela Bruna, 'Visioni neobarocche: Shakespeare e il cinema', in *Tragiche risonanze shakespeariane*, ed. Laura Di Michele. Naples: Liguori, 2001, 285–327.

143 Martin, Sara, 'Classic Shakespeare for All: *Forbidden Planet* and *Prospero's Books*, Two Screen Adaptations of *The Tempest*', in *Classics in Film and Fiction*, ed. Deborah Cartmell, I. Q. Hunter, Heidi Kaye and Imelda Whelehan. London and Sterling: Pluto Press, 2000, 34–53.

144 Marx, Steven, 'Progeny: *Prospero's Books*, Genesis and *The Tempest*'. *Renaissance Forum* 1:2 (Sept. 1996), www.hull.ac.uk/renforum/v1no2/marx.htm.

145 Marx, Steven, 'Greenaway's Books'. *Early Modern Literary Studies* 7:2 (Sept. 2001), 1.1–22, extra.shu.ac.uk/emls/07-2/marxgree.htm.

146 McKee, Alexander, 'Jonson vs. Jones in *Prospero's Books*'. *Literature/Film Quarterly* 35 (2007), 121–8.

147 McMullan, Gordon, '*The Tempest* and the Uses of Late Shakespeare in the Theatre: Gielgud, Rylance, Prospero', in his *Shakespeare and the Idea of Late Writing: Authorship in the Proximity of Death*. Cambridge: Cambridge University Press, 2007, 318–53.

148 Moser, Walter, '"Puissance baroque" dans les nouveaux medias: À propos de *Prospero's Books* de Peter Greenaway'. *Cinémas* 10:2–3 (printemps 2000), 39–63.

149 Murphy, Andrew, 'The Book on the Screen: Shakespeare Films and Textual Culture', in *Shakespeare, Film, Fin de Siècle*, ed. Mark Thornton Burnett and Ramona Wray. Basingstoke: Macmillan, 2000, 10–25.

150 Murray, Timothy, 'You Are How You Read: Baroque Chao-errancy in Greenaway and Deleuze', in his *Digital Baroque: New Media Art and Cinematic Folds*. Minneapolis and London: University of Minnesota Press, 2008, 111–33.

151 Murray-Pepper, Megan, 'The "tables of memory": Shakespeare, Cinema and the Writing Desk', in *The Writer on Film: Screening Literary Authorship*, ed. Judith Buchanan. Basingstoke and New York: Palgrave Macmillan, 2013, 92–105.

152 Palombo, Stanley R., '*Prospero's Books*: The Unconscious Visualized'. *Journal of the American Academy of Psychoanalysis* 23 (1995), 693–707.

153 Pascoe, David, 'The Book Depository', in his *Peter Greenaway: Museums and Moving Images*. London: Reaktion Books, 1997, 158–92.

154 Phelan, Peggy, 'Numbering Prospero's Books'. *Performing Arts Journal* 14:2 (41) (May 1992), 43–50.

155 Piazza, Antonella and Maria Izzo, 'Drop by Drop: Greenaway's Shakespearean Transformations'. *Shakespeare Bulletin* 29 (2011), 371–81.

156 Rodgers, Marlene, '*Prospero's Books* – Word and Spectacle: An Interview with Peter Greenaway', in *Peter Greenaway: Interviews*, ed. Vernon Gras and Marguerite Gras. Jackson: University Press of Mississippi, 2000, 135–46.

157 Rodman, Howard A., 'Anatomy of a Wizard', in *Peter Greenaway: Interviews*, ed. Vernon Gras and Marguerite Gras. Jackson: University Press of Mississippi, 2000, 120–8.

158 Rogers, Holly, '"Noises, Sounds and Sweet Airs": Singing the Film Space in *Prospero's Books*', in *CineMusic? Constructing the Film Score*, ed. David Cooper, Christopher Fox and Ian Sapiro. Newcastle: Cambridge Scholars Publishing, 2008, 141–64.

159 Ryle, Simon, 'Re-nascences: *The Tempest* and New Media', in his *Shakespeare, Cinema and Desire: Adaptation and Other Futures of Shakespeare's Language*. New York and Basingstoke: Palgrave Macmillan, 2014, 174–211.

160 Saal, Ilka, 'Taking on *The Tempest*: Problems of Postcolonial Re/presentation', in *Towards a Transcultural Future: Literature and Society in a "Post"-Colonial World*, ed. Geoffrey V. Davis, Peter H. Marsden, Bénédicte Ledent and Marc Delrez. Amsterdam and New York: Rodopi, 2004, 197–214.

161 Sapiro, Ian, 'The Filmmaker's Contract: Controlling Sonic Space in the Films of Peter Greenaway', in *Music, Sound and Filmmakers: Sonic Style in Cinema*, ed. James Wierzbicki. New York: Routledge, 2012, 151–64.

162 Schatz-Jacobsen, Claus, '"Knowing I Lov'd My Books": Shakespeare, Greenaway, and the Prosperous Dialectic of Word and Image', in *Screen Shakespeare*, ed. Michael Skovmand. Aarhus: Aarhus University Press, 1994, 132–47.

163 Schwenger, Peter, '*Prospero's Books* and the Visionary Page'. *Textual Practice* 8 (1994), 268–78.

164 Squeo, Alessandra, 'Shakespeare's Hypertextual Performances: Remediating *The Tempest* in *Prospero's Books*', in *Revisiting 'The Tempest': The Capacity to Signify*, ed. Silvia Bigliazzi and Lisanna Calvi. Basingstoke and New York: Palgrave Macmillan, 2014, 218–35.

165 Stalpaert, Christel, 'The Artistic Creative Process, Its Mythologising Effect and Its Apparent Naturalness Called into Question: An Interview with Peter Greenaway', in *Peter Greenaway's 'Prospero's Books': Critical Essays*. Ghent: Academia Press, 2000, 27–41.

166 Steinmetz, Leon and Peter Greenaway, 'The Library: *Prospero's Books*', in their *The World of Peter Greenaway*. Boston and Tokyo: Journey Editions, 1995, 104–15.

167 Tran, Dylan, 'The Book, the Theater, the Film, and Peter Greenaway', in *Peter Greenaway: Interviews*, ed. Vernon Gras and Marguerite Gras. Jackson: University Press of Mississippi, 2000, 129–34.

168 Tribble, Evelyn, 'Listening to *Prospero's Books*'. *Shakespeare Survey* 61 (2008), 161–9.

169 Trimm, Ryan, 'Moving Pictures, Still Lives: Staging National Tableaux and Text in *Prospero's Books*'. *Cinema Journal* 46:3 (Spring 2007), 26–53.

170 Turman, Suzanna, 'Peter Greenaway', in *Peter Greenaway: Interviews*, ed. Vernon Gras and Marguerite Gras. Jackson: University Press of Mississippi, 2000, 147–53.

171 Tweedie, James, 'Caliban's Books: The Hybrid Text in Peter Greenaway's *Prospero's Books*'. *Cinema Journal* 40:1 (Autumn 2000), 104–26.

172 Vaughan, Virginia Mason, 'Prospero after Freud', in her *The Tempest*. Manchester and New York: Manchester University Press, 2011, 70–97.

173 Vaughan, Virginia Mason and Alden T. Vaughan, 'Tampering with *The Tempest*'. *Shakespeare Bulletin* 10:1 (Winter 1992), 16–17.

174 Voigts-Virchow, Eckart, '"Something richer, stranger, more self-indulgent": Peter Greenaway's Fantastic See-Changes in *Prospero's Books* et al.' *Anglistik und Englischunterricht* 59 (1996), 83–99.

175 Walker, Elsie M., 'The Aesthetic Construction of Musical Forms in *Prospero's Books*', in *Peter Greenaway's 'Prospero's Books': Critical Essays*, ed. Christel Stalpaert. Ghent: Academia Press, 2000, 161–79.

176 Wall, Geoffrey, 'Greenaway Filming *The Tempest*'. *Shakespeare Yearbook* 4 (1994), 335–9.

177 Washington, Paul, '"This Last *Tempest*": Shakespeare, Postmodernity, and *Prospero's Books*', in *Shakespeare: World Views*, ed. Heather Kerr, Robin Eaden and Madge Mitton. Newark: University of Delaware Press, 1996, 237–48.

178 Willoquet-Maricondi, Paula, '*Prospero's Books*, Postmodernism, and the Reenchantment of the World', in *Peter Greenaway's Postmodern/Poststructuralist Cinema*, ed. Paula Willoquet-Maricondi and Mary Alemany-Galway. Revised edn. Lanham: Scarecrow Press, 2008, 177–201.

179 Willson, Robert F., Jr, 'Recontextualizing Shakespeare on Film: *My Own Private Idaho*, *Men of Respect*, *Prospero's Books*'. *Shakespeare Bulletin* 10:3 (Summer 1992), 34–7.

180 Woods, Alan, 'Books and Language', in his *Being Naked Playing Dead: The Art of Peter Greenaway*. Manchester: Manchester University Press, 1996, 102–15.

181 Yacowar, Maurice, 'Negotiating Culture: Greenaway's *Tempest*'. *Queen's Quarterly* 99 (1992), 689–97.

182 Yiu, Mimi, 'Prospero's Book of Architecture'. *REAL: Yearbook of Research in English and American Literature* 29 (2013), 235–64.

183 Yong Li Lan, 'Returning to Naples: Seeing the End in Shakespeare Film Adaptation'. *Literature/Film Quarterly* 29 (2001), 128–34.
See also 47, 61, 64, 70, 71, 72, 73, 78, 82, 86, 88, 90, 93, 95, 100, 101, 103.

1.4   The Tempest. *Dir. Julie Taymor (USA, 2010).*

184 Buchanan, Judith, 'Not Sycorax', in *Women Making Shakespeare: Text, Reception, Performance*, ed. Gordon McMullan, Lena Cowen Orlin and Virginia Mason Vaughan. London and New York: Bloomsbury, 2014, 335–45.

185 Crowl, Samuel, Rev. of *The Tempest*. *Shakespeare Bulletin* 29 (2011), 177–81.

186 Friedman, Michael D., 'Where Was He Born? Speak! Tell Me!: Julie Taymor's *Tempest*, Hawaiian Slavery, and the Birther Controversy'. *Shakespeare Bulletin* 31 (2013), 431–52.

187 Garcia, Maria, '*The Tempest*'. *Cineaste* 36:1 (Winter 2010), 50–2.

188 Henderson, Diana E., 'Shakespearean Comedy, Tempest-Toss'd: Genre, Social Transformation, and Contemporary Performance', in *Shakespeare and Genre: From Early Modern Inheritances to Postmodern Legacies*, ed. Anthony R. Guneratne. New York and Basingstoke: Palgrave Macmillan, 2011, 137–52.

189 Lefait, Sébastien, 'Prospera's Looks: Adapting Shakespearean Reflexivity in *The Tempest* (Julie Taymor, 2010)'. *Literature/Film Quarterly* 43 (2015), 131–45.

190 Lehmann, Courtney, '"Turn off the dark": A Tale of Two Shakespeares in Julie Taymor's *Tempest*'. *Shakespeare Bulletin* 32 (2014), 45–64.

191 Magnus, Laury, with Elyssa Jakim, '*The Tempest* and Julie Taymor's Talkback at BAM for TFANA's Gala'. *Shakespeare Newsletter* 60 (2010–11), 43–4, 72, 74.

192 Moore, Don, 'Melted into Media: Understanding Julie Taymor's Film Adaptation of *The Tempest* in the Wake of 9/11 and the War on Terror', in *OuterSpeares: Shakespeare, Intermedia, and the Limits of Adaptation*, ed. Daniel Fischlin. Toronto: University of Toronto Press, 2014, 115–51.

193 P[endleton], T[homas] A., 'Ladies' Day on the Magical Island: Taymor's *Tempest*'. *Shakespeare Newsletter* 60 (2010–11), 41, 50, 58, 60, 62.

194 Quarmby, Kevin A., 'Behind the Scenes: Penn & Teller, Taymor and the *Tempest* Divide Shakespeare's Globe, London'. *Shakespeare Bulletin* 29 (2011), 383–97.

195 Taymor, Julie, 'Rough Magic', in *Living with Shakespeare: Essays by Writers, Actors, and Directors*, ed. Susannah Carson. New York: Vintage Books, 2013, 466–82.

196 Vaughan, Virginia Mason, 'Un-Masquing *The Tempest*: Staging 4.1.60–138'. *REAL: Yearbook of Research in English and American Literature* 29 (2013), 283–95.

197 Vaughan, Virginia Mason, '"Miranda, where's your mother?": Female Prosperos and What They Tell Us', in *Women Making Shakespeare: Text, Reception, Performance*, ed. Gordon McMullan, Lena Cowen Orlin and Virginia Mason Vaughan. London and New York: Bloomsbury, 2014, 347–56.
See also 64, 66, 113, 114.

2.   Television Adaptations

2.1   The Tempest. Dir. George Schaefer (NBC, 1960).

198 González Campos, Miguel Ángel, '"Here Is a Box/What's in't Is Precious": Versiones televisivas de *The Tempest*', in his *Adaptaciones a la pantalla de 'The Tempest' de William Shakespeare*. Málaga: Universidad de Málaga, 2006, 285–339.

199 Vaughan, Virginia M., 'The Forgotten Television *Tempest*'. *Shakespeare on Film Newsletter* 9:1 (Dec. 1984), 3.
See also 40, 66, 78, 90, 97.

2.2   Burza/The Tempest. *Dir. Krystyna Skuszanka (Telewizja Polska, 1964).*

200 Fabiszak, Jacek, 'The 1964 *The Tempest*, or the Benignity of the Island', in his *Polish Televised Shakespeares: A Study of Shakespeare Productions within the Television Theatre Format*. Poznań: Motivex, 2005, 69–77.

201 Fabiszak, Jacek and Natalia Brzozowska, 'Magic Storms on Polish Television: The Case of *The Tempest*'. *Shakespeare Bulletin* 29 (2011), 359–69.

2.3   The Tempest. *Dir. John Gorrie (BBC, 1979).*

202 Charney, Maurice, 'Shakespearean Anglophilia: The BBC-TV Series and American Audiences'. *Shakespeare Quarterly* 31 (1980), 287–92.

203 Fenwick, Henry, 'The Production', in *'The Tempest': The BBC TV Shakespeare*, ed. Peter Alexander et al. London: British Broadcasting Corporation, 1980, 17–26.

204 Grundy, Dominick, 'The Shakespeare Plays on TV: *The Tempest*'. *Shakespeare on Film Newsletter* 5:2 (May 1981), 3–4.
    See also 40, 61, 66, 72, 78, 90, 97, 198.

2.4   La tempesta. *Dir. Giorgio Strehler (stage) and Carlo Battistoni (RAI, 1981).*

205 Griga, Stefano Bajma, '*La Tempesta*: Dal Lirico alla TV', in his *'La Tempesta' di Shakespeare per Giorgio Strehler*. Pisa: Edizioni ETS, 2003, 29–71.

206 Tempera, Mariangela, 'Giorgio Strehler's *La Tempesta*, from Stage to (Comic) Screen', in *Shakespeare in Performance*, ed. Eric C. Brown and Estelle Rivier. Newcastle: Cambridge Scholars Publishing, 2013, 223–34.

207 Vaughan, Virginia Mason, 'Postwar *Tempests* in Continental Europe', in her *The Tempest*. Manchester and New York: Manchester University Press, 2011, 127–50.

2.5   The Tempest. *Dir. William Woodman (Bard Productions, 1983).*

208 'The Bard/Britannica *Tempest* on TV Cassette'. *Shakespeare Newsletter* 34:2 (182) (Summer 1984), 20.

209 Vaughan, Virginia Mason, 'The Bard *Tempest*'. *Shakespeare on Film Newsletter* 15:1 (Dec. 1990), 11.
    See also 40, 66, 78, 97.

2.6   Burza/The Tempest. *Dir. Laco Adamik (Telewizja Polska, 1991).*

210 Fabiszak, Jacek, 'The 1991 *The Tempest*, or Prospero's Island as an Electronic Illusion', in his *Polish Televised Shakespeares: A Study of Shakespeare Productions within the Television Theatre Format*. Poznań: Motivex, 2005, 176–84.
    See also 61, 201.

2.7   Burza/The Tempest. *Dir. Krzysztof Warlikowski (stage) and Kasia Adamik (Telewizja Polska, 2008).*

211 Fabiszak, Jacek, 'Theatre, Television, Shakespeare? On (Counter-) representation of Stage Performances of Shakespeare's Plays on Television: The Case of Warlikowski's *Burza* [*The Tempest*]', in *Against and Beyond: Subversion and Transgression in Mass Media, Popular Culture and Performance*, ed. Magdalena Cieślak and Agnieszka Rasmus. Newcastle: Cambridge Scholars Publishing, 2012, 102–13.

212 Sakowska, Aleksandra, 'No "Happy Wrecks" – Pessimism and Suffering in Krzysztof Warlikowski's Adaptation of *The Tempest* by William Shakespeare'. *Shakespeare Bulletin* 29 (2011), 327–38.
See also 61, 201.

3.   Derivatives and Citations

3.1   Island of Lost Souls. *Dir. Erle C. Kenton (USA, 1932).*

213 Buchanan, Judith, 'Roguish Interventions: American Shakespearean Offshoots', in her *Shakespeare on Film*. Harlow and New York: Pearson-Longman, 2005, 90–118.

3.2   Yellow Sky. *Dir. William Wellman (USA, 1948).*

214 Brown, Eric C., 'The Bard Comes to *Yellow Sky*: Shakespeare's Tempestuous Western', in *Shakespeare in Performance*, ed. Eric C. Brown and Estelle Rivier. Newcastle: Cambridge Scholars Publishing, 2013, 138–54.

215 González Campos, Miguel Ángel, '"The Wealthy Kingdoms of the West": Recreaciones de *The Tempest* en el oeste', in his *Adaptaciones a la pantalla de 'The Tempest' de William Shakespeare*. Málaga: Universidad de Málaga, 2006, 61–103.
See also 88.

3.3   Forbidden Planet. *Dir. Fred McLeod Wilcox (USA, 1956).*

216 Buchanan, Judith, '*Forbidden Planet* and the Retrospective Attribution of Intentions', in *Retrovisions: Reinventing the Past in Film and Fiction*, ed. Deborah Cartmell, I. Q. Hunter and Imelda Whelehan. London and Sterling: Pluto Press, 2001, 148–62.

217 Caroti, Simone, 'Science Fiction, *Forbidden Planet*, and Shakespeare's *The Tempest*', in *Shakespeare in Hollywood, Asia, and Cyberspace*, ed. Alexa Huang and Charles S. Ross. West Lafayette: Purdue University Press, 2009, 218–30.

218 González Campos, Miguel Ángel, '"There Is Some Space": Recreaciones futuristas de *The Tempest* en el espacio', in his *Adaptaciones a la pantalla de 'The Tempest' de William Shakespeare*. Málaga: Universidad de Málaga, 2006, 105–43.

219 Jensen, Michael P., 'Forbidden Tempest?' *Filmfax* 88 (Feb.–March 2002), 64–5, 90–1.

220 Jolly, John, 'The Bellephoron Myth and *Forbidden Planet*'. *Extrapolation* 27 (1986), 84–90.

221 Karrer, Wolfgang, 'Fantasy-Elemente in Shakespeares *The Tempest* (1611) und MGMs *Forbidden Planet* (1956)'. *Anglistik und Englischunterricht* 59 (1996), 71–82.

222 Knighten, Merrell, 'The Triple Paternity of *Forbidden Planet*'. *Shakespeare Bulletin* 12:3 (Summer 1994), 36–7.

223 Lanier, Douglas, 'According to Shakespeare: Allusion and Citation', in his *Shakespeare and Modern Popular Culture*. Oxford: Oxford University Press, 2002, 50–81.

224 Lerer, Seth, '*Forbidden Planet* and the Terrors of Philology'. *Raritan* 19:3 (Winter 2000), 73–86.

225 Miller, Anthony, '"In this last tempest": Modernising Shakespeare's *Tempest* on Film'. *Sydney Studies in English* 23 (1997–98), 24–40.

226 Morse, Ruth, 'Monsters, Magicians, Movies: *The Tempest* and the Final Frontier'. *Shakespeare Survey* 53 (2000), 164–74.

227 Pilkington, Ace G., '*Forbidden Planet*: Aliens, Monsters and Fictions of Nuclear Disaster', in *The Fantastic Made Visible: Essays on the Adaptation of Science Fiction and Fantasy from Page to Screen*, ed. Matthew Wilhelm Kapell and Ace G. Pilkington. Jefferson and London: McFarland, 2015, 43–59.

228 Trushell, John, 'Return of *Forbidden Planet*?' *Foundation: The Review of Science Fiction* 64 (Summer 1995), 82–9.

229 Willson, Robert F., Jr, 'Selected Offshoots: Shakespeare at War, on Broadway, in the Mob, in Space, and on the Range', in his *Shakespeare in Hollywood, 1929–1956*. Madison and Teaneck: Fairleigh Dickinson University Press, 2000, 74–129.

230 Youngs, Tim, 'Cruising against the Id: The Transformation of Caliban in *Forbidden Planet*', in *Constellation Caliban: Figurations of a Character*, ed. Nadia Lie and Theo D'haen. Amsterdam and Atlanta: Rodopi, 1997, 211–29.

231 Zabus, Chantal, 'The Pleasures of Intergalactic Exile', in her *Tempests after Shakespeare*. New York and Basingstoke: Palgrave, 2002, 181–204.
See also 40, 61, 70, 73, 78, 86, 88, 97, 143, 172, 213.

3.4   Age of Consent. *Dir. Michael Powell (Australia, 1969).*

232 González Campos, Miguel Ángel, '"I Have Used Thee with Human Care": Derivativos humanistas de *The Tempest*', in his *Adaptaciones a la pantalla de 'The Tempest' de William Shakespeare*. Málaga: Universidad de Málaga, 2006, 237–83.

233 Salwolke, Scott, 'Something More Personal', in his *The Films of Michael Powell and the Archers*. Lanham and London: Scarecrow Press, 1997, 237–48.

3.5   Tempest. *Dir. Paul Mazursky (USA, 1982).*

234 Bruster, Douglas, 'The Postmodern Theatre of Paul Mazursky's *Tempest*', in *Shakespeare, Film, Fin de Siècle*, ed. Mark Thornton Burnett and Ramona Wray. Basingstoke: Macmillan, 2000, 26–39.

235 Coppedge, Walter R., 'Mazursky's *Tempest*: Something Rich, Something Strange'. *Literature/Film Quarterly* 21 (1993), 18–24.

236 Haspel, Paul, 'Ariel and Prospero's Modern-English Adventure: Language, Social Criticism, and Adaptation in Paul Mazursky's *Tempest*'. *Literature/Film Quarterly* 34 (2006), 130–9.

237 Knapp, Peggy A., 'Reinhabiting Prospero's Island: Cassavetes' *Tempest*', in *Transformations: From Literature to Film*, ed. Douglas Radcliff-Umstead. Kent, OH: Romance Languages Dept., Kent State University, 1987, 46–54.

238 O'Dair, Sharon, '*The Tempest* as *Tempest*: Does Paul Mazursky "Green" William Shakespeare?' *Interdisciplinary Studies in Literature and Environment* 12 (2005), 165–78.

239 Taylor, Geoffrey, *Paul Mazursky's 'Tempest'*. New York: Zoetrope, 1982.

240 Yogev, Michael, '"Music for nothing": Shakespeare's and Mazursky's *Tempest*s'. *JTD: Journal of Theatre and Drama* 5–6 (1999–2000), 81–100.

See also 40, 61, 70, 73, 78, 88, 93, 97, 100, 172, 225, 232.

3.6   Iguana. *Dir. Monte Hellman (USA, 1988).*

See 213.

3.7   Resan till Melonia/The Voyage to Melonia. *Dir. Per Åhlin (Swedish TV, 1989).*

241 Formisano, Carmela, 'Diario di bordo di una *Tempesta* per bambini', in *Shakespeare: Una 'Tempesta' dopo l'altra*, ed. Laura Di Michele. Naples: Liguori, 2005, 213–23.

242 Roudevitch, Michel, 'Si Shakespeare m'était conté: Roméo, Prospero, Titania et les autres'. *Positif* 388 (juin 1993), 56–9.

3.8   The Little Mermaid. *Dir. Ron Clements and John Musker (USA, 1989).*

243 Finkelstein, Richard, 'Disney Cites Shakespeare: The Limits of Appropriation', in *Shakespeare and Appropriation*, ed. Christy Desmet and Robert Sawyer. London and New York: Routledge, 1999, 179–96.

244 Finkelstein, Richard, 'Disney's *Tempest*: Colonizing Desire in *The Little Mermaid*', in *The Emperor's Old Groove: Decolonizing Disney's Magic Kingdom*, ed. Brenda Ayres. New York: Peter Lang, 2003, 131–47.

245 Hateley, Erica, 'Of Tails and Tempests: Feminine Sexuality and Shakespearean Children's Texts'. *Borrowers and Lenders: The Journal of Shakespeare and Appropriation* 2:1 (Spring/Summer 2006), www.borrowers.uga.edu/783082/show.

3.9   The Tempest – Shakespeare: The Animated Tales. *Dir. Stanislav Sokolov*
        (Great Britain and Russia, 1992).

246 Andreas, James R., 'The Canning of a Classic: *Shakespeare, The Animated
     Tales'. Shakespeare Yearbook* 11 (2000), 96–117.
247 Boltz, Ingeborg, '*Shakespeare: The Animated Tales*: Vom Trickfilmstudio in die
     Schule'. *Shakespeare Jahrbuch* 133 (1997), 118–33.
248 Osborne, Laurie E., 'Poetry in Motion: Animating Shakespeare', in *Shake-
     speare, the Movie: Popularizing the Plays on Film, TV, and Video*, ed. Lynda E.
     Boose and Richard Burt. London and New York: Routledge, 1997, 103–20.
249 Rubio, Gerald J., 'Shakespeare – The Animated Tales'. *Canadian Children's
     Literature/Littérature canadienne pour la jeunesse* 23:1 (85) (Spring/printemps
     1997), 86–8.
250 Semenza, Gregory M. Colón, 'Teens, Shakespeare, and the Dumbing Down
     Cliché: The Case of *The Animated Tales'. Shakespeare Bulletin* 26:2 (Summer
     2008), 37–68.
     See also 53, 56, 57, 78, 198, 242.

3.10   Trois couleurs: Rouge/Three Colours: Red. *Dir. Krzysztof Kieslowski
         (France, Poland and Switzerland, 1993).*

See 232.

3.11   The Tempest. *Dir. Jack Bender (NBC, 1998).*

251 Coursen, H. R., 'Shakespeare on Television: Four Recent Productions', in
     his *Shakespeare in Space: Recent Shakespeare Productions on Screen*. New York:
     Peter Lang, 2002, 53–70.
252 Hoenselaars, Ton, 'Gone with *The Tempest'. Folio: Shakespeare-Genootschap
     van Nederland en Vlaanderen* 8:1 (2001), 46–8.
253 Monteiro, Flávia R., 'Brave New Media: They That Sow the Secession,
     Shall Reap *The Tempest'*, in *III Congresso Internacional da ABRAPUI: Lan-
     guage and Literature in the Age of Technology* (2012), www.abrapui.org/anais/
     ComunicacoesCoordenasLiteratura/6.pdf.
     See also 78, 215.

3.12   Je rentre à la maison. *Dir. Manoel de Oliveira (France and Portugal, 2001).*

254 Delord, Frédéric, '"Mon vieux cerveau est troublé" (*La Tempête*, IV.I.159): *Je
     rentre à la maison* – De la différance à l'incongru', in *Shakespeare on Screen
     in Francophonia*, ed. Patricia Dorval and Nathalie Vienne-Guerrin, www
     .shakscreen.org/analysis/analysis_je_rentre.

Index